W9-BEE-087

FLORIDA STATE
UNIVERSITY LIBRARIES

MAR 25 1996

TALLAHASSEE, FLORIDA

Beyond Quebec

Beyond Quebec

Taking Stock of Canada

Edited by
KENNETH McROBERTS

McGill-Queen's University Press
Montreal & Kingston • London • Buffalo

© McGill-Queen's University Press 1995
ISBN 0-7735-1301-9 (cloth)
ISBN 0-7735-1314-0 (paper)

Legal deposit second quarter 1995
Bibliothèque nationale du Québec

Printed in Canada on acid-free paper

McGill-Queen's University Press is grateful to the Canada Council for
support of its publishing program.

Canadian Cataloguing in Publication Data

Main entry under title:
  Beyond Quebec: taking stock of Canada
  Includes bibliographical references
  ISBN 0-7735-1301-9 (bound)
  ISBN 0-7735-1314-0 (pbk)
  1. Canada – Politics and government – 1993 – 2. Canada – Economic
conditions – 1991 – 3. Canada – Civilization – 1945 – 4. Regionalism –
Canada. 5. Canada – Forecasting. 6. Quebec (Province) – History –
Autonomy and independence movements. I. McRoberts, Kenneth, 1942 –
FC635.B49 1995   971.064'8   C95-900253-7
F1034.2.B49 1995

This book was typeset by Typo Litho Composition Inc.
in 10/12 Baskerville.

Contents

Thus even if the referendum should fail, the question necessarily arises as to just how cohesive is "Canada Outside Quebec" and to what degree it would require and support a greater role for the federal government than does Quebec. At the end of this volume, after reviewing the nature of Canada Outside Quebec, we will return to this matter of the most appropriate political arrangements.

There is a final rationale for studying this question: it provides an ideal opportunity to explore the relationship between various forms of social change. By most accounts, the economy of Canada Outside Quebec has in recent decades become increasingly fragmented. Yet many observers would argue that the political life of this part of Canada has displayed increased cohesion, thanks in particular to constitutional repatriation and the adoption of the Charter of Rights and Freedoms. Moreover, by many accounts the cultural life of Canada Outside Quebec has undergone unprecedented development as anglophone Canadian writers and artists have secured international prominence. Thus the recent experience of the Canada "beyond Quebec" seems to offer a paradox: economic fragmentation and decline is accompanied by political integration and cultural growth.

Accordingly, this book brings together a distinguished group of scholars from a variety of disciplines. These contributors take stock of recent trends in a large number of key dimensions of Canada Outside Quebec: the political economy of regions, the impact of national political institutions, the integration/fragmentation of the "national" economy, the viability of English-language cultural production, the role of Native arts, and the strength of dominant social and political identities. In most cases, the authors use their "stocktaking" to extrapolate how Canada Outside Quebec would be affected by Quebec sovereignty or by conversion of Canada's federalism to asymmetrical and condederal variants. (To be sure, most contributors tend to focus more upon Quebec sovereignty than upon the latter possibilities.)

A rapid overview of the basic findings of each chapter and of the kind of general argument that emerges from these findings prepares the reader for the book that follows. The discussion below also provides more background about how this book originated and about the assumptions that underlie the insights it provides.

DEFINING TERMS

First, however, we need to return to the problem noted at the outset: the lack of a single agreed-upon vocabulary for our enquiry. In effect, the competing terms of "English Canada" and "Canada Outside Quebec" (or its several variants) contain different assumptions about the fundamental divisions within Canada and indeed what distinctions can be legitimately introduced to political life in general. The history of their usage reflects important developments in how Canada is generally understood. And the contemporary debate about their relative appropriateness tells us much about the challenges that would be faced if Quebec were no longer a province within Canada, at least not on the present basis.

Over a long period of time a large number of scholars from a wide range of disciplines found it quite appropriate to centre their studies around "English Canada" or a variation thereof. This can be seen simply by reviewing the range of scholarly works in which the term "English Canada" or its variants, appears in the very title. Many works have been devoted to "English-Canadian literature" as a distinct corpus (Ballstadt 1975; Beckow 1974; Craig 1987; Davey 1993; Fagel 1984; Grayson 1981; Grayson and Grayson 1978; Hutcheon 1988; James 1987; Moss 1974; Pache 1980). Several studies have traced the historical emergence of an English-Canadian cultural community, with its own institutions and networks (Tippett 1986, 1988 and 1990; Vipond 1980). Another scholarly tradition has explored the nature of a distinctly "English-Canadian" social and political thought (Allen 1987; Bell and Tepperman 1979; Breton 1988; Cole 1980; Cook 1985; Levitt 1980; Meisel 1977; Prang 1986; Resnick 1977; Rotstein 1978; Smith 1976. And there have been a good number of empirical studies of the attitudes and beliefs held by different categories of "English Canadians" or "Anglophone Canadians" (Gibbins and Ponting 1981; Grabb 1980; Hunter 1977; Lazko 1978; Ogmundson 1980; Young 1977).

Nonetheless, the fact that some of the more recent studies have defined their focus as "anglophone" or "English-speaking" Canada does betray a certain unease with the term "English Canada." We can understand this by examining the term's historical roots – roots which some people claim it can never escape.

"English Canada" originally denoted an entity which was not simply culturally distinct but ethnically if not racially distinct as well. By definition, English Canadians were descended from British immigrants or, arguably, were descendants of immigrants from other countries who were totally assimilated to English-Canadian culture. With Anglo-Saxon values and Protestantism at its core, this English-Canadian culture included a firm belief in the superiority of British institutions and traditions – especially the monarchy, parliamentary government, and British conceptions of justice – as well as in the virtues of the English language and the cultural achievement that it has produced (Breton 1988; McRoberts 1993).

This notion of an "English Canada" was, of course, sustained by Canada's long-standing dependence on Great Britain and the flow of immigrants that came from it. It was also sustained by nationalists in Quebec for whom it was the logical counterpart to the conception of nation that they had articulated in Quebec – that of a French-Canadian nation. French Canada too was conceived in cultural, in fact ethnic, terms. Quebec nationalists had every reason to envisage the rest of Canada in similar terms. In fact, the notion that Canada is composed of two founding peoples, English Canada and French Canada, became a cherished belief in Quebec. To be sure, not all versions of an "English Canada" conceived Canada in such dualist terms. Within some versions, Canada and English Canada were, in fact, one and the same. Canada was conceived, figuratively if not in fact, as if Quebec or French Canada were no longer part of it.

As Raymond Breton (1988) has shown, a variety of processes served to undermine the notion of an ethnically defined English Canada, whether as merely part or as the virtual essence of Canada. Not only did a French-Canadian society persist in Quebec and French-Canadian nationalists fight to maintain a French-Canadian presence in the other parts of Canada (admittedly, with little success), but by the turn of the century the notion of an ethnically rooted English Canada was threatened by the increasing prominence of non-Britishers among immigrants to Canada. While most immigrants became English-speakers, their presence within English-Canadian society weakened the possibility of defining this society in terms of religion, culture, or historical origins. Beyond that, of course, the decline of the British Empire served to undermine any definition of English Canada, or Canada, in terms of Britishness.

Out of these changes emerged a new conception of English Canada, or Canada per se, which Breton dubs a "civic nationalism." Within this new nationalism, cultural differences are seen as secondary if not irrelevant and even improper to any understanding of Canada. To the extent that there is a recognition of such differences, it is on the basis of "multiculturalism": a formula that incorporates an infinite number of cultural differences on precisely the same basis.

Thus in 1966 Kenneth McNaught articulated what he dubbed "the national outlook of English-speaking Canadians." He flatly rejected the juxtaposition of an English Canada and Quebec, branding such a duality a misrepresentation fostered by Quebec nationalists. His complaint was that this notion presumed that English-speaking Canadians shared a "racial"conception of nation comparable to that of Quebec nationalists, when in fact they held a "non-racial view of nationality" (McNaught 1966:63) and had come to accept "multi-racialism, or multiculturalism" since "their national loyalty is to national diversity" (Mc-Naught 1966:66). While recognizing that in such instances as the United Empire Loyalist tradition, the Imperial Federation movement, the Protestant Protective Association, the suppression of French-language schools and the two conscription crises "there was undoubtedly, on the part of Canadians of British descent, a feeling of racial identification," this component of the English-speaking outlook had steadily declined in significance (McNaught 1966:63).

Within this perspective, however, the very legitimacy of distinguishing an *English* Canada can come into question. To be sure, it might be claimed that in contemporary Canada the adjective refers to language alone, as in the phrase "English-speaking Canada." But since the term does have roots in a nationalism that was more broadly cultural, in fact ethnic or even racial, McNaught's claims notwithstanding, it is not surprising that a good many Canadians should remain suspicious of it. In any event, even if they were convinced that the distinction were purely linguistic, many Canadians would see no reason to differentiate among Canadians even on that basis.

Not only is the very existence of an "English Canada" increasingly questioned, but it has been widely argued that the term cannot be used, as it frequently has, to juxtapose Quebec and the rest of the country. Recent years have seen an increased self-consciousness among at least two groups outside Quebec which, by definition, cannot be accommodated within any notion of English Canada, however loosely defined.

First, in most provinces French-speaking minorities have become increasingly politically prominent. While this activism has not succeeded in arresting the demographic decline of the francophone minorities, it has at least heightened general awareness that in parts of Canada there are "official language minorities" who by definition are not part of any English Canada. Second, throughout Canada, Aboriginal peoples have been increasingly vigorous in making the claim that they constitute distinct "First Nations." Indeed they have secured considerable sympathy among non-Aboriginals. Clearly, they too stand outside any notion of an "English Canada." Also, an opposing problem with English Canada when used for these purposes is that by some readings it would extend to parts of Quebec where English-speakers are in large numbers.

There is a final complication: the obverse to "English Canada," "French Canada," has also fallen out of favour. The notion of a culturally defined French Canada has been replaced by a territorially defined Quebec nation. English Canada, as a culturally defined entity, sits uncomfortably with a territorially defined Quebec nation.

For all these reasons, then, the term "English Canada" has come into dispute. In particular, it has been discredited as a label for describing the entity with which we are concerned: the Canada that would remain if Quebec were to become sovereign or were to assume a significantly different status as a province. The result has been the invention of "Canada Outside Quebec," and its many variations such as "Canada Without Quebec" and "The Rest of Canada."

To be sure, "English Canada" continues to be employed. In 1991 Jack Granatstein and Kenneth McNaught edited a book entitled *"English Canada" Speaks Out*, although they were careful to insert the term in quotation marks, declaring that it "caused some difficulty" since it will suggest to some that "only the English-speaking or those of British origin" are entitled to speak out about the country's future (Granatstein and McNaught 1991:12). This was clearly not their intent.

More recently, Philip Resnick has published an essay forthrightly entitled *Thinking English Canada* (1994), in which he argues that while not ethnically exclusive, English Canada exists as a "sociological" nation, possessing all the traits normally associated with nations (as differentiated from states). He makes a similar argument in his chapter in this volume.

Nonetheless, the newly controversial status of "English Canada" has been confirmed by no less a source than *The Globe and Mail Style Book* which says: "Not a good term when differentiating Quebec and the nine other provinces and two territories. Its implication is that everyone in Quebec speaks French, and everyone outside speaks English. Prefer such terms as the rest of Canada" (MacFarlane and Clements 1990:94).

While consonant with the prevalent understanding of Canada and better suited to dealing with the Quebec question, terms such as "Canada Outside Quebec" do have an obvious flaw: they denote an entity on the basis of what it does not contain rather than what it does. It is the Canada that remains after Quebec has been removed.

Nonetheless, "Canada Outside Quebec" does serve our purposes. Defined in wholly geographical terms, it excludes no social category, including official language minorities and Aboriginal peoples. It is open ended, bearing no assumptions about the degree of cohesiveness within the population it demarcates. And of course it responds perfectly to the political development with which we are concerned: indeed it was invented for that purpose.

Generally speaking, this term will orient the various chapters that follow. At the same time, we see no reason to preclude contributors from using "English Canada" and its variants, especially when it is clearly understood to refer to something less than Canada Outside Quebec.

OUR APPROACH TO THE QUESTION

The primary question to which this book seeks to respond can now be simply stated as "How cohesive is Canada Outside Quebec?" Our approach is straightforward: in each of a large number of areas we examine general trends within Canada Outside Quebec over the last few decades, assessing the extent to which they demonstrate cohesiveness. For greater clarity, the response to this question is organized in the broad categories of politics, culture, economy, and society. To what extent are Canadians outside Quebec bound by a common allegiance to a shared political community and to national political institutions? How successful has Canada Outside Quebec been in fostering and supporting cultural activity? To what extent does Canada, with or without Quebec, function as a "national economy"? And how do established notions of identity in Canada Outside Quebec treat subordinate social groupings such as Aboriginal peoples, women, and "new Canadians"?

We have already indicated that we are also concerned with a second question: "How cohesive would Canada Outside Quebec be if Quebec were to: (a) become a sovereign state or (b) assume an asymmetrical or confederal status?" Any answer to this question must be very tentative.

In effect, we will extrapolate from the current condition of Canada Outside Quebec how cohesive it would be if Quebec's status were to change. This presumes, of course, that current trends will continue into the immediate future. Even with this assumption, the answer can only be partial for a couple of reasons.

First, the very absence of Quebec could trigger changes within the rest of Canada, even reversing trends presently evident. For instance, if, through Quebec sovereignty or the adoption of confederalism, Parliament were no longer to contain M.P.s from Quebec, then the relative strength of party caucuses could be radically different. To take an especially dramatic case, if the Reform Party were to continue to be relatively unpopular in Quebec then its chances of forming a majority government will remain very limited; without Quebec it would be a different story. We will attempt to take such possibilities into account.

Second, the very process of changing Quebec's status could itself have effects for Quebec – and for Canada Outside Quebec. For instance, numerous economists have insisted that accession to Quebec sovereignty and especially the negotiations leading up to it would have important transition costs: postponed or cancelled investment plans, higher costs for foreign borrowing, outmigration of labour, etc. Within most analyses, such costs would not be restricted to Quebec, they would also fall to a lesser degree on the rest of Canada as well. While we at various points attempt to take account of such effects, they are not our central focus.

In short, our examination of recent trends in Canada Outside Quebec can provide only part of the answer to the question before us. But it is a part that has been rarely attempted. In fact, these pages constitute the first collective effort by scholars from a wide variety of disciplines to do so.

ORIGINS OF THIS BOOK

This book is the result of a project organized by the Robarts Centre for Canadian Studies at York University, Toronto. In the late spring of 1994, over twenty nationally known scholars from all parts of Canada Outside Quebec were invited to prepare papers. They represented a wide variety of disciplines – in effect, the full scope of Canadian Studies. Virtually all those invited accepted.

Each invitee was asked to address within the particular area of their expertise the recent trends that were evident in Canada Outside Quebec, with an eye to the level of cohesion that resulted. And they were asked to extrapolate from this what would be the cohesion of Canada Outside Quebec if Quebec's status were to change. In preparing their papers, they were left free to answer these questions in whatever way they felt appropriate.

In late April of 1994 these scholars gathered at the Robarts Centre for a three-day symposium. Copies of most of the papers had been distributed to the participants well beforehand. As a result, the three days could be devoted to extensive discussion of the papers and exchanges of views. Most of the participants then extensively revised their papers in light of that discussion, as well as suggestions from the editor. Thus this book constitutes the result of a sustained and truly collective effort.

CONTRIBUTORS' FINDINGS

The Persistence of National Sentiment

The first set of chapters deals with the politics of Canada Outside Quebec, seeking in particular to assess the extent to which its residents continue to be united through allegiance to a shared political community and would likely remain so even if Quebec were to withdraw from the federation. With varying degrees of qualification, the authors respond in the affirmative.

In the opening chapter, H.V. Nelles examines Ontario's position within Canada and within a Canada Without Quebec. He makes a spirited argument for continuity in both cases. General impressions to the contrary, Ontario's historically dominant position within the Canadian economy has not declined over recent years. In fact, such measures as Ontario's proportion of the national Gross Domestic Product and the relative personal incomes of its residents suggest that "Ontario's economy has become more rather than less dominant." Nor would Quebec's withdrawal from Canada seriously threaten Ontario's economic position.

By the same token, Nelles argues, even if Quebec were to withdraw, the political stance of Ontarians and their government would remain the same. They would want Canada to persist, even in abbreviated form, and would continue to affirm the values of multiculturalism, bilingualism, and commitment to the Charter of Rights and Freedoms. Ontario would even want to play a mediating role between the new Canada and Quebec.

In the next chapter Roger Gibbins argues that Western Canadians also remain strongly attached to Canada. Tracing the history of national sentiment in Western Canada, Gibbins finds that from the outset its residents identified strongly with idea of a Canadian nation. To be sure, their vision of the nation closely reflected Western Canadian experiences and values: Canada was seen as a culturally homogeneous community modelled on British political institutions. There was little room for Quebec's claims to cultural distinctiveness.

At the same time, Western Canadians acquired a strong sense of alienation from Central Canada and its domination of Canadian government and economy. Devolution of powers to the provinces is not really a remedy, the jurisdictions that are most salient to Western Canada must remain lodged with the central government. Thus in recent years regional alienation produced proposals to reform institutions in Ottawa so as to afford Western Canadians their rightful role. The Reform Party has been especially successful in capturing this sentiment with its slogan "The West wants in" and its proposal of a Triple E Senate.

Thus, with respect to Western Canada, Quebec's accession to sovereignty would raise an intriguing paradox. A Canada Without Quebec would conform more closely to the Western Canadian variant of Canadian nationalism. But reforms for a Triple E Senate and the principle of equality of the provinces would have even less appeal to Ontario than they do now, since it would represent close to half the population of the new Canada.

In the third chapter, Robert Finbow examines Atlantic Canada's relationship to Canada Outside Quebec. Like Western Canadians, Atlantic Canadians display a long-standing loyalty to Canada which is tempered by an equally long-standing sense of grievance against Central Canada. Unlike Western Canada, however, the sense of regional grievance is also checked by a strong sense of economic dependence on the central government. Thus Atlantic Canadians have even more reason than do their Western counterparts to look to the national government for redress of their problems and to focus on securing a stronger regional role at the centre. Unlike Westerners, they have worked within the established national parties to secure this.

Finbow surveys the range of federal policies that have been designed to reduce regional disparities: equalization grants, transfer payments to governments and individuals, and regional development initiatives. While these policies have served to integrate Atlantic Canada more fully into national economic and political institutions, they have also reinforced a sense of dependence along with a strong sense of cynicism.

Atlantic Canadian concern with maintaining a strong regional presence in national political institutions was very much in evidence during the recent constitutional discussions. Atlantic Canada can be expected to resist any scheme for general decentralization of powers in the federal system. It would be preferable that Quebec be accommodated through asymmetrical arrangements.

As for Quebec sovereignty, it would raise the spectre of a physical separation of the Atlantic region from the rest of Canada. And the region can ill afford the economic costs that would accompany a long and rancorous transition to sovereignty. Moreover, there would be apprehension over Ontario's dominance of the Commons of a new Canada. However, Atlantic Canadian interests and loyalties will remain attached to Canada, with or without Quebec, provided that federal leaders honour national commitments to similar levels of public service and opportunities for all Canadians.

The next chapter, by Philip Resnick, argues that linking together the residents of all three regions is a common membership in a nationality that he straightforwardly labels "English Canada." While eschewing any ethnic connotation to the term "English Canadian," Resnick insists that the overwhelming majority of residents of Canada Outside Quebec share a commonality rooted in the English language, "the lingua franca of the inhabitants [of Canadian society outside Quebec] from Bonavista to Vancouver Island, with exceptions for pockets of francophones, Aboriginals, and first generation ethnic communities."

At the same time, Resnick argues for the need of English Canadians to develop a fuller consciousness of their distinct identity and of their common political interests, especially relative to Quebec and Aboriginal peoples. He notes how the recent constitutional debate saw "the beginnings of such an intra-English Canadian dialogue." As Quebec enters a new debate over its future, he argues, English Canadians must develop new political institutions that will enable them to address their collective identity and to define how their society should be organized and what type of relations it should maintain with Quebec. Accordingly, he outlines his proposal for an Estates General of English Canada.

Finally, F.L. Morton explores the effect that the Charter of Rights and Freedoms has had on Canada Outside Quebec and would be likely to have if Quebec were to withdraw from Canada. Morton recognizes that the Charter has become a powerful national symbol in Canada Outside Quebec, although not in Quebec itself, and to that extent is a unifying force. But he argues that the Charter is also a source of political conflict in Canada Outside Quebec since citizens are deeply divided over the policy objectives that should be pursed through application of the Charter. Disputing the contention of some scholars that outside Quebec virtually all citizens have become "Charter Canadians," he seeks to demonstrate that substantial numbers of Canadians are opposed to use of the Charter to promote equality of results for groups. Their political vision, rooted in individual rights, has been reflected in support for the Reform Party and opposition to the Charlottetown Accord.

With Quebec gone, he opines, the latter vision would be in a stronger position. In effect, this new Canada would be more clearly united around the Charter as a symbol of political community but perhaps more profoundly divided over the agendas to be pursued by the Charter. He speculates about whether this division might take on a regional character, Ontario versus the West, or by providing a non-territorial basis for political conflict might actually contribute to the unity of a Canada without Quebec.

To summarize, in political terms Canada Outside Quebec displays a high degree of cohesion: national symbols and institutions continue to command allegiance in the various regions, including Western Canada where the sense of political alienation has been strongest. If anything, political cohesion has been growing in recent years. The potential for decentralizing Canadian federalism is limited. By the same token, if Quebec were to withdraw from the federal order, the disposition in the rest of Canada would be to continue to function as a political community. However, in both East and West there would be a concern that national institutions be modified to prevent domination by Ontario.

The Rise of Anglophone Literature, Film and the Arts

The second part of the volume brings together six chapters on the cultural life of Canada Outside Quebec. First, in an overview of recent trends in anglophone-Canadian literature, criticism, and the arts, Frank

Davey traces how the established notion of a "national" culture, at least as anglophone Canadians have experienced it, has been undermined and fractured. For instance, leading Canadian artists increasingly are participating in a global culture, publishing their works with multinational corporations and assuming the role of celebrity-commodities on an international market. At the same time, the anglophone-Canadian cultural community is being fractured through disputes over such issues as cultural appropriation and racism and access to institutional recognition. In addition, many artists are rejecting the organization of cultural activities on uniform, national bases with conceptions based on local or particular circumstances and geared to redressing wrongs.

Davey in part traces these various changes to globalization and the many even contradictory influences it exerts. At the same time, he notes that those changes need not mean the end of anglophone-Canadian literature as long as "the writers of various groups continue to argue with one another" and scholars continue to construct it as a focus of study.

If the direction of anglophone cultural life has become less certain and subject to open debate, there can be little question that at the same time it has reached an unprecedented dynamism and vibrancy. Joyce Zemans traces the essential role which national institutions have played in bringing this about. She details how in the course of this century the federal government elaborated a complex of institutions to develop and support cultural life including the National Gallery, the CBC, the National Film Board, the Canada Council, and the National Arts Centre. While their responsibilities and mandates have been regularly challenged by Québécois cultural and political elites, they are widely recognized in Canada Outside Quebec as being essential to the future of cultural activity, as well as instrumental to the development of a sense of national community.

Thus, during the recent constitutional negotiations no other province endorsed Quebec's position that jurisdiction for culture belonged exclusively to the provinces. The artistic community across Canada Outside Quebec mobilized in defense of national cultural institutions and the federal government's role in supporting them.

Canada's national cultural institutions face a variety of challenges, which Zemans documents. But with respect to Canada Outside Quebec they can count upon the active support of their constituency. In this, Canada Outside Quebec has demonstrated real cohesiveness – and a marked divergence from Quebec.

In the next chapter Ted Magder surveys the dramatic growth that has taken place in English-language film production in Canada. Characterizing Canada as "Hollywood North," Magder notes that together Toronto and Vancouver represent the second largest production centre in North

America for English-language feature films and television programs. In particular, Canada has become a major producer of programs for television – and in fact is the world's second largest exporter of them.

This radical change from the situation less than two decades ago is largely due to the active support that the federal government has provided for feature film production, starting with the creation of the Canadian Film Development Corporation in 1968. Magder acknowledges that this film industry remains highly dependent upon state support. Moreover, much of it is geared to the perceived needs of the American market, especially for television programming. And Canadian films remain largely absent from movie theatres in Canada.

Nonetheless, anglophone Canada is now producing feature films at a level that would have been unthinkable twenty years ago. In a number of cases, these films have been recognized for artistic excellence not only in Canada but internationally. After surveying the possible rationales for continuing to support such an industry, Magder argues that the values of artistic expression are alone sufficient justification. Quebec's withdrawal from Confederation would have little effect on English-language film production, based as it is in Canada Outside Quebec and heavily geared to the American television market.

In her examination of English-language television in Canada, Mary Jane Miller seeks to determine whether it is likely to remain distinctive, especially if Quebec's status were to change. Her answer is qualified: "Probably." But the qualifications have mainly to do with factors other than Quebec's future status. Miller documents at length how over the years English-language television has developed a distinctive "footprint," with accomplishments in a wide range of areas such as news and public affairs, children's programming, and adult drama. Whether it will be able to maintain this distinctiveness is partly to do with whether it can meet the challenges of radical changes in technology. This, in turn, has a lot do with the stance of the Canadian state.

Quebec and the French fact have figured only marginally in English-language television. Even the CBC has functioned quite independently of Radio-Canada. To the extent the CBC has fulfilled the important role of providing the "symbolics" of nationhood it has done so independently of Radio Canada. On this basis, little would change if Quebec were to become sovereign or if, through some sort of asymmetrical federalism, the Quebec provincial government were to assume control of Radio-Canada.

Finally, Rowland Lorimer surveys the state of English-language book publishing in Canada, demonstrating that here too an enormous transformation has taken place. Not only do Canadian-owned publishers dominate along several indicators, such as numbers of firms, new title production, own-title trade sales, and publication of Canadian authors, but Canadian books enjoy national and regional attention in the mass media.

Lorimer argues that despite the processes of globalization, the Canadian English-language publishing industry has the capacity not only to survive but to continue to develop, and that the departure of Quebec would have little direct impact on the industry. On the other hand, Lorimer acknowledges that anglophone publishing could be indirectly jeopardized to the extent Quebec's departure would reinforce the position of forces, such as the Reform Party, that are opposed to state subsidization of cultural activity.

In short, over recent decades cultural life, at least in English, has flourished in Canada Outside Quebec. Whether the focus be literature, film, television, or book publishing, the trend is the same. Moreover, this activity is largely independent of French-language cultural life in Quebec. Unlike Quebec, the cultural community has firmly resisted devolution of jurisdiction over culture. By the same token, future development of cultural activity in Canada Outside Quebec would probably be essentially the same whether or not Quebec becomes sovereign.

Nonetheless, the final piece by Alfred Young Man compellingly demonstrates a fundamental deficiency of Canada's cultural institutions: their systematic refusal to recognize as art the work of Canada's Native artists. Drawing upon reproductions to make his points, Young Man shows how mainstream attitudes toward Native art have been fundamentally shaped by anthropological assumptions as to the nature of Native culture. The artistic production of Natives is thus judged in terms of its congruence with these stereotypes. If it conforms with them, then it is assigned to anthropological institutes and museums. If it not, it is ignored.

At the same time, the presentation in museums of traditional Native artifacts, as well as skeletal remains, raises important questions of appropriation. The display of what are considered to be sacred objects outrages First Nations people. Typically, museums make fundamental errors in their presentation of Native items. By the same token, both academics and commercial interests have increasingly intruded upon native ceremonial activities. In effect, the Canadian state's treatment of Native art has closely reflected the same stereotypes and assimilationist objectives that have guided state policy in general with respect to First Nations peoples.

Decline of the National Economy

The next set of papers focuses upon the economics of Canada Outside Quebec. Both contributors choose not to treat Canada Outside Quebec in isolation: in economic terms, it continues to function with Quebec in a single system. Yet, they also find that this system has been considerably weakened in recent years. In terms of such indicators as the importance of the internal market, the capacity of the federal state to regulate the economy, the condition of public finances, and the viability of federal social programs, Canada has very much declined as a "national economy." Moreover, the profound challenges this poses for Canada Outside Quebec would be largely the same whether or not Quebec remains a province.

To be sure, as one might expect, the two analysts' judgments differ markedly about the overall effects of the changes the Canadian economy has undergone and thus about the relative importance and severity of the different problems now facing the economy.

Focusing upon Canada's relations with the United States, Stephen Clarkson traces the steady integration of Canada within the North American continental economy and the concomitant narrowing of the autonomy of the federal and provincial governments. He roots these processes in the federal government's post-war strategy of encouraging u.s. direct foreign investment and undertaking public projects that support continental integration. This continentalist economic strategy served to compromise the post-war construction of a welfare state under federal aegis and ran at cross-purposes to a federal effort to create an indigenous Canadian cultural sphere.

With the arrival of Pierre Trudeau to power, the federal government embarked on a nation-building effort to counter Quebec separatism. But its effort to develop a third National Policy, through an interventionist industrial policy and enhanced staple development, was undermined by Canada's advanced degree of continental integration.

The Mulroney Conservatives pursued continental integration with a new zeal, resulting in the Free Trade Agreement (FTA) and the North American Free Trade Agreement (NAFTA), both of which were designed to constrain state intervention. Indeed the Mulroney years saw a scaling down in the activities of the federal government, especially in the cultural sphere. These developments had the effect of mobilizing popular support for a continued role for Ottawa, especially in social programs. This was a central concern of the broad-based coalition that opposed the Free Trade Agreement. These reactions served to distinguish English Canada from Quebec, where they were not in evidence.

Clarkson is pessimistic about the prospects for a post-separation Canada. As English-Canadian opposition to the Free Trade Agreement might suggest, the citizens of the new Canada might well remain strongly attached to their national government, expecting it to maintain social programs superior to those of the United States. But thanks to the forces of economic integration, formalized and reinforced through the NAFTA, the federal government would not have the capacity to do so. The new Canada would have "neither the economic viability nor the international raison d'être to form a successful nation state."

Melville McMillan offers a more positive reading of the effects of external forces upon the Canadian economy. His review of economics studies seeking to measure the effects of the FTA and NAFTA on the performance of the Canadian economy suggests that on balance they have been beneficial, especially in terms of the volume of exports. He acknowledges that trade liberalization may reduce the capacity of the Canadian state but claims that the constraint may be more in terms of means than ends – for which alternative measures such as direct tax-transfer systems are still available.

At the same time McMillan suggests that the importance of Canada's internal economy may not have declined so much as some analysts have argued, despite trade liberalization. In fact, external trade agreements may serve to enhance interprovincial trade through forcing the elimination of internal non-tariff barriers.

But McMillan also points to an internal process which has greatly weakened the Canadian economy and the federal state: the mushrooming of the Canadian public debt. He details the pressures that this places on the federal government's structure of social programs, which he sees as instrumental to maintaining a sense of Canadian political community. Not only will there be severe pressures to reform and scale down these programs but any such changes will complicate federal-provincial relations.

As for the future of a Canada from which Quebec has withdrawn, McMillan sees a mixture of changes. There might be some gains in the ease of reducing internal trade barriers, the burden of federal equalization programs, and the ability to secure federal-provincial agreement in such areas as social policy. After a transitional period, the economic costs of Quebec's separation for the new Canada would likely be "moderate." However, the new Canada would be confronted with the geographical separation of Atlantic Canada. And, as a smaller entity, it would carry less weight internationally.

Society: Dominance and Marginality

The final dimension of this "stock taking" of Canada Outside Quebec focuses upon its society. More specifically, this section seeks to assess the extent to which the predominant understandings of the nature of this society, especially as articulated by governments, effectively encompass the various social categories contained within it. We see how established notions of identity in Canada Outside Quebec have failed to come to terms with at least three of the social groups that compose it – Aboriginal peoples, women, and "new Canadians" – and provide a precarious recognition to a fourth group: francophones.

The opening chapter, by Frances Abele, explores the place of Aboriginal peoples within the dominant conception of Canada Outside Quebec, an "English Canada." She examines the several components of the idea of English Canada, as defined by Philip Resnick, and shows how in each case they are understood differently by Aboriginal peoples.

For instance, whereas language, represented by a common knowledge of English, is a defining feature of English Canada, for Aboriginal peoples speaking English is a "politically and emotionally charged experience," since their own languages not only are severely threatened by the normal pressures of twentieth century life but historically have been the objects of deliberate suppression by state and religious authorities. Similarly, whereas democracy is a presumed common value of English-Canadian culture Aboriginal peoples have had their own governing traditions replaced by arrangements that were most definitely not democratic. And the Aboriginal understanding of history and land are far different from the English-Canadian conceptions.

Abele argues that the need for Canada to find ways to include strong collectivities will not pass with resolution of the future of Quebec. The project to include Aboriginal peoples in Canada may ultimately require constitutional change; it will certainly entail a deeper and different understanding of Canadian history and ultimately a revised conception of the meaning of Canada.

In the next chapter, Michael Lanphier and Anthony Richmond examine ethnicity in Canada Outside Quebec with particular reference to the ability of programs of multiculturalism to accommodate diversity. In a survey of the Canada Outside Quebec's principal regions they show a high degree of variation both in the ethnic composition of regional populations and in the development and efficacy of provincial multiculturalism policies. Then, equating Canada Outside Quebec with English Canada, Lanphier and Richmond use recent census data to address the provocative question: "How 'English' is English Canada?" They show that in ethnic terms English Canada is not overwhelmingly "English." In fact, in 1991 only 26 percent of the population was exclusively of "British" origin. The authors show that within Canada as a whole in 1991, 2.3 million people used a language other than English or French as their home language, half of whom were located in Ontario. They conclude that

Canada Outside Quebec has lost whatever "English" social character it may once have had.

Lanphier and Richmond are uncertain what direction ethnic relations in a Canada of which Quebec is no longer part might take. While recognizing that biculturalism has already lost legitimacy, they note that multiculturalism as an ideal remains tentative and ambiguous. They evoke in particular the possibility of new global ethnic networks supported by electronic communication and advanced transportation. The political boundaries of Canada Outside Quebec would have no particular significance. Thus the conclusion becomes that Canada Outside Quebec "is in process of becoming a postmodern state in serious danger of fragmentation."

In the third chapter of this section, Janine Brodie traces the history of the women's movement in Canada Outside Quebec showing how this essentially English-Canadian movement has always followed a trajectory distinct from its Quebec francophone counterpart. Moreover, the development of the movement was closely shaped by the evolution of the Canadian state, with which it was closely linked, and by the definitions of women's identity that the state sought to foster.

The English-Canadian women's movement emerged at the turn of the century, guided by maternal feminism and the laissez-faire state's relegation of women to the private sphere. On this basis, the women's movement was able to secure state protective reforms for women and children as well as the enfranchisement of women nationally and in all provinces but Quebec – testament to the much weaker position of women in that province.

The link between the English-Canadian women's movement and the federal state was sealed through Ottawa's post-World War II construction of a Keynesian welfare state, in which the focus was the administration of income and social services for the family. Within this new state discourse women were defined as mothers, and as such they succeeded in securing both a substantial range of federal policies and a new claim to a voice in politics. In the process the disjunction between English-Canadian women and Quebec francophone women was further reinforced. This disjunction became manifest in the constitutional debates of the early 1980s, as English-Canadian women successfully lobbied to secure sexual equality provisions in the Charter whereas the Quebec movement viewed the adoption of the Charter without Quebec's consent as a betrayal.

As the 1980s progressed the women's movement was increasingly challenged by the neo-conservative discourse that came to dominate the Mulroney government, stressing a rollback of the state so as to respond to the pressures of globalization. Within the new discourse, the state was no longer to assume the Keynesian welfare functions. Within the same discourse, women no longer had a specific claim for state action and their movement was marginalized.

While recognizing the profound challenges presented to the English-Canadian women's movement by this new state discourse and new definition of women's identity, Brodie notes that the movement has become a key element among progressive forces in Canada Outside Quebec. By the same token, with its long history as a distinctly English-Canadian movement, it would be well placed to exercise a leadership role in determining the future of a Canada without Quebec.

Finally, Phyllis LeBlanc examines the evolution of notions of collective identity among the Francophones of "Canada Outside Quebec." She begins by tracing how after being unable to locate an effective identity for a Canada as a whole, historians turned to the exploration of regional identities and the histories associated with them. She then shows how students of the francophone communities outside Quebec were also driven to recognize the extent to which identities were fragmented by region. Beyond this fragmentation among francophone communities, there is also a fragmentation or marginalization of each community with respect to its territorial and social milieux.

LeBlanc then assesses the extent to which the federal government has been able to offset these processes of fragmentation through active support of the francophone minorities. She notes how beyond increasing budgetary constraints federal action is presently hampered by widespread lack of strategic planning. Of the provincial governments only New Brunswick has given French official equality with English. In any event, by definition action of the provincial governments cannot overcome the fragmentation that has affected francophones outside Quebec.

Just as the rise of Quebec neo-nationalism contributed to this fragmentation among francophones elsewhere in Canada, so the withdrawal of Quebec from Canada would pose a major challenge for them. In the new Canada the existing constitutional guarantees of linguistic rights, including New Brunswick's, could not be taken for granted.

The Future of Canada Outside Quebec

In a final set of chapters, three distinguished scholars of Canada offer their personal reflections of the future of Canada Outside Quebec, drawing in part on their reactions to the many contributions to this volume.

Abraham Rotstein speculates on the recent upheaval in Canadian federal politics and what this portends for any transition of Quebec to sovereignty. He interprets the rise of the Reform Party and the Bloc Québécois as direct reflections of the most powerful subterranean forces in Canadian politics: English-Canadian populism and Quebec nationalism, and argues that they constitute fundamentally incompatible worldviews. The individualism and egalitarianism of English-Canadian populism is on a collision course with the collectivism of Quebec nationalism. As a consequence, Rotstein fears that any attempt of Quebec to secure sovereignty is bound to be accompanied by an escalation of conflict between English Canada and Quebec.

Marjorie Griffin Cohen situates the future of Canada Outside Quebec within the forces of globalization which are both undermining the capacity of democratic governments to respond to their citizenry and forcing societies into increasingly rigid and extreme structures of stratification. She contends that the future of Canada Outside Quebec will be determined by these forces, largely for the worst, rather than by whether Quebec remains part of the federation. For this reason, she disagrees with the general optimism about the future of Canada Outside Quebec which she sees in most of the contributions to this volume. She sees a real possibility that if Quebec were to withdraw from the federation Western Canada would pursue its already developing linkages with neighbouring u.s. states. Atlantic Canada would be cast adrift by its new physical separation from the rest of the country. Given the extent to which its capacity has been undermined by international economic integration, the Canadian state would not be able to pursue the market-correcting social policies that historically have provided the "glue" needed to bind these regions to Canada.

In the final commentary, Tom Courchene outlines a series of ways in which Quebec's withdrawal would affect Canada Outside Quebec, all moving it in the direction of the American Creed: decline in tolerance of legal and institutional pluralism and in support for regional redistribution, multiculturalism, and collective rights; increase in centralization; rise of non-territorial cleavages; and a shift toward individualist capitalism. At the same time, Courchene argues that over the long term the pressures of globalization will inexorably lead to political decentralization in Canada, even if Quebec should no longer be there to champion provincial autonomy. Finally, he argues that the prospects for Canada Outside Quebec's surviving as an independent political entity are heavily dependent upon strengthening it as a state, not a nation, as well has having successfully addressed the challenges of the transition.

In a concluding chapter to this volume, we will explore more fully how the findings of these many contributors bear upon the future of Canada Outside Quebec, whether with a sovereign Quebec or in a reconfigured federal system. Now, however, we invite the reader to examine the chapters first hand.

BIBLIOGRAPHY

Allen, Richard. 1987. "Providence to Progress: The Migration of an Idea in English Canadian Thought." *Canadian Issues* no. 7.

Ballstadt, Carl, ed. 1975. *The Search for English Canadian Literature.* Toronto: University of Toronto Press.

Beckow, S.M. 1974. "From the Watchtowers of Patriotism: Theories of Literary Growth in English Canada, 1864-1914." *Journal of Canadian Studies* no. 9:3-15.

Bell, David, and Lorne Tepperman. 1979. "The English-Canadian Identity Puzzle." In *The Roots of Disunity*, 72-1070 Toronto: McClelland & Stewart.

Breton, Raymond. 1988. "From Ethnic to Civic Nationalism: English Canada and Quebec." *Ethnic and Racial Studies* no. 11:85-102.

Cole, Douglas, ed. 1980. "Anglo-Canadian Nationalism and Social Communication," special issue, *Canadian Review of Studies in Nationalism*, no. 7.

Cook, Ramsay. 1985. *The Regenerators: Social Criticism in Late Victorian English Canada.* Toronto: University of Toronto Press.

Craig, Terrence. 1987. *Racial Attitudes in English-Canadian Fiction, 1905-1980.* Waterloo: Wilfrid Laurier Press.

Davey, Frank. 1993. *Post-National Arguments: The Politics of Anglophone Canadian Fiction Since 1976.* Toronto: University of Toronto Press.

Fagel, Stanley. 1984. *A Tale of Two Countries: Contemporary Fiction in English Canada and the United States.* Toronto.

Gibbins, Roger, and J. Rick Ponting. 1981. "The Reactions of English Canadians and French Québécois to Native Indian Protest." *Canadian Review of Sociology and Anthropology* no. 18:222-38.

Globe and Mail. 1991. 2 April, A4.

Grabb, Edward E. 1980. "Differences in Sense of Control Among French- and English-Canadian Adolescents." *Canadian Review of Sociology and Anthropology* no. 17:169-75.

Granatstein, J.L., and Kenneth McNaught. 1991. *"English Canada": Speaks Out.* Toronto: Doubleday.

Grayson, J. Paul. 1981. "The English-Canadian Novel and the Class Structure." *Canadian Journal of Sociology* no. 6:423-45.

– and L.M. Grayson 1978. "Class and Ideologies of Class in the English-Canadian Novel." *Canadian Review of Sociology and Anthropology* no. 15:265-83.

Hutcheon, Linda. 1988. *The Canadian Postmodern: A Study of Contemporary English-Canadian Fiction*. Toronto: Oxford University Press.

Hunter, A.A. 1977. "Comparative Analysis of Anglophone-Francophone Occupational Prestige in Canada." *Canadian Journal of Sociology* 2:179-93.

James, William C. 1987. "Religious Symbolism in Recent English-Canadian Fiction." *Canadian Issues* no. 7.

L'Actualité. 1991. "Le refus global", March 15:25.

Laczko, Leslie. 1978. "English Canadians and Québécois Nationalism: An Empirical Analysis." *Canadian Review of Sociology and Anthropology* no. 15:206-17.

Levitt, Joseph. 1981. "Race and Nation in Canadian Anglophone Historiography." *Canadian Review of Studies in Nationalism* no. 8:1-16.

– 1900. "English-Canadian Nationalists and the Canadian Character, 1957-74." *Canadian Review of Studies in Nationalism* no. 12:223-38.

McFarlane, J.A., and Warren Clements. 1990. *The Globe and Mail Style Book*. Toronto: Infoglobe.

McNaught, Kenneth. 1966. "The National Outlook of English-speaking Canadians." In *Nationalism in Canada*, ed. Peter Russell. Toronto: University of Toronto Press.

McRoberts, Kenneth. 1991. *English Canada and Quebec: Avoiding the Issue*. North York: Robarts Centre for Canadian Studies, York University.

– 1993. "English-Canadian Perceptions of Quebec." In *Quebec: State and Society*, 2nd ed., ed. Alain G. Gagnon , 116-29. Scarborough: Nelson.

Meisel, John. 1977. "Who are We? Who Are They? Perceptions in English Canada." In *Options: Proceedings of the Conference on the Future of the Canadian Federation*, 13-33. Toronto: University of Toronto Press.

Moss, John. 1974. *Patterns of Isolation in English Canadian Fiction*. Toronto: McClelland & Stewart.

Ogmundson, R. 1980. "Toward the Study of the Endangered Species Known as the Anglophone Canadian." *Canadian Journal of Sociology* no. 5:1-2.

Pache, Walter. 1980. "English-Canadian Fiction and the Pastoral Tradition." *Canadian Literature* no. 86:15-30.

Prang, Margaret. 1986. "Networks and Associations: The Nationalizing of Sentiment in English Canada." In *National Politics and Community in Canada*, ed. Kenneth Carty and W. Peter Ward, 13-14. Vancouver: University of British Columbia Press.

Resnick, Philip. 1977. *The Land of Cain: Class and Nationalism in English Canada, 1945-1975*. Vancouver: New Star Books.

– 1994. *Thinking English Canada* Toronto: Stoddart.

Rotstein, Abraham. 1978. "Is There an English-Canadian Nationalism?" *Journal of Canadian Studies* no. 13:109-18.

Smith, Allan. 1976. "The Continental Dimension in the Evolution of the English-Canadian Mind." *International Journal* no. 31:442-69.

Tippett, Maria. 1986. "The Writing of English-Canadian Cultural History, 1970-85." *Canadian Historical Review* no. 67:548-61.

– 1988. *The Making of English-Canadian Culture, 1900-1939: The External Influences* North York: Robarts Centre for Canadian Studies, York University.

– 1990. *Making Culture: English-Canadian Institutions and the Arts before the Massey Commission.* Toronto: University of Toronto Press.

Vipond, Mary. 1980. "The Nationalist Network; English Canada's Intellectuals and Artists in the 1920s." *Canadian Review of Studies in Nationalism* no. 7:32-52.

Young, Robert A. 1977. "National Identification in English Canada: Implications for Quebec Independence." *Journal of Canadian Studies* 12 (July):69-84.

PART TWO

Politics/Persistence of National Sentiment

2 Ontario "Carries on"

H.V. NELLES

Anyone who took newspaper headlines literally would have to be forgiven for thinking that Ontario had fallen into a precipitous decline. "Ontario Hopes PM Will Stem Bleeding" (*Globe and Mail* 20 Dec. 1993); "Rae invite Ottawa à aider l'Ontario" (*Le Devoir* 9 Nov. 1993); and most recently, "Demise of a Fat Cat" (*Maclean's* 4 April 1994). One gets the impression of a recession-battered economy rapidly sinking, calling out to its neighbours for help. But *has* Ontario been "declining" relative to the others?

Let us begin with arithmetic and recent history. Has Ontario been a declining economic centre? Since we are concerned here with those parts of Canada outside Quebec, it would be useful to consider this question both including and excluding Quebec from the calculation. Statistics Canada's time series *The Provincial Economic Accounts* (13–213P) provides some quantifiable insight into this matter. Surprisingly, over the past decade the Gross Domestic Product (GDP) of the centre (defined by Statistics Canada as Quebec and Ontario) has actually grown relative to the rest of the country; and since Ontario has expanded more and contracted less than Quebec, Ontario's relative growth is more pronounced with Quebec out of the picture.

In 1983 the economy of the centre accounted for 58.5 percent of the total national economy, a proportion that had risen to 62.5 percent by 1992. This represented a slight fall back from the high of 63.9 percent reached in 1988 before the recession. In a hypothetical economy excluding Quebec, Ontario's proportion of the total would climb from 46 percent in 1983 to the most recent figure of 51 percent – an increase of 5 percentage points over the decade. In recent years, then, Ontario's economy has become more rather than less dominant.

At the same time Ontario citizens have become richer than their neighbours. Personal Income Per Capital in the procince of Ontario rose from 7 percent above the national average in 1983 to almost 13 percent in 1989 before slipping back to 9 percent in 1992. Removal of the Quebec figures, which are consistently but only slightly below the average, would not change the picture significantly.

Over the decade the relative size of the Quebec and Ontario economies has been shifting. In 1983 the Gross Domestic Product of Quebec was 61 percent that of Ontario. As Ontario boomed in the 80s Quebec's economy slipped to 55 percent that of Ontario. In the recession differential rates of contraction have brought Quebec up to 57 percent – still, it should be noted, a relative slippage of 4 percent over a decade. As it stands the Quebec economy is slightly more than half the size of that of Ontario and shrinking. In the centre it is the Quebec economy that is in relative decline.

Current data as they become available do not greatly change the overall picture. Ontario growth fell behind the national average, in the recession and through 1993. Data for 1994, however show an Ontario economy pacing economic growth as a result of increases in marchandise exports particularly in the auto sector. (*Canadian Economic Observer* December 1993, March 1994, June 1994, September 1994; Statistics Canada *The Daily*, 13 October 1994, 2–14.)

During the 1980s the two economies at the centre became less important to each other as markets for "exports." The table belows shows the relative importance of various markets for provincial manufactures in 1974, and 1984, and a calculation for 1989. In 1974 Ontario shipped 11.45 percent of its manufactures to Quebec, a proportion that had fallen to 5.89 percent in 1989, an almost 50 percent decline. By contrast Quebec's dependence upon Ontario as a market for goods dropped from 19.17 percent to 14.51 percent, a slippage of 20 percent.

Were political change to lead eventually to economic constraints, removing Quebec trade from the Ontario economy would be a big shock, but not so major a shock as it would have been in the past. The reverse is true, though not to the same degree, in Quebec. In the event that trade between the two economies should be disrupted for political reasons, it is clear that by this admittedly crude measure Ontario is twice as important as a market for manufactured goods to Quebec as Quebec is to Ontario. Both would face significant burdens of adjustment, but one more than the other. Ontario would be looking to replace roughly 6 percent of its shipments, Quebec 14 percent. At the

Table 1
Interprovincial Exports as a Percentage of Total
Manufacturing Shipments, 1974–89

	Ontario to Quebec	*Quebec to Ontario*
1974	11.45	19.17
1984	7.96	16.93
1989	5.89	14.51

Source: Statistics Canada, *Destinations of Shipments of Manufactures*, 1979, 1984, 31–530. The 1989 data are estimates calculated by Arthur Donner for an 18 February 1991 article in the *Toronto Star.*

same time the 10.3 percent of Quebec's manufacturing shipments to the rest of the country would be in jeopardy.

To sum up, the withdrawal of Quebec from the economy of Canada poses a much greater challenge to Quebec than it does to Ontario or the other provinces. Canada accounts for 25 percent of Quebec's manufacturing shipments; Quebec as a market for Ontario amounts to only 6 percent. Looking at the numbers alone it would not seem on the face of it that political disruption would cause a dramatic decline in the manufacturing exports of Ontario relative to the rest of the country. That, of course, is not the extent of the direct interconnections between the two entities, much less the indirect linkages, but it is an indicator of relative magnitudes. Ontario's economy has been growing relative to that of Quebec over the past decade, though the differences have diminished somewhat in the recession. In economic terms one part of the centre has been getting stronger, not declining. This trend would persist were Quebec excluded from the calculation.

Would such a hypothetical condition hold in the event of a real separation or an asymetrical restructuring of the Canadian federation? Again, clinging to the flimsy assumptions which govern this technical exercise, it is difficult to imagine the economic circumstances that would dramatically alter Ontario's position relative to the other provinces over a short period of time. Could continuing industrial restructuring, another oil shock, and a commodity price inflation like that of the 1970s combine to diminish an economy accounting for more than half of all national economic activity? Possibly. And that might well be a good thing from some perspectives as long as the growth in all cases was absolute. But other scenarios seem more likely, ones in which the centre would grow at or above the national average. Ontario's continued economic growth is driven by factors within the province, its large and growing foreign markets, and its economic union with the rest of the country. By comparison Quebec plays a relatively minor pole. Forecasts for 1994 and 1995 suggest Ontario real growth in GDP will exceed the national average in both years (*Globe and Mail* 3 May 1994; *Canadian Economic Observer* June 1994).

All of this serves to remind us that it is not Ontario that is broke, it's the Government of Ontario, and that is quite a different matter. In these unaccustomed straightened circumstances the Government of Ontario, like other governments before it, has begun to demand its "fair share" from Confederation. The calculus of such matters is contentious to say the least. Let us, for the sake of argument, take the Ontario government's view of the situation, recognizing that the numbers might change under cross-examination. Seen from a Queen's Park telescope Ontario continues to provide disproportionately more federal revenue than other provinces (43 percent) and receive disproportionately less (31 percent) federal expenditure in return. (By contrast Ontario contains 37 percent of the Canadian population and 39 percent of Canadian GDP.) In 1991 Ontario by its own account (or at least Informetrica's) contributed on balance $15 billion, or 5.5 percent of its GDP for redistribution to other regions (Office of the Premier of Ontario 8 November 1993; Informetrica). Meanwhile its government has become in four short years the largest nonsovereign debtor on international markets. These two facts taken together account for the loud squealing from Queen's Park.

Quebec affects this fiscal situation only at the margin to the extent that it influences interest rates. Changes in the federal structure in and of themselves would not necessarily alter the underlying condition of the Ontario government's penury. At the same time it is not true that Ontario's days as the self-perceived milch cow of Confederation are necessarily over. In a restructured federalism citizens of Ontario and their provincial government would probably still be willing to "pay the price of being Canadian" through equalization programs and other measures, but in hard times there is rather more attention to the matter of price than before.

Since the mid–80s governments led by three different political parties in Ontario, under financial pressure at home, have adopted an ever more strident tone in setting forth Ontario's needs vis à vis the federal government. Premier Rae's pre-budget letter to Ontario's members of parliament, following upon his six-volume study of Ontario's fiscal burden within Confederation, are but the latest examples of a new Ontario-centred federal strategy. In this respect, then, Ontario has become a province like the others. Or to put the matter in the premier's more melodramatic metropolitan language of November 1993, "Ontario has for decades been the part of Canada that dared not speak its name. The country was based upon the premise that everyone else could speak ill of Ontario, and at the same time this inherently wealthy place would continue to bankroll Canada." The reality, he went on to say, is that "Canada cannot prosper if its largest and most dynamic province does not. This is not always a popular truth in the rest of the country, but it is true" (Office of the Premier of Ontario 1993: 3–4).

So, under the present administration the Province of Ontario has developed an extensive list of "grievances" against Ottawa with price-tags on each of them:

- Offloading deficits through Established Programs Financing (EPF) reductions that have cost Ontario $10 billion;
- The cap on Canada Assistance Plan (CAP) that now limits the federal share of expenditures to 28 rather than 50 percent of Ontario's costs;
- Immigration and job training grants bear no relation to the provincial caseload;
- The province pays more than $1.6 billion more in Unemployment Insurance premiums than it receives in benefits;
- An excessively restrictive monetary policy has disproportionately hindered export-related economic recovery in Ontario.

The recent federal budget did little to address this bill of particulars – the cap on CAP, for example, remains in effect – and as a consequence the Ontario government in late March 1994 had to make more cuts, raise user fees, and add to its deficit.

However much amusement or even gloating this might stimulate in other parts of the country (the West actually has much stronger grievances on this score), should Ontario's whining be taken as a sign of decline? How much of this complaining is for home consumption? Would changes in transfers translate directly to Ontario's bottom line? To what extent are the Ontario government wounds self-inflicted while blame is shifted to others? These are difficult questions to answer in an election year.

It is by no means certain that the Province of Ontario can gain much sympathy by shifting blame to the federal government. It is true that this sort of thing plays well electorally in the West (circling the wagons against the external threat), but what about Ontario? After all, Ontario citizens vote for both the federal and provincial governments, more for the former than the latter. And Ontarians are said to identify more strongly with national than provincial governments. (Elkins and Simeon 1980: 17; Norrie, Simeon, and Krasnick 1986: 23). Are these cries evidence of a weak province or simply of a weak provincial government? The latter seems more likely.

Would Ontario take the lead in a fundamental restructuring of fiscal federalism, something that would notionally be easier to do in a Canada without Quebec, the leading beneficiary of transfers? Recent press reports suggest that the historic compact that has linked the federal and Ontario governments has been broken and that as a result the Ontario government has gone beyond negotiating for slightly better terms toward rethinking the justification for interprovincial transfers. According to the terms of this tacit contract Ottawa would pursue policies across a broad range of economic and social fronts that would, in effect, represent an Ontario view of Confederation by giving proportionate weight to Ontario's interests. For that reason Ontario has typically supported the notion of a strong central government. Conservative policies designed to serve a Quebec-West coalition broke this historic alliance, so the argument goes. And to the extent that the Chrétien government pursues deficit reduction *and* equalization, the costs will continue to be doubly borne by Ontario.

Reporters speak of a rapidly deteriorating relationship between bureaucrats in Queens Park and Ottawa. Premier Rae for his part has turned up the heat on his "fair share" campaign, indeed in recent months he seems to be moving beyond "better terms" to "no way." In mid-February 1994 the *Globe and Mail* reported that "What Ontario Wants is a financial restructuring of Confederation." And in a feature story in *Maclean's* (4 April 1994:12) Rae attacked the concept of equalization arguing that fiscal transfers to poorer provinces simply subsidized the purchase of foreign goods by the recipients. Formerly, the premier noted, "We would send the money out and it would come back. Everybody would read the Eaton's catalogue and send their cheques. The economic logic of that has collapsed."

In the same *Maclean's* story Tom Courchene agreed that Ottawa's unilateral action had threatened the integrity of the entire transfer payments system. Ontario could, if it chose, cause a lot of trouble by going it alone on fiscal measures: "Ottawa had better do something, because if Ontario flexes its muscles, it can wreak absolute havoc on the whole transfer system. If this isn't sorted out, the poorer provinces are going to lose more than Ontario is going to lose" (4 April 1994:12).

Rae's homely proposition holds only if the transfer recipients have a greater propensity for import consumption than Ontario, a province that runs the largest *international* trade deficit in goods and services. Moreover, the system does not have to be a completely closed loop to work as long as there are some direct or indirect linkages. Besides, Ontario's *interprovincial* trade balance in goods and services stands at more than $20 billion (*Canadian Economic Observer,* January 1993; October 1993:3.7–3.14). Apparently people are still sending the cheques even though Eaton's isn't sending the catalogue any more.

Besides that, fiscal federalism is not predicated upon the assumption that the money will be returned to the sender dollar for dollar. The equalization program equalizes the fiscal capacity of governments to provide services at comparable levels of quality across the country. That, not reciprocity, is the underlying principle.

Premier Rae's standard pre-election speech reaches its high point with a threat – or is it a plea – "All we're asking for Ontario is Our Fair Share." Should the rest of the country take seriously this pre-election threat from Ontario to reconfigure fiscal federalism to reduce the burden on the centre? I think not. In the first instance the provincial government – as it enters its fifth year – would have to seek a mandate to renegotiate fiscal federalism. With that government's popularity bordering on single digits, the rallying cry seem unlikely to set the heather afire. The Conservative opposition is trained on more fundamental issues – taxation and spending – not on these abstract fiscal heights. The Liberals, who on the face of it have the best chance at forming the next government, will be negotiating with notional friends after all. That should both improve the prospects of negotiation and moderate Ontario's intransigence. In the short run, therefore, the existing structure of fiscal federalism seems safe from the nightmare of the spoiled child of Confederation's running wild. Discounting for bluster, this looks like a negotiating ploy for more tax points, not a disagreement over fundamental principle.

But in the aftermath of separation or a restructuring of federalism, taxes will have to be paid and revenues shared. Under those quite different circumstances, what will Ontario want? Would Ontario seize the opportunity to insist upon further reductions or the elimination of some costly elements of the system? Would Ontario continue to finance net transfers at present levels? At the very basic level it would not have to for the simple reason that the largest net recipient of these transfer payments would no longer be a participant in the redistribution process. The total bill for equalization and other regional programs would fall. Ontario, Alberta, and British Columbia would have a smaller burden to carry.

In a world in which Ontario was even bigger relative to its other partners than it is now, and it found itself under continuing fiscal pressure, would it use its muscle to reshape fiscal federalism to its better advantage? In these circumstances I believe another set of countervailing forces would come into play. I think Ontario's desire to retain federal institutions in Ottawa would somewhat compromise its bargaining position. For it is quite likely that without Quebec the balance within Confederation would shift westward, and Winnipeg or some prairie Brasilia/Canberra would be a more appropriate capital than the discredited gothic ruin on the Ottawa. Maintaining proportionately scaled down federal institutions in Ontario would take some doing, and would require some give as well as take. There are and certainly will be distinct advantages to Ontario of the locus of the federation's being situated in one of its not otherwise viable cities.

The second argument is social and more closely linked to the logic of equalization. The alternative to transfer payments from rich to poorer provinces is interprovincial migration. In the absence of these programs the social fabric of the have not provinces weakens with out-migration to regions of stronger economic opportunity – Ontario being one of those regions. While national efficiency and Ontario as a growth centre might be well served by such a major shift in population, the social costs of decay and the welfare costs associated with heavy inmigration would have to be paid. Is it a better bargain to maintain stable communities than it is to add to the social stress of urban industrial centres? Ontario and the West have both had recent experience with massive interprovincial migration, and it has not been entirely successful.

Third, fiscal transfers would be one of the ways Ontario might be able to play a keystone role in keeping the residual federation together. The have not provinces would, one assumes, have some options as well. Their allegiance to a new order would have to be bought. Some years ago a student wrote on a Canadian history examination paper, "Confederation was accomplished by accountants." That may have captured some of the calculation of those negotiations, or at least the spirit of the historiography. However, an accountant's approach to reconfederation in which Ontario adopts a narrow view of its self-interest is unlikely to be attractive to others.

For these reasons I believe that a post-Quebec set of fiscal arrangements would look much like the system we have at present. There is quite a lot of flex in the system for renegotiation of terms without having the scrap the whole thing (Courchene, 1989).

Arithmetic and federal-provincial posturing arise, the more important questions are, Would the citizens of Ontario want to preserve something called Canada if the Quebec question opened all options? and, if so, what that something might be? The first question can be answered with greater certainty than the second. The citizens of Ontario and their provincial government are deeply attached to the idea of a Canada, even one with Quebec in it. This passion is something that BQ and PQ leaders discover with some surprise on their trips to Toronto. It is not entirely a rational preference dependant upon the coarse calculus of costs and benefits discussed above. Even bad numbers wouldn't change many minds and hearts. Ontario will not want to let either the idea of Confederation or the notion of a relatively powerful central government die, even if it might be economically better off on its own or in some loose political arrangement with the United States. The Canada choice resides at a different level of the collective psyche, in the same realm as taste, love, and desire.

Quebec's aspirations theoretically present Ontario with quite a wide range of choices for itself ranging from sovereignty, sovereingty-association, and annexation, to various kinds of re-confederation. Were Ontario's objections to fiscal federalism as it is presently constituted categorical, Ontario might want to pursue a similar course to Quebec, perhaps in conjunction with Quebec. Or it might want to go it alone. However, I think that the Government of Ontario's range of practical choice is much narrower, and indeed can be reduced to only one option – a federal system much like the one we at presently have.

Despite the occasional conceit of autarchy, the Ontario provincial government has no independentist option. For example, recent Ontario budgets have unwittingly compared Ontario's size and rates of growth favourably to those of other *countries*. And of course on simply economic grounds, Ontario separatism makes more sense than that of Quebec. Ontario is actually less tied in to the national economy than Quebec and more integrated into the global economy. But this is beside the point. Ontario will not take the opportunity of Quebec's departure to separate or to declare its unilateral independence from the rest of the country. There is no basis for believing Ontario would prefer to go it alone or negotiate a bilateral political-economic arrangement with the United States. There is even less foundation for believing in Ontario separatism than Western separatism. The budget slips should be read as pride rather than incipient autonomatism. In an uncomplicated deal-maker's universe Ontario and Quebec might cook up some mutually beneficial arrangement between themselves vis-à-vis the others. There is no support for such an arrangement at the moment, and any dislocation associated with Quebec's withdrawal – in whole or in part – would tend to reduce the attractiveness of that option. Ontario does not believe in sovereignty, much less sovereignty-association. Nor should we exaggerate the possibilities open to other regions. Tô be accepted, statehood must be offered – in most cases an unlikely prospect. On this matter the fantasies of Lansing Lamont are worth pondering (Lamont, *Breakup*).

Ontario will want a Canada to persist, not out of spite, not to get its fair share, and not because of some imperial dream, but rather out of a sense of pride, history, and kinship. It would feel a special obligation to make certain that the centre holds. Canada is not some half-way house between one imperial destiny and another. Ontario's citizens have some considerable pride of ownership in the independence of a northern, transcontinental dominion as an alternative North American vision. Ontario has a history and it is not one of pending statehood. We are a mobile people bound together over the generations by webs of kinship and friendship that stretch across provincial boundaries. These are not temporary emotions to be jettisoned in the slightest political turmoil. Indeed, an argument could be made that political adversity might heighten integrative beliefs. I agree with Bercuson and Cooper on at least that point (Bercuson and Cooper 1991:161-3, 170-1). In my view the belief in the nation is much stronger than many of us suspect; at least it is not so weak in Ontario that it would collapse simply on account of Quebec.

The Province of Ontario would strongly support the continuation of Confederation and probably in some unthinking way even pay to ensure that outcome. But what kind of country might this Remaining Canada, Continuing Canada, or just plain Canada be? Would it be a country with an Official Languages Act, a Canada Health Act, a Charter of Rights and Freedoms, and some commitment to multiculturalism? (I am struck as a historian how relatively recent these attributes of Canadianism turn out to be and indeed how Trudeauian our contemporary conception of Canada seems to be.)

I am on less secure ground here. Much would depend upon the short run complications and controversies. For example to take the most contentious issue, about half a million or 49 percent of the francophones outside Quebec make their home in Ontario. New Brunswick, with a higher proportion of francophone residents (33 percent), would nevertheless account for only 22 percent of Canadian francophones were Quebec not in the calculation. (*Canadian Social Trends* 1993). Ontario would then become the home to the largest body of francophones in Canada. What might happen to them in a new dispensation without Quebec? It is conceivable that Franco-Ontarians might get caught up in some vindictive backlash against "The French." On the other hand they have strong natural defences as well as some tactical opportunities.

Francophones in Ontario might become a minority like other minorities. That is not necessarily a step backward from the point of view of community service. In the rainbow coalition francophones would account for some 5.3 percent of the Ontario population, and they would still be the largest "ethnic" group. On the electoral margin and scattered through low population ridings in the east and north, they do have and will continue to have an influence out of proportion to their numbers. Similarly Ontario's treatment of its francophone minority will in some measure influence and be influenced by Quebec's attitude toward its anglophone and allophone minorities which are, after all, a much larger proportion of the total population. (The same might be said of the Aboriginal population, though it is less their numbers than their strategic geography that matters in Quebec.) Franco-Ontarian power, the ability to forge internal alliances with other minorities, and a possible competition between Ontario and Quebec over the treatment of minorities suggest to me that Ontario's francophones would have realistic options other than doom.

Certainly Quebec separation would put Ontario's extensive though not official commitment to bilingualism to a test. But it is not a foregone conclusion as far as I am concerned that Ontario would revert to some intolerant Regulation 17 mentality. The gain Franco-Ontarians have made are real and substantial and rest more on their collective power than any broader notion of bilingualism – but the latter does have some salience. Ontario is not the Anglo bastion of old. A new pluralistic vision animates all three political parties, admittedly to different degrees. The Leader of the Opposition, Lynn MacLeod, is a Trudeau Liberal, and Mike Harris, the leader of the Conservative Party, comes from a town that is almost 30 percent French speaking. Both must appeal to an extraordinarily heterogenous electorate. The Toronto *Star*, for what it is worth, chose a slow news day in June to declare that it was time Ontario became officially bilingual (11 June 1994).

Can one go so far as to say that Ontario would champion the notion of a bilingual, multicultural Canada without Quebec? To argue the affirmative requires considerable ability to suspend disbelief, but again it is not inconceivable. Significant francophone populations in Ontario and New Brunswick will expect the values of Canada to endure. While I would expect some modifications of the Official Languages Act to reduce its scope and some attenuation of bilingualism in the public service, I do not expect that most people would immediately abandon the vision of a bilingual country. It not only appeals to our vanity, it is a practial expression of our history and our ambitions. French immersion education is not an effort to keep Quebec in Canada. It is a positive assertion of our new selves in the next generation. Besides, language is one of Canada's most effective non-tariff barriers as Wal-Mart is discovering in its clumsy wooing of Canada. So I for one would not expect official bilingualism to be blown away by western revanchism after any breakup. Moreover I would expect that Ontario, perhaps much to its surprise and internal embarrassment, might lead the defence.

The same might be said of the Charter of Rights. As much as Ontario grumbled at its introduction, I sense that the revolution of Charter federalism is complete and irreversible. I believe that the Charter, in which our previously discussed bilingual nature is enshrined, has become a permanant attribute of our polity. It has proved to be too useful to too many people to be dumped in a huff. Indeed, too much effort is being spent attempting to establish more rights, than to return to a world of no rights as all. The populist commitment to the Charter might be weak, but despite everything there is a great deal of common ownership of it by interest groups (not the least of which are the law societies). Ontario may have taken to this new vision of Canada with greater fervour than others, certainly not less (Cairns, 37–61). After partition I would not expect any weakening of resolve on this issue. I think that for Ontarians the Charter speaks to citizenship in a broader national community in which provincialism plays a very small part. A new symbolic universe has been created which largely suits Ontario's needs.

But I am not sure of these arguments, and I do not see much point in cross-examining other "attributes of Canadianism" Ontario might strive to eliminate or protect. There are simply too many possible contingencies to speak with any confidence about Ontario's post-separation national agenda. New issues would arise in the process of disentanglement, and those would probably be the most contentious matters. Certainly the abstract construct "Ontario" would not be of one mind. All sorts of political tendencies find support in a spirited debate within its boundaries. There is strong support for the Reform Party in Ontario, for example. The degree of Reform support (it came second in a large number of ridings in the 1993 federal election) has not yet been reflected in parliamentary representation, but it is there and will not be denied. Here I have simply tried to imagine where, after the pluses and minuses have been taken into account, the majority might fall.

I do not believe, as Bercuson and Cooper apparently do, that a major dismantling of the Official Languages Act, equalization, and perhaps other redistribution programs would be immanent, at least in so far as Ontario is concerned. Rather, I am inclined to think that what we see is what we should get: a province committed to charter federalism in which bilingualism and multiculturalism would play a continuing role. Culturally and politically Ontario long ago moved off what might be thought of as its George Drew identity. I have some difficulty thinking of evidence, apart from the obvious social changes, that might support this conviction, but the list of recent winners of the Ontario Trillium Book Prize is suggestive. Those authors (Ondaatje [2], Findley, Eksteins, Munro, Atwood [2], and Urquhart) speak to a citizenship in a broader world of the imagination. They do not reflect a hunkered down, pioneer, homestead protective mentality. Over the last three decades of economic growth, social change, and political discourse, Ontario has shaped a new literary and cultural persona for itself more in keeping with its cosmopolitan character. It is, I believe, more firmly wedded to pluralism and charter federalism than we imagine, and this would not be shaken by the departure of Quebec.

To conclude, I do not see much evidence that Ontario is or might be a permanently "declining centre," the economic difficulties and the fierce provincial rights mien of its government notwithstanding. In the spirit of suspended disbelief and controlled speculation that surrounds this paper I do not think that Ontario would suddenly change its spots with the departure of Quebec. It is true that much has been done to accommodate Quebec, but I do not believe that the rest of the country has necessarily distorted itself culturally or constitutionally in the process. Much of the Canada we see is a positive choice accepted and warmed to by an extraordinarily diverse collection of Canadians in all regions. Seen from a different perspective our "secular tribalisms" have in large measure replaced our provincialism. (Cairns 1992:99).

Beyond that I would venture that Ontario would in its own way want to be accommodating and play an ongoing mediating role between Canada and Quebec. I think this would be particularly the case because Ontario would never accept Quebec's withdrawal from Canada as permanent. It would always want to keep an open door out of interest, perhaps, but more likely out of sentiment.

NOTE

I am grateful to Ken McRoberts for his encouragement and criticism, and to Janine Brodie, Tom Courchene, and Reg Whitaker for their profound scepticism. As this paper was revised for publication all of the prudential qualifiers upon which such a hypothetical exercise was constructed were excised for reasons of space. They nevertheless remain operative.

BIBLIOGRAPHY

Bercuson D., and B. Cooper, 1991. *Deconfederation: Canada Without Quebec*. Toronto: Key Porter.

Cairns, A. 1992. *Charter versus Federalism: The Dilemnas of Constitutional Reform*. Montreal and Kingston: McGill-Queens.

Courchene, T. 1989. *What Does Ontario Want?* John P. Robarts Lecture, Robarts Centre for Canadian Studies, York University.

Elkins, D., and R. Simeon. 1980. *Small Worlds*. Toronto: Methuen.

Informetrica Limited. 1993. *Summaries of Papers Prepared for the Ministry of Intergovernmental Affairs, Government of Ontario*.

- Jenness, R.A. "Ontario and the Canada Assistance Plan";
- "Review of the Established Programs Financing System";
- McCracken, M. "The Consequences of Deficit Shifting for Ontario";
- "The Distribution of Federal Spending and Revenue: Implications for Ontario and Other Provinces";
- "Recent Canadian Monetary Policy: National and Regional Implications";
- and R.A. Jenness. "Labour Market Development and Training."

Lamont, L. 1994. *Breakup: The Coming End of Canada and the Stakes for America.* New York: Norton.

MacLean's. 1994. "Demise of a Fat Cat." 4 April: 10–12.

Norrie, K., R. Simeon and M. Krasnick. 1986. *Federalism and the Economic Union.* Toronto: University of Toronto Press.

Office of the Premier of Ontario. 1993. *News Release.* Address by Premier Bob Rae on the Future of Ontario and Canada, 8 November.

Statistics Canada. 1993. *Canadian Economic Observer.* January: 1.1–1.15; October: 3.1–3.14; December: 1.1–1.5. 1994. Statistical Supplement. February: 57–61; March: 3.1–3.8; June: 1.1–1.15; August: 1.1–1.15; September: 1.1–1.6. *Canadian Social Trends.* 1993. *The Daily. 1994.* 13 October: 18. *Destinations of Shipments of Manufactures.* 1979, 1984. *Provincial Economic Accounts, Annual Estimates.* 1981–1991; *Preliminary Estimates.* 1992.

Toronto *Star.* 1994. 11 June.

3 Western Canada: "The West Wants In"

ROGER GIBBINS

The central thesis of this chapter is straightforward. Until the mid-1980s, chronic regional discontent in western Canada lacked any coherent reform focus; while the problems were quite evident, the solution was not. A solution was then brought into focus by a regional emphasis on Senate reform and, more specifically, on the pursuit of a Triple E Senate – elected, equal, and effective. This solution was championed by the new Reform Party, which was growing in strength across the region. Hence the "Camelot" period, when a clear reform vision was yoked to a powerful political movement dedicated to its attainment. In recent years, however, that focus has been lost. When the constitutional debate collapsed with the 1992 referendum, the Reform Party all but abandoned its earlier emphasis on Senate reform and turned instead to a much broader populist assault on the institutional and political status quo. Although Reform's populism has western roots, those roots were rapidly eclipsed as the party reached for a national audience for its platform of democratic populism, social conservatism, fiscal constraint, and tax revolt. Yet the nationalization of Reform has undercut the coherent western Canadian vision of institutional reform which had emerged in the 1980s. That vision has been subsumed within a much broader populist crusade (Sharpe and Braid 1992) which, while drawing from western inspiration, seeks a national audience.

This institutional reform saga sheds some interesting light on "national sentiment" in western Canada. With only minor and inconsequential exceptions, regional alienation in the West has been a form of frustrated Canadian nationalism. "Western alienation" has been characterized by a search for inclusion in the national community, a search nicely captured by Reform's founding slogan, "The West wants in!" Thus western alienation has had little in common with the nationalist movement in Quebec or with the latter's goal of dismembering the Canadian state. At the same time, this western expression of Canadian nationalism is not one that has recognized the distinctive character and aspirations of Quebec; it has sought inclusion for the West, but not on terms which would provide for the inclusion of a constitutionally distinct Quebec. To the contrary, it has been associated with national visions which have little if any currency within Quebec, a reality that is clearly illustrated by the recent debate over Senate reform. To the extent that national sentiment in the West has sought to include Quebec, it has been on terms unacceptable to that province. Although it can be argued that western figures such as John Diefenbaker, Peter Lougheed, and Preston Manning have expressed an important variant of Canadian nationalism, it is a variant that is more divisive than unifying within a Canada defined in bicultural or binational terms. Put somewhat differently, it is a variant best suited to a Canada without Quebec.

Before embarking upon a more detailed exposition of these arguments, an important albeit conventional caveat must be made. Any discussion of "the West" is bedeviled by the fact that the four western provinces do not form and have never formed a homogeneous region (Gibbins 1980). While the inclusion of British Columbia within the broader regional community is particularly problematic (Barman 1991), the difficulties do not stop there. The very different success rates for Reform candidates in the 1993 general election illustrate how fragmented the regional community can be: Reform won 46 of the 58 seats in British Columbia and Alberta, but only 5 of the 28 seats in Manitoba and Saskatchewan. And yet, the "West" refuses to disappear as a political and analytical concept; it remains an integral part of Canadian political discourse and debate. I will therefore continue a long-standing scholarly tradition by painting with a very broad brush on a regional canvas stretching from the Ontario-Manitoba border to the Pacific coast. The reader can decide to what extent the portrait that emerges can be applied with any precision to the specific provincial communities encompassed by "western Canada."

THE EVOLUTION OF NATIONAL SENTIMENT IN WESTERN CANADA

Although any full understanding of national sentiment in western Canada must begin with an appreciation of the region's political and social history, it is not possible to review that history in any detail here. However, a number of points of particular relevance to the present discussion should be noted. First, political discontent has been persistent throughout the region's history. The historical landscape of western Canada is littered with protest movements and parties including the Cooperative Commonwealth Federation, the Nonpartisan League, the One Big Union, the Progressive Party, the Riel rebellions, Social Credit, the United Farmers of Alberta, and the Winnipeg General Strike. A great deal of discontent, moreover, has also been channeled through the Conservative and Liberal parties. Strong regional support for the Liberals in the early part of the century often reflected regional discontent, as did support for the Progressive Conservatives from 1958 through the 1988 election.

Second, the variety of protest movements and parties expressed a common belief that the political rules of the game were fixed in favour of a broadly defined central Canada, and more specifically in favour of the economic elites located in the east. (The belief that Quebec per se was the prime beneficiary is of more recent vintage.) There was, in other words, a perceived linkage between the litany of economic problems confronting western Canadians – bottlenecks in the movement of grain, excessive freight rates, high tariffs on agricultural equipment, exploitative interest rates, insensitive financial institutions – and the nature of the political system. The sinews of that linkage were provided by party discipline in the House of Commons, which made it difficult for western MPs to defend regional interests, and by a party and electoral system which lodged political power in the heavily populated central Canadian provinces.

Third, and directly related to the second point, a strong populist ideology infused regional political protest, one that drew its inspiration in part from the American progressive movement in the early decades of the century. Populism grew out of the perceptions that external elites were exploiting the region and that the political system was badly tilted toward those holding economic wealth and power. References by Alberta Social Credit to the "50 bigshots" who controlled Canadian financial and therefore political institutions captured a more general regional theme. Populist sentiment was also fed by the frustration western Canadians found with regional representation in the House of Commons, where western MPs appeared to become so entangled in partisan interests and constraints that voters back home were forgotten or ignored. Devices were therefore sought which would make MPs more receptive and responsible to their immediate constituents rather than to their parties, centred as the latter were in Ontario and Quebec. Thus we saw the early appeal to nonpartisanship, and to instruments of direct democracy such as recall. (The western enthusiasm for recall goes back to 1935, when the new Alberta Social Credit government introduced recall legislation which was itself "recalled" in 1937 when constituency unrest threatened Premier Aberhart.) It should also be noted that populist sentiment reflected cultural tensions between the agrarian West and the urban East. While it would be an exaggeration to say that regional mythologies pitted the "prairie yeomen" against the "effete elites" of central Canada, at times they came close.

However, this regional and populist discontent never coalesced into support for western independence, and despite a radical fringe (Barr and Anderson 1972; Pratt and Stevenson 1981), never threatened to rupture the national political community. If western Canadians had a "dream of nation," to use Susan Trofimenkoff's (1982) evocative phrase, the nation was Canada and not the West. The western quest was constantly framed in terms of inclusion within the national mainstream; the goal was to achieve political leverage equivalent to the region's contribution to the national economy. And here there should be no mistake; western Canadians have always seen that contribution in very positive, even exaggerated terms. Western Canadians felt that they were the ones breaking the soil and building the new country, and it was in the West that the furnace of Canadian nationalism burned the brightest. As W. L. Morton wrote (1950:viii) shortly after the Second World War, "The dominant note in the social philosophy of western people has been an unbounded confidence in themselves, a belief that their region was one with a great potential future if the hand of the outside exploiter could only be removed." Liberal MP David Kilgour (1988:262) provides a more contemporary expression of the same sentiment: "The Western region's overall experience in Confederation to date can be described as buoyancy and confidence encountering continuous disappointment at the hands of outsiders. Full economic and political equality ... continues to elude the region." Thus boosterism has been mixed with populism and regional discontent to form a potent political stew.

Regional boosterism found reflection in the distinctive form of Canadian nationalism that emerged in the West. Although the region is often seen as the heartland of multiculturalism, the emergent nationalist spirit was closer in many ways to the myth of the American melting pot, and to the associated American frontier experience, than it was to more contemporary notions of a multicultural mosaic. A polyglot and ethnically diverse frontier society generated strong pressures for cultural assimilation and the use of a single, unifying language, pressures that often compromised the constitutional rights of the small francophone minority in the West. As Howard Palmer has explained (1982; see also Sharpe and Braid 1992:173), anglo-conformity was more characteristic of western society than was sensitivity to ethnic diversity. Thus John Diefenbaker's clarion call for "one Canada" was an authentic reflection of the region's historical experience. As Bercuson and Cooper observe (1993:21A): "Diefenbaker was less a political philosopher than a consummate rhetorician; much of his so-called vision came out of his mouth virtually as he spoke. But, being western-raised, he gave voice to a concept of Canada that has been quintessentially western for at least five generations. His vision was that of 'One Canada' where citizens and provinces were essentially equal."

It is interesting to note in this respect the following comment by Morton (1955:66): "The West has been defined as a colonial society seeking equality in Confederation. That equality was sought in order that the West should be like, not different from, the rest of Canada."

Morton's comment is interesting for two reasons. First, it suggests that the West was not trying to impose a new national vision, but rather was buying into the existing national vision of Sir John A. Macdonald. As George Melnyk argued more recently (1993:119), when western Canadians describe themselves as "alienated" they are taking on an identity defined from the outside. In discussing the evolution of the term "western alienation," Melnyk notes that "it was not important what Westerners felt about themselves; it was important that they were *alienated from* the centre where all goodness lay. It was Westerners who were alienated, while Central Canadians were not. The burden of deviancy was the West's."

Second, it is by no means clear that the "rest of Canada" Morton had in mind included Quebec. Indeed, the monochromatic character of western Canadian nationalism was bound to run afoul of the more complex, bicultural visions that were to emerge from Quebec.

In summary, there has been significant continuity to western Canadian political life. The same themes emerge again and again, and the political protest of the moment draws from the symbols of the past. Icons such as inequitable freight rates, the National Policy, and the National Energy Program appear on the stage in contemporary debates, just as the loss of the CF-18 maintenance contract will appear in future debates. However, and notwithstanding this continuity, it took western Canadians a long time to reach agreement on an institutional answer to their host of economic, and therefore political, complaints.

THE ABSENCE OF A COHERENT VISION OF INSTITUTIONAL REFORM

There is no question that western Canadians have chaffed against the institutional and partisan status quo; the term "western alienation" captures a long-standing, even chronic regional discontent with parliamentary institutions and the national party system. (Within the litany of western grievances, particular prominence is given to the role of party discipline within parliamentary institutions, a role that is fundamental to the operation of responsible government.) At the same time, western Canadians until recently lacked any coherent reform strategy to address chronic discontent. Instead, several strategies were advanced, and failed. Western Canadians alternated their vote between the mainstream Liberal and Conservative parties, enthusiastically backed one of the two (as they did the Progressive Conservatives for most of the last thirty-five years), created new parties (including Social Credit, the CCF, the Progressives, and Reform), or rejected parties and partisanship altogether. Proposals were advanced to reform the House of Commons, the electoral system, and the Senate. Province-building strategies were also pursued with vigour in British Columbia and, when resource revenues permitted (Richards and Pratt 1979), in Alberta and Saskatchewan. There were reform targets galore, but there was no *systematic* assault on the institutional status quo. As a consequence, that status quo was left unscathed by generations of regional discontent as western Canadian protest left virtually no mark on the institutional structures of the Canadian state.

Part of the western incoherence stemmed from an ambiguous stance toward British parliamentary tradition. Despite the multicultural heritage of the West, or perhaps even because of that heritage, regional residents have been among the most staunch defenders of British traditions and the role of British symbols in Canadian political life. John Diefenbaker, for example, spent much of his career trying to ward off Liberal attacks on British traditions and symbols. The difficulty, however, of championing things British while at the same time identifying parliamentary institutions and conventions as the root cause of western alienation led to the search for partisan solutions, ones that would not call into question the fundamental nature of parliamentary institutions. To argue that the cure for western discontent could be found by replacing St Laurent with Diefenbaker, Trudeau with Clark, or Turner with Mulroney, carried less threat to the established institutional order than to argue that Parliament itself was flawed.

A much larger part of the regional incoherence stemmed from the awkward position westerners found themselves in with respect to the Canadian federal system. While they felt disadvantaged within national parliamentary institutions, the logic of federalism not only made those institutions of central importance for western Canadians but also precluded some of the strategies for political influence used so effectively by Quebec. To understand the dilemma in which western Canadians found and still find themselves, it is useful to refer to the classic distinction between intrastate and interstate federalism.

Intrastate federalism and its related institutional arrangements provide a number of potential avenues for regional representation and protection. Regional interests can be conveyed to the national government through MPs and senators, and can find expression on the floor of the House and Senate, and within both caucus and cabinet. Unfortunately, all these mechanisms either seemed flawed to western Canadians or were so constrained by party discipline as to be ineffective. MPs were seen as beholden to their party rather than to their constituents, senators were without stature or influence, and dynamics of the House were dictated by electoral strategies rooted in vote-rich Ontario and Quebec. While effective regional representation might take place behind the closed doors of caucus and cabinet, such representation could not be seen in action. All that could be seen were the results, which too often provided little indication that a western voice had been heard or heeded.

It might be assumed, therefore, that western Canadians would turn from intrastate federalism to the interstate protections provided by the division of powers. Certainly this was an approach that appealed to provincial premiers, and one that was pursued with some enthusiasm by W.A.C. Bennett and Peter Lougheed. Unfortunately, this option is of limited logical appeal. The basic dilemma is that the jurisdictional powers of particular importance to the West have always been those relating to interprovincial and international trade. The powers that count are those dealing with such things as tariffs, freight rates, interprovincial pipelines and railways, national interest rate policy, agricultural marketing, and agricultural supports. However, these are also powers which adhere intrinsically to the national government in federal states; to assign them to provincial governments would destroy the economic union upon which the political superstructures of federal states are built. Thus the promotion of a more decentralized federal system has faced important logical and structural constraints in the West.

The remaining option for regional representation is to rely upon the intergovernmental mechanisms of interstate federalism, executive federalism, and the first ministers' conference as the primary forums within which to protect regional interests. Certainly this option has also been of considerable appeal to provincial governments and premiers, and it was polished to perfection by Alberta's Peter Lougheed. However, it should be noted that executive federalism fits uneasily within the populist tradition of western Canada. Speaking indirectly through provincial elites was of limited appeal to those raised in the direct democracy tradition of the Progressives and United Farmers of Alberta. This tension between executive federalism and the region's populist impulse was contained by strong provincial leaders such as Lougheed, but arose to destroy weaker leaders such as Don Getty when they tried to sell elite compromises like the Meech Lake Accord. When western elites, including Lougheed, rallied behind the Charlottetown Accord, their efforts were not enough to salvage public support. Indeed, their participation may even have contributed to the massive defeat the accord suffered across the West in the 1992 referendum.

It is useful at this point to compare briefly the western Canadian and Quebec situations with respect to federalism. The various aspects of both intrastate and interstate federalism that have troubled western Canadians over the years have been far less problematic for the residents of Quebec. The constraints of party discipline and the secrecy of cabinet and caucus deliberations have seldom been identified as parliamentary conventions which work to the disadvantage of Quebec. Rarely have Quebecers lacked numerical strength within the government of the day, and thus electoral and party reform have never captured a significant provincial audience. In general, intrastate mechanisms have worked reasonably well, a conclusion supported by the fact that the prime minister has been from Quebec for thirty-five of the fifty years since the end of the Second World War, and at present both the prime minister *and* the leader of the opposition come from Quebec. (Western Canada and Quebec have contributed four prime ministers each since the end of the war, but three of the four westerners – Joe Clark, John Turner, and Kim Campbell – had rather abbreviated first ministerial careers!)

At the same time, the division of powers and executive federalism have worked well for Quebec. Although the former cannot provide an effective defence for regional interests in international and interprovincial trade, it can do so for matters of language and culture. For this reason, a more decentralized federal state has much greater appeal in Quebec than it has in the West. The notion of "an independent Quebec within a strong Canada" better fits the logic of Canadian federalism than does "an independent West within a strong Canada," for the powers the West would need to protect its economic interests would preclude a strong Canada. The basic point is that the various mechanisms for regional protection in the Canadian federal state – intrastate representation within national parliamentary institutions, intergovernmental relations, and the division of powers – all work better for Quebec than they do for the West, even though the population of the West is now significantly larger than that of Quebec.

The historical bind for western Canadians was that if legislative powers were to remain in Ottawa, they would also remain within central institutions that failed to reflect, or at least were believed to fail to reflect, western interests and aspirations. Hence the only logical solution seemed to be to reform those institutions, to make them more sensitive to the western Canadian electorate. However, this was not a strategy to be championed by leaders such as John Diefenbaker, who believed so strongly in the "golden thread" of the British democratic tradition. Nor was it to be championed by provincial premiers, who recognized quite clearly that they and their governments might well be eclipsed by revitalized central institutions. (Former Premier Don Getty's enthusiasm for Senate reform is a clear exception here.) The region therefore had to wait for the emergence of a leader freed from any strong emotional attachment to the British tradition and unencumbered by a vested partisan interest in the promotion of strong provincial governments. Enter Preston Manning, stage right.

CAMELOT: SENATE REFORM AND THE BIRTH OF THE REFORM PARTY

The logic of federalism prescribed an obvious institutional response to western discontent, and that was the reform of central institutions so as to provide more effective regional representation. The experience of other federal states suggested that the locus of reform was to be found in the Canadian Senate, and the lack of any significant public or political support for the existing Senate made that body a natural target of reform. Whereas MPs were vigilant in their defence of the House of Commons and its conventions of responsible government, the Senate lacked any effective defence. The 1982 Constitution Act had removed the Senate's power to block its own reform or abolition, leaving senators with only a suspensive veto on constitutional change. Perhaps more important, senators were held in such low public repute that they were unable to defend themselves or their institution in the public arena. All that was needed, therefore, were three things: (1) a regional consensus that the Senate provided the most promising avenue of institutional reform; (2) an acceptable model of reform; and (3) an effective champion of that model. All three were put into place shortly after the 1984 general election.

The 1984 election was to play a decisive role in the evolution of the institutional reform debate in western Canada, although this role was by no means apparent in the immediate aftermath to the election when western Conservative MPs emerged as central participants in the new national government. In the early 1980s the Liberals had toyed with institutional reform in the wake of their own chronic electoral weakness in the West, but such reform was not part of the 1981-82 constitutional reforms. The Conservatives had argued that all that was needed was a new government and a new prime minister, that the discussion of institutional reform was little more than a smokescreen to conceal Liberal indifference to the legitimate aspirations of western Canadians. Thus the 1984 election results set up a critical institutional test: would western alienation persist in the face of a new, broadly based national government in which western MPs played an important role within both the cabinet and governing caucus? Or did the search for institutional reform reflect little more than the inevitable regional angst caused by two decades of Liberal rule, angst that would dissipate with a new Conservative prime minister in control?

The answer was surprising, and surprisingly swift in coming. Western alienation did not fade away but instead seemed to gather momentum (Braid and Sharpe 1990). Western Canadians seemed no more content with the new Conservative government than they had been with its Liberal predecessor. Brian Mulroney appeared to step right into Pierre Trudeau's shoes, and his government was charged with similar indifference to western aspirations. The most immediate consequence of this disenchantment was the birth of the Reform Party of Canada and the emergence of a new regional champion, Preston Manning.

The birth of Reform is of particular importance for the present discussion because it coincided with the transformation of the Senate reform debate. In 1982 the Alberta government had released a reform proposal calling for a provincially appointed Senate. This proposal (Alberta 1982) was very much in keeping with the emphasis at the time on executive federalism and with the push by western premiers for a more prominent role for provincial governments (and particularly premiers) in national governance. However, when a special select committee of the Alberta legislature took this proposal before public hearings held across the province, they found virtually no support. Instead, they uncovered a great deal of support for a new reform vision featuring the direct popular election of senators. In the face of this public reaction, and in the face of mounting pressure from the Committee for a Triple E Senate and the Canada West Foundation, the committee jettisoned the provincially appointed model and recommended (Special Select Committee 1985) that the Alberta government promote a Triple E Senate. Despite the clear reluctance of Premier Lougheed to do so, the Alberta legislature and government climbed aboard the Triple E bandwagon and thereby fundamentally changed the institutional reform debate. When Don Getty replaced

Lougheed as premier, the provincial enthusiasm for Triple E increased substantially.

The Triple E model differed in one critical aspect from earlier visions of institutional reform: it was clearly unacceptable to Quebec. The problems were not ones of detail, but of basic principle and institutional design. The government of Quebec had no enthusiasm for provincial equality, no enthusiasm for the popular election of another tier of federal politicians who would compete with the Quebec government for a voice in Ottawa, and no enthusiasm for strengthened national legislative institutions. Thus Alberta and the broader Triple E movement had embarked upon a quest that would receive no support in Quebec, and indeed would antagonize political opinion within that province. The emphatic support of the Reform Party for the Triple E model, combined with Reform's explicit opposition to Quebec's constitutional objectives, made a bad situation worse.

By the late 1980s western Canada was launched on an institutional reform trajectory that bore no correspondence to Quebec's search for a more decentralized federal state. Indeed, it seemed for a while that the West's Senate reform agenda, backed by the abrasive politics of Reform, could well divide the country (Stark 1992:141–9). Then two things happened. First, the constitutional debate collapsed with the defeat of the 1992 referendum, and thus the Senate reform clash between the West and Quebec fell from the national agenda. Second, and more important for the present analysis, the Reform Party abandoned its earlier emphasis on Senate reform as it sought to expand its appeal beyond the West.

THE TRANSFORMATION OF THE REFORM PARTY

The early years of the Reform Party were marked by an aggressive emphasis on the need for improved regional representation. The first of twenty-one basic principles outlined in the Party's Blue Book addressed the issue of Senate reform: "We affirm the need to establish a Triple E Senate in the Parliament of Canada – that is to say, a Senate which is Elected by the people, with Equal representation from each Province, and which is fully Effective in safeguarding regional interests" (Reform Party 1991:4). The party's draft "Constitutional Amendment to Reform the Senate of Canada" notes that "a reformed Senate, if properly constituted, could perform the role originally intended for it and alleviate feelings of alienation and remoteness toward national affairs which exist, particularly in the less populous regions of Canada and among minority groups" (Reform Party 1991:7). There is no question that the party's central plank was Senate reform, and that the party was formed to pursue a regional agenda – "The West wants in!" However, there is also no question that as the party expanded to Ontario and Atlantic Canada, and now even to Quebec, the Senate reform plank became an electoral encumbrance. Thus Reform moved from its initial emphasis on the reform of central institutions in order to achieve more effective regional representation to a much broader populist assault on the status quo.

It should be noted, of course, that populism has always been a central element to Reform's platform and electoral appeal. In many ways, the *Blue Book*'s genuflection to "the common sense of the common people" reads as a populist manifesto: "We believe in the common sense of the common people, their right to be consulted on public policy matters before major decisions are made, their right to choose their own leaders and to govern themselves through truly representative and responsible institutions, and their right to directly initiate legislation for which substantial public support is demonstrated." Now, however, the populist elements of Reform have overwhelmed the earlier emphasis on improved regional representation. This in turn has badly weakened the institutional reform consensus in western Canada, not by putting Reform offside, which it is not, but rather by diminishing the importance of Senate reform to the party's agenda.

Reform's populist assault on the institutional status quo provides a potential bridge between regional discontent in the West and political discontent in the "rest of the country," outside Quebec. Such bridges have been sorely lacking in the past when one western protest movement after another broke up on the shoals of indifference encountered outside the region. In this sense, then, the Reform Party's crusade has been nationalized, and has been nationalized in a manner that might even include some appeal within Quebec. In the process, however, the distinctively western Canadian elements of the crusade – the stress on regional representation and Senate reform – have been lost. In a larger sense, a distinctive regional voice may also have been lost. It is interesting in this context to note Reform's enthusiastic support for the 1994 campaign to remove Ontario MP Jag Bhaduria, the errant member from Markham-Whitchurch-Stouffville, from office. Bhaduria provided a compelling illustration for Reform's advocacy of recall and helped broaden the populist appeal of recall well beyond western Canada. Nonetheless, the fact that the recall of an Ontario MP could be so important within the contemporary dynamics of Reform suggests how much the party has been transformed in recent years. The change from "The West wants in!" to "Bag the Jag!" underscores this transformation.

THE NATIONAL QUESTION IN WESTERN CANADA

Although the national transformation of Reform is clearly under way, Preston Manning remains the West's most prominent and articulate visionary. (The western premiers, preoccupied as they are with very conflictual provincial environments, have showed little inclination to take up the reins of regional leadership.) Manning's national vision is similar in many ways to that articulated by John Diefenbaker and by generations of regional leaders before him. It is a vision of "one Canada" based on a single national community sharing a commitment to the equality of individuals and, in a constitutional sense, to the equality of provincial communities. As Manning has written (cited in Stark 1992:148), Canada's national symbol has become the hyphen rather than the maple leaf: "Its federal politicians talk incessantly about English-Canadians, French-Canadians, Aboriginal-Canadians, ethnic-Canadians, but rarely about 'Canadians period.' It has become patently obvious in the dying days of the 20th century that you cannot hold a nation together with hyphens."

There is a historical continuity to the evolution of national sentiment in the West. At the same time, there is no evidence that this evolution has come to grips with the claims of Quebec for a distinctive position within the Canadian political community. National sentiment in the West, and its associated emphasis on the reform of central institutions, thus comes sharply up against competing visions emanating from Quebec, visions rooted in a binational framework alien to the western experience (Bercuson and Cooper 1991). The inclusive nature of western forms of Canadian nationalism – the desire to be part of rather than separate from the Canadian mainstream – has clear limits when it comes to the inclusion of Quebec on terms acceptable to that province. Hence the dilemma.

As noted above, the reform of central institutions does not provide a potential bridge between Quebec and the West, for the two regions would prefer to move Canadian federal institutions in very different directions. In fact, the very contemplation of such reform brings into play essentially incompatible visions of the Canadian political community. The Reform Party has become the vehicle for a new vision of Canadian nationalism, albeit one with deep historical roots in western Canadian soil. This new vision is based on the equality of individuals and provinces, on a single, all-encompassing national identity, and on reformed parliamentary institutions, and is one with no appeal whatsoever in Quebec. As Reform has carried this new vision further and further afield, it has shifted the emphasis toward populism and away from

the party's original stress on Senate reform. This altered vision may
have considerable appeal in Canada outside Quebec, and indeed
could become the dominant national vision should Quebec leave. Yet
should Quebec stay, or should the debate reopen on whether Quebec
should stay, even the altered Reform vision is unlikely to provide a constitutional common ground between Quebec and the West. After all,
populist visions of the political community and the majoritarian devices they imply will always be problematic for ethnic and linguistic minorities.

In conclusion, let me return to the Camelot analogy. Although the
analogy suggests that the western Canadian constitutional vision has
been lost, this undoubtedly overstates the extent of the loss. What has
been lost is the institutional reform focus; the larger vision lives on.
Nor is it clear that the loss of the reform focus is necessarily damaging
in the short run. As is generally the case in Canadian politics, all depends on what happens next in Quebec. The historical record is un-
mistakable on one point: western Canadians will not drive the
constitutional or institutional reform agenda by themselves. If the constitution or central institutions are to be opened to significant change,
it will be in response to events in Quebec and not in response to pressure from the West. To use another analogy, popularized by Preston
Manning, the West can be seen as a constitutional surfer, riding the
waves of political discontent generated by Quebec. If there are no
waves, the West will be left standing powerless on a tranquil shore, with
the Triple E surfboard lying beached on the sand.

If the threat of independence again recedes, and if the federal government continues to respond to Quebec's aspirations for a more decentralized federal state by delegating program responsibilities rather
than by formal constitutional change, then the lack of a reform consensus in the West is of little consequence. Nor, for that matter, would
the existence of a regional reform consensus be of any consequence;
the system will only move in response to an acute threat to national
unity, and western discontent will never be seen in such terms. However, the state of affairs in the West could be of some consequence if we
are once again thrust into the constitutional morass. Should that happen, then the country might best be served if both the West and Reform could recapture the earlier consensus on the need to reform
central institutions. This consensus could be a valuable counterweight
to the pressures for decentralization which will inevitably emerge from
Quebec and which, in the long term, may not serve the interests or aspirations of Canadians in the "rest of Canada," including the West.

And what if, at the end of the day, Quebec does leave? In some important respects, a Canada without Quebec would come closer to the

western Canadian national vision than does the status quo. The new country would have a single official language, the populist impulse could be more readily accommodated, and the cultural landscape would be less complex. In other respects, however, the problems of institutional accommodation between the West and Ontario alone would be as great as those that exist with Quebec still in Canada. If a Triple E Senate and the notion of provincial equality have little appeal to Quebec, they will have no more appeal to Ontario in the new Canada, a Canada in which close to half of the population will reside in Ontario. Here, then, western Canadians find themselves between a rock and a hard place: satisfactory institutional reform is unlikely if Quebec stays and unlikely if Quebec goes.

It is in this context that the most recent transformation of the Reform party takes on particular importance. A Reform Party wedded to the objectives of Senate reform and provincial equality would be poorly positioned to form the national government in a new Canada for it would have a constitutional posture with little appeal in Ontario. Nor would Reform be well positioned to ease the transition of western Canadians into the new national order. Indeed, the party would be more likely to serve as the vehicle for ongoing regional discontent, discontent which could quickly destabilize the new national community. However, a Reform Party with a diminished emphasis on Senate reform and provincial equality would have appeal in Ontario, and could serve as a bridge between the western Canadian national vision and the Ontario electorate. In short, the recent transformation of Reform can be seen as an appropriate strategic response to the challenges posed by Quebec's potential departure from the Canadian political community.

BIBLIOGRAPHY

Alberta. 1982. *A Provincially Appointed Senate: A New Federalism for Canada.* Edmonton: Government of Alberta.

Barman, Jean. 1991. *The West Beyond the West: A History of British Columbia.* Toronto: University of Toronto Press.

Barr, John, and Owen Anderson. 1971. *The Unfinished Revolt.* Toronto: McClelland & Stewart.

Bercuson, David J., and Barry Cooper. 1991. *Deconfederation: Canada Without Quebec.* Toronto: Key Porter.

– 1993. "Why Voters Are Rallying Around Reform." *The Globe and Mail,* 14 October.

Braid, Don, and Sydney Sharpe. 1990. *Breakup: Why The West Feels Left Out Of Canada.* Toronto: Key Porter.

Gibbins, Roger. 1980. *Prairie Politics and Society: Regionalism in Decline.* Toronto: Butterworths.

Kilgour, David. 1988. *Uneasy Patriots: The West in Confederation.* Edmonton: Lone Pine.

Melnyk, George. 1993. *Beyond Alienation: Political Essays on the West.* Calgary: Detselig.

Morton, W.L. 1950. *The Progressive Party of Canada.* Toronto: University of Toronto Press.

– 1955. "The Bias of Prairie Politics," *Transactions of the Royal Society of Canada,* Series 3, vol. 49, June.

Palmer, Howard. 1982. *Patterns of Prejudice: A History of Nativism in Alberta.* Toronto: McClelland & Stewart.

Pratt, Larry, and Garth Stevenson, eds. 1981. *Western Separatism: The Myths, Realities and Dangers.* Edmonton: Hurtig.

Reform Party of Canada. 1991. *The Blue Book: Principles and Policies, 1991.* Calgary: Reform Party of Canada.

Richards, John, and Larry Pratt. 1979. *Prairie Capitalism: Power and Influence in the New West.* Toronto: McClelland & Stewart.

Sharpe, Sydney, and Don Braid. 1992. *Storming Babylon: Preston Manning and the Rise of the Reform Party.* Toronto: Key Porter.

Special Select Committee of the Alberta Legislature. 1985. *Strengthening Canada.* Edmonton: Government of Alberta.

Trofimenkoff, Susan Mann. 1982. *The Dream of Nation: A Social and Intellectual History of Quebec.* Toronto: Macmillan.

Weaver, R. Kent, ed. 1992. *The Collapse of Canada?* Washington, DC: The Brookings Institution.

4 Atlantic Canada: Forgotten Periphery in an Endangered Confederation?

ROBERT FINBOW

The region of Canada least equipped to deal with the breakup of Confederation is Atlantic Canada. Not only would it be physically isolated from the rest of the country; if the national will dissipated or if federal authority declined precipitously after Quebec's departure, this area could face hard times. Although Atlantic Canadians have long had a sense of being disadvantaged by the workings of national politics and economics, few informed citizens would welcome the breakup of the country. This reflects the dilemma of this peripheral region. Within Confederation its political and economic weight has been overshadowed by more prosperous regions, and political decisions have often been adverse. Without the existing support of the national regime, however the region's prospects could become even more marginal, and living standards might be difficult to sustain. Hence Atlantic Canadians exhibit an ambiguous mixture of loyalty to Canada and cynicism regarding its economic and political institutions. Confederation is often blamed for regional problems, yet national action is also considered essential for regional revival. Hence Atlantic Canadians have sought more sensitive national policies and more regional influence at the centre.

For the purposes of this essay, the idea of an Atlantic "region" is used only as a label of convenience; it is debatable whether the diverse character and politics of these four provinces justifies their classification as a single, cohesive region. Any brief essay purporting to treat them as a unit is undoubtedly inadequate to the task. These provinces are quite disparate internally, in geographic, historical, ethnic, and economic terms, with urban centres integrated to the continental community and rural enclaves still culturally and economically distant from it. And the existence of four distinct political units also widens social and economic divisions, as provincial governments and institutions fashion political loyalties and social existence on a provincial, not a regional, level. These provinces often act as rivals for limited economic prospects rather than as allies in a regional project of economic renewal. Nonetheless, as marginal economic participants in the continental economy, these four provinces share a vulnerability which would create serious problems of adjustment if Quebec separation ruptured the Canadian union. And, while short-term political pressures often induce competition among these provinces, the long-term well-being of the regional population in an endangered confederation may well rest on the ability of political leaders to look beyond provincial interests and to act collectively in the interests of all of Atlantic Canada.

HISTORICAL GRIEVANCES

The Atlantic provinces were reluctant participants in Canadian confederation. Anti-confederates were prominent in the Maritimes in 1867; no popular mandate was ever secured for union in Nova Scotia, and New Brunswick and Prince Edward Island opted out of union for several years. Local and Empire loyalties caused resentment of union, and there were fears that the Maritimes would lose control of their political destiny. Maritime delegates stressed the Senate as the protector of regional interests, and demanded equal representation in it. Fear of economic disruption from Canadian tariffs and economic policies was also expressed by local business elites dependent upon international trade. After Confederation, Maritime leaders attributed economic stagnation to federal policies which undermined regional industries. Maritime political strength in Ottawa declined with each redistribution of seats, and the region's ability to influence policy diminished (Howell 1977:187). Regional protest emerged periodically as regional citizens and business elites pushed for better terms in Confederation. Grievances centred on declining representation in the national parliament and resultant adverse federal decisions over intergovernmental transfers, banking, tariffs, and railway freight rates. The Maritime provinces sought to return to the numerical balance of seats of 1867; the only concession was the granting of the Senate floor for Commons representation in 1914. Increased subsidies were given to all provinces, but there was no recognition of the Atlantic region's special needs in federal policy, as political and fiscal calculus ensured favourable treatment of more populous provinces.

Post-war decline in the 1920s revived regional discontent. Forbes describes how the federal consolidation of the Intercolonial Railway into the Canadian National system (with management in central Canada) led to a dramatic increase in rates at a time when postwar recession ravaged regional industries. This prompted the emergence of the Maritime Rights Movement to agitate for improved federal grants to the region and restoration of Maritime control of the railway (Forbes 1989:103 ff.). Protest at that time led to an upward adjustment of grants in the 1920s and a reduction of freight rates. But there was no comprehensive effort to rectify regional economic disparities or provincial fiscal incapacity. The Rowell-Sirois report of 1938 recommended grants to allow provinces to provide comparable levels of services to their citizens. But wealthier provinces rejected such recommendations for many years, and the onset of World War II delayed serious consideration. Indeed, Forbes notes how the federal government's policies during the war directed most meaningful infrastructure and industrial development to the central provinces, even in areas of regional advantage like ship building and ports (Forbes 1989:198–9).

Newfoundland stayed aloof from Confederation for decades, and experienced similar sharp divisions over accession before 1949. Confederation, added belatedly to the ballot, gathered the support of only 52 percent of the population in a referendum which left many in mourning for the loss of sovereignty. With the help of federal transfers, Premier Smallwood persuaded many voters of the benefits of union, but critics remained. In fact, some saw the Smallwood approach to development and resettlement as a threat to the distinctive lifestyle and culture of the island province; transfers also fostered a harmful dependence on federal largesse (Matthews 1979:98). Fuelled by the prospect of indigenous development based on offshore oil revenues, there was a surge of "neo-nationalism" in the province by the late 1970s. This culminated in pronounced criticism of federal policy and a desire to promote provincial authority. Led by Premier Brian Peckford, this province posed some profound challenges to the federal government by the early 1980s, and studies of public opinion show a stronger allegiance to province than to nation (Overton 1979; House 1986). Diminished prospects for offshore wealth and the decline of the fisheries engendered a return to a preference for a strong national regime under Premier Clyde Wells (Brown 1990).

As provincial responsibilities assumed new importance, fiscal deficiencies became so pronounced that Atlantic leaders occasionally proposed transferring powers to the federal regime. Regional leaders pressured the federal government to adopt programs to alleviate the worst effects of regional disparity. Since the 1950s unconditional equalization grants, and conditional grants in health care, social services, and education have partially addressed the fiscal hardship of the Atlantic provinces. These payments have attenuated regional differences in the quality of public services by adding significantly to the revenues of "have-not" provinces. Regional development programs were also established to promote economic growth. These policies constituted a watershed in federal attitudes, replacing ad hoc responses to regional protest with a more comprehensive approach to regional disparities. While the open hostility of the wealthy provinces diminished, regional policies still faced opposition. This forced Atlantic premiers to seek protection against the uncertainties of intergovernmental bargaining and induced support for federal authority and federal aid to "stimulate the catch-up process" (Alexander 1980:38).

Political economists have vigorously debated the causes of regional economic decline. While regional political and business elites often articulated a sense of grievance at federal policy and national economic forces, it seems clear that geographic factors of location relative to changing continental and international markets and the nature of regional resource staples did not equip these provinces to become an industrial heartland. The workings of market forces and their agglomeration effects worked against regional expansion as development shifted first to the centre and then west and south on the continent. Historical evidence makes clear that Confederation did not immediately promote the demise of the Maritime economy, which briefly flourished in certain manufacturing centres under the National Policy Tariffs. But such prosperity was shortlived. T.A. Acheson (1977) notes how the development of national commercial enterprises hurt regional industries, which were largely consolidated under central Canadian control. The development of national banking institutions, instead of the dynamic state-level banks of the United States, prompted an outflow of regional savings into investments elsewhere. Subsequent federal politics and policies can be seen as insensitive, as the region's declining influence left its MPs unable to prevent undesirable policies on tariffs, freight rates, St Lawrence Seaway, and abandonment of a domestic merchant marine. For regional analysts, later redistributive policies are merely compensation for this discrimination, and the revenues from transfers have largely circulated back to the centre in the form of purchases of goods and services from central Canadian enterprises, corporate taxes on company profits derived in part from the region, and exports of skilled labour.

Problems of economic malaise and declining political influence persisted despite federal policies. These concerns engendered scepticism toward Ottawa and coloured these provinces' approaches to constitutional issues. In fact the Atlantic provinces hold the distinction of producing the original separatists in Canada. Nova Scotia's legislature passed a secession motion in 1887 as a tactic to secure better terms in confederation (Canada 1951:19). But anti-Confederate leaders like Joseph Howe and W.S. Fielding were quickly assimilated into the Canadian political elite via appointments to the federal cabinet. This began the Maritime practice of lobbying for change from within the federal regime, and through the two established parties, which contrasted with the third party populism of Western protest. Atlantic premiers and regional ministers sought federal redistributive policies to compensate for the adverse workings of the national economy federal policies. Hence Atlantic Canadians remained very ambiguous in their loyalties as Canadians. Deeply cynical about national political and economic institutions, Atlantic Canadians are nonetheless forced to rely heavily on those institutions for supportive programs. Fiercely loyal to local community, Atlantic Canadians have been forced by lack of opportunities to emigrate in large numbers to other regions. Ties to Canada were strengthened by the more supportive post-war federal policy, as both state and business elites and the wider population became accustomed to support from the central regime, and as the symbols of post-war Canadian nationalism supplanted traditional ties to Great Britain. While pride in region remains great, both pragmatic necessity and socialized loyalties make this region among the strongest supporters of a continued Canadian federation, as long as commitments to equalization and to national standards in social programs are fulfilled (Bickerton 1990:335, 342).

POLICIES TO ALLEVIATE REGIONAL DISPARITIES

Equalization was designed to reduce differences in fiscal capacity between the provinces, to permit provision of modern government programs and facilities in all regions. Although sometimes criticized for distorting the economy, equalization has beneficial effects – by equalizing human resource and infrastructure in all regions and reducing differences in tax burdens – which would hamper the flow of factors of production to optimal uses in have-not regions. The formula for calculation has changed over time, and since the resource boom of the early 1970s, fossil fuel royalties have been excluded, meaning that these grants fall far short of allowing for comparable service levels with comparable tax burdens. Established Programs Financing (EPF) transfers have been crucial to maintenance of quality post-secondary education and health services. Canada Assistance Plan (CAP) funding was also essential to creation of social assistance programs in this region. Because of its equalization entitlements, the Atlantic region is more dependent on federal transfers to governments than other provinces, though Quebec, Manitoba, and at times Saskatchewan have also been net beneficiaries. By the early 1990s federal transfer payments made up from 37 to 40 percent of Atlantic provincial revenues. Equalization dependence has been declining (due mostly to reduced growth in Ontario), and EPF and CAP funding is also being decreased to deal with federal budget deficits (APEC 1991f:23). However, most analysts agree that such funding is essential to the current level of services and to middle-class government employment, which makes up a higher share of the total workforce than in any other region.

Transfers to individuals also make up a high percentage of regional income. Notably, high unemployment rates and a regionalized benefit system make unemployment insurance a major source of income for many; benefits from this program exceed premiums paid by regional residents. Newfoundland residents receive three times the national average in per capita benefits, with the extended benefit period for persons in the seasonal fisheries as a major factor. Amendments to the unemployment insurance system since the late 1980s have reduced the benefit periods available. Newfoundland and Ottawa are negotiating a new system of guaranteed minimum income, which would eliminate the phenomenon of twenty weeks of work followed by forty weeks of benefits for seasonal workers, which has been a disincentive to worker adjustment. Experiments in New Brunswick with new forms of welfare and training are also welcomed as a way to direct benefits to the needy while reducing dependency effects. The region supports such changes as necessary to end abuse and overspending, to encourage worker adjustment to economic change (especially in light of the decline in the fisheries), and to target spending more effectively on the most impoverished.

Efforts have also been made to reduce regional dependence on transfers by regional development initiatives. Since the early 1960s a variety of programs and approaches have been tried – from the rural-oriented development plans of the Diefenbaker period to the growth pole model of agglomerative industrial development – and various levels of centralization and decentralization in policy development and administration have also been pursued. Yet these costly initiatives produced no appreciable closing of the gap between have and have-not provinces as measured by per capita income or unemployment rates. Moreover, by pursuing bilateral agreements with the provinces (under considerable pressure from them) rather than regional initiatives, federal policy was fragmented and did little to foster intraregional co-operation. And the value of these initiatives from an Atlantic view-point was dissipated, as political pressure forced governments to extend regional development assistance to ever larger areas eventually covering 93 percent of the country (Savoie 1990:37). The Mulroney government pledged to reemphasize regional disparities rather than national sectoral development and resource mega projects. The Atlantic Canada Opportunities Agency (ACOA) was designed to focus on regionwide needs rather than provincial initiatives, to emphasize private lead growth by promoting innovation, education, and training, and by providing assistance to local entrepreneurial development (Dewolf, McNiven, and McPhail 1988:324). However, the Mulroney government's concern with deficit reduction prevented the government from committing adequate resources as ACOA experienced repeated funding reductions.

DISILLUSION WITH REGIONAL POLICIES

Although integrating the region more fully into national economic and political institutions, these policies have become the source of great disillusionment in recent times because they are perceived to have treated the symptoms and not the causes of regional disparities. Measures to induce industries to locate (through a variety of grants, subsidies, and tax breaks) have largely been costly mistakes, which have transferred scarce public funds to private interests while creating only limited, temporary employment. The list of costly failures is lengthy, from heavy water plants, oil refineries, and the Bricklin automobile to the Sprung Greenhouse. Studies indicate that subsidies have been used to augment profits and have not significantly affected corporate choice of the region as a locus for investment. Moreover, the percentage of funds for development initiatives has been but a fraction of that devoted to transfers to governments and individuals, and more is generally spent on similar initiatives in other regions. Even the new ACOA programs have been plagued by political pressure to focus on short-term job creation, not long-term development of entrepreneurial orientations. Several high-profile failures of firms receiving ACOA support in the run up to the 1988 election did little to establish the agency's credibility. And political pressures inevitably led to creation of separate offices for western Canada and northern Ontario, again dispersing resources ineffectively.

There has been much discussion of the dependency effects of federal policies; and in some instances, these effects appear significant, especially concerning the regional component of unemployment insurance, which has encouraged short-term seasonal employment and inhibited migration out of such industries as the fisheries. However, equalization and EPF transfers in education and health have done much to support development of a modern economy in the area, even if disparities have not been eliminated. As well as its above noted efficiency effects, equalization can be defended on ethical grounds as a measure promoting "fiscal equity" or equal treatment of persons for tax purposes no matter what part of the country they live in. EPF transfers can also be seen as contributing to the federal government's constitutional responsibility to equalize provincial capacities to provide vital public services. Such transfers are surely crucial if Canadians everywhere are to have the opportunity to adjust to rapidly changing global economic conditions. However, federal cuts are dramatically affecting these vital transfers, which already do not account for anomalies such as Nova Scotia's high intake of out of province university students, including many from Ontario, who pay tuition equal to local students but produce no compensation from their home province (Nova Scotia 1991:95–6).

Policy developments in recent years indicate that lack of political influence in the federal government comes with continued costs. The failure of Ottawa to promote meaningful investment has continued, in contrast with the U.S. practice of dispersing major government investments throughout the country (as with development of space-related centres in the South). Recent decisions, such as continued subsidization of the St Lawrence Seaway (including icebreaking) and new investments in the Space Agency or NAFTA environmental headquarters, show the federal responsiveness to larger provinces with more electoral strength. Perhaps most perversely, political pressures led to the "nationalization" of regional development, with program expenditures diffused throughout the country, so that federal programs to stimulate the Atlantic economy actually compete with similar federal initiatives elsewhere. Spending on regional development dropped steadily in the Atlantic region from the early 1970s compared to other regions, and ACOA has minimal funding when compared to other government programs. In fact, by 1988 transfers to businesses by the federal government were $135 per capita nationally but only $111 per capita in Atlantic Canada (Northumberland Group 1991:10). Atlantic representation in the Mulroney government was minimal, and this may have affected what was perceived in the region to be very disadvantageous cuts to the region in military, transportation, and other programs; for instance federal employment in the Atlantic provinces declined by 3.7 percent (6.7 percent in Nova Scotia) as compared to 0.7 percent nationally between 1985 and 1989. Communities like Summerside, PEI, heavily dependent on the military base, were forced to adjust drastically to loss of their central employer (APEC 1991b:26–7). Finally, fiscal and monetary policies, notably the emphasis on high interest rates to support the dollar and to dampen inflation in the more prosperous regions, also worsened economic conditions in what is almost perpetually a recessionary regional economy (APEC 1990).

Nonetheless, these discriminatory practices have not encouraged many inhabitants of the region to support a greater decentralization of powers. Most commentators argue that Ottawa has to retain its current spending power to allow for continued equalization and cost-sharing ventures with the provinces. Have-not provinces require federal involvement in order to maintain programs of national quality in these areas, which are crucial both for the equity of citizens' treatment by government and efficiency of national labour markets (to prevent massive migrations of citizens to provinces with more generous programs or diminution in labour quality in poorer provinces). To be sure, federal policies which gave more support to genuine regional development without the distortions imposed by currently biased fiscal, monetary, and procurement policies, would lessen the need for interregional transfers, and would allow the Atlantic governments a better fiscal base from which to run their own programs. Thus the real solution the region has pursued has not been a reduction in federal authority but a sensitive, consultative approach to regional and economic policy.

CONSTITUTIONAL CRISIS AND THE ATLANTIC REGION

This concern for a strong regional presence in a strong national government was a major motivation for the stalling of the Meech Lake Accord by Atlantic premiers Wells and McKenna. For although raising the concerns expressed by various interests (women, First Nations, etc.) concerned about threats to their existing rights, issues of provincial equality and central institutional reform were paramount on these premiers' agenda. This was the motivation for Premier Wells' insistence on a Triple E Senate: "Economic balance will only be achieved when we achieve political balance" (Wells 1991:8).

Regional governments have historically been inclined to support a strong federal regime capable of delivering programs and services to reduce regional disparities or alleviate their worst effects. However, these governments have not been blind followers of federal proposals in constitutional negotiations, and they have sought guarantees for sympathetic federal programs to prevent adverse changes to meet electoral demands from more populous provinces. In rare displays of unity, these governments secured some guarantees for federal redistribution, notably in section 36 of the 1982 constitution, which committed Ottawa to the equalization of provincial revenues and service levels. Such successes have been rare, as regional divisions precluded further gains on offshore resources and development programs (Forbes 1993). Some forms of decentralization have not been opposed and some have at times been promoted, notably respecting offshore resources, fisheries, development programs, etc.; Finbow 1994). So there is a potential for flexibility in regional positions despite an aversion to radical decentralization.

Regional opinion also reflects this flexibility. Not only did the Spicer Commission reveal similar (and in Newfoundland higher) regional support for provincial over federal powers; but the supportive referendum result for the Charlottetown Accord in three provinces indicated an acceptance of some of its potentially decentralizing elements. Nonetheless, radical decentralization of authority from Ottawa to all the provinces would be detrimental to the maintenance of existing regional redistribution and development initiatives, and is opposed by most Atlantic commentators on that basis. Elimination of federal functions across the board would hardly be desirable, given that some redistributive efforts contribute to efficiency of the economy. Loss of programs like EPF and equalization would be problematic for regional adjustment to the global economy. If the region is left unable to promote human resource development, not only will the regional economy fail to adapt to new global reality but the quality of emigrants to the rest of Canada will decline, forcing other provinces to spend more on welfare and education. Hence preservation of central authority is still crucial from a regional perspective, and generalized decentralization will likely be resisted by Atlantic political leaders.

However, Quebec sovereignty would be a more threatening scenario. As Ian Robertson (1991:163) has argued, the immediate concern for the region after Quebec independence would be lack of territorial connection to the rest of Canada. It is unlikely that his proposal for the creation of a land corridor through Quebec to the rest of Canada could be realized without a high level of possibly violent conflict, which the majority of Canadians would likely dismiss as not worthwhile. Thus Atlantic Canada would be forced to exist in isolation from the rest of the country, and would rely on whatever deals Ottawa could strike with Quebec and the United States for transport of goods and people. A rancorous "divorce" with Quebec could maximize disruptions to the movement of people and goods to the rest of Canada, with disastrous consequences. In addition, the survival of the federal state in its current form could come into question, especially if the western provinces sought greater decentralization to avoid Ontario dominance of the federation. It is feasible that centrifugal pressures would cause a rupture of the federation entirely, as regions acted in concert or reoriented their focus to contiguous American and overseas regions. The prospects for the "Bangladeshization" of Atlantic Canada as an isolated forgotten periphery are real in these circumstances. However, all Canadian regions would be impoverished and weakened in their relations with the u.s. and others by such a scenario; hence Atlantic Canada could probably collaborate with other provinces to prevent the loss of these essential economic and political ties.

REGIONAL RESPONSES TO CRISIS

Ideally, Atlantic Canada would avoid dramatic alterations in interstate federalism, and might prefer pragmatic administrative adjustments. But this scenario may no longer be viable, given Quebec's dissatisfaction. This suggests that from an Atlantic viewpoint, some form of asymmetrical arrangement allowing greater powers for Quebec in certain fields might be the best risk. From the region's viewpoint, limited decentralization only to Quebec might be preferable in theory. However, outright special status would presumably encounter opposition from those who believe in the equality of the provinces. Authors like David Milne argue that flexible arrangements could be devised to allow for "concurrency with provincial paramountcy" to give provinces the option of exercising powers themselves or retaining federal involvement in many policy areas. This would preserve equal provinces and reduce tensions in the federation, as different arrangements were devised to serve each province's unique needs (Milne 1991:302 ff.). Interdelegation of powers between levels might also allow Ottawa to reach unique agreements with individual provinces, according to their needs. Such arrangements would risk degenerating into radical decentralization, or federal inaction, since Ottawa would receive no political credit in the large provinces which opted out. But these might be risks worth taking to prevent collapse of the federation.

If Quebec opts for independence, events then may be moving beyond this. How can the Atlantic region respond creatively to the challenge of Quebec sovereignty should it arise? Few potential benefits could be envisioned. In many areas (notably defence and shipbuilding and maintenance) Atlantic Canada has been a direct competitor for federal contracts with Quebec; this competition would presumably be lessened as political decisions in Ottawa were reoriented away from Quebec. It might even be possible to secure some major modern projects like the space centre, which would be supported by the region's developed higher education infrastructure. A campaign could be launched to secure a share of the *émigrés* and investments from the anglophone and allophone diaspora from Montreal; though many people and much money would go to Ontario, the Atlantic region's attractive, affordable urban areas might be a more appealing choice in this era of instantaneous communications via the information highway. Regional consumers and businesses could also press for relocation of corporate service and distribution centres from Montreal to the region, using the threat of purchases from American alternatives in this free trade environment.

However, such prospects are unlikely to compensate for the economic disruptions and drop in living standards which would follow from the physical rupture of the country. For instance, APEC has estimated a drop in living standards as high as 20 to 35 percent in the worst case scenario of an acrimonious breakup and diminution in federal programs. (APEC, 1991b:27). A report by the C.D. Howe Institute suggested that Newfoundland could lose 50 pecent of its population if separation led to elimination of transfers (Beauchesne 1991:21). The outcome would be destabilizing, but vigorous efforts would have to be made to maximize marginal opportunities and minimize the losses, however daunting the task.

The Atlantic provinces face difficult dilemmas in assessing prospects for constitutional reform. On interstate matters, insensitivity in federal exercise of its powers or in development of cost-sharing programs in areas of provincial jurisdiction has always been a difficult problem for this less populous, less politically influential region, but too much decentralization would also be undesirable. Whether transferring powers over the offshore or development programs to the provinces would compensate for loss of national cost-shared programs is a speculative and risky proposition, especially in light of the fisheries collapse and the less lucrative returns from offshore oil.

As for intrastate reforms to better reflect regional concerns at the centre, the Triple E Senate proposal has drawn some support in the region, notably from Newfoundland's Clyde Wells, but on occasion from the premiers of the other provinces as well. Whether a Senate with adequate powers could be developed is questionable; the Charlottetown proposal limited the powers of the Senate. While the region would compose a full 40 percent of the seats in an equal Senate, the prospect for paralysing conflict between Senate and Commons (as in the U.S.) could become a barrier to national programs, many of which have benefited the region. The majoritarian bias of the system has been a problem in the Commons, since the region has often had few voices in the governing coalition (as in the Mulroney years) or inadequate opposition representation to raise regional issues (as in the current Chrétien government). Regional ministers have been able to exercise clout on some issues, but have not had the backing of a large regional caucus within government compared to the central provinces; whether these powerful figures have represented regional interests or largely chan-nelled patronage to their own ridings remains a matter for investiga-tion. Some proportional representation formula to equalize voter intentions and party seat totals in the Senate or Commons might make governments more inclusive of all regions, reduce the parochial minis-terial concern with their riding, and strengthen the effectiveness of re-gional representatives in Ottawa (Bakvis 1991:300–1).

The breakup of the country could lead politicians in other provinces to question policies that are seen as a drain on their economies. Trans-fers to persons and governments have been criticized by provincial leaders and federal Reform politicians. However, the departure of Quebec could provide an opportunity to streamline programs like Un-employment Insurance and equalization; with Quebec (a net recipient of federal transfers) gone, burdens on the have provinces should be lessened, making the sustainability of such programs greater if the eco-nomic price of breakup in interest rates, currency exchange, and lost investment did not take too high a toll. However, the dominance of Ontario in an unreformed Commons would be greater than ever. The Atlantic region would still have problems securing sensitive policies, such as tax compensation for the impact of high interest rates in chronically recessionary regions, as suggested by Wells. Institutional re-form is needed to ensure that an Ontario-centred government does not further undermine genuine regional economic prospects in ex-change for the palliative panacea of transfers.

MULTIPLE CRISES AND REGIONAL PROSPECTS

While the constitutional crisis has simmered, the region has coped with the depletion of its most important resource, northern fish stocks. Industry participants have held government policies responsible; lack of enforcement against foreign factory trawlers, government-spon-sored overdevelopment of corporate fishing interests, and inadequate incentives for small producers to leave the industry have all been con-sidered factors. The result has been a decline in quotas and employ-ment throughout the region, producing a devastating effect on the regional economy. Prospects for the economy are being shaped by new technologies. This poses a challenge for policy makers as they seek to promote a competitive climate while protecting workers from adverse effects. Atlantic industries need to upgrade labour force quality to the level of technical competence required in an information economy. Only a few urban areas have sufficient critical mass to support development of expensive information infrastructures, though some centres are gradually improving their capacities. Moncton, for instance, with its bilingual workforce and the advanced telephone services of NB Tel, is attracting telemarketing and data processing firms. Only a few such centres will emerge in the region, and these will rely on government support for infrastructure – notably fibre-optics upgrading to communications networks and sponsorship of advanced training programs (Lamarche 1993). There is fierce regional, national, and continental competition for such industries, but technological change could reduce the isolation of the region after separation if adequate infrastructure is put in place soon.

Free trade also poses difficult challenges. While historically the Canadian tariff structure was considered discriminatory against regional interests, most existing Atlantic industries are not of sufficient scale to compete effectively in continental markets; there will be a dramatic winnowing out of inefficient enterprises, and job losses can be anticipated. Regional industries are often competitive (especially in primary sectors) with those in nearby New England, and complementary trade may be difficult to develop. Transportation routes are also competitive with American east coast centres, and in the free trade climate and post-separation era Maritime rail and port facilities will become even less viable. Regional development initiatives such as low cost loans to attract industries or regional transportation policies could be challenged under the Free Trade Agreement (FTA) as unfair subsidies, provoking American countervailing duties or quotas against Atlantic goods (Higgins 1990:268). Desjardins argues that regional resources and manufactures are not major imports of the United States or Mexico, and that the region needs to diversify its products and markets beyond the NAFTA region (especially to Europe) if it is to benefit significantly from trade liberalization (Desjardins 1994:64). Thus Atlantic leaders are faced with a series of challenges which are largely beyond their control. This is not an auspicious time for the region to deal with the breakup of Canada.

INTRAREGIONAL COOPERATION AS A SOLUTION?

These disruptions will place a greater premium on intraregional cooperation. Removal of barriers to commercial exchange among these four provinces is a necessary first step to equip the region to face these challenges. These barriers include restrictions on interprovincial flows of goods, services, capital, and labour or local preferences for government procurement, tenders, and contracts. Provincial governments in the region have often used such barriers as a source of protection for weak provincial economies, but these barriers are generally considered to have impaired economic efficiency and growth. Some cooperation has developed through a regional agreement to end provincial preferences in government procurement and to encourage money-saving bulk purchases by all four governments. Since the early 1990s the three Maritime provinces, in consultation with Newfoundland, have pursued greater cooperation in removing economic barriers involving transportation regulations, corporate registration, professional licensing, and mobility (CMP 1991). Intergovernmental agreements on policy harmonization are also desirable to eliminate competing provincial industrial policies and incentives which squander money with few tangible benefits. Declining fiscal transfers could force these governments to consider joint delivery of expensive programs like education and health care. Trade and tourism promotion, electric generation, environmental protection, and management of scarce resources like the fisheries could also benefit from more cooperation and less competition among provinces. And innovative capital generation through joint savings and investment initiatives, based on Quebec's Caisse de Dépôt, could increase local capital supplies. While greater regional integration and policy harmonization will not be a cure-all, such efforts could help these provinces make more effective use of shrinking resources.

The age-old spectre of political union has been revived as a response to fiscal crisis, globalization, and Quebec separation. Liberal MP Douglas Young of New Brunswick has argued that one united Atlantic province could more effectively influence national politics and constitutional reform than four disparate and competing ones (Young 1991:3 ff.). Union could help generate considerable fiscal savings from elimination of multiple bureaucracies and legislatures in what is one of the most overgoverned regions in any liberal democracy.

Past constitutional negotiations certainly reveal that the region's credibility and influence in constitutional discussions has been limited by internal divisions. Despite the ethnic and occupational diversity of the population, it has more similarities than the populations of other more integrated regions. However, historical loyalties to existing provinces will be hard to sweep aside in the name of unity. Prince Edward Islanders would be unlikely to give up their accessible legislature; New Brunswick's Acadians would not welcome a regional government more dominated by anglophones, especially with national bilingualism threatened by Quebec separation. Newfoundland's historic identity, based on its independence as a dominion, its isolation, and its unique resource base and way of life, make its citizens' loyalty to the "rock" greater than existing allegiance to Confederation, let alone a new regional regime; Nova Scotia's regional and occupational diversity as well as its old patronage habits already make it peculiarly difficult to govern.

Moreover, the disruption to displaced civil servants and politicians would be substantial, and the regional economy might not produce sufficient opportunities for the middle class in the private sector. And then there is the question of the regional presence in the constitutional amending formula; four provinces carry a combined veto and a large voice in federal-provincial negotiations. Thus Atlantic Canada's gains in economic efficiency and political credibility might not outweigh potential losses. As an APEC study suggests, this "is a highly emotional issue in a region where the component parts (provinces) pride themselves on their independence and political maturity and where the four smallest provinces nevertheless are equal partners in Confederation" (APEC 1991a:36).

Greater economic and policy cooperation on a voluntary basis among the four governments is a more viable option; such a model could gradually increase interprovincial coordination without full union. Nonetheless the existence of four governments, especially in a region with a high dependence on government employment and finances, induces a competitive ethos to many endeavours. Thus regional politicians squabbled for years about where to locate a police school, veterinary college, and other joint facilities. Such disputes are unavoidable under the existing regime of sovereign provinces. Yet the dire consequences of separation and regional isolation must foster a more cooperative spirit if these provinces are to maintain their political influence and living standards. New approaches must be devised to go beyond creation of a single economic space to the development of policy coordination and efficient program delivery. Cooperative measures must be forged to promote the best interests of all regional citizens, and not merely those of self-interested state elites bent on preserving autonomous provincial authority at whatever cost to taxpayers. Given the strength of entrenched elites, internal efforts alone may not be sufficient to secure the necessary level of cooperation. Ottawa could play a role by revising its approach to regional development to avoid a bilateral emphasis on deals with individual provinces and to focus on genuinely regional initiatives in future. Constitutional reforms must also address the fragmentation of service provision, bureaucratic resources, and jurisdictional competence in the Atlantic region, with four small provinces with historically arbitrary rather than jurisdictionally optimal boundaries.

Perhaps Atlantic governments should seek a constitutional clause which will permit constitutionalization of intergovernmental agreements (federal-provincial and interprovincial) on the delegation of powers and the sharing of revenues, services, and programs. This clause would not only achieve a long-standing regional goal of attaining greater certainty in cost-sharing and regional development arrangements with Ottawa. If used interprovincially, it would allow regions such as the Atlantic provinces, Maritimes, or Prairies to entrench agreements providing for joint services and bureaucracies, with advance notification for termination by any party. This could allow for more economical and efficient provision of essential provincial services, to improve rather than reduce their quality in times of restraint. It would also help overcome the limited capacities and narrow vision of governments responding to their own local constituency at the expense of effective regional policy or service provision. While full political integration might be more efficient, a less comprehensive integration could produce considerable savings – without jeopardizing provincial loyalties or the region's weight within national institutions.

CONCLUSION: CONTINGENT LOYALTIES?

Thus, although Atlantic Canadians are critical of the workings of the national economic and political structure, their interests do not lie in the breakup of Canada. It is probably true, as dependency theorists suggest, that regional economic fortunes have been disadvantaged by the workings of capitalism, as the region became a net exporter of surplus capital and skilled labour. Political forces have also been disadvantageous. Nonetheless, a refined dependency model must recognize that initial deficiencies in resources and location led to the region's subordination in politics and economics and generated regional political and economic elites who profit from the peripheral place of the region in national political and economic institutions. Hence creation of a separate Atlantic state would be unlikely to end the region's peripheral status. And there is no realistic salvation in a socialistic delinking from the national economy. While free trade may hold open the prospect of shopping for better deals and diversifying economic connections, this region seems destined to remain someone's periphery, if not Central Canada's then that of the United States or the Far East.

Atlantic Canadians have consistently supported Confederation in the past few decades, based on material interest and emotional loyalties built up over more than a century of union. Regional strategy must focus on reform of federal institutions and policies to maximize prospects for regional development; what remains to be seen is whether regional elites have either the motivation or ability to secure such changes. But erosion of the status quo from economic as well as constitutional upheaval appears inevitable. Can the region help to sustain the country against centrifugal and transnational pressures? Appeals can certainly be made to national loyalties, to constitutional principles like equalization, to common national standards in government services, and to self-interest in preservation of a common economic space, with or without Quebec. It is in no one's interests for this prosperous nation to become a scattered collection of satrapies at the mercy of unpredictable American political and economic forces and an unreliable free trade agreement. Those in other regions who share a common vision of the nation and a common recognition of our mutual interests must surely recognize that the abandonment of the eastern periphery is the beginning of the end for the transcontinental vision of the Canadian nation, that shared history and loyalties make continuation of the union desirable, and that the total collapse of Canada would diminish all its citizens to provincial ambitions, ending the wide open opportunities of Canadianism.

However, regional politicians and citizens should not rely on the goodwill of those in other parts of the country; they must at once pragmatically pool the limited resources of the region more effectively and flexibly but firmly negotiate for a more regionally sensitive national regime and national policy. Opportunity, not charity, should be the regional goal in a restructured Canada; provincial and federal leaders would need to work to reform policies to reduce dependency on transfers and provide for greater regional economic self-sufficiency. But Atlantic loyalties will rest on continued recognition that efficiency cannot be divorced from equity, and that a shared Canadianism requires national commitments to similar levels of public service, similar fiscal burdens, and similar opportunities for citizens to continue to enjoy the fruits of national prosperity and to prepare for the challenges of global integration and technological change. Atlantic allegiance to Canada was earned through the post-war welfare state consensus, which gave substance to common Canadian citizenship. If these commitments go unfulfilled, then former Nova Scotia Premier John Buchanan's musings about American statehood could gain credibility, as the attractions of Canadian citizenship diminish.

BIBLIOGRAPHY

Alexander, David. 1980. "New Notions of Happiness: Nationalism, Regionalism and Atlantic Canada." *Journal of Canadian Studies* 15, no.2 (Summer), 29–42.

- Atlantic Provinces Economic Council (APEC). 1990. *Strategies and Options for the Atlantic Economy in the 1990s*. Prepared for the APEC Annual Meeting, St John's, October 1990. Halifax: APEC.
- 1991a. *Atlantic Economic Cooperation: An Exploration of the Concept, its Benefits and Costs*. Prepared for the APEC Annual Conference, Dartmouth, N.S., June 1991. Halifax: APEC.
- 1991b. *Restructured Federalism and its Impacts on Atlantic Canada*. Halifax: APEC.
Bakvis, Herman. 1991. *Regional Ministers: Power and Influence in the Canadian Cabinet*. Toronto: University of Toronto Press.
Beauchesne, Eric. 1991. "Breakup 'devastating' for region, report says" *Daily News* (Halifax), 11 December, 21.
Bickerton, James. 1990. "Creating Atlantic Canada: Culture, Policy and Regionalism." In *Canadian Politics: An Introduction to the Discipline*, ed. J. Bickerton and Alain Gagnon, 325–44. Peterborough: Broadview.
Brown, Douglas. 1990. "Sea Change in Newfoundland: From Peckford to Wells." In *Canada: The State of the Federation, 1990*, ed. R. Watts and D. Brown, 199–229. Kingston: Queen's University Institute of Intergovernmental Relations.
Canada. 1951. *Dominion-Provincial and Interprovincial Conferences From 1867-1926*. Ottawa: Queen's Printer.
Council of Maritime Premiers (CMP). 1991. *Challenge and Opportunity: A Discussion Paper on Maritime Economic Integration* Halifax: CMP.
Desjardins, Pierre-Marcel. 1994. "Trade in Atlantic Canada: Trends and Opportunities Under Trade Liberalization" (Northumberland Group Discussion Paper No. 1). Moncton: Canadian Institute for Research on Regional Development.
DeWolf, A. Gordon, James McNiven, and Donald McPhail. 1988. "ACOA in an International and Historical Context". *Canadian Journal of Regional Science* 11, no. 2 (Summer), 313–25.
Finbow, Robert. Forthcoming. "Dependents or Dissidents? The Atlantic Provinces in Canada's Constitutional Reform Process, 1967–1992."
Forbes, Ernest R. 1989. *Challenging the Regional Stereotype: Essays on the 20th. Century Maritimes*. Fredericton: Acadiensis Press.
- 1993. "Looking Backward: Reflections on the Maritime Experience in an Evolving Canadian Constitution." In *The Maritime Provinces: Looking Towards the Future*, ed. D. Savoie and R. Winter. Moncton: Canadian Institute for Research on Regional Development.
Higgins, Benjamin. 1990. "Subsidies, Regional Development and the Canada-U.S. Free Trade Agreement." *Canadian Journal of Regional Science* 13, no. 2/3:259–72.
House, J. D., 1986. "The Mouse that Roared." In *Regionalism in Canada*, ed. R.J. Brym, 161–96. Toronto: Irwin.

Howell, Colin. 1977. "Nova Scotia's Protest Tradition and the Search for a Meaningful Federalism." In *Canada and the Burden of Unity*, ed. David Bercuson, 169–91. Toronto: Macmillan.

Lamarche, Rodolphe. 1993. "The Maritime Provinces in an Information Economy." In *The Maritime Provinces: Looking Towards the Future*, ed. Donald Savoie and Ralph Winter, 7, 69–97. Moncton: Canadian Institute for Research on Regional Development.

Matthews, Ralph. 1979. "The Smallwood Legacy: The Development of Underdevelopment in Newfoundland" *Journal of Canadian Studies* 13, no. 4:89–108.

Milne, David. 1991. "Equality or Asymmetry: Why Choose?" In *Options for a New Canada*, ed. R. Watts and D. Brown, 285–307. Toronto: University of Toronto Press.

Northumberland Group. 1991. "Looking Ahead: A Maritime Perspective." Moncton: Northumberland Group (mimeo).

Nova Scotia. 1991. *Reports of the Nova Scotia Advisory Committees on Constitutional Issues.* Halifax: Province of Nova Scotia.

Overton, James. 1979. "Towards a Critical Analysis of Neo-Nationalism in Newfoundland." In *Underdevelopment and Social Movements in Atlantic Canada*, ed. R.J. Brym and R.J. Sacouman, 219–49. Toronto: New Hogtown Press.

Robertson, Ian. 1991. "The Atlantic Provinces and the Territorial Question." In *English Canada Speaks Out.* ed. J.L. Granatstein and K. McNaught, 162–71. *English Canada Speaks Out.* Toronto: Doubleday.

Savoie, Donald. 1990. "Regional Development Policy: The Canadian Experience." In *Regional Policy in a Changing World*, ed. Niles Hansen, Benjamin Higgins and Donald Savoie, 15–40. New York: Plenum.

Wells, Clyde. 1991. "Notes for Remarks by the Honourable Clyde K. Wells, Premier of Newfoundland and Labrador to the Special Colloquium of the School of Public Administration, Carleton University, Ottawa, 5 June 1991.

Young, M. Douglas. 1991. "Atlantic Canada Political Union." Presented to the Atlantic Provinces Political Studies Association Annual Meeting, Saint John.

5 English Canada: The Nation that Dares not Speak its Name

PHILIP RESNICK

When in Book 9 of *the Odyssey* Odysseus, outwitting and blinding the cyclops Polyphemus who threatened to devour him and his companions, says that his name is "Nobody," the raging Polyphemus is reduced to lamenting: "O my friends, it's Nobody's treachery, no violence, that is doing me to death" (Homer 150).

English-speaking Canadians are not quite in the same plight as Odysseus and his crew, nor does a cyclops bar our path. Yet in an odd sort of way we too are given to thinking of ourselves collectively as "no-nation," and to denying vigorously that the twenty million Canadians who are neither Québécois nor Aboriginals might constitute an English-Canadian nation. The very term this book adopts, "Canada outside Quebec," and the earlier term which was bandied about in the lead-up to Charlottetown, Rest of Canada (ROC) help to highlight the problem. For there is a remarkable unease on the part of many English-speaking Canadians, not least academics or intellectuals, to define themselves as English Canadians. How many readers would feel altogether comfortable with the statement, "I am an English Canadian"? Not every one, I wager. There would be much less problem with, "I am a Canadian."

If this were a volume dealing with Quebec – one of those perennial collections on identity, modernity, and the like – there would be few among the francophone readers who would have any difficulty defining themselves as Québécois. Some, it is true, might well see themselves as Canadians, no less than Québécois; others, of a Péquiste or Bloc persuasion, might see themselves as exclusively Québécois. But the Québécois pole of identity has become a defining one for a vast majority of Quebec's inhabitants, including, interestingly enough, a good number of Anglo-Québécois and of Quebec's allophone population as well.

In similar fashion, were this a volume dealing with First Nations people, can there be any doubt about how the overwhelming majority of Aboriginal readers would define their identity? Not that the term "Aboriginal" would necessarily mean the same thing for everyone, nor that there would be anything resembling agreement about the full implications – constitutional, political, or what have you – of Aboriginal status in this country. But the notion that Aboriginal People constitute a distinct nationality or grouping of nationalities within Canada has made giant strides in recent years.[1]

This is a volume, however, primarily addressed to English-speaking Canadians from a diversity of backgrounds living outside Quebec. Its very theme may for some be a source of embarrassment and unease. How comfortable are Acadians and other Franco-Canadians, that is non-Québécois francophones, likely to be with a concept such as English Canada? What linguistic and cultural rights are they likely to retain in a hypothetical English Canada with a new, as yet undefined relationship, with Quebec?

What about the close to 50 percent of the population of Canada outside Quebec whose origins cannot be traced back to the British Isles? Can they be comfortable with a term "English Canada" that, for some at least, connotes a privileged place not only for a language, English, but perhaps for an ethnic group as well, those of English or British stock? It is not surprising that in an increasingly multicultural country, one with visible and audible minorities of all sorts, the term "English Canada" may seem like a provocation or worse.

Even a good number of English-speaking Canadians whose origins go back to the British Isles may find the term "English Canada" offensive. They have grown up with the assumption that they were Canadians by nationality, not hyphenated English-Canadians.[2] They would resist any attempt to redefine Canada outside Quebec as "English Canada" as giving in to the worst tendencies of Quebec nationalism in recent decades. For it is Quebec nationalists, so the argument goes, who have needed to invent an English Canada as part of their rationalization of a two-nation Canada and of their own claims to some form of Quebec sovereignty. It ill behooves us in the rest of Canada to play the separatist game.

The question of nomenclature is, therefore, a pivotal one. It is partly one over terms – what exactly are we to call ourselves: Rest of Canada, Canada outside Quebec, English Canada, English-speaking Canada,

Canada *tout court?* We could organize numerous conferences debating the terminology we should use without, I suspect, reaching any consensus. We could initiate a Canada-wide contest on the topic, with big prize money to induce participation, and the outcome would probably be the same. For the question of terms touches a much deeper matter altogether, namely the question of identity.

That is why in my recently published *Thinking English Canada* (1994), I spend relatively little time on our favourite academic pastime, the constitution, and a great deal more trying to explore the sociological, cultural, and even geographical contours of English-Canadian identity. For in truth we cannot hope to find a way out of our quagmire as a federation unless and until the majority group, by which I mean English-speaking Canadians, begin to reflect more seriously on their own underlying values.

I would contend that the term "English Canada" or "English Canadian" is not an entirely artifical one, and that it can be traced back to the underlying duality between English and French speakers that was to mark Canada from the time of Confederation on. If French Canadian (or the earlier term *Canadien* in contradistinction to *les anglais*) was the term commonly used to describe the French-speaking inhabitants of Canada down to the time of the Quiet Revolution, then it is no great surprise to find the term "English Canada" or "English Canadian" being used in a variety of political, historical, or cultural contexts.

André Siegfried, the French political scientist, in his landmark 1906 study, *The Race Question in Canada*, titled chapter 17 "The Attitudes of French and English Canadians Towards the United States"; Thomas Guthrie Marquis published a study in 1913 titled *English Canadian Literature*; historian Frank Underhill (1964:50), for his part, wrote in 1964 that "the root of our current difficulties is that French-Canadians and English-Canadians have different pictures in their minds of what the meaning of Confederation was in 1867"; Peter Waite (1987:370) notes, more recently, in reference to the 1890s that "The French-Canadian nationalists of O Canada and English-Canadian nationalists of Canada could not meet"; and Ramsay Cook (1987:413) argues with respect to 1914–18 that "given the divisions created by the pre-war debates over minority schools and imperial relations, it was almost inevitable that the war years should witness a bitter quarrel between French and English Canadians." Nor has there been a shortage of titles using the term English Canada. Examples might include: *English-Canadian Points of Views on Biculturalism* (O'Hearn and Ferguson 1964), *English-Canadian Furniture of the Georgian Period* (Webster 1979), *English Canadian Theatre* (Benson and Connolly 1987), *"English Canada" Speaks*

Out (Granatstein and McNaught 1991), and *English Canada and Quebec: Avoiding the Issue* (McRoberts 1991).

It is true that the term "English Canada" might seem to better fit the image of a society where until World War II a clear majority of the population was of British origin, and where Loyalist imagery and British references, to Crown and Empire, for example, prevailed. In other words, there was an undoubtedly ethnic character associated with the term "English Canada" in an earlier period of Canadian history, as when George Parkin (1985:159) wrote in 1888: "The emigrant is encouraged or even assisted in leaving the old Britain; he is heartily welcomed in the new Britain beyond the seas." This ethnic dimension – those of British stock as the founding people and dominant group on the English Canadian side – helps explain the antipathy of many, especially of non-British origin, to the term.

I would argue that somewhere between the first half of the twentieth century and today, Canada outside Quebec crossed the line between a more ethnically rooted concept of identity and one a good deal more pluralistic in character. This was the inevitable consequence of the opening up of Canada, for example, of the west, to waves of immigration from continental Europe, and in a more recent period, especially since the 1960s, to large-scale immigration from Asia, Latin America, and the Caribbean. The weakening of the British connection with the waning of the Empire also played an important role, as did Canada's increased tropism toward the United States.

To use the term "English Canada" today as referring to a British charter group, for example, is a non-starter. As someone of Jewish and East European background myself, I would be the last to want to make the case for such a usage. But to use the term in reference to the linguistic and cultural characteristics of mainstream Canadian society outside Quebec is another matter. Can anyone deny that English is the lingua franca of the inhabitants of that society from Bonavista to Vancouver Island, with exceptions for pockets of francophones, Aboriginals, and first generation ethnic communities?[3] Can anyone deny that our politics, media, educational system, cultural, and sporting events, and much besides, reflect this? There is nothing ethnic about this use of the term English, nor is it meant to imply for one moment that people of a variety of linguistic and cultural backgrounds have not made giant contributions to the culture of Canada outside Quebec. The fact remains, nonetheless, that the vast majority of the inhabitants of Canada outside Quebec, regardless of their origins, are and will continue to be English speakers, and that English will continue to mark the public sphere and most of the private as well. It is only realistic, therefore, to use the terms English Canada and English Canadian to describe our society.

To the degree that language is one of the primary poles of identity in the modern world, to the degree that in other multilingual federations like Switzerland or Belgium or India it is a key feature of internal differentiation, to the degree that is has served as a historical marker between Quebec and the rest of the country, to that degree we can hardly deny that we are English Canadians. And it is precisely in this fashion that I have used the term in my recent essay.

Still, I recognize that the term "English Canada" is something of an ugly duckling, and that beneath resistance to its use lies something deeper. In their heart of hearts, a majority of English Canadians think of themselves as Canadians – period. Whatever Quebec's ultimate status, the rest of us would want to continue to call ourselves Canadians. And the same would be true vis-à-vis First Nations people, were they to achieve some form of Aboriginal self-government.

I share this sentiment, and cannot claim that "I am an English Canadian" comes more easily to my lips than "I am a Canadian." We outside Quebec have been socialized to think of ourselves as Canadians; if any other term might spring to mind, it is far more likely to be a provincial or regional term of identity like Westerner or British Columbian or Ontarian than English Canadian.

This doesn't get us off the hook where thinking about our relations with Quebec or with Aboriginal peoples is concerned. To the degree that their identities are caught up with a form of national self-identification, in other words that they define themselves as nationalities vis-à-vis the rest of us, we really have no choice but to ask ourselves the hard question. What are we but a nationality as well? If so, do we need a term to distinguish the pan-Canadian dimension of our identity, including Québécois and Aboriginals, from the more specifically English or English-speaking component?

It is here that we really enter the debate of the mid-1990s, the post-Meech, post-Charlottetown debate. Once upon a time, no doubt about it, the backbone of a certain Anglo-Canadian nationalism lay in defining ourselves as against Great Britain or the United States. For some people, particularly those of a Tory persuasion, close imperial relations with Great Britain were the bedrock of our resistance to absorption into the United States. For others, more often Liberals, Canada was a North American nation *par excellence* (Dafœ 1935); the faster it made its peace with that reality the better for all. For still others, I am thinking of a few hardy social democratic intellectuals in the 1920s and 1930s and of the newer current of Canadian nationalism that surfaced in the 1960s, we would have to cultivate our independence as against the United States, no less than as against Great Britain in an earlier period.

The more difficult debate, however, is the one that has been sparked by the emergence of a new Quebec nationalism in the aftermath of the Quiet Revolution. Where an earlier French-Canadian nationalism was content to resist any and all encroachments into Quebec jurisdiction as spelled out in the BNA Act and to look to religion as a bulwark of self-defence, contemporary Quebec nationalism was to take another turn. The emphasis would now be on modernizing Quebec society and politics as quickly as possible, in promoting francophone control over the economy, and in making language the chief component of identity. Where Quebec relations with Canada were concerned, this meant enhancing Quebec's powers at the expense of Ottawa's. Some, as in the Quebec Liberal Party, were still prepared to define themselves as federalists, even while pressing for forms of special status. Others, as in the PQ, openly called for a sovereign Quebec, with or without some ongoing association with the rest of Canada.

It is only in the 1990s that the full implications of Quebec nationalism, *nouvelle vague*, and of the newer Aboriginal nationalism that has arisen since are coming home. In the late 1960s or 1970s a few observers, a few publications were prepared to take Quebec nationalism on its own terms – the Canadian Union of Students, *Canadian Dimension*, *Canadian Forum*, the Waffle movement in the NDP, academics like Abe Rotstein (1973) or Dennis Smith (1971). But the large majority of Canadians outside Quebec were under the spell of Pierre Trudeau (as were many inside Quebec), and assumed that the Official Languages Act and bilingualism at the federal level would resolve matters. The PQ victory in 1976 and Bill 101 which followed shook some of their complacency; but the outcome of the 1980 referendum on sovereignty-association, Trudeau's subsequent Charter cum repatriation of the constitution, and the defeat of the PQ in 1985 seemed to put the spectre of sovereignty to rest.

We know better that this was but a hiatus, and that from the Meech Lake Accord of 30 April 1987 to the defeat of Charlottetown on 26 October 1992, we were to live constitutional politics on a full-time basis. I do not intend to revisit those debates in any detail. What I would stress, however, is the emergence of a new consciousness within English Canada of the potentially destabilizing character, from its own point of view, of Quebec (and potentially of Aboriginal) demands, and of the unacceptability of any kind of constitutional package that does not win explicit popular approval.

Although sections of English-Canadian public opinion were prepared to go along with a decentralizing political agenda that transferred powers to all the provinces, a significantly larger component was just as firmly opposed.[4] Coming at the same time as the Canada-

U.S. Free Trade Agreement with its weakening of the powers of the federal government, Meech Lake and Charlottetown were seen by many of its opponents as an unacceptably high price to pay for the fickle favours of a Robert Bourassa or the political gamesmanship of a Brian Mulroney. Moreover, important sections of English-Canadian public opinion were far from convinced that distinct society status for. Quebec or open-ended provisions regarding Aboriginal self-government might not make the equality provisions of the Charter or the putative equality of the provinces nul and void. And though a few groups like the National Action Committee on the Status of Women or the signatories to a 1992 declaration in *The Toronto Star* (4 February: A17) were prepared to think of Canada in terms of three nations, these were but minority voices in English Canada.

What was heartening about the period between the demise of Meech and that of the Charlottetown Accord was the degree of discussion within English Canada, especially in milieux that did not normally live or breathe politics. There was an epidemic of grassroots discussion, both in spontaneous meetings and in bodies like the Citizens' Forum on Canada's Future or the constitutional conferences between January and March 1992. There were the beginnings of an intra-English Canadian dialogue, in which traditional party allegiances played a very small part indeed, and in which, according to one observer, "a more thoughtful and heartfelt English-speaking sense of community [was] in the making, and growing quickly" (Spicer 1991:3). There were demands for democratic empowerment, spurred on by the disenchantment of large sections of public opinion with the top-down style of politics of Meech, and culminating in the repudiation of much of the Canadian political class in the referendum of 1992.

The federal election of 1993 was to confirm something of the new mood in the land. The two political parties that had opposed Charlottetown – Reform in English Canada and the Bloc in Quebec – scored signal electoral breakthroughs, even as the Conservatives and the NDP in effect died. And though the Liberals were back as the governing party, it remains to be seen just how well equipped they are to bridge the faultlines between English Canada and Quebec.

What can one expect by way of a reaction in English Canada to the ongoing question of Quebec? At one level, there is profound constitutional fatigue and a new preoccupation with issues of public finance, debt, social programs, employment, and the like. Globalizing forces, of which the FTA and NAFTA were manifestations, have suddenly made many of the old assumptions about Canadian political economy and public policy much less certain. Neither Smith nor Keynes, let alone

Marx, is really the prophet of the new age that beckons. Perhaps the beast slouching towards Bethlehem bears the face of Malthus.[5]

At another level, the politics of national self-affirmation seems to be part of the same postmodern meltdown that brought the end of communism and of the Cold War. For despite homogenizing trends in a capitalism that is planetary in character,[6] forms of cultural resistance are everywhere. From Islamic fundamentalism to the ethnic nationalisms of the Balkans or Central Asia, from the debates over citizenship and immigration in Germany or France to the Zapatista rebellion in Mexico, identity politics are the flavour of the decade. And we in English Canada may be no more immune to its charms than are our counterparts in Quebec.

What shape might the debate about English Canada take? Some of it will involve academic types from across English Canada, talking heads participating in conferences like the one that the Robarts Centre organized for the contributors to this volume. There will be representatives, male and female, from different regions, from different disciplines, from different cultural communities, from different parts of the political spectrum. And this being English Canada, every one will be very polite, at least at first, though before long differences and conflicts will surface.

Some participants will reject the very notion of an English Canadian identity in the name of something else – region, nation state, multicultural diversity, for starters. Others will take solace from deconstructing the very notion of nationality, arguing that, as denizens of postmodernity, we have gone beyond such nineteenth century artifacts. Still others will dream their ideological dreams – an English Canada based upon rational choice models, for example, one involving a more regulated capitalism with a human face, or perhaps a market socialism, with distinctly green and feminist components.

The debate will leave the rarified atmosphere of the academy and take on a more popular hue. The hot line shows will be opened up, along with the letter columns of the newspapers. *Maclean's* will lock twelve representative English Canadians, with half a dozen facilitators, away in Lake Louise for a week to reflect on the English-Canadian psyche. *Prime Time News* will stage a series of town-hall meetings with Pamela and Peter. And the cry will go up from one end of the country to the other, "Bring Back Keith Spicer!"

On a more serious note, as I suggested at the conference and first argued in *Thinking English Canada* (Resnick 1994), we may well have to envisage something like an Estates General for English Canada. Back in the 1960s when the debate about Quebec was beginning to heat up, Jacques-Yvan Morin, a constitutional law professor at the Université de Montréal and future PQ cabinet minister, had the idea of convening an

Estates General of French Canada. This involved a series of local and regional meetings, primarily in Quebec but also involving French Canadians outside Quebec, organized under the auspices of groups such as the St Jean Baptiste Society. These meetings culminated in a larger gathering in Montreal in 1967 of about 2000 delegates, who wrestled with such questions as the identity of French Canada and the future of Quebec.

We in English Canada have never really had occasion to address our collective identity in the way Quebec francophones and Aboriginal People have. Our debate about the constitution, for example, both over Meech and Charlottetown, was very much caught up with Quebec and Aboriginal demands. More foundational questions – the nature of English-Canadian political culture, the dialectic of nation and region within English Canada, the implications of NAFTA and of globalization for English-Canadian identity, the subject of multiculturalism – we have been remarkably inept at debating among ourselves.

In Eastern Europe, social movements and intellectual figures played a seminal role in the revival of civil society in contradistinction to the state.[7] We in English Canada may not need to invent civil society, but we do need to find a way to give voice to sentiments about identity and nationality that motivate ordinary Canadians at the grassroots level. We need to ensure that if there is to be some fundamental restructuring of the Canadian federation – along asymmetrical confederal lines (Resnick 1993, 1994), no less than in the meltdown scenario that Quebec sovereignty would pose – that we do not as a society sleepwalk through it blindly. Nor can we simply leave it to elected politicians, like Jean Chrétien who keeps telling us the constitution is not worth discussing or Preston Manning with his nostrums about ten equal provinces, to preempt the debate. We need something more broadly representative.

What I have in mind is a series of regionally organized forums, within each of the provinces other than Quebec and the two territories, to address certain key questions. Is there such a thing as English Canada (or whatever other name we choose to call it)? What, if any, are some of its core values? How do we, as English-speaking Canadians, envisage the powers of the federal government and those of the provinces? What sort of changes, if any, in our relations with Quebec or with Aboriginal peoples are we prepared to entertain? What about bilingualism or multiculturalism within English Canada? What about our place on the North American continent or within the larger world?

The focus would not be on coming up with hard constitutional formulae. Rather, it would be on eliciting a wide range of views on what makes English Canada the type of society it is. The forums could be organized by significant social actors – business, labour, cultural organizations, farmers, ethnic communities, women's groups – rather than by governments or political parties. A majority of those attending the forums would be ordinary Canadians, chosen by some sort of lottery, perhaps in the way that juries are selected. But some of the other participants would indeed represent key social interests.

These regional gatherings would eventually culminate in a single English Canada-wide gathering with delegates from all the regions. This would be the Estates General of English Canada, properly speaking, and would meet for a week or two in Ottawa or any other city we agreed to in full view of the media. Delegates would strive to reach agreement on key issues, and take stock of others on which there was strong disagreement. For once, English(-speaking) Canadians from a broad variety of backgrounds would be meeting among themselves, and they just might be laying the foundation for a new sense of collective self.

Perhaps I am letting my imagination run amok. We are still at a very early stage in our self-reflections; a Quebec referendum, if the proponents of sovereignty were to lose, would still any serious discussion for a time, though a significant "Yes" vote for sovereignty, 47 or 48 percent of those voting, would certainly keep the issue alive. Before we can envisage an Estates General for English Canada, moreover, English-speaking Canadians still face the difficult problem of whether to begin to see themselves as a nation. Are we ready for the conceptual leap that this would represent – thinking of Canada as a multinational federation, disaggregating the specifically English-Canadian component from the pan-Canadian? Do we have the stamina for a whole new round of debates, within English Canada first and foremost, but eventually with Quebec and with Aboriginal People?

In Homer's *Odyssey*, when Odysseus and his sailors are safely aboard ship, he reveals his real name to the blinded Polyphemus; he and his crew then barely escape the cyclops' boulders with their lives. Are we in English Canada finally prepared to stop calling ourselves "no-nation"? And what furies will we face, both within and without, when we finally cease being a nation that dares not speak its name?

NOTES

I have benefited from helpful suggestions from the book's editor, Kenneth McRoberts, as well as from discussions at the original conference at the Robarts Centre, 29 April–1 May 1994.
1 Among of variety of possible sources, I would list Englestad and Bird (1992); and Mercredi and Turpel (1993).

2 It may be worth noting that 765,095 respondents to the 1991 census identified themselves as Canadians by origin, disdaining the other ethnic origins that were available (Statistics Canada 1991). Such respondents would
probably find a hyphenated term such as "English-Canadian" quite unacceptable.

3 The 1991 census shows 79 percent of respondents in Canada excluding
Quebec identify English as their mother tongue (Statistics Canada 1991,
table 6.5, p. 22). But close to 87 percent of respondents in Canada outside
Quebec identified English as the language spoken in the home (Statistics
Canada 1991, table 1, pp. 8–9, 18–19).

4 See, for example, The Citizens' Forum on Canada's Future (1991, fig. 2,
p. 158), which shows clear majorities in every province other than Quebec
for maintaining or strengthening the powers of the federal government as
opposed to increasing provincial powers. See also the CBC/ *Globe and Mail*
poll results in the *Globe and Mail*, 22 April 1991, A4.

5 For an apocalyptical forecast, the reader might profitably turn to Kaplan
(1994).

6 Two good discussions of this are Chesneaux (1989); and Barnet and
Cavanagh (1994).

7 Useful sources on this theme include Keane (1988; part 3); Cohen and
Arato (1992); and Tismaneanu (1992, chaps. 4, 5).

BIBLIOGRAPHY

Barnet, Richard, and John Cavanagh. 1994. *Global Dreams: Imperial Corporations
and the New World Order.* New York: Simon and Schuster.

Benson, Eugene, and L.W. Connolly. 1987. *English Canadian Theatre.* Toronto:
Oxford University Press.

Chesneaux, Jean. 1989. *Modernité-Monde.* Paris: La Découverte.

Citizens' Forum on Canada's Future. 1991. *Report to the People and Government of
Canada.* Ottawa: Canadian Government Publishing Centre.

Cohen, Jean, and Andrew Arato. 1992. *Civil Society and Political Theory.* Cambridge: MIT press.

Cook, Ramsay. 1987. "The Triumph and Trials of Materialism." In *Illustrated
History of Canada*, ed. Craig Brown, 375–466. Toronto: Lester & Orpen Dennys.

Dafoe, John. 1935. *Canada: A North American Nation.* New York: Columbia University Press.

Englestad, Diane, and John Bird, eds. 1992. *Nation to Nation: Aboriginal Sovereignty and the Future of Canada.* Concord, Ont: House of Anansi Press.

Granatstein, J.L., and Kenneth McNaught, eds. 1991. *"English Canada" Speaks
Out.* Toronto: Doubleday.

Homer. 1946. *The Odyssey.* Trans. E.V. Rieu. London: Penguin.

Kaplan, Robert. 1994. "The Coming Anarchy." *The Atlantic Monthly* (February).

Keane, John, ed. 1988. *Civil Society and the State.* London: Verso.

McRoberts, Kenneth. 1991. *English Canada and Quebec: Avoiding the Issue.* North York, Ont: Robarts Centre, York University.

Marquis, Thomas Guthrie. [1913] 1973. *English Canadian Literature.* Toronto: Brook and Co. Reprinted for the Royal Society of Canada by University of Toronto Press.

Mercredi, Ovide, and Mary Ellen Turpel. 1993. *In the Rapids: Navigating the Future of the First Nations.* Toronto: Viking.

O'Hearn, Walter, and George Ferguson. 1964. *English-Canadian Points of View on Biculturalism.* Montreal: Montreal Star.

Parkin, Sir George. [1888] 1985. "The Reorganization of the British Empire." In *Canadian Political Thought,* ed. H.D. Forbes, 156–65. Toronto: Oxford University Press.

Resnick, Philip. 1993. "The Crisis of Multinational Federations: Post-Charlottetown Reflections." *Review of Constitutional Studies* 1, no. 2.

– 1994. *Thinking English Canada.* Toronto: Stoddart.

– forthcoming. "Towards a Multinational Federalism: Asymmetrical and Confederal Alternatives."

Rotstein, Abe. 1973. *The Precarious Homestead* (especially "After the Fall," 118–24). Toronto: New Press.

Siegfried, André. 1966. *The Race Question in Canada.* Toronto: McClelland & Stewart.

Smith, Dennis. 1971. *Bleeding Hearts ... Bleeding Country: Canada and the Quebec Crisis* (especially chap. 7). Edmonton: Hurtig.

Spicer, Keith. 1991. Chairman's Forward to *Report to the People and Government of Canada,* Citizens' Forum on Canada's Future. Ottawa: Canadian Government Publishing Centre.

Tismaneanul, Vladimir. 1992. *Reinventing Politics: Eastern Europe from Stalin to Havel.* New York: The Free Press.

Toronto Star. 1992. "Three Nations in a Delicate State." 4 February, A17.

Underhill, Frank. 1964. *The Image of Confederation.* Toronto: CBC.

Waite, Peter. 1987. "Between Three Oceans: Challenges of a Continental Destiny." In *Illustrated History of Canada,* ed. Craig Brown, 281–374. Toronto: Lester & Orpen Dennys.

Webster, Donald Blake. 1979. *English-Canadian Furniture of the Georgian Period.* Toronto: McGraw-Hill Ryerson.

6 The Charter and Canada outside Quebec

F.L. MORTON

In 1982 Canada made a fundamental change to its constitution. To its 125-year-old tradition of parliamentary supremacy cum federalism, Canada grafted a constitutionally entrenched Charter of Rights and Freedoms with explicit authority for the courts to interpret and to enforce these rights. A decade later, this bold experiment of "Charter democracy" is widely viewed as a success in all parts of the country except Quebec. I survey the nature of the Charter's success in Canada outside Quebec (COQ), as well as the reasons for Quebec's disenchantment. I then extrapolate the effect of Charter politics in a post-partum COQ.

Contrary to the conventional view of the Charter as a unifying force in COQ, I argue that the Charter is also a source of political conflict. Specifically, I argue that there is a tension between the Charter qua symbol and the reality of Charter politics, between a liberal regime of equality of opportunity for individuals and a post-liberal regime of equality of results for groups. The latter is championed by a new Court Party, which is content to use judicial and administrative fiat to pursue its version of democracy (group equality) if legislatures are not forthcoming. The former is most closely identified with the new Reform Party, whose understanding of democracy emphasizes electoral-legislative primacy complemented by referenda and other populist devices. The Court Party is strongest in the "Charter Belt" of southern Ontario, while the Reform Party's primary base of support is in the West. In this respect Charter politics reproduces a long-standing pattern of centre-periphery conflict in Canadian politics. Conflict between the Court and Reform Parties could divide a post-partum Canada along regional lines. However, it is just as probable that this conflict would cut along educational, occupational, and urban-rural lines. That is, the Charter would divide Canadians, but by dividing along non-regional lines, could actually contribute to a more unified nation state.

THE CHARTER AS A UNIFYING SOURCE IN ENGLISH CANADA

Polling done on its tenth anniversary found wide support for the Charter. An Angus Reid poll found that Canadians who thought that the Charter had been "a good thing" outnumbered those who thought it had been "a bad thing" by a margin of three to one (*Reid Report* 1992). A different survey found a 76 percent support rating (Ouellette 1991:9). In a similar vein, pollsters found widespread public opposition to the "notwithstanding clause," the Charter section which allows a government to insulate legislation from any Charter challenge (*Reid Report* 1992). The *Reid Report* (1992) found 53 percent support for abolishing section 33, while the Justice Department study (Oullet 1991) reported that 62 percent of Canadians were "opposed" to section 33. A decade after its adoption, the Charter has been hailed as the leading institutional symbol of a new pan-Canadian nationalism.

This popularity is not an accident. The Charter was the centrepiece of the constitutional package that Pierre Trudeau sold as the "the People's Package" in 1982. Trudeau's nation-building objectives are well documented (Knopff and Morton 1985), and – at least in English Canada – they have been largely realized. The Charter has acquired its own constituency – a loose coalition of feminists, civil libertarians, the disabled, Aboriginals and other "visible minorities," official language minorities, social reform activists, and ethnocultural organizations. Cairns has aptly labeled these groups "Charter Canadians" (Cairns 1988). They have been somewhat less charitably but more accurately described as "the Court Party" (Morton and Knopff 1992). Whatever the label, their new influence has been evident ever since they helped to defeat the 1987 Meech Lake Accord and then played a leading role in the consultative process that culminated in the 1992 Charlottetown Accord. These groups are now as much a part of Canada's unwritten or social constitution as the Charter is a part of the written constitution.

The new status and influence of these Charter Canadians is widely viewed as an index of the democratization that has swept Canada in the wake of the Charter. In a series of influential essays, Alan Cairns (1991, 1992a) has chronicled the Charter-induced struggle between the the "governments' constitution" and the "the citizens' constitution";

between "constitutional insiders" and "constitutional outsiders"; between "Charter Canadians" and "non-Charter Canadians." Cairns makes it clear whose side democracy is on. "The Charter," he writes, "was an instrument to relocate sovereignty in the people, rather than in the governments of Canadian federalism" (1992b:7). In a similar vein, Cairns (1992b:11) declares: "The Charter gives the constitution a popular base. It bypasses governments and speaks directly to the citizenry." After only a decade, Cairns (1992b:8) described the net effect as a new "participant constitutional culture stimulated by the Charter." Outside Quebec, those foolish enough to disagree with these Cairnsian panegyrics have been stigmatized as constitutional Luddites, and written off as a handful of "left- and right-wing Charterphobes" (Sigurdson 1993).

Charterphilia, however, has not penetrated French Quebec. Quebec nationalists have vehemently opposed the Charter ever since it was "imposed" without their consent in 1982. Successive Quebec governments have fought an ongoing battle to blunt the impact of the Charter on their policy-making autonomy, first via the systematic invocation of the section 33 override, then by the "distinct society" clause of the failed Meech Lake Accord, and finally by a watered-down version of "distinct society" in the equally ill-fated Charlottetown Accord (Morton 1994). Each defeat has further embittered Quebec's view of the Charter as a threat to its cultural survival. As Cairns (1992b:2) has observed, "From the perspective of the nationalist Quebec elites, the Charter is partly seen as a weapon of the victors, rather than a liberating instrument for the citizenry." This disillusion with the Charter is reflected in surveys of public opinion, which found that Quebec was the only province in which pluralities supported the section 33 "notwithstanding" clause (*Reid Report* 1992:12; Oullett 1992:10). Quebec's continued opposition to the Charter has thus thwarted its ultimate "nation-building" purpose. It also legitimates other criticism of the Charter, and, more importantly, guarantees that the section 33 override – the bane of the Court Party – will not be repealed as long as Quebec is part of Canada.

QUEBEC'S DEPARTURE: A RENAISSANCE
OF CHARTER DEMOCRACY?

There appear to be two contradictory but equally plausible scenarios about the effect of Quebec separation. The first predicts a more democratic, more integrated Canadian state. According to this scenario, Quebec's departure would remove the severest critic of the Charter, and also the strongest sociological source of the decentralist impulse in Canadian federalism. Under these conditions, it is easy to imagine a Charter "renaissance" and a more democratic, more unified Canadian society. I will call this the "big happy family" scenario.

The alternative scenario predicts that Quebec's departure would be the catalyst for still more fragmentation along regional lines. The primary evidence for this consists of increased north-south integration of provincial economies with their u.s. counterparts. I shall call this the "big bang" theory of Canadian federalism. The impact of economic integration on Canadian federalism is addressed by other contributors to this volume. I will consider the potential of the Charter to further aggravate the tendency toward regional fragmentation.

The nation-building potential of the Charter has two main premises: that the Charter is a democracy-enhancing institution and that this democracy would unleash a pent-up consensus that would strengthen key Charter values. The Charter as an instrument of democracy can be traced to Trudeau's constitutional marketing strategy of the "the People's Package." As noted above, the democratizing influence of the Charter has been subsequently elaborated through the influential writings of Alan Cairns.

The thesis of the Charter as a force for democracy can be supported in several respects. It has clearly democratized the process of constitutional amendment by expanding the number of constitutional players. Executive federalism and first ministers' conferences have been discredited as the exclusive vehicle for constitutional amendment. After Meech and Charlottetown, any significant "package" of constitutional amendments will almost certainly have to be put to a national referendum. This is democracy with a vengeance.

The Charter has also democratized the policy process in the sense of creating new access points: the courts. No longer are the Cabinet and senior bureaucracy the only access points for citizen input. Moreover, litigation privileges different resources than the traditional lobbying process. While money and supporters are not irrelevant to successful Charter litigation, "the right argument" (or a sympathetic judge) can make up for a lack of the former. Groups that lack the resources required to be effective in electoral-legislative arenas may possess those required to win in court. This leads to a third way the Charter may be said to have democratized Canadian politics: it has facilitated some political victories for historically underrepresented or marginalized groups: women, Aboriginals, other ethnic minorities, disabled people, gays, and francophones outside of Quebec. Commentators such as Sigurdson (1993) describe the Charter as democratic because it has produced more equality of results for the underprivileged.

The corollary to this new democracy is a belief that with Quebec's departure coq would experience an outpouring of support for an even "stronger" Charter. Thus, Cairns (1992b:13) has approvingly quoted Patrick Monahan (1992) as to the likely constitutional agenda in a new COQ: "Thus a constituent assembly convened in the COQ would likely produce a list of proposals along the following lines: a strengthening of the Charter of Rights and Freedoms through the addition of social and economic rights, or the removal of the notwithstanding clause; a Triple-E Senate; enhancement of constitutional protections for multiculturalism, gender equality, environmental rights and disabled rights ... recognition of the right to Aboriginal self-government; and entrenchment of a Canada Clause in the constitution." In short, the departure of Quebec would set in motion a Charter renaissance. COQ would support the Charter, and the Charter would support COQ. The result would be a more democratic, more integrated, more coherent state. For the first time in many decades, we could again talk about a Canadian "nation."

CHARTER AS A SOURCE OF CONFLICT

There are reasons to believe that the "big happy family" version of COQ is overly sanguine, at least as far as the Charter is concerned. First, there are problems with characterizing the Charter as a democratizing force. Second, while the Charter qua symbol is popular, the same is hardly true of the policy agendas of the interest groups who have most effectively used the Charter to advance their policy objectives. In sum, there are many citizens in COQ who would challenge both the process and the substance of the Charter qua politics. Much of this Charter angst has begun to appear, at least implicitly, in the policy agenda of the new Reform Party of Canada.

To understand this we must first unravel the concept of the Charter as a democratizing force, an argument that has been uncritically accepted. Anyone who has struggled through one of the Supreme Court's typical eighty-plus-page Charter judgments quickly realizes the absurdity of Cairns' claim (1992b:11) that the Charter "speaks directly to the citizenry." The Charter does not speak directly to anyone. Like the Bible in preliterate societies, the Charter speaks only through official prelates (judges), and they in turn speak a language foreign to normal citizens. There are just over 2000 of these judicial priests in Canada, and in the end only nine of them really count: those on the Supreme Court of Canada. These nine enjoy a monopoly on authoritative interpretations of the meaning of the Charter and are accountable to no one for their decisions. Unless we discard the principles of participation and accountability, this is hardly a recipe for democracy.

Of course Cairns' statement is not so much wrong as incomplete. As noted above, the Charter has had a democratizing influence in several other respects. However, none of these other "democratic" aspects of the Charter change the fact that it is anti-democratic in the most fundamental sense that it allows unelected and unaccountable judges to overrule the policy decisions of elected governments. This is Mandel's (1989:33) point about the Charter when he writes, "Law has been a way of getting around the people ... Law [is] used to achieve an end too difficult to achieve by exclusive reliance on representative institutions or other democratic methods." While he does not emphasize it, even Cairns (1992b:16) concedes this anti-democratic element of the Charter: "The basic Charter message is to limit the policy discretion available to governing majorities over time and across space."

In this sense, the Charter, rather than representing a break with the "old style" Canadian politics of elite accommodation, is a novel extension of it. True, judges now play a more influential role than previously. True also that there are some new players among the elites. But the essential remains: the Charter is a way of insulating politically sensitive decisions from the direct influence of public opinion, especially at the local or provincial level. This is especially true with respect to minority language rights (see below), but it applies more generally to other Charter issues. And while senior appellate court judges are not the same as the federal Cabinet, they are appointed by the Cabinet, and most certainly share a similar commitment to the values of the national political class. Anyone who doubts this should ponder how these judges would have voted, if they could vote, in the 1992 Referendum.

The reason for the anti-majoritarian component of Charter politics becomes clearer when we focus on the real-world agenda of Charter politics. The same dynamic that fueled the politics of elite accommodation in pre-Charter Canada explains its new form under the Charter: distrust of democracy, or more bluntly, weak political support for elite agendas. With the exception of language rights, there is of course overwhelming public support for the core meaning of the general principles explicitly mentioned in the Charter. But for this very reason, these values are almost never infringed and thus rarely litigated. In the real world of Charter politics, it is not the core meaning of the enumerated rights that are contested but their peripheral meaning. As I have argued elsewhere (Morton and Knopff 1992; Morton 1992), criminal lawyers and the various interest groups that constitute the Court Party are always "pushing the Charter envelope" to try to persuade the courts to adopt new and often unintended meanings to basic Charter principles.

The lack of popular support for extending bilingualism into provincial jurisdictions hardly requires proof. This is why Trudeau wanted constitutionally entrenched minority language rights and later refused to allow them to be subject to the section 33 notwithstanding clause. Both Quebec and the Prairie provinces subsequently fought the extension of minority language education rights in court but lost. In these cases, they had no choice but to grudgingly comply with the courts' decisions. But in other language rights cases – *Ford* and *Devine* in Quebec and *Mercure* in Alberta – where section 33 or new legislation was an option, provincial governments have continued to resist successfully the extension of national bilingualism. A variation on this theme is found in Ontario and New Brunswick, where political elites support provincial bilingualism but face popular opposition. Their solution has been to actively encourage judicial decisions in other jurisdictions that would force all provinces to adopt such policies, and then to use "the Charter excuse" – "the Charter made me do it" – to justify the adoption of such policies to provincial voters (Manfredi 1994).

A similar pattern exists for certain other Charter-based "minorities" and their policy agendas. While there is no serious opposition to the principle of sexual equality, there is hardly overwhelming support for the feminist movement and its "official" (i.e., state-funded) representatives. In 1985, the year section 15 took effect, a study commissioned by the federal government found that the majority of Canadian women did not view themselves as a disadvantaged minority (Butler 1985:7). A 1991 Decima poll found that 66 percent of Canadian women do not consider themselves feminists. A 1993 Angus Reid poll found that only 14 percent of Canadians believed that the National Action Committee on the Status of Women (NAC) represents Canadian women.

While everyone supports the principles of non-discrimination and equality of opportunity, these are no longer the primary concerns of section 15 of the Charter. Indeed LEAF and other members of the "Section 15 Club" worked hard to prevent the court from adopting this traditional (small-L) liberal understanding of equality. Responding to the persistent urging of the Court Party, the Supreme Court in its 1988 *Andrews* decision adopted an interpretation of section 15 that stressed "equality of results" rather than equality of opportunity. This is the constitutional equivalent of employment equity policies now being pushed by the federal and some provincial governments. The Butler Report (1985) found strong and widespread opposition to employment equity programs on the grounds that they were unfair, unnecessary, and too expensive. Nor has eight more years in Charterland changed the public's mind. According to a 1993 Gallup Poll, three out of four Canadians still oppose race- or gender-preference hiring policies.

The *Andrews* ruling also effectively restricted the application of section 15 to "historically disadvantaged groups." Thus, in the 1993 case of *Schattschneider v. The Queen,* in which a married couple challenged provisions of the Income Tax Act that taxed them more heavily than a similarly situated common law couple, Canadians were treated to an earnest explanation by a Federal Court judge that section 15 does not protect married couples against government discrimination because they are not part of a historically disadvantaged group. Even the *Globe and Mail* ("More equal than others" 1993) was outraged by such reasoning!

The case of Aboriginal rights is more problematic. Again, there is certainly support for the principle that Aboriginals should be treated fairly and be able to obtain what is rightfully theirs. It is just as clear, however, that when the practical consequences of this principle entail high private or public costs, support dissipates (Butler 1985:9). In British Columbia, for example, the public reaction to the Supreme Court's ruling in *Sparrow* – which was perceived as threatening the salmon fishery and non-Native fishermen – was very negative. It may explain why British Columbia recorded the largest NO vote in the Referendum: 68 percent of the voters rejected a constitutional package in which the entrenchment and extension of Aboriginal rights was a leading components. Perhaps more telling was the insistence of Native leaders that the "right to Aboriginal self-government" in the Charlottetown Accord become "justiciable" within three years of adoption. Such eagerness to turn to the courts belies much more confidence in the federally appointed judges than in public support.

In sum, the Charter has set in motion a form of minoritarian politics – new to Canada – that pursues a certain type of democratic agenda – equality of results – but via an undemocratic process – litigation and judicial edict. The means chosen are appropriate, perhaps even necessary, given the evidence of public opposition to the policies being promoted.

Thus it is not surprising that the support for the Charter qua symbol (reported above) may be as thin as it is wide. When asked to give an example of a specific right protected by the Charter, 44 percent of the respondents in the 1992 Reid poll could not name a single right. Nor do the rights that were mentioned inspire much confidence. The most frequently named right was freedom of expression (29 percent). But does this square with actual record? Every freedom of expression claim decided by the Supreme Court under the Charter has been rejected except Nazi-propagandist Ernst Zundel's challenge to the false news provision of the Criminal Code. During this same period, the Supreme Court has upheld censorship provisions for both pornography (*Butler v. The Queen*, 1992) and "hate speech" (*Keegstra v. The Queen*, 1990). At a conference celebrating the tenth anniversary of the Charter, Peter Russell (1992b) observed that in his thirty years of university teaching in Canada, he had never seen the environment more hostile to freedom of thought and expression than the present. Is it really accurate to say that freedom of expression is better protected now than before 1982?

In a similar vein, the second most frequently cited right in the Reid (1992) poll was equality (19 percent). Yet as explained above, the Supreme Court has operationalized the meaning of equality to exclude protection for anyone who is not a member of one of the "discrete and insular minorities" listed in section 15 or an analogous "historically disadvantaged group." In other words, the Canadian middle class has been almost completely excluded from the protection of section 15, while "official minorities" can claim not only a negative right not to be discriminated against, but a positive right to preferential treatment. It seems improbable that a majority of Canadians would be enthusiastic about these *details* of section 15 equality rights. Consultants' advice to the federal government on how to handle the analogous issue of employment equity is apropos: try to avoid public discussion, but if forced to, then stress generalities not specifics and "appeal to the public's emotional rather than rational side" (Butler 1985:10-11).

Perhaps this explains why 39 percent of the respondents in the Reid Poll (*Reid* 1992:15) responded in the negative when asked whether "Canadians like you" had been affected by the Charter. When asked to identify who had benefitted, the most frequent responses were "minority groups" (66 percent), people accused of crimes (60 percent), and lawyers (54 percent). This is hardly a recipe for political popularity. The last two groups are perennial losers in every public opinion poll. As for minority groups, the Butler Report (1985) found strong public opposition to any preferential treatment of these groups, and the recent controversy over the government of Ontario's "minorities only need apply" advertisement suggests continued public anxiety ("Ontario barring white applicants for senior positions" 1993).

To summarize, public support for the Charter is ambivalent. At the symbolic level, support is high indeed: Who can be against rights? But at the more concrete policy level, there is equally strong evidence of public suspicion and ignorance. While this pattern is consistent with public opinion in other democracies (McClosky and Brill 1984), it also means that the Charter – or more likely, the courts – could be vulnerable to a political attack that articulated the public's specific concerns.

It should also be noted that the various minority group agendas that have come to be associated with the Charter may suffer further erosion of support should Quebec depart. Quebec has provided the "group rights" paradigm that until now has legitimized the other group rights most closely associated with the Charter and the Court Party. The departure of Quebec would remove the constitutional blueprint upon which other collectivities have modelled their claims. It seems probable that public support for national bilingualism and French-language education services would quickly disappear, at least in Western Canada. The various "francophones-hors-Quebec" groups would be reduced to just one of many threads in COQ's multicultural social fabric.

For the same reasons, official multiculturalism would likely suffer a similar setback. The elimination of special government funding for francophones-hors-Quebec groups would remove the original reason for government funding of other ethnic groups. Multiculturalism has always piggybacked on bilingualism. With the demise of bilingualism, multiculturalism would probably go also, at least outside Toronto. The Reform Party has already put the privatization of culture on the political agenda. I would second Gibbins' (1993:271) prediction that Quebec's departure would fuel support for this reform.

The same dynamic would challenge the most recent form of multiculturalism – employment equity and other forms of preferential public policy for visible minorities. Indeed, employment equity would be eroded on two fronts. First, it would lose the legitimizing "halo" that it has always enjoyed from official bilingualism. The lack of public debate – compared to the United States – over the introduction of employment equity policies is almost certainly explained by the fact that preferential hiring and ethnic hiring "goals" were already in place in the federal civil service as part of official bilingualism. With the demise of the latter, this debate would be more difficult to avoid.

Second, the face of multiculturalism has changed since 1970. The original multiculturals – white Europeans of non-French and non-English origin – are no longer its only or even its primary constituents. Indeed public policies such as employment equity – which privilege non-whites – operate against the employment interests of the children and grandchildren of the original proponents of multiculturalism. As awareness of this spreads among the non-visible minorities, a reaction seems inevitable. Indeed, there is already abundant anecdotal evidence of growing opposition to employment equity ("Employment equity given little support" 1993). The Reform Party has already tapped into this sentiment, and will continue to push to define equal opportunity as a "colour-blind" policy of non-discrimination rather than a "colour-sensitive" policy of ethnic hiring "goals." As Jeffrey Simpson (1993:123) and others have observed, the Reform model is basically an assimilationist model. As long as Quebec has been a part of Canada, the policy of cultural and linguistic assimilation has been stigmatized as illegitimate. But with Quebec's departure, why would the stigma remain?

The discrediting of "group rights" and the ascendancy of the assimilationist model would pose a serious challenge to the Aboriginal rights movement (Gibbins 1993:272), one of the primary constituencies of the Court Party. The two primary claims of contemporary Aboriginal leaders and their apologists – the demand for self-government and the settlement of land claims – are both modelled after and derive much of their legitimacy from the example of Quebec. The "First Nations" metaphor plays off (and indeed trumps) the "Two Founding Nations" model. If the French Québécois have a right to pursue a nationalist politics of minority survival through territorially based self-government, why shouldn't Aboriginals? Rhetorically, this is a powerful argument, but only so long as Quebec is still a part of Canada. If Quebec leaves, why would COQ want to embark on a new version of the "Two Founding Nations" model when the first one had just exploded?

To summarize, while Quebec's departure would remove the strongest and oldest centrifugal dynamic from Canadian federalism, there are good reasons to doubt that this would trigger some new form of Canadian unity driven by a Charter renaissance. While the Charter qua symbol may enjoy considerable popularity in COQ, the Charter qua minority-group politics does not. Not only are the various collectivist agendas of the members of the Court Party already contentious, but they would lose an important source of legitimacy with the departure of Quebec.

Perhaps a better indicator of the lack of consensus over the agenda of the Court Party has been the rise, over the same period, of the Reform Party. In some respects, the Reform Party can be understood as a middle-class backlash against the perception that the primary beneficiaries of the Charter are minorities. This interpretation has been advanced by Jeffrey Simpson (1993:95, 121) "The middle-class resentments that simmer in the Reform Party are directed against elites, to be sure, but also against welfare cheaters, uppity social activists, feminist rhetoricians and other minoritarian pleaders, who ... twist public priorities to assist themselves, leaving excessive burdens of taxation and burgeoning regulations to restrict the freedoms of the hardpressed, overtaxed and underappreciated majority."

Preston Manning, the founder and leader of the Reform Party, has been sensitive to the popularity of the Charter as symbol, and has tried to ensure that Reform not be perceived as anti-Charter. There is nothing in the party's *Blue Book* (1991), for example, that explicitly criticizes the Charter. On the other hand, a more careful reading of Reform documents and speeches discloses various policy proposals that show thinly veiled antagonism toward policy issues promoted by the Court Party through Charter litigation. Reform supports the reduction of immigration and has indicated that it is ready to amend the constitution, if necessary, to do so. It is opposed to the current form of bilingualism, the heart of Trudeau's vision of the Charter. It also favours "privatization" of cultural support, spelling an end to state-supported multiculturalism, and the addition of property rights to the Charter, anathema to the egalitarian redistributionist factions of the Court Party. In his speeches, Manning has made various "crime control" pronouncements, including toughening the Young Offenders Act, abolishing parole, and holding a referendum on capital punishment. Perhaps nothing exudes anti-Court Party sentiment more than Manning's oft-repeated support for "the equality of all persons," a direct challenge to the multi-tiered preferential system constructed around section 15 of the Charter.

More systematic demographic and attitudinal profiles of Reform Party members have confirmed sharp differences from groups associated with the Court Party. Reformers are overwhelmingly middle-class, middle-aged, and small-town/suburban in outlook. There are "few single mothers, welfare recipients, or unemployed people [but] also few really well-to-do executives of large corporations, lawyers, doctors" (Flanagan and Ellis 1992:7–8). Reform members are more male than female, and are more frequently found among those with a high school diploma than those with college degree. Support rises with income but not uniformly. Most studies show a dip in support in the $60,000 to $80,000 annual income range, after which it rises again. Occupationally, Reform support is highest among sales people and farmers. There is no difference between blue-collar and white-collar support (Clarke 1993).

Attitudinally, Reform Party supporters in the 1993 election appear to be consistently more "conservative" on various social issues than those who voted for any of the other parties. Preliminary analysis of the *1993 Election Study* indicates that Reform voters were more likely than voters for other parties to hold negative attitudes toward each of the various "minorities" in Canada – francophones, immigrants, racial minorities, Aboriginals, and homosexuals. They were more distrustful of politicians and more likely to support capital punishment. They were also more supportive of the traditional homemaker role for married women (Nevitte 1994). Consistent with the Reform's demographic base, the differences between Reform and Progressive Conservative voters were not as great on economic issues, although Reform voters were still somewhat more conservative (Nevitte 1994).

This portrait of Reform support – especially the way it cuts a swath through the Canadian middle class – looks strikingly similar to the conservative side of the "postmaterialist" division of the American middle class. Recent studies have showed that middle-income Americans have become increasingly divided by "social issues" between a "new" and a "traditional" middle class. Despite the same income levels, these two groups disagree sharply on issues such as abortion, divorce, extra-marital sex, homosexuality, the environment, and race relations (Ladd 1977). The key to this new cleavage is education and occupation (Wilson 1986:120). The "traditional" middle-class voter lives mainly in the suburbs, goes to church, works in a small or large business, and votes Republican. "New Class" members are more likely to live in cities, to attend church, have postgraduate degrees, be professionals, and vote Democratic. College education, once a reliable predictor of support for the Republican Party, has, since 1964, correlated more strongly with support for the Democrats (Ladd 1977).

In both Canada and the United States the relation between economic status and political attitudes has weakened considerably, and differences of education and occupation have become more accurate predictors of conservative-liberal cleavages on noneconomic issues. The Court Party/Reform Party cleavage in Canadian politics bears a strong resemblance to the new class/traditional class cleavage in American society. In the U.S. the Republicans have successfully exploited these new post-materialist cleavages. The "Reagan-Democrat" phenomenon is the result of Republicans' successful exploitation of such court-related issues as abortion, school busing, capital punishment, affirmative action, crime-control, and judicial appointments.

Until now, the Reform Party has only exploited similar or analogous issues indirectly and avoided linking them to Charter politics. This may now be changing. One of the leading candidates for policy proposals to be debated and voted on at the 1994 Reform Party national assembly is the repeal of section 15(2) – the reverse discrimination clause – of the Charter. Another is to repeal the Charter completely ("Manning may have to fight," 1994)!

To conclude, the "democratizing" effect of the Charter has been paradoxical and unstable. Both the Court Party and the Reform Party embrace the Charter and its "new" democracy. But the meanings they attach to this democracy are very different. The Court Party understands Charter democracy as the promotion of equality of results for officially designated ethnic and racial groups, achieved if necessary through litigation. The Reform Party understands Charter democracy as equality of opportunity for individuals, and increased use of referendums and recalls. The democratization that the Charter has encouraged at the constitutional and judicial levels has also stimulated a new participatory ethos that threatens the agenda of the Court Party at the political level. The Reformers' emphasis on equality through accountability and participation could very easily collide with the Court Party's agenda of equality of groups results.

Imagine national referenda on issues like employment equity, gay rights, the RCMP's "Sikhs only" turban policy, and so forth. Would referenda in COQ support such policy initiatives for minorities? Perhaps in Ontario? But this then raises the spectre of renewed centre-periphery regional conflict.

CHARTER CLEAVAGES IN A
POST-PARTUM CANADA

There is strong evidence that Charter politics would become the focus of partisan political conflict in a Canada without Quebec. There is inconclusive evidence, however, on *how* Charter politics might divide COQ. Would Charter politics mobilize electoral competition along non-territorial lines, crosscutting and thus weakening traditional regional cleavages? Or would Charter conflict follow and thereby aggravate existing regional tensions and threaten to further fracture the Canadian state? The remainder of the paper briefly canvasses the evidence for the latter scenario, and then considers the contrary evidence.

During the past decade and a half of macro-constitutional politics,[1] there has been a consistent pattern of centre-periphery conflict. The centrist banner – in the name of national unity – has been carried primarily by an Ottawa-Ontario-Quebec federalists alliance, with varying support from the Maritime provinces. The periphery includes not just the Western and Maritime hinterlands, but also the nationalist-separatist elites in Quebec (a "sociological hinterland" from the perspective of Westmount and Ottawa). The primary object of this game is to preserve national unity by allowing the centre-coalition to control the divisive and untoward tendencies of the hinterlands.

The initial focus of this alliance was provincial language policy, and it was quickly achieved through the Supreme Court of Canada's monopoly over authoritative interpretation of section 23 – the minority language education rights section – of the Charter. In a series of landmark decisions (*Quebec Protestant School Board*, 1984; *Manitoba Language Rights Reference*, 1985; *Mahé v. Alberta*, 1989; *Ford and Devine v. Quebec*, 1989) the Supreme Court brusquely swept aside a variety of provincial attempts to restrict bilingualism. As Shapiro (1981) and Bzdera (1993) have pointed out, once in place, the Charter – through the Supreme Court – can become an instrument of national control over a host of other hitherto provincially controlled policy areas.

In each of the three major "rounds" of macro-constitutional politics – Patriation and the Charter (1980–82), Meech Lake (1987–90), and Charlottetown (1991–92) – Ontario has been Ottawa's strongest and most consistent ally. This is especially significant, because Ontario was governed by three different political parties during this period. For all three Ontario governments, whatever their partisan orientation, the same regional interest was stronger than any party differences. This point becomes clearer if we think of constitutional politics as analogous to foreign policy. From this perspective, Ontario's foreign policy has been sustained through Ottawa. Likewise, the strongest opposition (in COQ) has come those provinces on the periphery, especially the West. Again, this opposition transcended changes in partisan government in British Columbia, Saskatchewan, and Manitoba.

Governments also participate in micro-constitutional politics by intervening in Charter cases and presenting legal arguments that attempt to influence how judges interpret and "operationalize" enumerated rights. Governments' micro-constitutional strategies toward the Charter have thus far been neglected by scholars. However, preliminary research indicates that certain provincial governments active in macro-constitutional politics have pursued parallel strategies at the micro-constitutional level. For example, in the *Quebec Protestant School Board* (1984) and *Mahé* (1990) cases, Quebec's factums to the Supreme Court presented legal arguments that tried (unsuccessfully) to mitigate the impact of the Charter in the area of language rights.

The same dichotomy between Ontario and the Western provinces that exists at the macro-constitutional level has reproduced itself at the micro-constitutional level. Even prior to the adoption of the Charter, Ontario frequently allied itself with Ottawa against most other provinces in key constitutional cases such as the 1976 *Anti-Inflation Reference* (Russell 1977) and the 1981 *Patriation Reference*. Since 1982, while most provincial governments participated in micro-constitutional politics in order to maximize their policy autonomy and discretion, Ontario took the side of the Court Party and judicial expansionism. This has occurred in a series of landmark Charter cases involving Aboriginal rights (*Sparrow*, 1999), equality rights (*Andrews*, 1989), language rights (Mahé, 1990), and the scope of the section 33 legislative override (*Ford and Devine*, 1988). In this last case, Ontario argued that the validity of a province's use of the section 33 legislative override was subject to review and reversal by the courts. As the Alberta and Saskatchewan governments pointed out, such an interpretation would reverse the very purpose of section 33, which was to give elected legislatures a check on the courts, not vice versa. The Supreme Court of Canada eventually adopted the Charter interpretations endorsed by Ontario in each of these cases (except the last).

A third and final body of evidence for regional conflict over Charter politics in COQ may be found in the distribution of the NO Vote in the 1992 Charlottetown Referendum and the support for the Reform

Table 1
Regional Distribution of NO Vote (1992) and Reform Vote (1993)

	NO Vote 1992	Reform Vote 1993
	(percent of total vote)	
British Columbia	68.0	36.1
Alberta	60.1	52.0
Saskatchewan	55.2	27.3
Manitoba	61.6	22.4
Ontario	49.6	20.6
New Brunswick	38.0	8.5
Nova Scotia	51.1	13.3
pei	25.9	1.5
Newfoundland	36.5	1.0

Party in the 1993 federal election. In both instances, there were sharp differences between Ontario (and the Maritimes) and the West. The regional distribution of the NO and Reform votes is illustrated in table 1. The Charlottetown Accord was rejected by a majority of voters in every province west of Ontario. In all, more than 60 percent of Western Canadians voted NO. By contrast, the Charlottetown Accord was accepted by a majority of the voters in every English-speaking province from Ontario east except Nova Scotia. In three of these provinces the YES vote was over 60 percent.

The regional distribution of electoral support for the Reform Party followed a similar regional pattern. Reform support was strongest in the West, especially in British Columbia and Alberta, where it received the largest number of votes of any party. By contrast, Reform received less than 15 percent of the votes in every English-speaking province east of Manitoba except Ontario. When votes are translated into seats, the regional cleavages becomes even starker. As illustrated in figure 1, Reform dominated but was restricted to the West; the Liberals dominated Ontario and the Maritimes; while the BQ swept Quebec.

While it would be simplistic to interpret these results as clear measurements of support for or opposition to Charter-related groups and agendas, it would be wrong to reject any connection. With respect to the 1992 federal election, we have already noted that a portion of Reform Party support flows from opposition to the minoritarian politics of group status that is associated with the Charter. Interpreting the referendum is more complex, since the Charlottetown Accord was de-

Figure 1
Percentage of seats won by political parties in 1993 Canadian election, by region

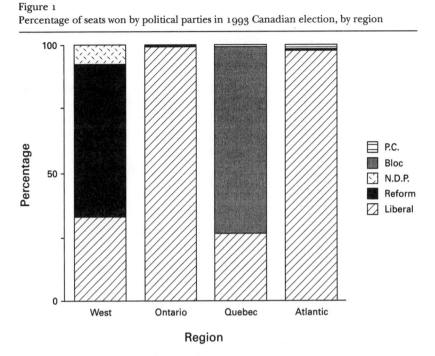

Source: Elections Canada 1994 and Neil Nevitte, *Electoral Discontinuity: the 1993 Election* (1994)

feated by "a coalition of opposites" (Johnston 1993:32). Admittedly, an important component of this coalition were pro-Charter groups who were rallied by Pierre Trudeau. Yet an equally important member of the anti-Charlottetown coalition were NO voters associated with the Reform Party. Recall that Reform was the only national political party to oppose the Accord. Moreover, an internal survey of Reform Party members found that 69 percent of the respondents wanted the party to publicly oppose the accord (Flanagan 1995: chap. 5). When Reform did go on the attack, it criticized the accord for its "unacceptable collectivist vision of ethnicity" and "special status for francophones and Aboriginals" (Flanagan 1995: chap. 5). The results suggest that these attacks played particularly well in the West.

Provincial differences in the macro- and micro-constitutional politics of the 1980s, the regional cleavages in the Charlottetown Referendum and the 1993 federal election: is it possible that Charter politics is just a disguised version of the well-established if not so venerable Canadian institution of centre-periphery politics? If so, it would be tempting to predict that these regional cleavages could aggravate the threat of further balkanization in a post-partum Canada.

Alas, things are not so simple. There is strong evidence that Charter cleavages also follow urban-rural and educational/occupational cleavages that could have just the opposite effect of suppressing regional differences. In the 1992 referendum, for example, metropolitan Toronto and Ottawa voted strongly YES, while most of the rest of Ontario voted just as strongly NO (Flanagan 1995: chap. 5). A similar urban-rural split was also evident in the West. In Alberta and British Columbia, the only constituencies in which the YES side won more than 40 percent of the vote were in Vancouver, Victoria, Calgary, and Edmonton (Flanagan 1995: chap. 5).

There was a similar urban-rural pattern to the Reform Party vote in 1993. While Reform swept the West, it barely held its own in Western cities. Calgary was its only urban sweep, and it did not win a single urban riding in Victoria, Winnipeg, Regina, or Saskatoon. In Vancouver, Reform carried the suburbs but was shut out in the seven inner-city ridings (Flanagan 1995: chap. 7). In Ontario the pattern was similar: Reform candidates did their worst in inner-city ridings and their best in the outer suburbs of Toronto, central Ontario and the Niagara Peninsula (Flanagan 1995: chap. 7).

There was also a class cleavage running through the referendum. The higher a constituency was on the socio-economic scale (SES), the more likely it was to vote YES, and vice versa. Thus in some higher SES ridings in the West – such as Manning's own, Calgary Southwest – majorities supported the Charlottetown Accord, while in some blue-collar constituencies in Ontario – Hamilton East and Hamilton Mountain, for example – the NO side prevailed (Flanagan 1995: chap. 5). The parallel breaks down, however, with the 1993 election. The Reform Party was not able to hang on to the blue-collar, low-income voters who had voted NO in the referendum. Also, support for Reform Party does rise with family income, but not uniformly (Flanagan 1995: chap. 7).

To summarize, there are cross-cutting urban/rural and class cleavages that may blunt any sharp east-west, regional fracturing. If the NO vote in the referendum and the Reform vote in the 1993 election are interpreted as proxies for opposition to the policy agendas of Charter-based interest groups, then both sides have substantial but unequal support in all regions except the Maritimes. While it elected only one MP from Ontario, the Reform Party did win 20 percent of the Ontario vote, more than the Tories and three times more than the NDP. In a similar vein, in every Western province except Alberta, more than 50 percent of the voters voted against the Reform Party.

CONCLUSION

Russell (1992) has persuasively argued that the democratizing impulse imparted by the Charter has increased the potential for conflict between Quebec and the rest of Canada. I have argued that this same potential exists within COQ. "Charter democracy" has come to mean two different forms of politics with two different agendas. The collectivist, judicially driven equality-of-results program of the Court Party is on a collision course with the individualistic, equality-of-opportunity, participatory politics of the Reform Party. What is not certain is whether this conflict will take on a regional character of Ontario (or the Ottawa-Toronto axis) versus the West.

Ironically, the new Charter-driven cleavages in COQ could actually become a source of unity to the extent that they replace the old regional cleavages. This possibility was identified as part of the Charter's nation-building potential at the outset (Knopff and Morton 1985). More recently, Gibbins has made a similar point: that an increase in political issues that cut through the country along nonterritorial lines such as the new social movements of feminism and environmentalism can be a cohesive force. This led him to predict that "the first post-Quebec national election would likely pit the NDP against the Reform Party ... in an ideological contest unlike any we have witnessed before in Canada" (Gibbins 1993:269).

This scenario is certainly consistent with my reasoning,[2] but it suggests that my original articulation of the alternatives – "big happy family or big-bang" – was wrong. If Quebec were to leave, Canada might find itself more of a big *unhappy* family, but still more of a family than it has known for its first 130 years.

NOTES

1 This concept and its counterpart – micro constitutional politics – have been elaborated by Manfredi. Macro-constitutional politics denotes attempts to amend the explicit text of the constitution ("first order rules") through the formal amending process. Micro-constitutional politics denotes attempts to amend constitutional meaning through litigation and judicial interpretation ("second order rules"). See Christopher Manfredi, "Litigation and Institutional Design: Micro-Constitutional Politics and the Canadian Charter of Rights and Freedoms." paper presented at 1993 Annual Meeting of Canadian Political Science Association Ottawa, Ontario.

2 While I have not developed it here, I would argue that the NDP is the most hospitable political party for Court Party activists. For example, it was the

NDP members of the Beaudoin-Dobbie Committee who proposed to amend the Charter to exempt the section 15 equality rights from the section 33 override. See *Report of the Special Joint Committee on a Renewed Canada* (Ottawa 1992), p. 36.

BIBLIOGRAPHY

CASES CITED

Andrews v. Law Society of British Columbia, [1989] 1 SCR 143.

Butler v. The Queen, [1992] 1 SCR 452.

Ford and Devine v. Quebec, [1988] 2 SCR 712; 2 SCR 790.

Keegstra v. The Queen, [1990] 3 SCR 697.

Mahé v. Alberta, [1990] 1 SCR 342.

Manitoba Language Rights Reference, [1985] 1 SCR 721.

Quebec Association of Protestant School Boards v. A.-G. Quebec, [1984] 2 SCR 66.

Schachttschneider v. The Queen, [1994] 1 FC 40.

Sparrow v. The Queen, [1990 1 SCR 1075.

SECONDARY SOURCES

Butler Research Associates. 1985. "An Assessment of Public Attitudes Toward Employment Equity, Final Report." Prepared for Employment and Immigration Canada. October.

Bzdera, André. 1993. "Comparative Analysis of Federal High Courts: A Political Theory of Judicial Review." *Canadian Journal of Political Science* 26:3–29.

Cairns, Alan. 1988. "Citizens (Outsiders) and Governments (Insiders) in Constitution-Making: The Case of Meech Lake." *Canadian Public Policy* 14:121–45.

– 1991. *Disruptions: Constitutional Struggles, from the Charter to Meech Lake.* Ed. Douglas E. Williams. Toronto: McClelland & Stewart.

– 1992a. *Charter versus Federalism: The Dilemmas of Constitutional Reform.* Montreal: McGill-Queens University Press.

– 1992b. "Reflections on the Political Purposes of the Charter: The First Decade." Paper presented at the Conference on the Tenth Anniversary of the Charter; organized by the Canadian Bar Association and the Federal Department of Justice, Ottawa, 14–15 April 1992.

Clarke, Harold. 1993. "The Dynamics of Support for New Parties and National Party Systems in Contemporary Democracies: The Case of Canada." Funded by the National Science Foundation. (Data reported in Flanagan, *Waiting for the Wave*)

"A Decade with the Canadian Charter of Rights and Freedoms." 1992. *The Reid Report*, vol. 7, no. 4.

Decima Poll. 1991. (Cited in *Alberta Report.* 1993. 9 August: 44.)

"Employment equity given little support." 1993. *Calgary Herald,* 24 December: A3.

"Employment equity's true colours." 1993. *The Globe and Mail*, 12 November: A4.

Flanagan, Thomas. Forthcoming. *Waiting for the Wave.*

– and Faron Ellis. 1992. "A Comparative Profile of the Reform Party of Canada," Paper presented at the Annual Meeting of the Canadian Political Science Association, June.

Gibbins, Roger. 1993. "Speculations on a Canada without Quebec." In *The Charlottetown Accord, the Referendum, and the Future of Canada*, ed. Kenneth McRoberts and Patrick Monahan, 264–73. Toronto: University of Toronto Press.

Johnston, Richard. 1993. "An Inverted Logroll: The Charlottetown Accord and the Referendum," *PS* 26 (March, 1993), 43–48.

Knopff, Rainer, and F.L. Morton. 1985. "Nation-Building and the Canadian Charter of Rights and Freedoms." Report of the Royal Commission on the Economic Union and Development Prospects for Canada, 1985. Vol. 33, *Constitutionalism, Citizenship, and Society in Canada*, 133–82.

Ladd, Everett Carll, Jr. 1977. *Where Have All the Voters Gone?* 2nd ed. New York: Norton.

Mandel, Michael. 1989. *The Charter of Rights and the Legalization of Politics in Canada.* Toronto: Wall&Thompson.

Manfredi, Christopher. 1994. "Constitutional Rights and Interest Advocacy: Litigating Educational Reform in Canada and the United States." In F. Leslie Seidle, *Equity and Community: The Charter, Interest Advocacy and Representation*, 91–113. Montreal: Institute for Research on Public Policy.

"Manning may have to fight for policy of moderation." 1994. *The Globe and Mail*, 29 September: A5.

McClosky, Herbert, and Alida Brill. 1983. *Dimensions of Tolerance: What Americans Think about Civil Liberties.* New York: Russell Sage.

Monahan, Patrick. 1992. *Constituent Assemblies: The Canadian Debate in Comparative and Historical Context: Background Studies of the York University Constitutional Reform Project.* Study no. 4. North York: York University Centre for Public Law and Public Policy.

"More equal than others." 1993. *The Globe and Mail*, 14 July: A20.

Morton, F.L. 1992. "The Charter Revolution and the Court Party." *Osgoode Hall Law Journal* 30, no. 3:627–52.

– 1994. "Judicial Politics Canadian-Style: The Supreme Court's Contribution to the Constitutional Crisis of 1992." In *Constitutional Predicament: Canada After the Referendum of 1992*, ed. Curtis Cooke, 132–48. Montreal: McGill-Queens University Press.

– and Rainer Knopff. 1992. "The Supreme Court as the Vanguard of the Intelligentsia: The Charter Movement as Post-Materialist Politics." ed., In *Canadian Constitutionalism, 1791–1991*, ed. Janet Ajzenstat, 57–80. Ottawa: Canadian Study of Parliament Group.

Nevitte, Neil. 1994. "Electoral Discontinuity: The 1993 Canadian Federal Election." Paper presented to the Israel Association for Canadian Studies Annual Conference. Hebrew University, Jerusalem, Israel, 1–4 May 1993.

"Ontario barring white applicants for senior positions." 1993. *The Globe and Mail*, 11 November: A4.

Oullet, Shirley Riopelle, 1991. "Public Attitudes Towards the Legitimacy of our Institutions and the Administration of Justice." Department of Justice Technical Report TR1991–5, Public Opinion Research Program, Research Section, June.

Reform Party of Canada. 1991. *The Blue Book: Principles and Policies, 1991*. Calgary: The Reform Party of Canada.

Reid, Angus. 1993. Angus Reid poll. (Cited in *Alberta Report*. 1993. August: 44.)

Russell, Peter H. (1977). "The Anti-Inflation Reference: Anatomy of a Constitutional Case." *Canadian Public Administration* 20:632–55.

– 1992a. *Constitutional Odyssey: Can Canadians Become a Sovereign People?* Toronto: University of Toronto Press.

– 1992b. "The Political Purposes of the Charter: Have They Been Fulfilled? An Agnostic's Report Card." Address to the British Columbia Civil Liberties Association Conference on The Charter – Ten Years After, Vancouver, B.C., 15–16 May 1992.

Shapiro, Martin (1981). *Courts: A Comparative and Politic Analysis. Chicago*. Chicago: University of Chicago Press.

Sigurdson, Richard. 1993. "Left- and Right-Wing Charterphobia in Canada: A Critique of the Critics." *The Charter, Federalism and the Constitution: International Journal of Canadian Studies* 7–8:95–116.

Simpson, Jeffrey. 1993. *Faultlines: Struggling for a Canadian Vision*. Toronto: HarperCollins.

Wilson, James Q. 1986. *American Government: Institutions and Policies*, 3d ed. Toronto: D.C. Heath.

PART THREE

Culture: The Rise of Anglophone Literature, Film, and the Arts

7 (Con)figuring a "Canada": Some Trends in Anglophone-Canadian Literature, Criticism, and the Arts

FRANK DAVEY

The range of the current struggles over how anglophone-Canadian culture should be read, configured, and interpreted is so wide that the distinctions one might in other circumstances make among literature, popular culture, literary criticism, literary theory, and cultural theory are largely inappropriate. Conflicts over structuralist critical theory, over what constitutes a prize-winning poem or novel, and over the staging of *Miss Saigon* or *Showboat* occur in the same general cultural site and reflect similar clashes of views over what should constitute social value. In this paper I address many of these widespread struggles, but with particular attention to my own field: literature. These are for me after all, as they are for many Canadians, autobiographical conflicts. All the trends I will be discussing in some sense position me, by sex and gender, sexual orientation, race, class, or regional or ethnic affiliations. Like most people, I cannot claim a disinterested position outside the various contentions we may call "Canada."

Also rendering complex my undertaking of this paper and its narrative constructions is the fact that one of the major elements in these contentions is a question rather unsatisfactorily taken as uncontentious in the theme of this volume: what, indeed, is "the rest of the country"; what constitutes "Canada Outside Quebec"; is there a Canada inside Quebec or are "Canada" and "Quebec" parallel terms? Moreover, should "Quebec" in these formulations be understood territorially, linguistically, or culturally? Can one be outside Quebec culturally while not being outside linguistically or territorially? Can one even use the term "Canada" to indicate the country's ten provinces other than provisionally, in quotation marks, as it were?

The title of a recent anthology of essays on "Canadian" literature published by the New York-based Modern Languages Association (MLA), *Studies on Canadian Literature*, reflected the implicit understanding that there is a Canada both inside and outside Quebec; the essay titles – which are largely by "Canadian" contributors – offer a panorama of terms and understandings for Quebec/non-Quebec distinction. One essay is entitled "English Critical Discourse in/on Canada," where "English" operates linguistically rather than geographically, and "Canada" is both singular and geographic. Another is entitled "The Evolution of French-Canadian Literature to 1960," in which "French-Canadian" may be both a linguistic and geographic designation. Another is subtitled "Teaching Canadian and Quebec Literature Outside Canada," where in the first four words "Canadian" and "Quebec" appear to be mutually exclusive geographic terms, while in the subsequent three both the literature and the country are paradoxically named as singular. Yet another essay is titled "Native-Canadian Literature," where "Native" operates as cultural modifier of "Canadian" but leaves ambiguous the geography signified by "Canadian." Overall, however, the anthology's u.s. editors have attempted to create a symmetry by including eight essays on what they generally call English-Canadian literature, eight on what they call Quebec literature, three on topics that involve both language groups, and the one on "Native-Canadian" literature. This general configuration implies a French-English equivalence disturbed by the presence of Aboriginals.

At a slightly earlier stage in the debates over how to configure the relationship between the two literatures, Canadian literary and cultural theorists who, like Ronald Sutherland or Philip Stratford, resided on Quebec territory but outside Quebec francophone culture, insisted on bicultural and bilingual rather than territorial understandings of Canada. In this bicultural model, they themselves could remain part of anglophone-Canadian culture, while inviting their francophone "twins" to give up sovereigntist dreams in exchange for having francophones declared fifty percent of Canadian culture. This was the period of the 1973 founding of The Association for Canadian and Quebec Literatures, in which the plural form of last word indicated an agreement that there were two distinct, parallel, and equal literatures. One can see this understanding continuing in the structure of the MLA anthology. In recent years, however, literary and cultural theorists from other regions have joined the debate with arguments that there are more than two Canadian literatures. Beginning with E.D. Blodgett's 1982 study *Configurations: Essays on the Canadian Literatures*, theorists like Blodgett, Anthony Purdy, and W. H. New have argued that there are multiple Canadian literatures, perhaps even inside the territory of

Quebec. Purdy in particular has moved toward deconstructing the idealized view of francophone-Quebec literature as an homogeneous body of texts. Within the territory of Quebec, writers like Linda Leith and Ken Norris have attempted to demonstrate the existence of an anglophone-Quebec literature. Francophone theorists like Régine Robin, Pierre Nepveu, and Sherry Simon have pointed to feminist, gay, and ethnic heterogenization within francophone Quebec writing.

A current trend in anglophone-Canadian theory seems to be to problematize both the cultural homogeneity of Quebec as a geographic space and the presumed linguistic, cultural, and ideological homogeneity of Quebec literature: that is, to insist on the presence in the territory of Quebec of anglophone, Aboriginal, Haitian, Vietnamese, and other cultures, and of both francophone and anglophone cultures descended from non-British and non-French immigration. Accordingly, I will be defining Quebec here culturally, linguistically, and territorially, in that order, as the francophone culture of roughly the southern half of Quebec province. My provisional Canada outside Quebec will be the Canada outside that culture.

Anyone even casually watching the arts in Canada in recent years would probably have noticed two phenomena: the increased participation by established Canadian artists in global culture, and the increasingly ill-tempered disputes among many of them over questions of cultural appropriation, racism, and access to juries, awards, and publication within Canada. These two phenomena frequently interact, as in 1989 when the international group that lobbies globally on behalf of imprisoned writers, PEN (Poets, Essayists, and Novelists), held its annual conference in Toronto and Montreal, and its Toronto organizers were accused by local black writers of racism in their selection of Canadian participants. An extremely important subtext of this particular conflict was the wide divergence of views on individual and collective rights. PEN's entire program is directed to constructing and protecting the individual rights of authors against state or state-sanctioned restriction. Its most celebrated recent case is that of Salman Rushdie, whose individual "right" to depict the prophet Muhammed has clashed with strongly held collective views in Islamic communities. PEN's accusers were not arguing the right of any one individual to participate in the conference, but rather the collective right of non-white individuals currently self-constructed as "people of colour" to representation in sufficient numbers to redress historical under-representation.

Similar conflicts have affected numerous other Canadian cultural institutions. In 1988 Women's Press was fractured by a dispute of the "appropriation of voice" issue, a dispute which saw some writers who espoused individualist freedom-of-expression beliefs that a writer should be free to write in whatever "voice" she chose challenged by other writers, largely writers of colour, who argued that only writers of specific racial minorities should write in those minority voices. Many of those who argued the freedom-of-expression position later left to found Second Story Press.

In the same year, this issue affected the Writers Union of Canada when, after the general membership voted disapproval of attempts to restrain the artistic freedom of writers, a group of Aboriginal, black, and Asian writers formed a Racial Minority Writers Committee within the union. Subsequent and related conflicts within the Writers Union have seen repeated accusations of racism against one of its founders, June Callwood, and her spring 1994 resignation from the union.

The appropriation of voice dispute reached the Canada Council in 1992, when its advisory committee on racial equality in the arts recommended that the Council take a position on the issue, and the Council chair of the time, Joyce Zemans, was quoted in the national media as having observed that Council juries would be sensitive to matters like appropriation of voice. Her remarks precipitated nearly a full page of letters to the *Globe and Mail,* some from established writers, several of whom (including Timothy Findley) attempted to equate their impending subjection to minority sensitivity with the atrocities suffered by Jews during the Holocaust.

In October 1993 accusations of racism fractured the Association of National Non-Profit Artists' Centres, the national association of Canadian artist-run art galleries colloquially known as ANNPAC, even more violently than it had Women's Press. After a badly managed and seemingly misunderstood attempt to implement an anti-racism initiative at the 1993 general meeting in Calgary, the British Columbia and Prairie associations resigned from the association, as did several individual galleries across the country.[1] Again you may have noticed the extent to which almost any Canadian, including my fellow contributors or me as an executive member of an ANNPAC gallery, can be implicated in these contentions and in various narratives about them.

Conflicts such as the ones at PEN, Women's Press, the Writers Union, and ANNPAC almost always involve struggles over who and what ideology is going to control the institution. There have been at least two trends here. One has been a conflict between individualist and collectivist conceptions of art: between art based on concepts like "freedom of expression" and "free enterprise," in which Wordsworthian notions of individuality, Benthamite conceptions of liberty, and Adam Smith's economic theories construct an individual artist with whose conceptions it would be immoral for a society to interfere, and an art based on cultural specificity, group histories, and group loyalties, and protected by policy and legislation. The concept of the individualist artist was evident in the Free Trade debate, when sixty-two artists and writers who supported free trade published an advertisement in which they announced that they were "not fragile" and welcomed the competitive global environment which free trade promised. It was evident later in the *Globe and Mail* protests against Joyce Zemans' Canada Council comments on cultural appropriation, as when poet Richard Outram argued that "no spurious concepts of 'intellectual property' or 'intellectual copyright' can be allowed to constrain the human imagination" (letter 28 March 1992, D7).

The collective concept of art was visible in the Massey Commission Report in its conception of a national culture, and has been visible since then in attempts to protect Canadian magazines through discriminatory taxation policies, in the state assistance to Canadian-owned publishers and Canadian film producers, in Canadian broadcasting regulations, and in attempts to regulate film distribution as well as in the positions of Aboriginal artists and writers of colour on cultural appropriation. The second trend has been a conflict between, on the one hand, national conceptions of institutional organization, based on uniform national standards and opportunities and on protective by-laws and regulations, and on the other hand, asymmetrical conceptions of institutional organization, based on policies and structures that not only address particular local circumstances but also redress wrongs. Interestingly, this conflict, which at least indirectly affected the Common Agenda Alliance for the Arts (an umbrella group made up mostly of national and Ontario-based arts organizations, but which attracted no special-constituency members) during its Charlottetown Accord campaign against the "devolution" of responsibility for arts funding from the federal government to the provinces, strongly resembles the national constitutional conflict between symmetrical and asymmetrical conceptions of federalism.

As I turn to Canadian publishing, my narratives risk again becoming explicitly personal. I have been an editor of the Canadian-owned literary publisher Coach House Press since 1976, and have edited for Vancouver's Canadian-owned Talonbooks since 1982. I have had books published by western presses like Turnstone, NeWest, and New Star, and by the Ontario-based University of Toronto Press. Like many Canadian writers and academics, I have a particular stake in certain kinds of publishing. When I use the phrase "in Canadian publishing," I am, as before, telling something of a personal story.

In Canadian publishing, the contrasts between collective and individualist notions of authorship, and between limited and national conceptions of audience and of cultural policy evident in the PEN and Writers Union debates, have been largely reflected in differences among publishing houses whose primary objectives are commercial and those, like Women's Press, or NeWest Press, whose primary objectives have been to aggrandize particular groups or regions. The general trends in book publishing have been the strengthening of these special-constituency publishers, about which I will have more to say later, a weakening of Canadian-owned commercial publishing, and the growing participation in the Canadian book market of foreign-owned publishers. It is in this increasing participation in Canadian publishing, either as branch plants (in the case of presses like Viking-Penguin, Doubleday, Random House, or HarperCollins) or as co-publishers (in the case of Alfred Knopf or Farrar, Strauss, and Giroux), of foreign-owned presses that the trend in Canadian literature toward globalization has been most evident. In many co-publishing agreements, the non-Canadian press looks after the editing of the Canadian manuscript and the Canadian press publishes the resultant text (Carol Gerson of Simon Fraser University has recently discovered that this was the case for the McClelland & Stewart/Alfred Knopf co-publication of Margaret Laurence's *The Diviners*, and that the Knopf editor's non-Canadian expectations may have decisively changed that novel's structure).

Increased international publication has led to increasing participation of anglophone-Canadian fiction in international prizes like the Booker Prize, and to overlappings between Governor's General and international award nomination. While some journalists have argued that this increased international participation reflects an increase in the quality of the Canadian text, there is considerable evidence in Canadian fiction that what it may actually signal is the development of desocialized transnational texts that are largely unconnected to local, regional, or national politics and practices or that attempt to subordinate social questions to aesthetics. Canada's best-known international novelists, and most frequent nominees for the Booker Prize, Robertson Davies, Margaret Atwood, and Michael Ondaatje, all write novels that imply disdain or radical mistrust of political process and that subordinate politics to transcendental, individualist, or aesthetic values. This global market in fiction is emphatically a late-capitalist formation, which treats the text as a commodity and the author as both an individual producer and as a potential fetish-object that can be commodified in conjunction with his or her texts – as in, "Have you read the latest 'Atwood'?" The value of the text is not constructed in terms of its social impact within its own community – the kind of impact Atwood's

Survival, Dennis Lee's *Civil Elegies,* or Dave Godfrey's *Death Goes Better with Coca-Cola* had in the 1960s – but rather in terms of its sales and its themes of transnational humanism.

The change evident here is one which Horkheimer and Adorno (1972) described as a shift from cultural politics to cultural industries, from art that interrogates the prevailing order of society to art that acquiesces to it. In Canadian theatre, this shift has been seen less in original plays than in the large English-Canadian productions of musicals like *Cats, Kiss of the Spider Woman, Les Miserables, The Phantom of the Opera,* and *Miss Saigon.* In fact, under the Mulroney government, the development of profitable "cultural industries" was constructed to Canadians not as the threat to culture it was to Horkheimer and Adorno but as the basis of a culture policy. Mulroney's 1985 "Baie Comeau" cultural policies assumed the existence of Canadian commercial publishers that wished to produce and distribute transnational texts, but overlooked the existence of numerous other Canadian publishers, both commercial and noncommercial, that aimed to produce texts which had meaning chiefly in terms of material and social issues specific to Canada.

Another increasingly problematical aspect of the growth of branch-plant publishers in the Canadian market has been their tendency to attract authors whose reputations and audiences have been developed by small, Canadian-owned presses. Author development is an expensive aspect of publishing in which a publisher often produces two or three low-selling titles by an author before that author becomes widely enough known for a title to have wider sales potential. When faced with direct competition for authors by branch-plant publishers, all but two or three of the largest Canadian-owned presses are rarely able to continue to publish books by the newly established authors whose reputations they have developed. Their loss of authors like Brian Fawcett, Audrey Thomas, and Mordecai Richler to much better capitalized branch plants which can afford large advances and promotional budgets, in turn, limits the possibility that the Canadian publisher will ever be able to outgrow its dependency on state subsidy (see Lorimer on this phenomenon, 1988:207). The result of a situation in which most author development is done by the smaller Canadian commercial and special constituency presses, and most of the well-known authors are published by branch plants, is an industry in which the branch plants, according to current Association of Canadian Publishers estimates (passed on to me by my friend and editor, Talonbooks owner, Karl Siegler), publish only 20 percent of Canadian authors, but hold a 73 percent market share of sales of Canadian-authored titles.

Federal government investment policy, rather than opposing this trend toward multi-national branch-plant domination of Canadian publishing, has actually encouraged it. Current federal legislation requires that a branch-plant publisher, whenever its parent company is purchased by another non-Canadian company, either be sold to Canadian buyers at a fair market price or else show that its remaining under non-Canadian control will be of direct benefit to Canada and to Canadian authors. The "fair market price" provision, a price guaranteed by the federal government acting as a purchaser of last resort, has been successfully interpreted by companies such as Paramount and Gulf & Western as an international fair market price, a price far higher than the value of Canadian-owned publishing houses, which can, by the legislation, be sold only to Canadian buyers (see Mumford 1992:6; and Ross 1994:C2). But, of course, the very sale of a branch-plant publisher converts it from a higher-value international company to a lower-value Canadian company, and makes it instantly worth less than the international fair market price the non-Canadian company has demanded. The "direct benefit to Canada and to Canadian authors" provision under which – because of the seller's successful overestimation of the branch-plant publisher's value – most of the these situations are now resolved, merely invites the branch plant to raid the writer assets of Canadian-owned publishers. Obliged to publish Canadian authors, the branch plant can use its financial resources to skim more of the most profitable Canadian authors and texts to its lists, thus *appearing to* benefit Canada while leaving the subsidized Canadian-owned presses with lists dominated even more by difficult-to-sell titles.

If one combines this tendency with the long-term decline in federal publishing subsidies – Canada Council Block Grant funds are now 5 percent lower than they were in 1986 while the number of titles funded by the program has increased by 58 percent – and with the budget deficits that are plaguing all levels of government in Canada, the future of Canadian-owned publishing looks extremely bleak. In decades of relative prosperity, federal policy was not able to help Canadian-owned commercial publishers overcome their grant dependency (in fact, it can be argued that the investment legislation discussed above doomed them to grant dependency); today, the government's ability to sustain any meaningful level of subsidy looks doubtful.[2] Yet without an active Canadian-owned publishing sector that develops new authors, would there even be Canadian authors for branch-plant publishers to skim off? Who would develop new Canadian authors if the subsidized Canadian-owned presses could no longer be subsidized?

The antipathy that has been evident in the appropriation of voice debates between commercially successful writers like Atwood, Davies, Findley, and Richler on the one hand, and writers like Keeshig-Tobias, Brand, and Nourbese Philip, who view writing as done at least partly on behalf of a community, on the other, is likely to become an even more pronounced trend as the growth of multinational publishing causes the gaps between these positions to expand. The growing influence of Canadian lives of the GATT and NAFTA promises not only an increasing subordination of culture to commerce and a consequent commodification of art, but also an increasing estrangement of minority communities from what they perceive as elites that have become – much like throughout his terms in office, Brian Mulroney became less and less distinguishable from George Bush – indistinguishable from elites in other countries. With the recent federal approval of repurchase of the Ginn publishing company by Paramount, and of the acquisition by Paramount of Macmillan, Prentice-Hall, and Simon & Shuster, and the U.S. purchase of the Lucinda Vardey Agency, the proportion of Canadian publishing controlled by multinational companies continues to expand, as does also the number of Canadian-authored books consciously or unconsciously structured to appeal to more than one national market.

Meanwhile, the two parallel trends – the relative weakening of Canadian-owned commercial publishing, particularly at the national level, and the growth of special constituency publishing – have continued. Only one new Canadian-owned national publishing company, Key Porter, has been formed in the last decade while several – Hurtig, Lester & Orpen Dennys, and House of Anansi – have gone out of business or ceased independent operation. In the same period special constituency publishing has expanded: older regional presses like Breakwater Books in St John's, Talonbooks in Vancouver, Turnstone Press in Winnipeg, have grown, while numerous other presses have been founded or dramatically expanded including feminist presses like Press Gang, Ragweed, Sister Vision, and Second Story; First Nations presses like Theytus and Pemmican; and Acadian presses like Perce-neiges and Quatres Saisons. What is especially interesting about these new special-constituency or "niche" publishers is that they have taken on many of the legitimation functions that in the past have been the exclusive functions of national publishers. Unlike small presses in the 1960s and 70s, they have published not only poetry and fiction, but also anthologies of poetry and fiction, volumes of selected poems, and volumes of literary criticism that examine many of the texts which the press has previously published. While many of the earlier small presses saw themselves as the unacknowledged "farm teams" of larger publishers to whom their writers would "move up" and become nationally legitimized once they had received national attention, these presses have tended to see themselves as parallel and alternative to Toronto publishers. Rather than wait for larger publishers to resolve the canonicity claims of emerging writers (which many of the newer branch-plant publishers are not interested in addressing), they have set about establishing their own literary norms and canons and their own critics, historians, anthologists, and "major" writers. In this situation, the national literary scene has become threatened from two directions: international publication lures its most successful writers to write for multiple audiences – even its less-known writers like Susan Swan, Barbara Gowdy, Carol Shields, and Brian Fawcett are led to seek U.S. or British publication – while special constituency publication spurns both the concept of a national literary scene and any notion of national authority.

One important consequence of this, as I note in a recent book, is that the national Canadian poetry canon has changed very little since the mid-1970s. While proposed additions to the canon in the 1970s were usually the unanimous choices of the editors of the competing anthologies, in the 80s and 90s they have tended to be choices made by one editor, but dissented from by others. The editors of national anthologies themselves have continued to be from the generation of editors that emerged in the 1960s and 70s – my generation. Meanwhile, the younger generations of anthologists have been producing mostly regional, ethnic, racial, or feminist anthologies, and publishing them with the new special constituency presses. What may be developing here in the place of a national canon is a number of specialized canons: of regional poetries, feminist poetry, First Nations poetry, Black poetry. The next large national anthology – and I speak here as a publisher's editor who has attempted to imagine the next large national anthology – may have to be an anthology of anthologies.

In fiction, the main consequence has been to increase the number of criteria by which canonicity can be conferred. As one of my graduate students observed this spring, to construct a course in Canadian fiction, one currently appears to take three steps: 1) select one novel by each canonical author; 2) consider and select from canonical texts authored by non-canonical authors; 3) select one novel each from each of four canonical constituencies – Aboriginal, lesbian-feminist, Asian, and gay.[3] I would add, in my identity as academic and course designer, that a fourth step also appears to take place: the selections of work by canonical authors are re-sorted for regional and period representation. Thus, in contemporary fiction, one selects from among titles by

George Bowering, Jack Hodgins, Audrey Thomas, and Robert Harlow a B.C. novel; from titles by Rudy Wiebe and Robert Kroetsch a prairie novel; from titles by Atwood, Davies, and Richler a Central Canadian novel; and a work by David Adams Richards is by default the Atlantic novel. Elsewhere, Joy Kogawa's *Obasan* has become the Asian novel and Timothy Findley's *The Wars*, the gay novel, while one must select from titles by Jane Rule, Daphne Marlatt, and Gail Scott a lesbian novel, and from among ones by Thomas King, Jeannette Armstrong, and Beatrice Culleton, an Aboriginal novel. In the latter category, however, and in Black writing, the literary and critical communities await the writing of the acceptably representative novel: the novel that can arguably "stand for" the writing of these constituencies as *Obasan* currently stands for Asian fiction. Overall, the fiction canon over the past decade has thus changed, but only in very particular ways. Writers have been added, but only in very particular ways: to represent previously under-represented regions, cultures, or constituencies. There has been no "need" here for more Central Canadian writers, more writers who are merely "women writers" (except perhaps a strong woman novelist from Atlantic Canada), or male writers except from the Arctic. This situation, in turn, has encouraged Toronto writers to situate themselves within international writing where the development of a transnational, commercial, "postmodern" canon appears to invite Canadian participation.

Some mornings when, while driving to my university office, I reflect absent-mindedly on the current situation of writing and literary criticism in Canada, the following exaggerated scenario comes into my head. Most of the big-name writers, and many of the most ambitious Toronto ones, have turned their backs on the Canadian literary scene, hired agents to find them British and U.S. publishers, and begun trying to write what was once known as "transatlantic" literature. They are bored with what they see as the petty politics of Canadian literary contention; they are understandably happier keeping company with other internationally famous writers in New York or Rome or even at Toronto's "world-class" Harbourfront International Festival of Authors than they are defending themselves against charges of racism or elitism at meetings of the Canadian chapter of PEN or of the Writer's Union. The country's national institutions – the Writer's Union, the League of Canadian Poets, the Canada Council juries – are now largely operated by coalitions of regional and special constituency interests. There is no national literary audience: there is an international audience that responds to prizes and celebrity, and there are special constituency audiences that respond to various constructions of marginalized identity.

Writers who have not managed to affiliate themselves with any of these audiences, who construct literature neither as entertainment nor as a displacement of power contentions, have difficulty finding publishers and readers. Some of these belatedly begin scrambling to claim minority standing, finding themselves a Métis great grandfather, or reasserting nearly forgotten Irish, Cornish, or Pennsylvania Dutch heritages.

Would such a scenario be the end of anglophone-Canadian literature? Not necessarily, and particularly not if the writers of various groups continued to argue with one another. Moreover, critics like myself could and would continue to construct anglophone-Canadian literature as the collectivity of texts written by anglophone Canadians, even if many were not written specifically for Canadians. Further, even without the direct participation of many of the writers who had turned toward global audiences, there would still be a textual field of power relations in which such writers implicitly participated. Their texts would still be used, as the transatlantic texts of expatriate fiction writers Mavis Gallant and Elizabeth Smart have been used by some feminist critics, for specific political purposes by anglophone-Canadians working within anglophone Canada.

If there has been a trend in anglophone-Canadian literary criticism, it has been toward both participation in literature as a form of cultural struggle and constructing Canadian literature as such as a field of power relations, and away from constructing it as a collection of individual aesthetic productions. While much textual explication and humanistic appreciation continues to be published, a higher proportion of work is now published in what might loosely be termed "cultural studies." Among these I think of Terry Goldie's *Fear and Temptation: The Image of the Indigene in Canadian, Australian and New Zealand Literatures*, Sylvia Soderlind's *Margin/Alias: Language and Colonization in Canadian and Québécois Fiction*, Susan Rudy Dorscht's *Women, Reading, Kroetsch*, Robert Lecker's anthology, *Canadian Canons: Essays in Literary Value*, Arun Mukherjee's *Towards an Aesthetics of Opposition*, and the six volumes to date of the University of Alberta Research Institute for Comparative Literature's *Towards a History of the Literary Institution in Canada* (*HOLIC*). An even more pronounced trend in the periodical literature suggests that large numbers of similar kinds of books are likely to appear. Again, however, I am in no way "outside" – to return to that keyword of this volume – the matters I describe. The preceding part of this paragraph describes the direction of my own thoughts about Canadian literature as well as, self-reflexively, my thoughts in this chapter. It describes many of the articles by others that I have published in a journal I edit, *Open Letter*. Terry Goldie is a contributing editor of that journal, and Susan Rudy Dorscht has edited two of its special issues; I have contributed to two of the University of Alberta's Research Institute's volumes. We in this volume may be to some extent our own trends.

The above literary criticism falls into three or four general areas. Some of it involves contention for coveted positions of marginality: arguments that particular writers have hypocritically constructed themselves as marginal, as in Soderlind's book, or that particular writers are worthy of attention because they have been marginalized or write from marginalized positions. Some of this criticism involves contention for interpretive and ideological possession of an author's work, as in various books and articles offering competing postmodernist, feminist, and modernist understandings of Robert Kroetsch's fiction, articles offering competing modernist, feminist, and lesbian feminist readings of Phyllis Webb's poetry; articles offering rival postmodernist, essentialist, or materialist readings of Daphne Marlatt's poetry, or articles offering rival postmodernist, Marxist, or postcolonial understandings of Michael Ondaatje's fiction. In many cases these understandings of a writer's work are used to help legitimate and advance particular social views and programs. And some of the most interesting current critical work is being done in the interrelated areas of canonicity and literary history. Is a history of the Canadian literatures possible? asks my friend and HOLIC organizer, E.D. Blodgett, in the article that opens a recent issue of the journal *Essays on Canadian Writing*. English-Canadian literary history has been coming under scrutiny from a number of viewpoints. The question what is "Canadian" expands from the question of whether a history should include Quebec francophone writing to whether Aboriginal writing and writing in languages other than English and French has been sufficiently acknowledged. The question of what is "literary" opens from the assumption implicit in Klinck's 1967 *Literary History of Canada*, and includes a large area of what we might often understand as "cultural," from writing in the physical and social sciences to debates on whether "literature" as an aesthetic category may be largely a Eurocentric conception. The question of what is history focuses on both perspective and rhetorical mode. Is history necessarily perspectival; are there hierarchies of perspectives; should the rhetoric of literary history be narrative and risk telling a single story, or should it be archaeological, and offer cross-sections of historical moments? Moreover, is the practice of literary history itself inextricably tied to concepts of nationhood, national culture, and nationalism and to the narratives of national histories, as Klinck assumed, and thus to the reading of texts through the problematics of national cultural formation, or can there be useful literary histories that address Canadian writing while also cutting across nationalist constructions? And what can be my own position here, when the academic chair I hold at the University of Western Ontario is itself historicized by the name "The Carl F. Klinck Professor of Canadian Literature"?

The general trend evident in these and other critical disagreements appears to be toward viewing Canadian writing as a postcolonial literature, that is, as a literature produced by power differentials both within the country and in relationship to events elsewhere. Here the nation is increasingly viewed not as an entity but as a specific field or complex of power relationships. A history of the literature of such a nation would be less a narrative than a narrative of contentions among narratives.

A third, but less focused, area of intense activity in anglophone-Canadian literature criticism has been the question of identity – which here has become not only the old and somewhat naïve question of whether Canada or anglophone Canada has a national identity but also the epistemological question of what actually constitutes "identity." I say that this activity has been less focused because in general identity has not yet been explicitly identified as a conceptual problem, as canonicity and literary history have been, but rather has been approached through a variety of more specific questions: the question of the reliability of authors' intentions, and of the epistemological status of interviews and autobiography; the question of the generic nature of life writing – are this and other forms of autobiography species of fiction, is scholarly writing a species of autobiography or fiction, is some fiction perhaps veiled autobiography; the question of the critical value of author-focused criticism, and of canons that are founded on authors rather than on texts; the question of whether it is appropriate to create celebrity author-identities to help market books and interest students; the question of whether personal identity itself may be a textual construction, something historical and contingent rather than essential. The poststructuralist conception of identity as something that is not stable and uniform but is rather multiple, contingent, and continually negotiated has been particularly useful to some critics, like E.D. Blodgett and Smaro Kamboureli, in working toward a theory of a multicultural Canada. At the same time idealist notions of identity have been politically useful to Aboriginal peoples and ethnic minorities in arguing for proprietorship over their narratives, viewpoints, and experiences. The identity politics that inspires the formation of a women's press or a First Nations publishing house can also manifest itself, as it did two years ago in the widely publicized case of my colleague, James Miller of the University of Western Ontario, in white lesbian students refusing to "allow" a white, gay, male professor to teach the texts of Audre Lorde, an Afro-American, lesbian cultural theorist.

A fourth tendency to note is that of anglophone-Canadian literary and artistic cultures being held together – like perhaps myself in this chapter – by overlapping fractures. The long-evident regional separation of Atlantic Canada from the rest of "the rest of Canada" has if anything increased in recent years. The catalogues of most Atlantic-Canadian publishers describe books only in terms of their regional marketplace; these books rarely appear in bookshops outside that region. None of the publishers construct themselves as national publishers. The west coast and prairie regions are preponderantly represented by similar regionally focused presses; a large proportion of their writers, however, receive notice in other parts of Canada and at least two of their publishers, Talonbooks and Douglas & McIntyre, both based in Vancouver, present themselves in their catalogues and manuscript selection as both regional and national publishers. First Nations writing, women's writing, and racial and ethnic constituency writing, however, create other fracture lines which, paradoxically, operate to reconnect regional solitudes. While Toronto's Women's Press is primarily an Ontario regional press, Prince Edward Island's gynergy books is a national press that publishes feminist and lesbian feminist writing from across the country. The various anthologies of First Nations writing that have been published in Canada in the last decade, including those from Native-operated Pemmican and Theytus presses, have all been defined as nationally Canadian in that their contributors come from all parts of Canada and mostly from within Canada.

I will conclude by pointing to three recent events which to some extent serve as metonymies for some of the trends I have been discussing. The first event concerns the novel, *Cantique des plaines*, by Calgary-born novelist Nancy Huston, and co-published by the Quebec press Leméac and the Paris literary press Actes Sud, which won the 1993 Governor-General's Award for what the Canada Council terms French-language fiction. Huston first learned French as a young woman in Boston and New York. She then moved to Paris, where she has lived for more than twenty years, and published in French a dozen works of fiction and non-fiction. There she married a well-known Bulgarian-born literary theorist, Tzvetan Todorov (who in the last decade has moved from his early work on structuralist genre theory to cultural theory, and in books like *Nous et les autres, Face à l'extrême*, and *Les morales de l'histoire*, has focused on ethnic difference and otherness in societies in which homogenous cultures mix and clash). In remarks published in *L'Actualité* and *Le Devoir*, Huston commented not only that she has felt little attraction to her Alberta roots but also that she and her husband have no French friends – their domestic visitors are from America and Eastern Europe (Halpern 1994:70).

Cantique des plaines was published roughly simultaneously with an English-language version of the novel, *Plainsongs,* published by the Toronto branch of HarperCollins, which was not shortlisted for the Governor-General's Award in English-language fiction. Huston has said that she created this English version first, the first writing that she had done in English for over fifteen years, and that she then wrote *Cantique des plaines* by translating the English-language text. The action of the novel, while not specifically autobiographical, concerns a young woman's growing up in and near Calgary.

The novel's winning of the French-language award created a small tempest in Quebec; Huston did not live in Quebec, some commentators complained, she was not francophone, she had never lived in a Canadian francophone community; moreover, the book was a translation rather than an original novel. The novel and its award apparently operated in Quebec to destabilize various linguistic and cultural categories and to demonstrate the messy effect of "otherness" on idealized cultural forms. Together with the personal history of the author – her Calgary birthplace, her American French, her Bulgarian-born French-intellectual husband, her Paris residence, her French writing career – the novel illustrated both the globalizing and deterritorializing of Western culture and the cultural collisions, fears, and misunderstandings which had been the subjects of Todorov's last three books. As Huston observed to *l'Actualité,* "I am not a prairie writer, nor a Quebec writer. I am Canadian, I am French, but I am not French-Canadian."

Such globalization has been a trend in English-Canadian writing for some time, evident in a small scale in David Fennario's bilingual plays set in working-class Montreal, in a somewhat larger scale in Paris-based Mavis Gallant's fictional accounts of post-war Europe, some of which contributed to her winning a Governor-General's Award for English-language fiction in 1981, and in a yet larger scale in the winning of the same award in 1984 by Czech expatriate Josef Skvorecky for a novel, *The Engineer of Human Souls,* translated from Czech into English by someone other than himself. It is particularly and ironically interesting in these instances that one of the main elements of the global can be the "otherness" or special-constituency status of the author: the expatriate position assumed by Gallant, the refugee and political dissident position of Skvorecky, the triple otherness of Huston, refugee from Calgary, expatriate in Paris, perceived interloper in Canadian francophone culture. The expatriate, refugee, or immigrant – the potential special constituency subject – becomes a global phenomenon as the twentieth century closes. But what is perhaps most important to note is that in the global figuration this expatriate is most often alone, without affiliation or the support of a constituency. When Huston's novel wins its award, no community celebrates and many in one community are offended.

The second event I wish to point to is the recent opening in Toronto of the Canadian-written and produced musical *Napoleon*. Rick Salutin of the *Globe and Mail* has astutely pointed out how utterly non-Canadian this production is – how devoid of reference it is to the particularities of living in Canada, except ironically, through its now very Canadian story of someone abandoning their home for a dream of conquering the world. Salutin sees the musical as representing the abandonment by Canadian politicians, businessmen, and artists of the everyday business of negotiating a Canadian polity – of the abandonment of art in favour of industrial entertainment, with each production having "the familiarity of a room at the Holiday Inn, no matter where in the world you book it." *Napoleon* is another face of globalism, not the face of the lost individual expatriate, as was the case of Nancy Huston, in which every human subject seems part of yet another diaspora, but of the synthetic global homeland, in which indistinguishable movies are played on indistinguishable airliners that land at indistinguishable airports and send similar planeloads of passengers to indistinguishable chains of international hotels.

The third phenomenon I want to note is the development in Canada of the closed-audience conference: the conference to which registration is restricted to a particular sex, sexual orientation, ethnic, or racial constituency. In religious communities, in communities that perceive themselves to be under threat, or even in service clubs, meetings are routinely closed to members or adherents; the closure of such meetings reflects not only difference, but also the conviction that only people who share that difference and its codes can be trusted with knowledge of it, and the suspicion that the presence of others could alter these codes or cause adherents to alter them. In the arts in Europe and North America, the general assumption about the dissemination of ideas for the past three centuries has been the liberal humanist one that the widest possible circulation of ideas is preferable, that censorship is undesirable, that cultural codes are generally intelligible, and that ideas and cultural expressions which encounter difficulty in achieving wide circulation or which weaken when circulated, do so not because they have been repressed or attacked but because they have been intrinsically uncompetitive with other ideas and expressions.

The trend toward closed meetings and conferences in the arts reflects both a mistrust of the general community and the belief that some cultural constructions have been "uncompetitive" in the general community not because of their own merits but because of power differentials among the constituencies in that community – that even the mere presence of members of a dominant group can stifle or distort the productions of the less powerful. One of the first closed meetings I became aware of was a 1982 meeting of feminist writers in a large city of southern India; men of whatever background, including my own, were forbidden to attend because the women had noticed that many among them were reticent to speak with men present or would speak differently than they would otherwise. The next was the enormously successful Women and Words conference (successful in terms of texts published, the number of writers claiming to be helped, and in the number of workshops and conferences that have ensued from it) held in Vancouver in 1983, most of the sessions of which were also closed to men. The most recent is the "Writing Thru 'Race'" conference organized by the Racial Minority Writers Committee of the Writers Union of Canada for 30 June 30 to 3 July 1994, and advertised as "limited to First Nations writers and writers of colour." Conference organizer Roy Miki explained this limitation by expressing his wish that the writers in attendance be able to speak "without the mediating screen of a binary 'white/coloured' dichotomy" (quoted in Fulford 1994:C1). These closed conferences are in a way viewable as explicit manifestations of a phenomenon already evident in special-constituency writing and publishing in Canada, particularly by feminist, Black, and First Nation writers: the construction of texts on the basis of cultural norms specific to a minority community – of texts that imply that community as an audience and that are later legitimated in anthologies and critical essays also written on the basis of that community's understandings of what is literary.

I choose these three phenomena not only because they all in different ways trouble the notion of Canada Outside Quebec but also because although in some ways they represent conflicting trends, they are also closely related to one another. Global shifts in which writers become rootless and transportable from one language or culture to another, and in which their books move from market to market according to individual success of a "product," make it difficult for both national and special constituency cultures to present distinct identities. This assault on national and group identity is more painful for groups and for individual subjects whose own identities are founded on group membership than it is for individuals who have gained success and power within the global culture and its institutions. Those who have most eagerly embraced the closed audience model, either explicitly in conferences, or implicitly in the kinds of texts they write and publishing institutions they build, have been those who historically have believed themselves outside significant cultural, political, and economic power. The macro trend here seems to be for these various positions to become increasingly separated – for the spaces that separate the individual Canadian artist, the Habourfront International Festival of Authors, and groups like the Racial Minority Writers Committee, or the spaces that separate HarperCollins, Newfoundland's Breakwater Books, and Sister Vision Press, to become wider, and for national culture, at least as anglophone Canadians have experienced it, to become lost, or at least fractured, between.

When Christian Rioux of *Le Devoir* asked her about Canada, Nancy Huston replied, "I don't know what this thing is, Canada. Do you know? I believe that all identities are false that Canada has truly no identity ... I think that we are pseudonyms, usurpers of identity, but that exiles know this better than others" (1994:c1). One major trend in many of the arts in Canada today may be toward a scramble for such pseudonyms, for assumed and often reductive identities: for that of the self-sufficient citizen of the world or of the new world economic order or for identity as First Nations-Canadian, Chinese-Canadian, Canadian of colour, and so on. In a sense there is no audience for an artist without identity, without the illusion of a fixed point which artist and audience share, much as there is no political power without the imagination of shared interests and objectives. With religious and national identities no longer seeming effective, with diaspora experiences becoming commonplace, with cosmopolitan identities looking to many Canadians like disguised versions of the United States or of Eurodisney, and with one's own identity, like mine in this chapter, increasingly subject to conflict, fracture, and promiscuous complicity, an insistence on regional, racial, and ethnic identities may appear to many artists to be the only effective life or professional strategy.

NOTES

1 The passion of the ANNPAC and other debates over racism suggests that these debates may be serving as substitutions for initiatives which marginalized groups find themselves unable to conduct effectively in the general culture. The anti-racist supporters often seem to expect their interventions in cultural organizations to accomplish social change the organization itself is powerless to deliver. For example, the changes which the proponents of the "Minquam Panchayat" initiative sought to bring about in ANNPAC could have had at best a symbolic impact on the policies of ANNPAC member galleries.

2 It is uncertain whether a policy which presently appears to be under consideration by the federal government – requiring branch-plant publishers that are taken over by new international owners to sell their book distribu-

tion businesses to Canadian-owned publishers – would be useful to any but the largest Canadian publishers. It is also unclear whether such a policy would survive U.S. threats of counter-measures.

3 I am indebted to Caroline Sin for this analysis.

BIBLIOGRAPHY

Blodgett, E.D. 1982. *Configuration: Essays on the Canadian Literatures* Toronto: ECW Press.

– 1993. "Is a History of the Literatures of Canada Possible?" *Essays on Canadian Writing* 50 (Fall):1–18.

– and A.G. Purdy, eds. 1988. *Problems of Literary Reception. Towards a History of the Literary Institution in Canada*, vol. 1. Edmonton: Research Institute for Comparative Literature.

– and A.G. Purdy, eds. 1990. *Prefaces and Literary Manifestos*. Towards a History of the Literary Institution in Canada, vol. 1. Edmonton: Research Institute for Comparative Literature.

Davidson, Arnold, E. ed. 1990. *Studies on Canadian Literature: Introductory and Critical Essays*. New York: Modern Language Association.

Fulford, Robert. 1994. "George Orwell, Call Your Office." *Globe and Mail*, 30 March, C1.

Goldie, Terry. 1988. *Fear and Temptation: The Image of the Indigene in Canadian, Australian and New Zealand Literatures*. Montreal: McGill-Queen's University Press.

Halpern, Sylvie. 1994. "Cantique des plaines." *L'Actualité* (February):68–73.

Horkheimer, Max, and Theodore W. Adorno. 1972. *Dialectic of Enlightenment*. New York: Herder and Herder.

Huston, Nancy. 1993. *Cantique des plaines*. Montreal: Leméac.

Kamboureli, Smaro. 1993. "The Technology of Ethnicity: Law and Discourse," *Open Letter* 8, no. 5–6:202–17.

Klinck, Carl F., Alfred G. Bailey, et al. eds. 1965. *Literary History of Canada*, 2 vols. Toronto: University of Toronto Press.

Lecker, Robert, ed. 1991. *Canadian Canons*. Toronto: University of Toronto Press.

Leith, Linda. 1990. "Quebec Fiction in English During the 1980s: A Case Study in Marginality." *Studies in Canadian Literature* 15, no. 5:1–20.

Loriggio, Francesco. 1989. "History, Literary History, and Ethnic Literature." *Canadian Review of Comparative Literature* 16, no. 3–4:575–99.

Lorimer, James. 1988. "Free Trade and Book Publishing in English Canada." In *Scholarly Publishing in Canada: Evolving Present, Uncertain Future*, ed. Patricia Demers, 202–14. Ottawa: University of Ottawa Press.

McLaren, I.S., and C. Potvin, eds. 1991. *Literary Genres*. Towards a History of the Literary Institution in Canada, vol. 5. Edmonton: Research Institute for Comparative Literature.

– eds. 1991. *Questions of Funding, Publishing and Distribution*. Towards a History of the Literary Institution in Canada, vol. 5. Edmonton: Research Institute for Comparative Literature.

Mukherjee, Arun. 1988. *Towards an Aesthetic of Opposition: Essays on Literature, Criticism, and Cultural Imperialism*. Toronto: Williams-Wallace.

Mumford, Ted. 1992. "Proofs in Pudding." *Quill & Quire* (March):1, 6, 8–9.

Nepveu, Pierre. 1988. *L'Écologie du réel: Mort et naissance de la littérature québécoise contemporaine*. Montreal: Boréal.

New, W. H. 1989. *A History of Canadian Literature*. London: Macmillan.

Norris, Ken, and Andre Farkas, eds. 1977. *Montreal: English Poetry of the Seventies*. Montreal: Vehicule.

– and Peter Van Toorn, eds. 1982. *Cross/cut: Contemporary English Quebec Poetry*. Montreal: Vehicule.

– eds. 1982. *The Insecurity of Art: Essays on Poetics*. Montreal: Vehicule.

Pivato, Joseph, ed. 1990. *Literatures of Lesser Diffusion*. Towards a History of the Literary Institution in Canada, vol. 4. Edmonton: Research Institute for Comparative Literature.

Potvin, C., and J. Williamson, eds. 1992. *Women's Writing and the Literary Institution*. Towards a History of the Literary Institution in Canada, vol. 6. Edmonton: Research Institute for Comparative Literature.

Rioux, Christian. 1994. "Qui a peur de Nancy Huston?" *Le Devoir*, 17 January, C1.

Robin, Régine. 1989. *Le roman mémoriel*. Longueil: Le Préambule.

Ross, Val. 1994. "Who's Driving the Bus? Publishers Have a Right to Wonder." *Globe and Mail* 2 March, C2.

Rudy Dorscht, Susan. 1991. *Women, Reading, Kroetsch*. Waterloo: Wilfrid Laurier University Press.

Salutin, Rick. 1994. "This little emperor went to market." *The Globe and Mail* (1 April):C1.

Simon, Sherry. 1991. "Espaces incertains de la culture." In *Fictions de l'identitaire au Quebec*, 13–52. Montreal: XYZ.

Soderland, Sylvia. 1991. *Margin/Alias*. Toronto: University of Toronto Press. 1991.

8 The Essential Role of National Cultural Institutions

JOYCE ZEMANS

Margaret Atwood has written, "Canadians are forever taking the national pulse like doctors at a sickbed." Portraying Canada as "an unknown territory for the people who live in it ... a state of mind ... that kind of space in which we find ourselves lost" (Atwood 1972:18). Atwood has explored this theme throughout her writing. Her premise is that the single unifying and "informing symbol at [Canada's] core is 'survival'"; survival against hostile elements, survival in crisis, and cultural survival. The most recent variation on the survival discussion comes from those "who believe Canada is obsolete" and survival is seen as the "vestige of a vanished order which has managed to persist after its time is past" (Atwood 1972:32–3).

Northrop Frye defined Canada's national dilemma as the familiar existential search – with a significant twist: not, "Who am I?" but "Where is here?" Summarizing his thoughts in 1980, he wrote that Canadian culture is "not a national development but a series of regional ones" (Frye 1980:84). He also observed that though, in a world increasingly united and uniform, Canada would remain within the American orbit, culturally "both nations should run their own show"; and that it was "of immense importance that there should be other views [than that of the United States] of the human occupation of this continent, rooted in different ideologies and different historical traditions." He concluded by applauding Canada's achievement in "responding to the world with the tongues and eyes of a mature and disciplined imagination" (Frye 1980:84).

I am somewhat surprised to find myself going back to Atwood and Frye, but the fact is that they have identified a number of the key themes central to this paper – Canada outside Quebec: fragmentation or integration and the future of Canada's national cultural institutions; the importance of place in the definition of the Canadian experience; the continual Canadian search for identity; the danger of simplifying and misunderstanding the question of nationhood and national strategies to achieve that goal; and the constant presence of the u.s. as a key factor in shaping Canadian cultural policy – all form continuous threads in my discussion.

Though understandings of the terms *nationhood* and *identity* and how they might be achieved have differed, these concepts have been at the heart of Canadian policies designed to support cultural development, and the national institutions have been Canada's principal instruments for the creation and delivery of cultural policy. In 1949 the Massey-Levesque Commission which recommended the creation of the Canada Council was established on the premise that "it is desirable that the Canadian people should know as much as possible about their country, its history and traditions and about their national life and common achievements." In 1988 the new broadcasting policy for Canada was based upon "its major role in defining our national, regional, local and even our individual identities." In the March 1992 debates leading up to the Charlottetown Accord, the Liberal Party's cultural position paper posited "maintaining national unity and cultural sovereignty as the goal for federal cultural institutions and policy" as a "fundamental policy principle" (Finestone 1992:3).

To understand the future of national cultural institutions, one must be aware both of the historical conditions that shaped them and the current political, economic, and cultural environment in which they operate. I intend, therefore, to examine the institutions, albeit briefly, with special attention to the following factors:

1 their historic evolution and current roles;
2 the restructuring discourse arising from the ongoing debate regarding federal-provincial jurisdictions, particularly regarding the debates leading up to the Charlottetown Accord (including the claims of Quebec on the cultural portfolio);
3 the shift toward decentralization and devolution in government in light of the competing pressures of globalization and regionalism, and the response of the artistic community in Canada outside Quebec to these events;
4 the impact of the new global order in which the repositioning of boundaries between national and international activities is calling into question the validity and the role of the nation state (with particular reference to the implications of current trade agreements which increasingly challenge the state's ability to address national issues);

5 the demise of the Keynesian model and the public paradigm, the shift toward the reduction of the public role and the expansion of the private market, and the shift of responsibility from government to the private sector in social services, job creation, training, and arts support, etc.;

6 the changing demographics of Canada;

7 the changing technological environment.

Although each of these factors might appear to militate against continued support for national cultural institutions, I will argue that these institutions would remain essential to defining the experience of Canadian life in the event of an asymmetrical federal arrangement with Quebec, and even more so in the event of Quebec's separation. Survival will, however, require strategic responses from government and from the agencies themselves to ensure their capacity to carry out their missions within the politically and economically restructured environment.

THE HISTORY OF NATIONAL INSTITUTIONS IN CANADA

In their comparative research on government policy on the arts, Milton Cummings Jr and Richard Katz identify a number of reasons for a state to intervene in the arts and cultural sector (Katz and Cummings 1987:350–68). The political and cultural objectives which, they suggest, lead most countries into arts and culture might very well have been drawn from a Canadian case study. First is the establishment (and subsequently the reinforcement) of national identity; joined to this is a policy of "cultural defence" resulting from the fear of "cultural imperialism," along with the preservation of artistic and cultural heritage and the need for cultural development. Cummings and Katz also outline other motivating factors (economic, social welfare, employment), and the intrinsic value of the arts (Katz and Cummings 1987:350–68). (While the latter is the motivating factor for artists and arts supporters, it has seldom been the principal motive for government involvement.)

Researchers have documented the enormous growth in government support for the arts in Europe and North America between 1945 and 1975 (Schuster 1987, 1990; Katz and Cummings 1987). Governments' significantly increased financial and to a certain extent legislative presence during the post-World War II period, represents a major trend during this period. By the 80s, public involvement in the arts had become a permanently established government responsibility, and Canada was no exception. Although Canada has employed a variety of strategies to support culture, its national cultural institutions have had the greatest longevity and the highest profile – in large measure because their impact has been evident and the institutions have taken on a symbolic role in Canadian life.

Although Saskatchewan pioneered the establishment of an arts council in Canada in 1948, provincial entry into the cultural policy field was relatively slow and uneven. Perhaps this can be attributed to the fact that the federal government was already a presence in the arts, but it is more likely that when provinces did enter, the decision, except in the case of Quebec's creation of the Ministère des affaires culturelles in 1961, was motivated as much by social or industrial strategies as by the compelling vision of nationhood and national identity which dominated the discourse at the federal level.

A brief review of the historic and current mandates of several national cultural institutions will help us to understand the policy objectives which led to their formation, the reasons why national institutions were selected as the instruments for creation and delivery of policy in the cultural sector, and the evolution of the roles these institutions have played.

The National Gallery

If the support of national cultural institutions in Canada burgeoned in the post-war years, it did not begin then. Though the colonial period saw no royal or aristocratic arts patronage of a financial nature, it was the Governor-General, Lord Lorne, who in 1879 urged that Canadian artists should have their own national association – the Royal Canadian Academy – and he obligingly provided the royal charter so that Canadians could emulate their British counterparts. He also recommended the formation of a national gallery, anticipating, as Dennis Reid points out, the first federal government involvement in the destiny of Canada's art (Reid 1979:274). In the absence of private benefactors, anxious to establish their social and political positions such as could be found among their neighbours to the south, Canadians would have to wait thirty years before the gallery was actually incorporated and a century before a building was constructed to house the country's national treasures.

Minutes of board of trustees meetings when the gallery was established in 1913 reveal the members' political purposes: to instil national pride, to encourage a sense of national identity, and to create appropriate values in this heterogeneous new and culturally diverse country with its rapidly growing population (National Gallery of Canada 1:102). (Like their British counterparts, the trustees believed that art could serve as a principal agent of education and moral improvement.) Issues relating to French and English Canada remained a subtext, while regional service and commitment to creating artistic resources that would serve a country with few provincial institutions were clear priorities.

The National Gallery, a heritage institution which until 1977 received on deposit the diploma pieces of Canada's academicians, also had a mandate to serve contemporary artists. Indeed from its inception, this institution, designed to offer visual confirmation of the nation and proof of its civilization, had a two-pronged role: to foster Canada's artists through collecting, exhibiting, and disseminating their work and to build an international historical collection of quality that would educate and elevate Canadian citizens and provide a resource for the Canadian people (Boggs 1980:10).[1]

Today the gallery, finally ensconced in its new building, represents pride and ownership for many Canadians. Its collection, though sometimes controversial, is considered to be outstanding. It is on the list of must-sees for most Ottawa visitors. It has established its role as a national centre of research. With its historical role as provider of exhibitions, expertise, and educational materials to the underdeveloped provincial institutions now less relevant because of the exponential rise of provincial and municipal galleries, the gallery's role has shifted toward one of partnership. It still tours exhibitions regularly; it co-curates exhibitions with provincial partners. Its new affiliate, The Canadian Museum of Photography (though still defining its role), has broadened not only the scope of the collection but access to it, permitting the gallery to tour exhibitions more widely and less expensively, with fewer demands on the physical space required for museum standard exhibitions. The gallery distributes videotapes documenting its exhibitions and collection through the National Film Board system and is planning to document its collection on CD ROM. Through the Canadian Heritage Information Network, data relating to the collection are accessible to museums and scholars (Shirley Thomson, director of the National Gallery, telephone interview 26 March 1994).

The most significant challenges to the gallery from artists have arisen regarding representation in the collection and particularly the breadth and diversity of its representation of Canadian artists. But if the gallery's practices are questioned, the symbolic and real importance of the national institution is generally acknowledged. The response to recent controversies, such as the Gallery's expenditure on Barnett Newman's *Voice of Fire* and the exhibition of Jana Sterbak's *Vanitas: Flesh Dress for An Albino Anorectic,* suggests that the well-orchestrated protests reflected as much on the public's sense of ownership of the gallery as its outrage.

The CBC

In 1928, fifteen years after the National Gallery was incorporated, the Canadian government established the Royal Commission on Radio Broadcasting. Chaired by a pillar of free enterprise, Sir John Aird, president of the Canadian Bank of Commerce, the commission nevertheless recognized the impossibility of a private sector solution to the problems facing Canadian broadcasting. Only the centres of large population were even minimally served. French-language broadcasting was almost totally absent. Owners and advertisers were not profiting if they provided programs of high quality. Nor was radio realizing its potential to link the disparate regions of the country (Peers 1988:18).

The greatest threat of all lay in the "power and penetration of American stations" and the fact that, by 1929, stations in Toronto, Montreal, and Calgary were scrambling to attach themselves to the two American networks. To have left radio in the hands of private owners whose revenues would be based purely on advertising was a recipe for ensuring the complete domination of programming interests (Peers 1988). Great Britain and Europe provided the model: some form of public broadcasting and a willingness to use regulatory instruments to further national policy goals.

The commission recommended a nationally owned broadcasting system to span the country and the abandonment of privately owned stations supported exclusively by advertising. Introducing the bill to establish the Canadian Radio Broadcasting Commission (the CRBC, forerunner of the CBC) in 1932, Prime Minister Bennett warned that broadcasting must be under complete Canadian control "free from foreign interference or influence." Only public ownership could ensure equality of service "without regard to class or place"; the airwaves were a natural resource that should be reserved for "the use of the people" rather than for "private exploitation" (Peers 1988:15). Not without controversy from a federal/provincial jurisdictional viewpoint, the national mandate for broadcasting was affirmed when the Judicial Committee of the Privy Council of the U.K. upheld the Supreme Court ruling over a challenge brought by Ontario and Quebec.

The Aird Commission's research and hearings had made it clear that Canadians wanted a reflection of Canada on their airwaves. Even a government essentially opposed to such interference in the market place recognized that only through government intervention, coordination, and support could a network be established that would reflect not only the regions to themselves and to one another but national and international issues from a Canadian perspective. While affirmation of a unique culture was essentially a defensive response to an external threat, it also provided the means of articulating and expressing that unique Canadian culture and enabling Canadians to communicate with other Canadians.

If the railways had been the physical glue that bound this country, the CBC (established by the King government in 1936 as the successor to the CRBC) would have to provide the intellectual and spiritual community with a clear mandate to create both national identity and national unity. Regional development was perceived as critical and the public/private partnership that constituted the network at least paid lip service to the pre-eminence of public need. In its 1951 report, the Massey Commission would label the CBC Canada's "greatest single agency for national unity" (Royal Commission 1951:279). (Elsewhere in this text, Mary Jane Miller argues that the parallel development of the English and French networks and limited cross-over programming has served, in fact, to further isolate the two solitudes, although the CBC radio's success in linking Canadians outside Quebec is, I believe, undeniable.)

Analysts have noted how similar in thrust the successive broadcasting inquiries have been – from Aird to Massey, Fowler to Caplan-Sauvageau, and as Frank Peers points out, how congruent have been the instruments of public policy: the CRBC, the CBC, and the objectives set out for the CRTC and the broadcasting system in 1968 (Peers 1988:27). The environmental factors have until recently remained remarkably constant: the nature and distribution of the Canadian population, two main languages, regional and sectoral interests, and the virtual omnipresence of American culture.

Rearticulated in the political and economic climate of 1990 under the pragmatic leadership of Gerard Veilleux, the text of the CBC mandate remains strikingly similar to the earliest mission statement (despite the fact that the possibility of achieving it was becoming ever less likely and the irony that cuts to regional programming initiated in the same period severely limited the corporation's ability to fulfill that mandate, while significantly enhancing the tensions between the regions and the centre). Describing the responsibility entrusted to it as "noble, essential and unique," the CBC described itself as a "cornerstone, not only of the Canadian broadcasting system, but of Canada itself." It warned: "Whatever changes take place in Canada or in the Corporation, this mission remains a constant, unifying force to guide the CBC in responding to those changes" (CBC 1990:1).

Hearkening back to the CBC's original goals with deference to the current Canadian reality, the 1990 mission statement pledged the CBC to contribute to the development of a shared national consciousness and identity; to reflect the regional and cultural diversity of Canada by, among other things, presenting each region to itself and to the rest of the country; to reflect the changing realities of the Canadian experience and of the world in which we live, as seen by Canadian eyes, heard by Canadian ears, investigated by Canadian minds and explored by Canadian imaginations; and to contribute to the development of Canadian talent and culture. It also pledged, impossibly, to be all things to all people: "To inform, entertain and enlighten both general and specialized audiences" (CBC 1990:1).

On 23 March 1994 CRTC Chair Keith Spicer berated CBC's new president Anthony Manera for the CBC's unwillingness to redefine how its mandate, in so far as it applies to television, can viably be fulfilled within the current economic and technological environment. Spicer criticized the corporation's reliance on American programming and predicted that, without a clearer focus, CBC television would not survive. These were tough words from the nation's broadcasting regulator – and problematic in light of the financial dilemma of reduced government funding and the CBC's reliance on American popular fare to generate required revenue dollars. Spicer also predicted that the Canadian state's capacity to regulate the market would soon end (Cuff 1993:A12).

Controversy continues over the role and value of a national broadcaster, particularly in the case of English television, in light of diminishing resources and the options that will be provided for viewers in the new technological universe. Without doubt, CBC television will have to forego the desire to be all things to all people and determine what it can do best – most likely returning to its original mandate of reflecting Canada to Canadians and to the world. In so doing, it should keep in mind that, although the CBC audience share figures have dropped substantially over the last ten years (from 17 percent of the all-day audience in English Canada to 9.9 percent), the public broadcaster captures at least 50 percent of Canadians watching Canadian programming – a signal that must be clearly read if the CBC is to successfully define its future (Winsor 1994:A4).

The NFB

In 1939, faced with impending war in Europe and both the need to enhance and enforce national identity in a culturally and regionally diverse country and to foster a commitment to battle for the values this nation held sacred, the King administration hired John Grierson, the leader of the British documentary movement, to establish the National Film Board. In a country with "no films that dramatized the idea of Canada and brought it into the imagination of the home country," Grierson recalled MacKenzie King worrying, "Has Canada got an identity –

this everlasting, frustrating, humiliating question" (Jones 1981:388).[2] The Film Board's goal was to "help Canadians in all parts of Canada to understand the ways of living and the problems of Canadians in other parts" of the country (Jones 1981:200).

From the government's perspective (as Robert Fothergill's 1993 play, *Public Lies*, so aptly illustrates), the NFB was often viewed as an agency at the service of government in the task of creating images of Canada that would strengthen the local citizen's sense of Canadian identity. For Grierson, the mission was to create a team of expert artists second to none in the field of documentary film and he often walked a tightrope in insuring both that "public lies will not be told" and that "the king's shilling must not be abused." It has been said that Grierson's "greatest single discovery in the development of documentary came with the realization that its logical sponsorship lay with governments and with other bodies conscious of their public responsibilities." Sponsorship, not simple patronage, reflected the close link between the needs of the government and the needs of film makers (Jones 1981:200).[3] Speaking on CBC in 1940 he described the Film Board as "the eyes of Canada, [which] will, through a national use of cinema, see Canada and see it whole – its people and its purposes."

In the fifty years since it was established, the NFB has provided an international model of government financial support for film production (Feist 1990:5). In the first years it tended to select safe rather than contentious issues and remained faithful to its documentary mandate. Pierre Maheu would claim: "The film board is an instrument of colonization; it is a gigantic propaganda machine whose role it is to put the public to sleep and to exhaust the creative drive of the film makers" (Jones 1981:108). The NFB has nevertheless been able to bring together the finest group of filmmakers ever assembled in Canada, and artists like Michel Brault, Gilles Carle, and Denys Arcand, among others, have had an enormous impact on the development of the Canadian film. With maturity, the board's scope broadened significantly. Studio D was dedicated to giving voice to women film makers; more recently, the board has directed resources to artists of Aboriginal and minority communities, continuing to provide "Canadian perspectives on issues of importance to Canadians" and to offer "alternative points of view across the spectrum" (Schwartzberg 1994:S10). Focusing on education, it is pursuing development in children's and young people's programming (Michele d'Auray, NFB Director of Communications and Corporate Affairs, telephone interview 26 March 1994). Production facilities, located in eight major centres, provide service and training facilities for film makers, though Quebec continues to absorb the lion's share of the resources.

Excluded from commercial distribution by the American stranglehold on Canada's movie theatres, the NFB originally took its films into the communities.[4] Later it focused on direct distribution to libraries and the educational market. Distribution remains a major problem. The board is now taking advantage of advances in technology and developing niche markets and, though market penetration still remains limited, sales in Canada outside Quebec have increased 150 percent in the last year. It continues to explore new distribution strategies including television and direct to home and direct to work broadcast capability in partnership with the private sector (Drainie 1994:C3).[5]

The major challenge to the Film Board continues to revolve around its relevancy in an increasingly market-driven environment, especially since many of its productions are also funded by Telefilm and the Canada Council. A current examination of its mandate by an externally appointed evaluator is but one of a string of government commissioned studies of the board. The fact remains, however, that many of the most important Canadian films, most recently Alanis Obomsawin's internationally acclaimed *Kanehsatake: 270 Years of Resistance*, have been Film Board projects or received Film Board support.

The Canada Council

Like the National Gallery, the CBC, and the National Film Board, the inspiration and model for the Canada Council, Canada's principal instrument of government support to artists and arts organizations, was British, and a primary impetus for its creation was the domination of American product in the Canadian market.[6] Claude Bissell has called the Massey-Levesque Commission which recommended the creation of the council "a spectacular farewell to the colonial era in our cultural life" which gave us "the ability to move forward on our own into a period of intense nationalism and pride" (Bissell 1982:21).

When the Massey-Levesque Commission reported in 1951, its recommendations were clear and precise. Its report emphasized the importance of recognizing the artist's role in society and the need to support arts activity through national leadership and to recognize research in the social sciences, the humanities, and the arts. The commissioners were committed to finding new means of supporting the creative experiences of Canadian life. They abhorred the artistic vacuum which was being filled from the U.S. and the mass media of the powerful U.S. conglomerates; they called for infrastructure development that would nurture and protect Canada's best talents, and they saw that only through a coherent national strategy could such goals be achieved (Litt 1991:375–87).[7]

Key words throughout the Massey-Levesque report include *unity*, *identity*, and *access*. Though personally sceptical, in 1957 St Laurent was persuaded to create the Canada Council from windfall death duties representing an original endowment of $50 million. In so doing, St Laurent adhered directly to the Massey Commission's recommendations that the council, the government's principal instrument for funding artists and arts organizations, should be established at arm's length from government.

Though it represents a minute portion of the federal government's approximately $2.9 billion cultural budget, the council has been instrumental in the development of an indigenous professional artistic community in Canada (Statistics Canada 1993).[8] Recognized primarily as a direct funder supporting arts organizations and individual artists, its role in providing services, advising on and developing arts policy through program innovation and implementation, and providing national and international networks is often overlooked. In partnership with provincial governments and agencies, it has been the catalyst for artistic infrastructure development across the country. For artists, its support is the ultimate mark of recognition of achievement. As such, it has been an important agent in encouraging private sector investment in the arts. The parallel gallery system in the visual arts, the Canada Council Art Bank which has placed the work of Canadian artists in government buildings and public spaces across the country and significantly enhanced the appreciation of contemporary Canadian art, and the public lending right for Canadian authors are just a few of the results of Council initiatives.

It is this record of achievement and particularly the council's emphasis on artistic rather than political significance that has made it important to artists and arts organizations across the country. It also led a number of Quebec artists, despite their political reservations and the history of French-Canadian critics' argument that the Massey-Levesque Report was a centralizing document in an area where centralization was expressly forbidden by the constitution, to speak out for the importance of the council and to demand a parallel support system for the arts in Quebec (Bissell 1982:14–15). In fact, the recent constitutional debates on culture generated a small irony. Despite the fact that Quebec politicians have often disparaged the arm's length model of arts funding, arguing that it is an English creation and has no history or validity in French culture, in 1992 the Quebec government announced the creation of an arm's length arts council modelled after the Canada Council.[9] Though Quebec's capitulation to the pressure for the establishment of an arts council was intended to pacify the province's artistic community in order to gain support from that constituency for the government in its bid for the devolution of the cultural portfolio to the province, the artists' position speaks clearly to the continued relevance and importance of the model for the Canadian artistic community.

As an arm's length agency advised by professionals in the arts community, the council's policies and achievements have historically set standards throughout the country. In recent years, while continuing to play a lead role in the development of national policy, the council has become much more of a team player, working with its counterparts across the country to address issues specific to particular place. Its success rests on its ability to keep in close touch with its constituency and remain responsive to the changing environment.

In 1992 the council was confronted with a government-imposed merger intended to bring the functions of the Social Science and Humanities Research Council, the Canada Council, and External Affairs' responsibility for the arts and education under the same umbrella. Though there had long been recognition of the need to develop integrated arts and cultural strategies at the national and international levels, and there would certainly have been significant benefit from a strengthened presence of the cultural sector at the federal level and in the international arena, an enforced marriage in which both parties felt themselves aggrieved and in which the government's only agenda seems to have been a misguided belief that the merger would result in significant cost reductions, was doomed to failure. In June 1993 the legislation was defeated in the Senate.

The first priority for a revitalized council will be a rearticulation of its essential role in Canadian life. The council provides the critical artistic and geographical link that can only be achieved at the federal level. It has played a unique role in research and development, which through training and development of artistic talent, nurturing and support of creation, and facilitation of production, has been a critical component of Canada's artistic and cultural life. Like other national cultural institutions and unlike other federal strategies which support the cultural industries, the council evaluates artistic significance rather than relying on economic impact as the principal criterion for support. The council is positioned to provide the critical linchpin in the new strategies that are developed to address the changing environment and to ensure that artistic values are not lost in the competitive rush.

The National Arts Centre

Of the national cultural agencies, the future of the National Arts Centre is perhaps most difficult to predict. Created as a centennial year project, like many other capital projects, it combines an ambitious and extremely large physical plant with a program mandate that is far from clear. Since its inception administrations have struggled with the contradiction between its mandate as a national cultural institution and its physical location and commitment to serve the Ottawa region.

Over the last few years, program changes effected in the name of cost reduction included the elimination of the centre's production facilities and the reduction of its French and English theatre programs, undermining, many would argue, its unique leadership capability in the production of the best this country has to offer in the performing arts. Seeking a new mandate which would better match its national mandate and overcome the limitations of its physical location in Ottawa, management shifted the centre's focus and to a certain extent its resources from programming and production to strategies for dissemination. First it embarked on a failed attempt to become the centre for the Canadian development of high definition television (HDTV); more recently it competed with the CBC in its bid to develop and operate a cable television specialty arts network.

In shifting the centre's focus from creation and the live arts to electronic distribution, the key issue which required resolution – the role of the performing arts in a high tech world – was never adequately addressed. The 1986 report of the Task Force on the National Arts Centre, the "Hendry Report," made clear that there had to be a partnership which would allow for national dissemination of Canadian productions focusing on "electronic touring," but it did not suggest that the NAC should achieve this at the expense of the live performing arts themselves. In fact certain co-production initiatives undertaken with private sector production companies and CBC, including Carbon 14's *Le Dortoir* (with Rhombus Productions) and Michel Tremblay's *La Maison Suspendue* (with Primemedia), illustrate the potential for successful partnerships in this field, especially if a national arts service is established. The centre has recently begun to reevaluate its strategies, reopening its production facilities in a limited way and increasing its theatre season. At the same time the National Arts Centre Orchestra has found greater support within the institution. But the central issues remain to be addressed.

I could have dealt with other national cultural institutions: the museums, the National Library, the Archives, and Telefilm, for example. But the institutions I have discussed represent the key elements in federal government policy in the arts sector. The creations of patriarchal governments concerned with strengthening national sentiment, each has been accused of elitism and had its current relevance questioned. Regional resentment of central Canadian institutions is a historical fact, as is the perception of inequities between the urban centres and the "hinterland"; in the case of the Film Board, the allocation of resources obviously favours Quebec; in all cases, Aboriginal artists have historically, and with legitimacy, felt that these institutions did not represent them or their interests; with some variation, the same is the case for a large percentage of Canada's culturally diverse artists. Faced with an environment of diminished government support and an increasing emphasis on economic as opposed to artistic and cultural bottom lines, each institution faces critical challenges from government, the public, and its own constituency, as it struggles to restructure. The second part of this paper will focus on that environment and its implications.

THE RESTRUCTURING DISCOURSE: FEDERAL/PROVINCIAL POLITICS

If we are to address the environmental factors affecting the future of cultural institutions in a new Canada, we should begin with the importance of federal-provincial relations. Despite an overwhelming shift in the western world toward decentralized arts and culture delivery service (a pattern which is reflected in the Canadian experience), no province other than Quebec argued during the Charlottetown discussions that the jurisdiction for culture should devolve exclusively to the provinces (or, in line with Quebec's constitutional position, that it already resided there).

During those debates, provincial arts constituencies argued the need for the leadership role that national cultural institutions can and must play, for multi-level government funding, and for the importance of artistically based decisions in the granting process. Artists in every part of English Canada argued that, if their identity began with particular place and ultimately led them to participation in the international arena, they saw themselves as Canadian and Canadian artists from across the country as their peers. Voicing the feelings of many, a *Toronto Star* editorial questioned whether a transfer of powers would benefit "ordinary Canadians" who consume cultural programming. The answer was clear. "Not if artists find themselves pigeonholed by provincial interests and further estranged from national interests" (*Toronto Star* 1992:A18). Even the regularly argued case for additional resources and provincial claims for a larger share of the federal pie were subdued in face of the perceived threat of devolution.

Nor was the artistic community alone in arguing the case for national cultural institutions. The Ontario government took a lead role in insisting on shared responsibility in the cultural sector, speaking particularly to the roles of the national cultural institutions. Though Keith Spicer's *Report of the Citizen's Forum on the Future of Canada's Constitution* contained limited direct reference to the question of cultural responsibility in a renewed Canada, the public did speak to the importance of sustaining national institutions. "Participants frequently and loudly told us they were dismayed at the government's perceived weakening of national institutions and symbols. This complaint ran the gamut from VIA Rail (for many outside Quebec) to the CBC (for many in Quebec, English speaking artists, intellectuals, many rural Canadians, Aboriginal peoples and people wanting news from a national perspective)."

The apparent ambiguity of the Charlottetown Accord which gave the provincial legislatures exclusive responsibility for culture "in the province" but then proceeded to assert a continued role for Ottawa with respect to "national cultural matters, including national cultural institutions" reflects the complexity of the situation. As Frye (1980) has pointed out, Canadian culture, like all culture, is regional; so, for the most part, is the infrastructure that supports it. However, the strength of that infrastructure varies dramatically, particularly outside the metropolitan centres. And while facilities are relatively widespread, strong institutions do not exist in large numbers. The need for leadership and concerted national strategies in the globalized environment make a provincial cultural head of power extremely problematic. In all the debates on this issue outside Quebec, there was clear recognition of Parliament's role with respect to national institutions and activities of a national or international nature. Any new federal state will find, as the European Community has discovered, that though culture is a regional and even local matter, there is likely to be an enhanced need for instruments of cultural policy and institutions with national and international mandates.

DEVOLUTION OR DECENTRALIZATION?

When the Massey-Levesque Commission reported out 1951, it described Canada as a cultural wasteland: "In a large part of Canada the schools [were] accepting tacit direction from New York they would not think of taking from Ottawa." One of the briefs they received reported that "out of thirty-four children in a Grade VIII class in a Canadian school, nineteen knew all about the significance of July 4 and only seven could explain that of July 1"(Royal Commission 1951:5–16). Few books were published in Canada, there were only four professional theatre companies, professional ballet was a fledgling operation (there was no modern dance company), and the Canadian feature film did not really exist. Hollywood controlled Canadian movie theatres, and American touring companies dominated Canadian performing arts venues. The U.S. Carnegie Foundation was a principal benefactor of Canadian libraries and university programs, and the Guggenheim Foundation provided virtually the only significant source of funding support for artists in Canada. Seven years later the Canada Council was established. Since then, the council, with its provincial counterparts, has been a key player in dramatically changing the picture.

The objectives of public funding in Canada have historically resulted in a decentralized production system. Unwieldy perhaps, if the economic bottom line is the only criterion for measuring success, this approach has been relatively successful in achieving broad national opportunities for the creation of cultural products (though it has been less successful in disseminating the results on a national basis – another key goal of federal policy). This decentralization reflects, as Frye (1980) suggested, a defining characteristic of Canadian culture, the recognition of the diversity of this country. Regional publishing houses and film co-ops, for example, have worked according to their particular place and circumstances, often evolving their own aesthetic and style. Far from a national strategy resulting in the creation of state approved national art forms, what is unique about Canada is its regional diversity – a diversity sustained through a coherent, though seldom clearly articulated and always tension-provoking, national strategy which has focused on decentralization. This decentralization is both Canada's strength and its Achilles' heel at a time when multi-national industries are increasingly determining that products must have broad international appeal, often requiring the elimination of the local and the specific. Without the combination of the Canada Council, the CBC, and the National Film Board, it is unlikely that the distinctive regional voices of this country will be maintained in English Canada.

Canada's problems have been and remain those of scale, market, and distribution. The national cultural agencies have in some measure provided resources and networks to address these issues through solutions that would have been, and will remain, impossible if left to the provinces or territories alone. Canada's record for reinvesting profits (except as required by CRTC) into cultural research and development is virtually non-existent. It has been the public sector institutions which have compensated, at least minimally, for the structural and economic domination of the Americans over every aspect of our communications network.

THE CURRENT TRADE ENVIRONMENT: BEING CANADIAN IN A GLOBALIZED WORLD

There are common threads in this history. The political agenda has remained constant and, one might add, critical to Canada's future and the key rationale for federal intervention in the cultural domain. The goals have been the cultivation of Canadian cultural identity, nation building, national unity, and cultural defence. The historic threat of Americanization is, if anything, enhanced in the globalized universe; Canada cannot change its geographic location, and the u.s. has a market which is greater than ten times that of Canada (Coleman 1988:96). (Elsewhere in this book, Mary Jane Miller refers to American popular culture's growing domination of the European market – a phenomenon the Europeans have labelled "Canadianization".) Discussing Canadian communications policy several years ago, former CBC president Al Johnson described Canadian policy as "Americanization by importation, by privatization and by fiscal deprivation" (Peers 1988:27). Today the overall extent of Canadian cultural domination by foreign-produced (principally u.s.) programs is effectively unparalleled among the OECD nations. Yet Keith Spicer has predicted: "Full pick and pay, beyond a few rock bottom, common national services can come only after this decade, but I believe it must come" (Spicer 1994:5). In such an environment, he has suggested, Canadian content regulations have a limited lifetime.[10] Tax incentives, like the Directors' Guild of Canada's venture capital mutual fund, announced in January 1994 to encourage investment in the Canadian film industry, represent one method of addressing this problem. These will be parallelled by other such investment and loan strategies. The establishment of a Crown foundation to provide preferred tax advantages for donations to the arts and cultural sector offers another potential strategy to enhance contributions to the sector, though the creation of such an instrument seems a long way off for a heavily indebted government. But without a coherent base of opportunities for artistic development across the nation, these schemes will have little in which to invest. History has proved that, through sheer numbers alone, American production will overwhelm Canadian.[11] Nor will the use of new lower-cost systems of production change the balance: greater integration of u.s. and Canadian production systems under free trade is likely to reinforce the predominance of u.s. type production systems and inhibit experimentation (Parker 1988:82).

In the case of film, Canada will once again have to decide whether it can afford to make films that are specifically Canadian in content, and whether it should be providing training and research and development opportunities for film makers and for the film industry. With five major Canadian film companies having recently gone public the larger question is can we afford not to. Bronwyn Drainie reports that, at a 1994 conference on Canadian film, Michael MacMillan of Atlantis Film, "spoke to the fears of many producers ... when he urged continued government support, especially for movies that tell specifically Canadian stories." In the world of international deals, he noted "the homogenization of program content is inevitable. We're not supposed to talk about that but it's happening, and only government support will ensure that our own stories keep getting told."(Drainie 1994:C3). Only through artistic creation will Canadian culture survive in the 500 channel universe; only through support of our creators will the product be there that can respond to the challenge.

The current restructuring in the private sector and the as yet undetermined impact of international trade agreements suggest that unless Canada is vigilant about its right to intervene in the cultural sector and to foster the unique voices that represent the cultures and the regions of this country, we may find ourselves in a vastly diminished artistic and cultural environment. If the free trade agreements do in fact limit Canada's ability to introduce new initiatives in the cultural field, they should not prevent the full utilization of current institutions in the support of the arts. Thus national cultural institutions represent the most viable instruments of support for artistic creation and policy development.

PUBLIC/PRIVATE: THE END OF THE WELFARE STATE

In 1986 the "Bovey Report," *Funding the Arts to the Year 2000*, calling for partnerships in support of the arts in Canada, outlined the roles of both the private and public sectors. Though the report emphasized the need for greater support from the private sector, it stressed the fact that in Canada all levels of government must continue to assume significant responsibility for funding the arts. Its conclusions clearly refute the neo-liberal belief that responsibility for arts and culture can eventually be shifted from government to the private sector.

Those who argue that commercial enterprises in the cultural sector are already self-supporting have seldom fully examined the situation. A false distinction has been created which has identified private-sector cultural production with a market-driven approach and public-sector cultural production with a policy-driven approach (Parker, Hutcheson, and Crawley 1988:xiii). As the Bovey commissioners clearly realized, the two are inter-related, and in Canada they have always worked in a symbiotic relationship. The private sector in the cultural industries in Canada has succeeded principally on the basis of public policy initiatives – initiatives intimately tied to the function of the national cultural institutions. (CRTC's quota guidelines, CBC's mandate to reflect Canada to Canadians and to contribute to the development of Canadian talent and culture, Telefilm's funds for film and broadcast production, and the Canada Council's publishing program are a few of the most obvious examples.) Support to individual artists through the Canada Council, Telefilm, and the National Film Board, like scientific grants in the academic community, provides a significant amount of the research and development upon which these industries are based. It is highly naïve to suggest that "industry" can be hived off to become fully self-supporting without the public infrastructure for support of training and creation that currently exists or that the arts will flourish in Canada without public support and a public-sector strategy.[12]

THE NEW CANADA: THE CHANGING DEMOGRAPHICS

On a 16 January 1994 CBC broadcast, Canadians of South African, East Indian, Macedonian, Ukrainian, and Chinese backgrounds discussed the immigrant experience in Canada. For many of them, especially the first generation, their focus was primarily on their homelands and the resolution of their problems in relationship to those lands. Others discussed the anxiety of trying to resolve the legacy of the cultural history they, their parents, or their grandparents had brought with them when they immigrated to Canada.

The discussion included not one mention of the "traditional" symbols of Canadian identity: the landscape and geography, the flag, the maple leaf, the Group of Seven. Nor were there references to Canada's colonial identity or the threat of American domination. Each person interviewed saw Canada as a place to work through earlier experiences and to create a future; their common vision was based on the country and its promise. The discussion pointed to the evolving truths about who we are and the need for new mythologies – mythologies the artists among them will help to create.

Canadian immigration patterns have historically brought people of widely disparate experience to a not always welcoming land. Regional and cultural disparities have always been present. The myth that there ever was or can be a single overriding narrative with the authority to speak for all Canadians has been dispelled in the postmodern era. The notions of national unity and national identity are often seen as Foucauldian strategies that states have historically designed to impose control. These terms and "cultural nationalism," which has been chiefly used to suggest that Canadians should have control over their own culture, have elicited suspicion that the state's purpose is to homogenize the different cultural traditions which represent the Canadian experience. In recent years, the key problem for national cultural institutions has been to ensure that barriers to full participation are eliminated and access provided to the plurality of our society and its multiple voices, ensuring that the evolving paradigm of what it means to be Canadian includes the broad range of regional and cultural experience.

Northrop Frye's definition of Canada may be reframed in a different voice – that of Marlene Nourbese Philip or Alanis Obamsawin in their contestation of official history and the dominant narrative. What are the colours of here? How do we make ourselves *here?* How do we understand histories *between* communities? If the search for identity remains the goal, collective belonging remains the challenge of national identity – an identity constructed through a sense of individual belonging, of understanding of difference as well as similarity, and through a sense of community – the capacity of the national institutions to reflect Canadians to Canadians.

THE NEW TECHNOLOGIES

David Ellis suggests that as space and time are globalized, the shape of human community is not entirely altered; the local play of substantive desire remains, and the utopian quest is not abandoned. If Canadians have come to terms with, or at least accepted, their position in a globalized world they have not, I would argue, accepted the thesis that this implies homogenization. For Canada the overriding factor that will determine the future will be the ability to deliver Canadian content. It is only through national strategies that we, as Canadians, have any hope of intervening to control the impact of the 500 channel universe and the main method left to us is to ensure a significantly increased capacity for creation.

Thus – though it might seem sensible to suggest that in an age of globalization, dominated throughout the western world by policies of diminished government intervention, deficit reduction and decentralization, federal strategies in the arts and cultural are anachronisms and will eventually disappear – I would argue that the need for distinctly Canadian creation and programming, especially in the dramatically altered environment brought about by new technologies, will demand a strengthened role for national cultural agencies.

CONCLUSION: A COHERENT STRATEGY FOR THE FUTURE

In this paper I have argued that, whatever the configuration of Canada in the future, national institutions will play a central role in the evolution of federal cultural policy. Alterations to the state, whether through asymmetrical federalism or the departure of Quebec, would enhance the need for national cultural institutions for both symbolic and very practical reasons. National strategies are required to maintain, within Canada, a consistent core of highly qualified artists, allowing Canada to fully participate globally.[13] Moreover, if free trade agreements have closed off options for new strategies to sustain cultural development, they do not limit government's ability to support culture through existing institutions. The challenge, however, is great and will require continued adjustments and restructuring within the institutions and a new level of cooperation and collaboration among them. What is required is a consistent approach as to how cultural creation can be stimulated and risk-taking assured in this new universe.

The recent constitutional discussions and the Charlottetown Accord have clearly indicated English Canada's commitment to maintaining a federal role in culture and the belief in the continued relevance of national cultural institutions. Advisory task forces, parliamentary committees, and civil servants working in the arts and culture field have echoed the arts community and the cultural industries in their commitment to the national institutions and in the repeated call for a coherent policy in the cultural sector. That goal is far from being realized. The list of commissioned reports and unaddressed recommendations is legion. As recently as 1992, *The Ties That Bind*, an all-party parliamentary committee report which examined the impact of constitutional proposals on the arts and was very much aware of public consensus outside Quebec on the subject, argued that culture is intrinsic to our sense of nationhood, to our shared identity, to our human spirit, and to our economic prosperity; the report also restated the importance of the national institutions.

My real concern lies less in the fear that the provinces, other than Quebec, will opt out of national policies, claiming the jurisdiction for themselves, than that governments will continue to address every situation in isolation or to so diminish their support to the national institutions as to destroy their effectiveness.

The 1993 creation of the Department of Canadian Heritage, which at the same time that it integrated the areas of multi-culturalism and sport into the cultural portfolio discarded communications, reflects the fact that a clear vision and strategy for cultural policy has not been identified. There is a critical need to reassess the strategy of separating culture and technology and of isolating issues of content and carrier. The Liberals' statements on the importance of the arts and culture and of the national cultural institutions notwithstanding, there is little evidence of a coherent approach in the sector or understanding of the domino effect of decisions that are taken.[14]

While this chapter has not specifically addressed the issue of finances, a significant aspect of the federal government's role lies in its spending power. As government moves generally to diminish its involvement and withdraw from certain sectors, the cultural sector appears exceedingly vulnerable. While there is a clear recognition that new strategies are required to meet the changing environment, it is possible that the pattern of continued reduction in spending, combined with the absence of a coherent overview of the role the institutions can play, may ultimately undermine their ability to function effectively.

As we face a global future which links us to every part of the world through instantaneous communication and in which a new generation of information is added every several years, there is growing awareness of the importance of the local, the human need for community and for belonging (the context within which the individual can see the world and identify), and the need to communicate our experiences to each other. Northrop Frye's insistence on the regional nature of Canadian experience should be updated by Robert Lepage's *Tectonic Plates* and his images of shifting and sometimes conflicting cultural realities. In the transnational, transcultural world of the future, the search for identity will remain an intensely desired objective, and the places where people find themselves and their lives reflected will be crucial to a stable environment. Canada's national cultural institutions are essential elements in any strategy to achieve these goals.

NOTES

1 Boggs writes that the National Gallery of Canada is the earliest national arts institution founded with a specific obligation to the contemporary art of its own land. In 1979, 79 percent of its collection was Canadian.

2 Grierson remembered that the prime minister said, "Wouldn't it be a great pity if Canada were to lose her sense of dependence on the Mother Country only to fall into a sense of dependence on ... our good neighbour to the south?"

3 Ibid, 12. Quotes Forsyth Hardy, ed., *Grierson on Documentary* (London: Faber and Faber 1966), Postscript.

4 It was originally suggested that American film distributors reinvest one quarter of their Canadian profits and distribute 40 to 50 NFB shorts a year, though this was never achieved.

5 Interview with Michele d'Auray, NFB, 26 March 1994. Drainie notes that NFB distribution currently includes Newsworld, Vision, TVO, the Movie Network, CBC, and Access Alberta.

6 Concern about Americanization was rampant in the submissions to the Massey Commission. Cultural organizations which appeared before

the commission across the country inexorably blamed American cultural imperialism for Canada's problems in developing its own art.

7 Litt deals in depth with the fears of American mass culture that dominated the discussion at this time and the perceptions of Americanization which preoccupied the cultural community in post-war Canada.

8 The total federal government expenditures were $2.889.228,000. The Canada Council's government allocation, which included UNESCO and the Public Lending Right, was $106,249,000.

9 Less surprising, in January 1994, an advisory committee struck by B.C.'s former Minister of Culture, Darlene Mazari, urged the provincial government to set up an arm's length arts council for the province. A Nova Scotia provincial advisory committee made a similar recommendation in the 1990 "Terris Report."

10 I do not agree with Spicer. While it will not be possible to regulate direct to home broadcast and telephone delivered pay for view in the way that is currently done, the possibility for general content requirements in terms of inventory and of commitment to the creation of Canadian content can be regulated.

11 The 1992 Liberal Party Cultural Policy document rearticulated the findings published in the federal government's 1987 discussion paper *Vital Links*, pointing out that in sound recording, "Canadian firms produce 72 percent of Canadian recordings. Twelve foreign firms produce only 28 percent of Canadian albums, yet account for 89 percent of total revenues derived from the sale of recordings in Canada; in publishing: Canadian firms publish about 78 percent of the Canadian titles. Foreign subsidiaries publish only about 22 percent of Canadian titles, yet earn 61 percent of total industry revenues; in film: Canadian companies distribute 95 percent of Canadian films. Although foreign companies – generally the Hollywood majors – generate about 90 percent of the nearly $1 billion in distribution revenues from Canada's film and video market, revenues from the distribution of Canadian films account for less than 1 percent of all the revenues earned in Canada by foreign firms. In broadcasting, Canadian businesses own and control all broadcasting and cable companies by law in Canada. And, Canadian content regulations of the CRTC ensure Canadian programs are carried on radio and television."

12 The government's *Vital Links* (1987) discussion paper illustrates the intricacy of the situation. If CBC radio has fulfilled the goal of providing local and national services for Canadians, television, particularly English television, remains dominated by foreign (read American) programming which represents three quarters of prime time viewing (48 percent of French TV programs in prime time are foreign in origin).

13 Initiatives such as those developed through the partnership of Telefilm, the NFB, and the CBC Development Fund, which in 1988–89 spent $203 mil-

lion (one of the highest levels of support in the world), offer examples of cooperative strategies required in the future. Such strategies will increasingly include federal and provincial funds; revenues from sales, advertising and royalty, patent and other copyright revenues; and private Canadian investment and foreign investment flows.

14 The recent sale of Ginn Publishing to U.S. entertainment conglomerate, Paramount Communications, offers ample evidence of this fact.

BIBLIOGRAPHY

Atwood, Margaret. 1972. *Survival.* Toronto: Anansi.

Bissell, Claude. 1982. "Massey Report and Canadian Culture." The 1982 John Porter Memorial Lecture. Ottawa: Carlton University.

Boggs, Jean Sutherland. 1980. *Ten Decades of Service, The National Gallery of Canada.* Ottawa: National Gallery of Canada.

Canadian Broadcasting Corporation. 1990. *Mission, Values, Goals and Objectives* (October). Toronto: CBC.

Coleman, John Traves. 1988. "Canadian Television: A Broadcaster's Perspective." *The Strategy of Canadian Culture in the 21st Century.* Toronto: TOPCAT Communications.

Cuff, John Haslett. 1994. "Some burning questions about the CBC." *The Globe and Mail* (8 February):A12.

Drainie, Bronwen. 1994. "Canadian filmmakers want it both ways for good reason." *Globe and Mail,* 12 February, C3.

Feist, Andrew. 1990. "Canada." *Cultural Trends 1990 Issue 5.* London: Policy Studies Institute.

Finestone, Sheila. 1992. "A Canadian Cultural Policy: Discussion Paper." 11 pp. Liberal Party position paper. March.

Frye, Northrop. 1980. "Insight." *The Toronto Star* (28 June): B1, 4.

Jones, D.B. 1981. *Movies and Memoranda: An Interpretive History of the NFB.* Ottawa: Canadian Film Institute.

Katz, Milton J., and Richard Cummings. 1987. *The Patron State: Government and the Arts in Europe, North America and Japan.* Oxford: Oxford University Press.

Kelly, Keith. 1991. *Why is Federal Responsibility for Culture an Issue?* Ottawa: Canadian Conference of the Arts.

Litt, Paul. 1991. "The Massey Commission, Americanization and Canadian Cultural Nationalism." *Queen's Quarterly* 98/29 (Summer):375–87.

National Gallery of Canada. *Meetings of the Board of Trustees.* vol. 1:102. Ottawa.

Parker, Ian. 1988. *The Strategy of Canadian Culture in the 21st Century.* Toronto: TOPCAT Communications.

– John Hutcheson, and Patrick Crawley. 1988."Introduction." *The Strategy of Canadian Culture in the 21st Century.* Toronto: TOPCAT Communications.

Peers, Frank W. 1988. "Public Policy Meets Market Forces in Canadian Broadcasting." *The Strategy of Canadian Culture in the 21st Century*. Toronto: TOPCAT Communications.

Reid, Dennis. 1979. *Our Own Country Canada*. Ottawa: The National Gallery of Canada.

Royal Commission on National Development in the Arts, Letters and Sciences, 1949–1951. 1951. Ottawa: King's Printer.

Schuster, J.M.D. 1987. "Making Compromises to Make Comparisons in Cross-National Arts Policy Research." *Journal of Cultural Economics* 11, no. 2 (December).

– 1990. *Cultural Trends 1990*. Issue 5. London: Policy Studies Institute.

Schwartzberg, Shlomo. 1994. "NFB sets new goals within a diminished budget." *Financial Post* 12 February, s10.

Spicer, Keith. 1993. "Broadcasting regulation: is it obsolete?" *Globe and Mail*, 8 June.

Statistics Canada. 1993. "Government Expenditures on Culture in Canada 1982–83 to 1986–87." Catalogue 87–206, Ottawa, Table 27 (a) *Canadian Government Support to Culture: Total Federal Expenditure by Function 1984–85 to 1990–91*.

Task Force on the National Arts Centre. 1986. *Report*. Ottawa: Queen's Printer.

"Time Out! A Reality Check on the Electronic Marketplace." 1994. Notes for an address by Keith Spicer, Chair, Canadian Radio-television and Telecommunications Commission, at the Annual Convention and CABLEXPO of the Canadian Cable Television Association, Montreal, 16 May.

Toronto Star. 1992. "Canadian Culture and National Unity." 26 May, A18.

Winsor, Hugh. 1994. "Debate over CBC's future a war of rhetoric." *The Globe and Mail*, 13 April, A4.

9 Making Canada in the 1990s: Film, Culture, and Industry

TED MAGDER

Spring 1994: As Hollywood revellers recover from the afterglow of another mega-moment in the history of Oscar, Quebec film director Denys Arcand is in London, England, a guest of the British Film Institute's and National Film Theatre's month-long salute to contemporary Canadian cinema. The head of programming at the National Film Theatre in London comments that the diversity of Canadian filmmaking is "fascinating. Not much is mainstream, and that, I find, is interesting. The variety. A movie like *I've Heard the Mermaids Singing* has got a gay community edge to it. Films like *Masala*, reached different ethnics here"(in Goddard 1994:B1). Arcand's new film, *Love and Human Remains*, is about to open in Toronto. It is his first feature film shot in English, and he has started to work on his second English-language feature, a one-picture deal with Alliance Communications Corporation, Canada's leading private producer and distributor of television programs and feature films. Also opening in Toronto, *D2 The Mighty Ducks*, Walt Disney's latest attempt to "synergise" its investment in a National Hockey League franchise and stoke the flames of Yankee pride. In this sequel to *Mighty Ducks*, a collection of "ringers" from around the United States join the team's Minnesota regulars and defy the odds to win an international goodwill tournament in California. Since the Soviets no longer constitute a threat, and since a team of slapshooting Arabs is beyond even Hollywood's sense of the believable, Team U.S.A. takes on a rough and tumble squad of Nordic trash from Iceland in the grand finale (a newspaper headline informs us that the Canadian contingent has been ousted by Team U.S.A. in a preliminary round). Wayne Gretzky makes a cameo appearance and there is a bit part for Canadian actor Jan Rubes. The Ducks win at the box-office too. In its first weekend of release in North America, *D2* pulls in $10.5 million, edging out *Naked Gun 33 1/3: The Final Insult*, starring Canadian-born actor Leslie Nielsen, which takes in about $8 million. (For all of 1993, the Canadian box-office total for the ten top-grossing Canadian feature films was a little less than $5 million; see Table 1, pg. 169). At the Cannes Film Festival, Atom Egoyan's *Exotica* becomes the first English-language Canadian feature film to garner the coveted International Critics' Prize.

Much has changed since the federal government's Canadian Film Development Corporation (CFDC), now Telefilm Canada, opened its doors in 1968 with a mandate to "foster and promote the development of a feature film industry in Canada" (Canada 1967; see Magder 1993: chapter 7). While hockey has become a California pastime, Canada has become Hollywood North. Outside Los Angeles, Toronto and Vancouver together constitute the second largest North American production centre for English-language feature films and television programs. In some recent years the production activity in Toronto alone has outpaced that in New York. According to Martin Knelman, "Canada's TV programming industry has grown into a $300 million-a-year-plus business, and made Canada the second largest exporter of TV programs in the world" (Knelman 1994:63). For a country that was in the backwaters of feature film and television production two decades ago, this is no small accomplishment.

This success, as measured in terms of dollar values and production activity, is tempered by some sobering facts about the state of feature filmmaking in Canada. Canadian feature films have only a tenuous connection with Canadian audiences; roughly five percent of annual screen time is allocated to the exhibition of Canadian films, and most English Canadians would have a hard time naming more than a handful of Canadian films. Moreover, without government support programs, very few Canadian feature films would be made. At Cannes, Egoyan himself made a point of thanking "Canada for letting me make *Exotica*" (*Globe and Mail* 1994c:C1). Most Canadian feature filmmakers are equally indebted to the largesse of the Canadian state. The moniker Hollywood North thus poses a quandary. If it is meant to imply that the Canadian feature film industry is now a stable and successful private commercial enterprise, it is misleading; it is even more unsuitable if it is meant to imply that Canadian feature films have come to resemble, in narrative form and content, Hollywood films. The Canadian feature film industry continues to exist from hand to mouth, unable to break free of its dependence upon government funding; moreover, Canadian cinema is still very much a cinema of the margins, the periphery, the underground, an "alternative" to Hollywood's over-arching and over-bearing definition of the medium. "Hollywood North" is far more appropriate as a description of Canada's television production industry. Companies like Alliance, Atlantis, Paragon, and Nelvana now hold significant positions in the international marketplace for television programs. By contrast Canadian feature filmmaking is still – in economic terms – something of a cottage industry. In cultural terms it would be hard to argue that Canadian feature films have played a formative role in representing Canada to Canadians, especially in English Canada.

THE STATE OF FUNDING

Year after year, Telefilm Canada, like the CFDC before it, has attempted to reconcile two principle objectives: first, to support the establishment and growth of a stable, private feature film (and, since 1983, television) production industry; and second, to support feature films and television projects that contribute to the articulation of Canadian cultural life. From the outset the CFDC was adamant that the first objective drove the second, and in the late 1960s it moved quickly to distinguish itself from the National Film Board of Canada (NFB). If the NFB was to "interpret Canada to Canadians," the CFDC was more a "specialized bank." As Georges Emile Lapalme, first CFDC chair, argued: "We are not filmmakers. We are just investing money and making loans ... If we were to judge our scripts from an intellectual and cultural point of view we would not be a bank anymore" (Magder 1993:133–4). The tension between film-as-culture and film-as-business would become the fulcrum around which CFDC policies were reviewed, debated, and altered. The artistic or critical success of feature films produced with the support of the CFDC did not often coincide with commercial success, and after the well-documented trials and tribulations of the tax-shelter boom of the late seventies, it appeared as if a stable, private industry in feature film production was an unrealistic objective.

In the work leading to the establishment of the CFDC, cabinet had been warned that the system of film distribution in Canada was controlled by the major Hollywood distributors through a series of long-standing business arrangements with Canada's exhibition chains (Magder 1993; Pendakur 1990). Canadian-made films would have a hard time breaking into the loop of theatrical distribution and exhibition, and the Hollywood majors would continue to repatriate the lion's share of box-office receipts. Without reasonable access to Canadian theatres, the Canadian feature film industry would remain hopelessly under capitalized. Throughout the 70s and into the 80s, secretaries of state, and then ministers of communication, raised the issue and threatened to reduce Hollywood's lock on screen time and box-office receipts in Canada. The most recent, and most notable, attempt came in the late 1980s, when the Progressive Conservatives introduced the Film Products Importation Act. The act died a thousand deaths, the victim of Hollywood's lobby efforts in the u.s. and Canada, one of the quid pro quos for the passage of the Canada-United States Free Trade Agreement in 1989[1].

While much attention throughout the 1980s focused on the issue of film distribution, a more significant confluence of events was transforming the marketplace for television programs and the structure and practices of the private production industry in Canada. In 1984 the Government of Canada introduced a new source of funding, the Canadian Broadcast Program Development Fund. It was designed specifically to promote the production of private and independent Canadian television programming. In 1992–93 Telefilm committed $66.2 million under the Broadcast Fund in the form of advances and investments to over 450 hours of television programming (Telefilm Canada 1993a:15). Because of Canadian content regulations, television broadcasting in Canada was (and is) a protected market. The fund also coincided with a staggering growth in new television services the world over, the first wave of the much ballyhooed "500 channel universe." In Canada the number of channels licensed by the Canadian Radio-televsion and Telecommunications Commission (CRTC) went from 87 in 1976 to 146 in 1991 (the expansion coming primarily in terms of pay-TV and specialty cable services). In Europe during the 1980s, over 60 private broadcasters began operations (Atlantis 1993:8–9). In the United States, the age of network dominance was coming to an end, as a wide range of new cable-delivered television services cut sharply into the conventional networks' (ABC, CBS, NBC) share of the viewing audience. Put simply, the new services increased the overall demand for television product; because of increased audience fragmentation and a corresponding drop in advertising revenues, there was also increasing demand for cheaper television programming (*The Economist* 1994). The architects of the Broadcast Fund may not have foreseen these developments, but the introduction of the fund could not have been more timely. It paved the way for independent, private television production in Canada. By the late 1980s the Canadian production industry was poised to become a major supplier of television programming in international markets.

In an attempt to redress the shift toward television production that resulted from the Broadcast Fund, the federal government introduced the Feature Film Fund in July 1986. Also administered by Telefilm Canada, the fund was established with an annual budget of $30 million; in September 1988 Telefilm was granted an additional $11.4 million a year to be administered as an auxiliary fund. As of 1992–93, the Feature Film Fund had four general objectives:

1 To stimulate investment in the production and distribution of high-quality, culturally relevant Canadian fictional feature films, created and produced by the private sector for commercial theatrical release;
2 To reach the broadest possible Canadian audience with these films, through distribution in all media in Canada by both Canadian and foreign sales companies, to ensure maximum exploitation abroad in terms of audiences, high profile and commercial revenues;
3 To assist the Canadian private sector in improving its financial capacity to develop, produce, promote and distribute Canadian fictional feature films, thereby ensuring its ongoing stability and professional and economic development;
4 To permit those working in this sector, in both creative and technical functions, to benefit fully from public funds made available to the Canadian film industry. (Telefilm Canada 1993b:2)[2]

Between 1986 and 1990 Telefilm spent $111 million (or 23 percent of its budget) on the development and production of approximately 24 feature films a year (Groupe Secor 1991). During this period the average production budget was $2.2 million; Telefilm's participation averaged 37 percent per project. By 1990 Telefilm's participation had increased to close to $1 million per project (or 45 percent). Over the four years, Telefilm recouped $3 million or 2.7 percent of its investment; in other words, these investments might be more properly referred to as subsidies. Some of the more notable films during this period: *The Decline of the American Empire* (Arcand), *Jésus de Montréal* (Arcand), *I've Heard the Mermaids Singing* (Rozema), *Life Classes* (MacGillivray), *Dead Ringers* (Cronenberg), and *Speaking Parts* (Egoyan).

The establishment of the Feature Film Fund coincided with the establishment of funding agencies in a number of English-Canadian provinces. The Ontario Film Development Corporation (OFDC) was established in 1986–87. Since 1989 the OFDC has operated the Ontario Film Investment Program, which provides cash rebates to Ontario investors of 15 to 20 percent for television productions and 20 to 25 percent for feature films to a total of $15 million a year. Eligible projects must have significant Canadian content, and at least three quarters of their budgets must be spent in the province. The OFDC also provides investment capital for medium- and low-budget projects. In 1991-92, it funded films including, *The Adjuster* (Egoyan), *Sam and Me* (Mehta), and *Masala* (Krishna).

In 1987–88 British Columbia established BC Film (1993 budget, $5 million), and Manitoba established the Cultural Industries Development Office (1993 budget, $1.5 million). In 1989-90 Saskatchewan established SaskFilm (1993 budget, $1.5 million). The Alberta Motion Picture Development Corporation was established in 1991–92 (1993 budget, $10 million). The provincial agencies have become a significant source of funding, especially in the production of feature films. In 1991 they collectively contributed 14 percent to the production of English feature films. Together with Telefilm's investment, the contribution of government sources to total feature film budgets was roughly 51 percent (Groupe Secor 1991:29).

Beyond the financial role played by government programs, Canadian feature film (and television) production also benefits from co-production treaties between the Government of Canada and 23 other countries, including, Great Britain, France, Australia, Germany, Italy, Israel, Mexico, New Zealand, and Argentina (Hoskins and McFadeyn 1993).[3] The treaties permit producers in two (or more) countries to pool resources and take advantage of legislated benefits (financial incentives, screen-quotas) in each jurisdiction. In 1991, of twenty-seven co-productions certified by Telefilm Canada, nine projects were feature films, of which *Léolo* (France) and *Naked Lunch* (United Kingdom) are the most notable.

Whatever the artistic and critical success of recent Canadian feature films, commercial success remains elusive. The average box-office receipts from a sample of English-language between 1986 and 1990 was just over $200,000 (Groupe Secor 1991). *Dead Ringers* recorded the highest return at the theatres with receipts of $1.4 million, while *I've Heard the Mermaids Singing* and *Bye Bye Blues* (Wheeler) recouped $500,000 each. Table 1 reveals that with respect to English-language features not much has changed since the late 1980s. It is much more likely that English-Canadian audiences will see a Canadian feature film on television than in a theatre. In terms of access to Canadian audiences, the Canadian Broadcasting Corporation's (CBC) introduction of the Cinema Canada series in 1991–92 was a major breakthrough (table 2).

Table 1
1993: Top Ten Canadian Feature Films, Box-Office Receipts (Canada)

La Florida	$1,600,000
Agaguk/Shadow of the Wolf	1,200,000
Matusalem	957,057*
Le Sex Des Etoiles	355,000
Les Amoureuses	152,000
Paris, France	150,000*
Manufacturing Consent	140,000
Thirty-two Short Films about Glenn Gould	110,000*
Calendar	83,000
Twist	75,000

* still being tracked
Source: Playback, 14 February 1994

HOLLYWOOD NORTH: THE TELEVISION VERSION

The inability of Canadian feature films to reach large theatrical audiences in Canada or to recoup production costs has to be measured against the recent success of Canada's independent television production industry. While the CBC recently embarked on a campaign to convince viewers to "go public," that same phrase has become something of a rallying cry for the larger players in the independent television production industry. Since June 1993 six companies – Alliance Communications, Atlantis Communications, Paragon Entertainment, Nelvana, Cinar Films, and Malofilm Communications – have made an initial public offering of shares. These companies have used Canada's partially protected market for television programming, government incentives, and the advantages of a relatively cheap dollar to vault themselves into the international marketplace for television production. This is Hollywood North.

Alliance Communications Corporation

Alliance is Canada's leading fully integrated producer and distributor of television programs and feature films (Alliance 1993; Playback 1993–94). Since 1985 Alliance has produced or co-produced close to 450 hours of television programming, including the series Night Heat (broadcast on CTV), Bordertown (CTV), E.N.G. (CTV), Counterstrike (CTV), and North of 60 (CBC). Night Heat and Bordertown are currently

Table 2
CBC Cinema Canada: Audience Figures (1993–94, to 16 March)

Week	Film Title	Avg Audience (000)	Avg Share %
1*	Hounds of Notre Dame	294	7
2*	Dead Ringers	304	8
3*	Une Histoire Inventée	260	5
4*	Techtonic Plates	154	3
5*	Night Zoo	271	6
6	Clearcut	241	10
7	Forbidden Love	413	14
8	Straight to the Heart	144	5
9	Understanding Bliss	86	3
10	Masala	180	8
11	Company of Strangers	168	6
12	Decline of the American Empire	236	9
13	Grocer's Wife	171	6
14	Mon Oncle Antoine	110	5
15	Paper Wedding	138	6
16	Perfectly Normal	103	4
17	Milk and Honey	345	10
18	Les Ordres	130	4
19	Chain Dance	429	15
20	Events Leading Up to My Death	209	8
21	Le Party	215	10
22	My Financial Career (R)	51	4
23	Jesus of Montreal	183	7
24	Termini Station	254	10
25	Les Bon Débarras	151	5
26	Deep Sleep	194	7

1993–94, Cinema Canada was aired on Thursdays at 11:00 pm on most stations, except in the first five weeks of the season (indicated by *), when most broadcasts occurred on Wednesdays at 10:00 pm.
Share: proportion of total viewing audience during that time period
Source: CBC Audience Research

in strip syndication. E.N.G. has been sold in almost fifty countries, and there are enough episodes of *E.N.G.* (ninety-five) and *Counterstrike* (sixty-six) to exploit the strip syndication market. Alliance has also produced a number of successful movies for television and mini-series, among them: *Family of Strangers*, broadcast on CTV and CBS (where it ranked third among movies for television shown in the United States in the 1992–93 season), and *Woman on the Run: the Lawrencia Bembenek Story*, broadcast on the CanWest Global System and NBC. Alliance is currently developing projects with a variety of U.S. broadcasters and cable networks, including ABC, CBS, Fox, USA Network, Family Channel, Nickelodeon, and MTV. In 1993 Alliance contracted with Harlequin Enterprises (a subsidiary of Torstar) to produce and distribute television movies based upon Harlequin's extensive library, as part of an effort to establish a "romance fiction syndicate" of international broadcasters. The contract called for six movies to be shot in Canada in the summer of 1994 (each with a budget of $3 million), and thirteen more in the near future. In September 1994, *Due South* became the first Canadian-produced series to be broadcast during network prime time in the U.S. (CBS).

Chair and chief executive officer, Robert Lantos, is not shy about the success of his company: "Alliance is a desirable supplier of television programming to pretty well every television scheduler in the world from small countries like Greece to new markets like Korea to the major U.S. networks" (*Globe and Mail* 1994a:B1). Lantos has come a long way from the uncertain days of tax-sheltered feature film productions. Aside from its near frantic production schedule, Alliance operates as a domestic distributor (Alliance Releasing) and international distributor (Alliance International Releasing) of film and television productions, and through a licensed subsidiary (Equicap) it arranges and markets structured financing for the Canadian production industry. The company's revenues have increased annually. In 1989 Alliance reported revenues of $43.6 million on expenses of $41.5 million. At its year end of 31 March 1993, the company had revenues of $132.1 million on expenses of $125.4 million. Cineplex Odeon is one of the company's principal shareholders.

Its initial share offering prospectus notes that although Alliance initially secured the majority of its financing through Canadian sources (producing programming designed to meet the Canadian content requirements of Canadian broadcasters), it has now built a solid foundation in international markets. European broadcasters, in particular, are increasingly interested in programming "with the widest possible appeal, which largely originates in North America" (Alliance 1993:10). Canadian production companies are well situated to supply this market, most especially because of the co-production treaties between Canada and many European countries. Likewise, the United States market has opened to foreign suppliers in two ways: first, the dramatic increase in television services means that there is greater overall demand for programming, especially programming which is cheaper than the conventional Hollywood supply. To the extent that Alliance can offer attractive programming partly financed by Canadian, and in some cases, European sources, it is well situated to be competitive in the new U.S. television marketplace. Second, The downward pressure on the costs of U.S. programming makes Canada an attractive site for location shooting, service productions, and coventures. Alliance, like other Canadian production companies, has benefited considerably from the long-term relative decline of the Canadian dollar. There is little doubt that Alliance sees its future in international sales and services. The story of its growth is a story of internationalization, first into Europe, then into the margins of non-prime-time network programming and the first wave of cable-delivered services in the United States, and now into the mainstream of the prime-time U.S. network market.

Television is not only a lucrative market for Alliance, it is also, relatively speaking, a safe one. Alliance will not normally begin production on a project until 80 percent of the production costs have been covered by a combination of licence fees from television services in the United States and Canada, contributions from co-producers, presales of foreign distribution rights, and government incentives. For the fiscal year ended 31 March 1993, of $81 million spent on program production, approximately $17.3 million or 22 percent was financed through government incentives (Alliance 1993:13). In other words, government equity investments, grants, and tax-abatements play a crucial role in the financial underpinning of Alliance.

Unlike a number of the other major production companies in Canada, Alliance is active in feature film production as well as television programming. In 1991, it produced *Black Robe*, a $12 million Canada-Australia co-production that won six Genies. In 1994 Alliance produced Atom Egoyan's *Exotica*, and Léa Pool's *Mouvements du désir*. These ventures notwithstanding, Alliance is not particularly bullish when it comes to the feature film market. Given Hollywood's dominance over screen time in most of the major markets, Alliance sees itself as producing "specialty films designed for niche markets" (Alliance 1993:14). The financial underpinning of these ventures relies heavily upon government incentives. According to Alliance's prospectus the budget of a recent feature film received approximately 50 percent of its funds from Telefilm and 27 percent of its funds from the Ontario Film Development Corporation (Alliance 1993:14). Alliance payed itself 13 percent to acquire world distribution rights to the film, and the remaining 10 percent was financed by the deferral of fees payable to creative personnel. As long as government agencies continue to subsidize close to 75 percent of the costs of feature film production, Alliance can afford to remain in the film business.

Atlantis Communications

Founded in 1978, Atlantis has concentrated its production activities in television programs, rather than feature films destined for the cinema, for over a decade (Atlantis 1993:4). Atlantis has produced over sixty titles comprising over 600 television programs or more than 400 hours of programming. Some of its more notable series titles include *Neon Rider* (CTV), *Maniac Mansion* (YTV, The Family Channel [U.S.]), and *The Ray Bradbury Theatre* (CanWest Global, The Movie Network, Superchannel, USA Network). In 1993 Atlantis production activities included: *Destiny Ridge* (CanWest Global and ARD [Germany]), *African Skies* (The Family Channel [Canada and the U.S.], Beta Taurus [Germany]), *White Fang* (Baton, M6, and Canal J [France], Beta Taurus), and *Tekwar* (television movies with MCA/Universal [U.S.] and William Shatner's Lemli Productions). *Tekwar* exemplifies the growing independence of Atlantis from Canadian sources of revenue; with Universal as its distributor, *Tekwar* went into production without a committed Canadian broadcaster.

Like Alliance, Atlantis' revenues have showed solid growth since the late 1980s. In 1990, on expenses of $40.8 million, Atlantis brought in revenues of $43.1 million. For 1993, the company forecast revenues of $75.9 million on expenses of $65.5 million (Atlantis 1993:5). Atlantis has also entered into a "strategic relationships" with the U.S.-based Interpublic Group of Companies (IPG) and Freemantle Corporation. IPG is one of the largest advertising organizations in the world, with agencies operating in over 75 companies, including McCann Erickson Worldwide, Lintas: Worldwide, and The Lowe Group. IPG also owns 80 percent of Freemantle International, the world's leading producer of television game shows. Freemantle International is affiliated with Freemantle Corporation, a major international distributor of television programs and now the sub-distributor of Atlantis programs in South America. The relationship with IPG gives Atlantis access to the growing market for "barter" television programming (Atlantis 1993:12).

Atlantis' business plans reveal a company eager to exploit foreign markets and to break free of any dependence upon government financing. Like Alliance, Atlantis will not normally proceed to production unless at least 80 percent of the budget has been covered by third parties. A commitment from broadcasters is key, and as Atlantis' (1993:14) prospectus notes: "Usually a broadcaster will make a non-recourse financial contribution to the development costs, participate in the choice of writer, director, and key actors, and approve the script, budget, schedule, and key production personnel. This active involvement by a broadcaster reflects its significant financial commitment to the program, assists in ensuring that the program will meet the needs of the target audience and enhances the likelihood that the broadcaster will be satisfied with the completed program."

For Atlantis, as for the other major independent Canadian production companies, many of the broadcasters who play this formative role are foreign. In the period between 1990 to 1993, close to 68 percent of the license fee revenue received by Atlantis came from broadcasters and distributors outside Canada. It is little wonder that audiences in Canada have trouble distinguishing Atlantis' productions as "Canadian."

Paragon Entertainment

Established in 1985, Paragon Entertainment is the corporate vehicle of producer Jon Slan, who has spent the last seven years building up Paragon's relationship with u.s. broadcasters from his home and office in Los Angeles. In June of 1993 Paragon was the first of the major Canadian production companies to go public. In 1992 spending on production amounted to $65 million (*Globe and Mail* 1993b:B1). Paragon's recent projects include *Sherlock Holmes Returns* (CBS), *Forever Knight* (CBS), and *Lamb Chop's Play-Along* (PBS). While most of Paragon's projects are produced in Canada, they are typically entended for the u.s. market, either as independent productions or as joint ventures with companies such as MCA, Spelling, and Tristar. As Slan has remarked: "Like other Canadian companies we too realized that there was limit to the growth that we could have as a Canadian company operating solely for Canadian broadcasters" (*Globe and Mail* 1993a:B1). In keeping with Paragon's emphasis on links with the U.S. market, Slan hired Gary Randall, former president of Spelling Television, to become president of Paragon Television u.s., effective August 1993.

Nelvana

In business since 1971, Nelvana is Canada's leading producer of animated television programs and feature films Nelvana's revenue for 1993 was $19 million; the company has forecast revenue $27.7 for 1994 and a profit of $3.6 million (*The Globe and Mail* 1994b:B20). Nelvana's line-up of animated shows include: *Babar* (HBO, CBC, Family Channel), *Care Bears* (ABC, Global, Société Radio Canada), *Tales from* the *Cryptkeeper* (ABC), *Jim Henson's Dog City* (Fox, YTV, Canal Famille), *Eek the Cat* (Fox), and *Cadillacs and Dinosaurs* (CBS). The company has also produced three Care Bear Movies, and the live action series, *The Edison Twins* (CBC, Disney Channel), *T and T* (Global, Tribune Broadcasting), and *The Twenty-Minute Workout* (CITY-TV) (Nelvana 1994: passim). In keeping with the marketing strategy of most U.S. children's programming, Nelvana has entered into master toy licence agreements for *Cadillacs and Dinosaurs* and *Tales from the Cryptkeeper*. In the fall of 1993 Nelvana signed a multi-year project to produce five animated feature films for Paramount Pictures. The first two features began production in the summer 1994; both are budgeted at approximately $20 million (*Playback* 1993:4). Nelvana relies heavily on the U.S. and international market for its success. In 1993, approximately 60 percent of its revenue came from the United States; in total, 88 percent of Nelvana's revenues came from sources outside Canada.

MAKING CANADA: FILMS AND CULTURE

The tenuous commercial footing of feature filmmaking in Canada and its dependence upon government incentives raises these simple questions: Is it worth the cost? What would be lost by transferring most of the government funds now available for the production of Canadian feature films to the production of Canadian television programming which is better able to reach large Canadian audiences and is increasingly successful as an export?

One way to attempt to answer this question is to consider the various rationales behind state support for the production of culture. I can think of three. Easily the most common justification for state support of indigenous cultural activities in Canada is an argument that begins with an analysis of markets and ends with an analysis of culture. In film and television – no less than in book and magazine publishing – the marketplace gives foreign products a sizeable advantage. Foreign products, especially those from the United States, are in a sense dumped into Canada after they have recouped their initial production costs in their home market. They are cheaper than Canadian products, they benefit from a far more effective regime of marketing (which is, in its own way, a function of economies of scale), and Canadians have come to accept them as part of the mainstream of daily cultural life. The evidence here is incontrovertible.

In the face of this evidence governments and academics have drawn the following conclusion: in the long run, foreign dominance of the cultural marketplace causes irreparable damage to national consciousness, to national identity, and ultimately to the continued viability of

Canada as a nation state. As the Royal Commission on National Development in the Arts, Letters and Sciences (the Massey Commission) pithily remarked sometime ago: "Hollywood refashions us in its own image" (Canada 1951:50). The first rationale for state intervention in culture is thus based upon a theory of the role of communications media in the construction of nationhood. Support for Canadian cultural activities is justifiable in terms of their ability to provide the foundations for a national identity, a *common* sense of Canada.

There has been much recent scholarship on the relationship between nation and state. The last 200 or so years suggest that the process of state formation is greatly enhanced by the ability to lay claim to the existence of a nation; no entity seems to have a greater claim to political sovereignty than what has come to be known as the nation state. Nationhood provides legitimacy for statehood. The question is, What makes a nation? Among others, Ernest Gellner has argued that nations and nationalism are not, in and of themselves, organized historical entities. Nations may have historical roots – in language, religion, ethnicity, culture, and so on – but as organized social phenomena they have to be culled and fabricated: "Nations as a natural, God-given way of classifying men [sic], as an inherent ... political destiny, are a myth; nationalism, which sometimes takes preexisting cultures and turns them into nations, sometimes invents them, and often obliterates preexisting cultures; that is a reality"(Gellner 1983:40). Nations take on meaning in relation to the pursuit of an organized political project; they are the product of "invention and social engineering"(Hobsbawm 1990:10). Nations and nationalism are constructions. Nationalism is less about preserving the past (though it will mine the past for useful symbols and myths) than it is about the articulation of a narrative that provides a common emotional bond. As Benedict Anderson puts it, the nation is "an imagined political community" (Anderson 1983:15). This "imagining" is continuous; it works through all the systems of public communication, including the various institutions of the media and education.

Like all political projects, the construction of a nation is open to abuse. One of the particular dangers inherent in the invention of nationhood is associated with the tendency to base nationalism on a politics of exclusion. One of the best ways to articulate a sense of national identity is to highlight and denounce those social characteristics, traits, values, which can be depicted as threats or unwarranted intrusions on the nation-to-be or the nation-that-is. As Hobsbawn puts it: "There is no more effective way of bonding together the disparate sections of a restless people than to unite them against outsiders" (Hobsbawm 1990:91). Ask an English Canadian to define what it means to be Canadian and chances are good that he or she will begin by distinguishing Canadian from American. While such a distinction might work well for establishing allegiances at sporting events, most political scientists and sociologists would regard it as an unruly form of generalization. Still it is a distinction that seems to work for many English Canadians, one that even provides a little glib comfort from time to time. This politics of distinction rarely begins and ends at borders, especially in a country such as Canada, a country with two conquering European "nations," and a country of immigrants. Within Canada the political stakes are higher. The process of constructing a nation or of appealing to the nation as a source of legitimacy can have a ugly face: it can be racist and ethnocentric.

Richard Collins recently took this line of thinking to one of its logical extremes. In a paper that raised hackles among Canadian communications scholars, Collins had the temerity to suggest that the term "national culture" is a "mystifying category error," and that there is no logical reason why "culture and political institutions must be isomorphic" (Collins 1991:225–6). Collins extends this argument in a book-length examination of Canadian broadcasting in which he claims that Canada's very lack of a national identity represents a "pre-echo of a post-national condition" for which it deserves high praise (Collins 1990:xii).[4]

Collins bases many of his theoretical claims on the literature on nationalism outlined above. But he adds an insight that comes from a background in communications that scholars and pundits of nationalism (and the symbolic construction of identity writ large) ignore at their peril. Briefly put it is this: the message sent is not necessarily the message received. In other words the relationship between the symbols and signs and discourses that are about (or are intended to be about) Canada and the attitudes and values that form and reform in the Canadian population is not at all one-directional or clear.[5] Personally, I feel more like a Canadian when I watch violent American television programming then when I watch *Anne of Green Gables*. I simply cannot identify with the gushing Victorian romanticism of Anne and her Gables; to some extent my reaction is that of an uninvited outsider, someone who, at that place and in that time, would not have fit in and probably would not have been allowed to. When I watch cops and robbers shooting it up in Los Angeles or Miami, I am reminded that the rate of urban violence is much less in Toronto than it is in *many* American cities (though there is an ongoing effort to change that view), and this thought is sometimes accompanied by a hint of nationalist smugness.

There are then at least two risks inherent in a strategy that supports the production of Canadian feature films on the basis of national claims. First, there is every possibility that projects will be evaluated in terms of their potential contribution to national identity, and that in this process political and cultural distinctions will be made that exclude or marginalize certain images or narratives about Canada and Canadian life. Second, the strategy is open to a test it may be unable to pass. If it can be shown that exposure to Canadian feature films does not increase sentiments of national identity, why bother?

As I suggested earlier, there are other rationales for state support to the production of Canadian cultural products. One of these is the argument that state support mechanisms of culture contribute to what is increasingly an important economic activity and export industry. From this perspective, government support to feature film production is justified as a business subsidy; in its early days, the CFDC used an "infant industry" argument to establish and to justify its investment priorities. As it turns out, this argument is far more applicable to the private production of television programs in Canada than the production of Canadian feature films. Companies like Alliance, Atlantis, Paragon and Nelvana have flourished as a result of the shift to television production; Canadian feature films play almost no role in their strategic business plans. Canadian feature film production remains a cottage industry. If the objective is profitability in the national or international marketplace, Canadian feature films are a very bad bet.

There is then one final rationale upon which government support to Canadian feature film might be justified. It may sound a little old-fashioned, but like a good Hollywood publicist I will try to give it a new spin. It is this: artistic expression. Not art for art's sake, but art as form of freedom of expression. What is valuable about much of contemporary Canadian feature filmmaking is precisely that it is not of the mainstream, that it does not fit neatly into a project to establish an overarching sense of national identity or unity. As Brenda Longfellow has argued in a very thoughtful essay, in feature films such as *Masala* (Krishna) and *Calender* (Egoyan) the narrative is constructed as a search for an identity in the spaces between official Canadian culture and the experiences of transnationalism, immigration, and exile (Longfellow 1994; *cf. Canadian Journal of Film Studies* 1993:2–3).

CONCLUSION

As we begin again to imagine the very real possibility of a Canada without Quebec, government programs of all types will have to be rethought. Certainly government support of Canadian feature filmmaking has done little to help stem the tide toward Quebec sovereignty; if anything it is arguable that it has helped to promote that tide by providing a national narrative. In English Canada, no such transformation of the collective psyche has taken place. Given the structure and dynamics of the marketplace for film (and television) in English Canada, there is no reason to believe that things would be much different in a Canada without Quebec. It is quite possible that the departure of Quebec would bring renewed attacks upon all federal government programs that support the production of cultural products by Canadians. The Reform Party certainly is no patron of the arts. It is also possible that there will be calls for a renewed attempt to construct (once and for all) an English-Canadian nation, and to do the job right this time.

The ever-present danger is that we downplay the importance of contemporary Canadian cinema because it does not (or cannot) fulfil the objectives some people had hoped it would. It isn't profitable, and it isn't an easy set of civic lessons on that elusive subject known as national identity. Instead this cinema of the margins provides us with a trenchant set of commentaries on the politics and experience of difference. It is a cinema of diversity, far more daring than the narratives of official multiculturalism. To ask Canadian feature filmmakers to do any less would be like asking Canada's literary community to focus its energy on coffee-table odes to the Great White North, heritage histories, and primary school readers. To expect that television programs can explore the same terrain as these feature films, with the same acuity and bravado, is to ignore everything we know about the limited range of narratives that are regarded as suitable for the broadcast audience. The only justifications for support to Canadian feature films is the creative energy of the films themselves and our willingness to support diversity in the realm of public communications.

NOTES

Research for this essay benefited from the financial assistance of York University.

1 Legislation regulating the distribution of feature films was passed in Quebec after intense negotiations with the Motion Picture Association of America. In the long run its most notable consequence was to limit the access of English-Canadian distributors to the Quebec market; the actual market share of Quebec distributors has not increased appreciably (see Magder 1993:222–4).
2 The Auxiliary Fund targets films that "make a significant contribution towards celebrating Canada's diversity," and "films with highly significant creative content" (Telefilm Canada 1993b:2).

3 With the emergence of provincial funding agencies, it is also now possible to arrange inter-provincial co-productions. Arcand's *Love and Human Remains* was originally structured as the first tri-provincial deal, involving Quebec, Ontario, and Alberta (and Telefilm). Alberta ultimately backed away from the project, claiming that not enough of the budget would be spent within its borders.

4 For a review of the responses to Collins see Attallah (1992).

5 For a thoughful review of the recent literature on audience reception see Corner (1991).

BIBLIOGRAPHY

Alliance Communications. 1993. "Prospectus for Initial Public Offering." 20 July.

Anderson, Benedict. 1983. *Imagined Communities: Reflections on the Origin and Spread of Nationalism.* London: Verso.

Atlantis Communications. 1993. "Prospectus for Initial Public Offering." 3 December.

Attallah, Paul. 1992. "Richard Collins and the Debate on Culture and Polity." *Canadian Journal of Communication* 17, no. 2:221–36.

Canada. 1951. Royal Commission on National Development in the Arts, Letters and Sciences. *Report.* Ottawa: Edmond Cloutier.

– 1967. Canadian Film Development Corporation Act. *Statutes of Canada* 1966–67 c.78.

Canadian Journal of Film Studies. 1993. 2, nos. 2–3.

Collins, Richard. 1990. *Culture, Communication, and National Identity: The Case of Canadian Television.* Toronto: University of Toronto Press.

– 1991. "National Culture: A Contradiction in Terms?" *Canadian Journal of Communications* 16, no. 2:225–38.

Corner, John. 1991. "Meaning, Genre and Context: The Problematics of 'Public Knowledge' in the New Audience Studies." In *Mass Media and Society*, ed. James Curran and Michael Gurevitch. London: Edward Arnold.

The Economist. 1994. "A survey of Television: Feeling the Future." 330, no. 7850 (12–18 February).

Gellner, Ernest. 1983. *Nations and Nationalism.* Oxford: Blackwell.

Globe and Mail. 1993a. "u.s. deals thrust Paragon into television spotlight." 11 March.

– 1993b. "Paragon Entertainment set to be publicly traded." 29 May.

– 1994a. "Alliance's top billing unchallenged at home." 17 January.

– 1994b. "Animation company Nelvana set to go public." 19 March.

– 1994c "Egoyan snares critics' prize." 23 May.

Goddard, Peter. 1994. "Denis Arcand carries the can at British fest." *The Toronto Star* 25 March.

Groupe Secor. 1991. "Evaluation of Telefilm Canada Feature Film Fund." 31 May (available from Telefilm Canada).

Hobsbawn, Eric. 1990. *Nations and Nationalism Since 1780: Programme, Myth, and Reality*. Cambridge: Cambridge University Press.

Hoskins, Colin, and Stuart McFadyen. 1993. "Canadian Participation in International Co-productions and Co-Ventures in Television Programming." *Canadian Journal of Communication* 18, no. 2:219–36.

Knelman, Martin. 1994. "Made-for-TV Movies." *Report on Business Magazine*. May:63–70.

Longfellow, Brenda. 1994. "The Crisis of Naming in Canadian Film Studies." Fine Arts Department, Atkinson College, York University.

Magder, Ted. 1993. *Canada's Hollywood: The Canadian State and Feature Films*. Toronto: University of Toronto Press.

Nelvana, Ltd. 1994. "Preliminary Prospectus." 17 March.

Pendakur, Manjunath. 1990. *Canadian Dreams and American Control: The Political Economy of the Canadian Film Industry*. Toronto: Garamond.

Playback. 1993. "Nelvana seals major feature deal with U.S." 8 November.

Playback. 1993–94. various issues.

Telefilm Canada. 1993a. *Annual Report 1992–93*.

– 1993b. *Feature Film Fund: Policies 1992–93*.

10 Will English-Language Television Remain Distinctive? Probably

MARY JANE MILLER

Will English-Canadian television services remain distinctive if Quebec separates from Canada?

The answer to this question depends on the answer to a more basic question which faces all broadcasters, public and private; that is whether the technological changes now in process will erode and eventually destroy television networks and services around the world. In turn the answer to that question will be specific to each culture as it responds to or ignores the challenge. Thus I would like to address the issue of technological change (to use a soap opera analogy, the "backstory"), as well as the specific problems faced by the rest of Canada, to demonstrate how I arrived at a conclusion reflected by the title of this chapter.

I have narrowed the focus from "broadcasting" to television because public radio is justly the fair-haired child of regulators and critics alike. CBC radio is distinctive, of high quality and appeals to a plurality of audiences from Generation X and the sports fans devoted to *The Inside Track* to the motley crew who love *Ideas*, the fans of *Double Exposure, Roots and Wings, Finkelman's 45's*, Clyde Gilmour, Jurgen Goth, Vicky Gabereau, and the inimitable Peter Gzowski (all on AM) as well as the local and regional supper hour and early morning shows. I don't think a case needs to be made for the survival of distinctive local or national public radio. Television is the question mark.

The much heralded environment of the 500 channel universe will be delivered by direct broadcast satellites or cable using fibre optics or, more cheaply, high-quality, unshielded, twisted pair wiring. Some observers – and participants – see this context as the death of distinctive television, not only in Canada, a small "postmodern" nation with marked episodes of cultural amnesia and a relatively short history, but also in countries with distinguished and distinctive regional and national cultures, like France, Italy, or India. Others see wonderful new opportunities for new talent to be offered to a viewer 500 times an hour, twenty-four hours a day, 365 days a year. For example, the CBC sees its purchase of time on a "deathstar" as the chance to sell and deliver current programming abroad without an intermediary. More surprisingly, given the corporation's usual amnesia about its own accomplishments,[1] this decision suggests that the CBC recognizes the quality and distinctive nature of their programs. It is generally agreed, however, that to survive, a network or an independent production company or even a successful program will have to have a "footprint" – that is be distinguishable from the other 499 choices.

DOES THE CBC HAVE A DISTINCTIVE FOOTPRINT?

The idea of a "distinctive footprint" as essential to survival in years to come is widespread. In *Turn Up the Contrast* (Miller 1987) I define that recognizable, although marginalized, "Canadian" voice in the North American context as a taste for ambiguity and ambivalence, a rejection of narrative closure, the demythologizing of individuals and public figures, diversity of subject and mode, regional diversity, and, I would now add, a more consistent focus on Aboriginal concerns.[2] Our successful docudramas, our long tradition of self-reflexive characteristics of visual, verbal, and plot satire and the conventions based on the mode of "realism," which flavours much of our programming, also separate Canadian television and its viewers from American television and its audience. It is the difference between *Degrassi High* and *Beverley Hills 90210*.

More elements in the distinctive trail of footprints of Canadian television are found on basic services or the least expensive tier of cable in this, the most "wired for cable" country in the world. The provinces have set up educational networks which exchange programs among themselves. YTV carries on and expands the over fifty-year tradition of distinctive children's programming by the CBC. Six days a week Vision TV provides a widely eclectic mix of documentary, alternative news, arts and drama, and even collections of music videos with an ethical focus. Both YTV and Vision also offer space for good anthologies like *Inside Stories* or weekly themed evenings of NFB films.

I will try to demonstrate that our television drama has remained distinctive even in the context of major changes in broadcasting over the last decade. Whether it will continue to do so will depend on whether the CBC continues as the designated national broadcaster, whether Telefilm survives as a partner for the CBC, CTV, Global, and independents, and on the proposed new broadcast fund of $300 million designated for children's and drama programming legislated by the CRTC in February 1994. It may also depend on whether a redefined CRTC survives.[3] If any one of those pieces disappear, then in my view only the purely local half hour supper shows will remain and distinctive Canadian television will fade – not "to black" but into "the snow" of permanent outside interference to the signal.

A RAPID OVERVIEW OF PROGRAMMING IN THE LAST FEW YEARS

News and Current Affairs

English Canadians, unlike Americans are addicted to news and current affairs. "In comparison with viewing to television programming as a whole, viewing of Canadian produced programs is skewed in favour of news and public affairs programs ... over half ... in 1988–89" (CBC Research 1991).[4] Our appetite for news and current affairs has evolved into the expectation that news and analysis will be available continuously on a basic cable channel such as Newsworld (Lochead 1991). For the 20 percent of English Canada not yet on cable there is access to basic CBC and CTV, local, national, and international news with some analysis continuously available week nights from 9 PM to midnight. The ratings continue to justify that kind of programming. Contrast CBS, ABC, and NBC with their underfunded half hour of news. Moreover their affiliates and the independent stations make local "news" programs which can be completely unrepresentative of their communities, even in markets as large as Phoenix.[5] More than fifty years after the start of commercial television in the United States, there are still no programs on the four major networks (Fox doesn't bother with news at all) which regularly provide American viewers with in-depth documentaries and analysis of domestic and foreign affairs in prime time.[6]

Children and Family

Canadian programming abroad has been strong for at least two decades. For an earlier generation it was *Adventures in Rainbow Country*,

The Friendly Giant and (still) *Mr Dressup*. Now it is *Fred Penner's Place, The Umbrella Tree*, and *Sharon, Lois and Bram*. The fact is that commercial American networks do not make this kind of programming. We do – with flair, imagination and distinctly Canadian elements.

The CBC also has a well-deserved reputation for successful programming for family viewing. *Fraggle Rock, The Raccoons, Beachcombers, Danger Bay*, and of course the two *Anne of Green Gables* miniseries and the cognate, long-running series *Road to Avonlea* have been seen around the world. The 1980s successes of *Kids of Degrassi, Degrassi Junior High*, and *Degrassi High*, and the strangely allusive fantasy *The Odyssey* had a contemporary appeal to a broad family audience. One distinctive element of Canadian family and children's programming is that it does not resolve all of the dramatic problems in the last five minutes. Ambivalent, open-ended, or even unhappy endings are permitted on *Degrassi* or *The Odyssey*.

Other Services

Vision TV is unique in the world. Surviving on donations and the sale of evangelical programming on weekends it brings us distinctive programming. Some shows are in familiar genres: music videos with ethical themes, alternative news, alternative current affairs, unfamiliar performers. Some represent a particular faith; Ba'hai, Muslim, the charismatic Catholic Kateri movement, *Spirit Connection* from that specifically Canadian institution the United Church. There are profiles of religious figures of all faiths. These are also regular programs on Native issues, the arts and the Third World.

Exports of Canadian-originated concepts are another measure of "distinctive success." Moses Znaimer's Toronto-based City TV has a place here simply because his concept for a local station has been sold and copied in foreign markets – the informal style of set, clothing, writing, improvised dialogue, live coverage, young reporters, and street corner *Talkback*, when anyone can buy one minute on video tape for one loonie and perhaps be included on the half-hour selection which is aired weekly. More directly City offers programs like *Media TV*, which is an often superficial but also quite smart and funny decoding of the ways television, magazines, and the music industry manipulate their audiences.

The educational channels like TVO are distinctive in three ways. They make or acquire programs which overtly teach something – from *Math Patrol* for the elementary schools to Tai Chi and sewing for adults. They also can and do clear their schedules to address a topical issue for a full week. Examples from TVO would be the week on the 1992

Earth Summit, a week of samples of television in Third-World countries in 1993, and energy and its consumption in 1994. Finally, like other specialty channels, the educational networks find programming of interest that is not snapped up by one of the bigger networks – documentaries, international films, Britcoms, or nature series. These channels have survived because so far there are enough selective viewers who look for programs like these.

Adult Drama: Movies and Mini-Series

One theme reiterated in the discussions on Canadian television since the 60s, and certainly in this paper, is the related issues of whether distinctive Canadian television drama exists, and if so how to make more of it (Peers 1969). I will present evidence that distinctive drama continues to exist on the CBC – and occasionally on CTV and Global/Canwest.

In the North American context of the 90s it may be one of the most distinctive things about Canadian culture that we do not yet see events on our front pages as fodder for the movie-of-the-week mill, nor ourselves, as we live our lives, as featured players for next week's video releases. In fact we still care very much about the differences between evidence, argument, reenactment and "make it up or leave it out," whichever makes a more entertaining television movie approach. We can still distinguish between docudrama (real people are characters), topical drama (foregrounds a contemporary issue) or historical drama (a mixture of real and fictional characters set in a time of which most viewers will not have first-hand knowledge).[7] The most recent example of historical drama is *The Valour and the Horror.* It is unimaginable that Americans would argue strenuously for months on end about the verisimilitude of both the documentary and dramatized segments of three programs about the Second World War.

When the CBC made *The Scales of Justice* a series of drama specials about well-known, sometimes sensational (sometimes only half-remembered) legal cases (e.g. the Susan Nelles/baby death case, the murder of Sir Harry Oakes, the case of wrongly accused Stephen Truscott), they hired well-known criminal lawyer Edward Greenspan[8] to advise on the scripts. He then served as an on-camera/voice-over guide for the viewer through the intricacies of the law. The parts of the script based on testimony and those based on speculation as well as the contradictions are explicitly pointed out. *The Scales of Justice* appears two or three times a year, bringing us our own judicial and social history without losing track of the ethical questions involved in docudrama.

If (as we so often do) we were to use the criterion of success abroad, we could look at the 1993 Cable Ace awards where *The Sound and the Silence*, a docudrama on Alexander Graham Bell made by Atlantis with several partners, was chosen "best international movie or miniseries" and *Road to Avonlea* was chosen as "best dramatic series." The New York Festival of International television handed eight gold medals to CBC programs including *The Boys of St Vincent, Road to Avonlea, and Blanche* and a silver medal to *The Odyssey*, more awards than to any other broadcasting company in the world. In fact 1993 was a fairly normal year for the CBC, which has been winning international honours for its television drama since the 50s.

Using the equally common criterion of ratings in other countries, early 90s miniseries based on some of our most painful short-comings as a society have been sold to primetime U.S. networks where they were ratings hits. Here again the voice is distinctive, however dissonant, to the English Canadian culture under scrutiny: *Love and Hate*, a four hour miniseries which not only explored the personalities involved but also the cultural context of the murder of Colin Thatcher's wife, Joann; *Conspiracy of Silence: the Story of Helen Betty Osborne* a searching account of the racism in La Pas. *Liar, Liar* looked at the possibility that a child may lie about child abuse[9]. Of them all, John Smith's *The Boys of St Vincent*, a 1993 CBC/NFB collaboration is the best example of the survival of a distinctive English Canadian television voice.

Adult Series

Longevity is one clear definition of success. *Beachcombers*, made in house, was the longest running dramatic series in English Canadian television. *Street Legal*, also an in-house production, was a popular series which averaged over a million faithful fans over its eight-year run. With its smart dialogue, stylish costumes, decor, and camera work and dollops of socially relevant issues in law, the ratings grew steadily. I argue at greater length elsewhere (Miller 1993) that the series did lose some of its most distinctive characteristics when the emphasis shifted from the topical issues to games of musical beds and improbable plot twists – but the ratings did go up significantly.

The changes in *Street Legal* coincided with Ivan Fecan's takeover as director of English television and his hands-on style of management. To Fecan there was no dramatic conflict, with three "nice" people as protagonists (interview 1989). Hence the introduction of Olivia and the foregrounding of the personal rather than the political and other topical elements. When the series was canceled at the end of the 1993–94 season, even John Haslett Cuff confessed that, although he regularly described *Street Legal* as too Americanized, he would miss Chuck, Oiliva, and Leon. That seems to be the quintessentially Canadian television reviewer's response: ignore any history of television in this country which might provide a context for what you watch and admit you like a popular cultural artifact only when it is safely put to rest. The fact is that our popular drama has always been competitive with 'theirs' when time and money is spent on it, from the success of *Wojeck*, *A Gift to Last*, *King of Kensington*, and *Hangin' In* to *Max Glick*, *Seeing Things*, and *North of 60*.

Regional and Aboriginal Motifs

These are the two most important motifs which could make our television distinctive. The regions are defined variously by governments, Crown corporations, agencies, boards, as well as by the people who live in them. Some parameters are established by official and other languages, by geography and by a bureaucratic convention. The CBC uses British Columbia; "the West" – lumping Alberta, Saskatchewan, and Manitoba into one conceptual unit; Ontario (which only those who live there seem to know is at least two places, Toronto and the rest); Quebec, which should be Montreal and the rest; and "The Maritimes," which conflates Prince Edward Island, Newfoundland and Labrador, Nova Scotia, and New Brunswick (Acadia included) into one "place." In fact these "regions" have often been mistaken for reality – to the cost both of those who live there and of the CBC's ratings. The problem is that, for much of its history the CBC has decentralized *making* but not *decision making*.[10] Moreover, as Gibbons and Resnick point out, the populist, inclusive, monochromatic vision of Canada creates unresolved tensions in a CBC which has been self defined as polychromatic, nationalist, *and* regional *and* bicultural. As Nelles points out, if Ontario begins to see its interests and identity separate from those of "Canada," a new region may emerge on our screens – along with the realization (at last) that Toronto is not Ontario.

As Wayne Skene, former director for B.C. television, documents in *Fade to Black: A Requiem for the CBC* (Skene 1993), CBC regions are forced to work in illogical and often impossible circumstances, made worse in 1990 by an indifferent and inept head office. The conflict is an old one but the stakes are much higher than they have ever been. Canadians, like most other North Americans, connect to their television services *first* at the level of local and then regional, news, weather, sports, entertainment, and information. Removing three stations and cutting down eight others, although a response to a real financial emergency, moved the patient onto the critical list. Recovery by the mid 90s is by no means a sure thing.

Another distinctive motif in Canadian television has been the representation of Aboriginal peoples. Intercultural, intertribal, and family conflicts and accomodations were the focus of the series *Cariboo Country, Beachcombers, Spirit Bay*, and the one-hour anthology or drama specials *A Thousand Moons, Dreamspeaker, Where the Heart Is, Where the Spirit Lives, Conspiracy of Silence, Medicine River, Spirit Rider*. I have traced this element in a limited way in chapters on anthology and docudrama (Miller 1987) as well as in extended analyses of *Caribou Country* and *Beachcombers*. The subject also reappeared sporadically in other places throughout the 70s and 80s (*Dreamspeaker, Where the Heart is, A Thousand Moons*, many episodes of *Beachcombers*, a few episodes of *Danger Bay*, and all of *Spirit Bay*, the short series for children). The subject reappears most notably and controversially in 1989 in *Where the Spirit Lives*, a historical drama about residential schools which was sold to PBS and around the world and rebroadcast in Canada three times.[11]

Since 1992 the CBC has presented three full seasons of *North of 60*, set on a reservation in the North West Territories. Unlike *Northern Exposure*, the American cult hit to which it is so often and so inappropriately compared, *North of 60* does not use Aboriginal People as an exotic backdrop. There were also two drama specials in 1993–94, *Spirit Rider*, a movie for Family viewing, and *Medicine River* based on a novel by Aboriginal writer Thomas King.

Since Oka, and in the midst of an ongoing debate about cultural appropriation, we have changed what we watch and how we watch it. Meanwhile, the long-running Aboriginal motif, which has changed significantly since Philip Keately and Paul St Pierre explored it in *Cariboo Country* 1960–66, has now been claimed by those whose lives it reflects. Frances Abele points to the fresh perceptions which could arise from First Nations writers, directors, and producers for whom speaking English is a politically charged act, who may perceived "history" and "geography" as identical, and whose sense of topography is radically different from the romanticism of the Wacousta syndrome, the "garrison mentality," or the empty "vistas" of tourist brochures. Their voices, heard directly without mediation, could considerably enrich our television drama.[12]

REPOSITIONING AS A CBC STRATEGY
FOR SURVIVAL

The CBC's strategy for survival in the 500 channel universe in 1992–93 and 93–94 was to create three mini-channels five nights a week, each intended to have its own distinct identity. Widely discussed in newspapers and periodicals 'repositioning' was intended to make the 7 to 9 P.M. time period a family and information network. From 9 to 10, a reworked news and documentary hour called *Primetime News* was intended to lure at least as many Canadians away from the most popular American programming as the old *The National/The Journal* had. Then from 10 to 12 P.M., the CBC, free of the economic imperatives of ratings at last, could entertain adults in "their own" slot – with adult humour like *Codco*, challenging BBC mini-series like GBH, and Canadian films for adults, as well as with "loss leaders" like *Adrienne Clarkson Presents*,[13] which some affiliate stations can and do drop in favour of *Magnum P.I.* reruns.

In May 1994 the CBC announced that *Primetime* would go to 10 P.M. In the late 80s and early 90s the CBC featured excellent family programming but provided little for the adult in search of alternatives to American network cop shows and tabloid TV. The major advantage of repositioning was that adult audiences could more easily reclaim their own programming "footprint." It remains to be seen whether adult programming other than news will survive this retreat. Creating a footprint by counter-programming is an old broadcasting strategy. Given that there is more and more evidence that viewers are choosing to watch programs, not networks, the CBC may fall back on a program-by-program rather than time-slot approach.

Other new factors will also change the broadcast context. Four decades late, the Chrétien government promised to stabilize CBC funding by supporting its annual $1 billion budget over several years – a stable financial situation which the BBC and most public broadcasting systems have enjoyed since the 30s. This means that at last rational program planning can be done. Since the 1960s, most dramatic and children's, arts, and science programming has required twelve to eighteen months lead time. Yet the budget has been renewed annually at the pleasure of parliament. The CBC is not even allowed to borrow money. The result is ridiculous inefficiencies and anomalies. Finished programs are literally put on the shelf for months before going to air so that the programs' costs will show on another year's budget (Winsor 1994).[14] Ominously, by October 1994 heritage minister Duphy refused to say whether this the promise would be kept.

The second policy change is that the government promises to find alternative sources of funding from levies on cable operators, perhaps with additional funding from the private networks as their ransom from CRTC directives to make Canadian children's and dramatic programming. There may also be another levy to Rogers as the price for permission to take over MacLean Hunter. Moreover the Mulroney cuts will be spread over several years so that further downsizing can be managed rationally even if no alternative sources of funding are found. Unfortunately those policy initiatives were referred in 1994 to yet another parliamentary committee whose mandate is to rethink the role of the CBC. To add to the confusion, the heritage minister is refusing to reassure the CBC after reports that he is unable to defend the promised rational budgeting from the more powerful finance minister's knife. Cuts of up to $400 million or close to half the CBC budget are widely feared within the corporation.

Another fundamental change at this critical time is the appointment as president of someone who has actually worked (for nine years) at the CBC. Regrettably, unlike his BBC counterparts, Anthony Manera, a senior vice-president, has never made a program, but at least he is familiar with the CBC corporate culture and what remains of its ethos, he has a memory, and more important he is trying to create a new relationship with the unions.

DOES CANADA NEED A NATIONAL SYMBOLICS TO SURVIVE?

Many Francophones do not believe that English Canada has a mature symbolics of culture. Collins (1990) and others have correctly pointed out that Canadians like American programming. He repeatedly argues that English Canada lacks a shared symbolic culture. But he also argues that as the world's first post-modern state, Canada will survive as a nation. I would argue that in fact we have two national symbolics – one in Quebec, one in the rest of Canada. Both are under attack by shrinking revenues, rising costs, and news technologies which can reduce or add to the costs of reprogramming. Of course, I would prefer to see the institutions on which our symbolic life depends strengthened – a necessity whether Quebec remains inside Canada or leaves.

INNOVATIONS IN TECHNOLOGY

In the 1990s there will be technological convergence – and casualties. A decade's worth of Japanese analog High Definition Television (HDTV) will disapear as American digital HDTV takes over. If enough on-demand programming becomes available from cable, the direct Broadcast satellites will not be the 'death stars' so often touted. The CRTC as a regulatory body of delivery systems may well disappear. FREENETS will plug those in major cities with modems into online inforation, e-mail from around the world. Sound and image capacity (a clip of the baby's first steps sent to grandma) which does not use huge amounts of memory will follow.

Choices will be everywhere *if* and only if ways of financing newsgathering, documentaries, and children's and adult drama can be found.

Choice is not the dilemma. Providing "software" (otherwise known as programming) is.

I would ask you to pause for a moment and look at these 500 'choices' not from the point of view of the broadcaster or business-executive or critic but that of one viewer. For any given viewer there are never 500 choices to be made but only two at any given time. The first decision she makes is whether to watch or not. If the choice is to watch then there are still only two choices – recognizably Canadian or American or imitation-American TV. If Canadian, then the most consistently and definably Canadian choice for general viewing available is the CBC. The other is something else. People can only concentrate on (not watch, concentrate on) one thing at a time – and there are many forms of television that still require attention spans of longer than five minutes. Thus though we began with 500 choices it still comes down to the CBC or "something else."

AUDIENCES AND ECONOMICS

As the ethnologists and reception theory specialists have been pointing out to academics and industry alike (with increasing success), what a person chooses to watch is dependent on time, place, day, hour, sex, age, race, mood, habits, weather, homework, telephone calls, and bladder capacity as well as who has possession of the channel-changer, the demands of the baby or dog, or the viewer's desire for company while eating, ironing, or painting the patio furniture. The Nielsen and BBM records of ratings and shares are limited in the information they provide. The choice to turn on the set and then to choose a program does not mean, "I like it," or, "I remember it five minutes later," or especially, "I will buy the sponsor's dish detergent" – or, even if the choice is the *fifth estate*, that "I will vote for someone who will support public broadcasting." As Ien Ang argues, "Public service institutions no longer address the television audience as citizens but as "consumers" – at least at a general organizational level ... Ratings discourse is too replete with ambiguities and contradictions to function as the perfect mechanism to regulate the unstable institution-audience relationship" (154). She continues, "The social world of actual audiences consists of an infinite and ever expanding myriad of dispersed practices and experiences that can never be and should not be contained in one total system of knowledge." (155).

Yet another answer to the question, "Will English Canadian TV services remain distinctive in the event that Quebec separates?" is, "Yes, if there is the political will" – which often translates into, "If there are the dollars to preserve a distinctive voice in a small market." All over the world it is a fact that commercials do not provide all the money needed to support drama and children's programming. Even in the huge U.S. market it is resales abroad and syndication at home that allows independent producers to make money.[15] In most countries, the producers must either be subsidized or through co-productions sell their products on the world market. The danger in such co-productions is that an effort to please the varied tastes of very different cultures may result in a brew tasting of thrice-used tea leaves or what the British call "Europud." "Europud" is defined as programs made for twelve different countries which satisfy none (Hutchinson 1993:16)[16]. For a recent example see *A Foreign Affair*, 100 episodes of an international soap opera shown on Global with lead actors from countries as diverse as Holland, Canada, and Brazil.

Since the mid-80s when the CRTC finally threatened to use its power to revoke licenses,[17] CTV and Global/Canwest have bought costly and distinctive of drama and children's programming.[18] Without that pressure, the "discipline of the market place," with its connotations of U.S. domination, has often dictated Canadian co-productions in which the partner with the most money and access to the widest audience determines the kind of game played, for example, Bordertown, Counterstrike, Katts and Dog, and Matrix. Yet even the U.S. system of independent productions houses and commercially driven networks is no longer powerful or affluent enough to go its own way on expensive mini-series. Long television specials (unless they are adaptations of novels by Danielle Steele) have almost disappeared on American television due to costs and minimal resale potential.

It is now also increasingly difficult to find the start-up costs of hour-long series. So we arrive at the reiterated and as yet unanswered vital question of where the supply of TV movies, mini-series, and series, or children's programs – the most popular and by far the most expensive programming – will come from to supply not only the existing services but more obviously the direct broadcast satellites. "On demand" cable will also need much more programming. At the moment movies and pay-per-view live concerts and sporting events seem to be the only steady source of supply. Everyone recognizes that distinctive programming will have a better chance than another rerun of *Gilligan's Island* in prime time, yet distinctive programming based on current models of films with high production costs remains difficult to finance.

PUBLIC BROADCASTING IN CRISIS WORLD-WIDE

Another major problem facing the CBC specifically in these difficult times is an apparent erosion of public support for the whole idea of tax support of public broadcasting. This erosion of public support for the CBC as a public broadcaster is not unique to Canada; there is a crisis in public broadcasting around the world.

The ebbing of support for public broadcasting did not happen overnight. Around the industrialised world conservative agendas – themselves perhaps the inevitable reaction of voters to the more left-wing and affluent 60s – have flourished since the mid-70s. What has happened to the CBC is a paradigm for what is happening wherever state-operated public broadcasting exists. In 1991 the lobby group Friends of Canadian Broadcasting sent its members a fact sheet based on "the Main Estimates of the Government of Canada as presented annually in the House of Commons … information on CBC employees comes from the CBC itself." This was intended to counter the information sent out by Conservative members of the House of Commons regarding the government's financing of the CBC. It showed in graphs that, adjusted for 1991 dollars, parliamentary appropriations for 1984 to 1991 had diminished from $1.2 billion to $0.8 billion that the CBC advertising revenues had increased by 62 percent from 1984 to 1989 (but had declined when the recession started be felt in 1990), that the total share of federal expenditure had declined by 20 percent, and that the CBC staff had been cut 25 percent – this in the context of a constitutional crisis which seemed to threaten Canada itself. The basic decline in purchasing power summarized in the "fact sheet" is documented in the CBC document, "CBC budgets 1984–1994: An Overview" (May 1989), and for 1989–94 by Nash (1994), who points out that "since 1984 cuts and the non-provision of funds for inflation totalled more than a billion dollars … a reduction in staff from more than 12,00 in 1984 to 9,370 ten years later" (538).[19] Telefilm, a partner in most independent drama production particularly for the private broadcasters, and the NFB are both rumoured to be on the Liberal chopping block. And yet the distinctive programming which helps create the symbolics which are still required by a post-modern state largely depends on the existence of the CBC, the NFB, Telefilm, and other cultural agencies.

THE FRENCH FACT – ITS ABSENCE AND ITS REFLECTION

Another distinctive element on the CBC which I have identified could be, paradoxically, the continuance of our French fact – which will survive in Acadia and many other places whatever the result of the next referendum.

We must begin by acknowledging what did not happen for thirty-five years – what Marc Raboy would call a missed opportunity. As the CBC itself admitted in its submission to the CRTC in 1978, "The French and English networks developed side by side during the 1940's and 1950's and into the 1960's ... the perception of the need to reflect the two linguistic communities to one another emerged in the CBC at about the same time as it emerged in the country – gradually over the last half of the 1960's and then early 1970s and then abruptly in the mid 1970s" (CBC 1978:39).[20] No mention is made of the CRTC's earlier far-reaching recommendations in its 1974 report, "Radio Frequencies are Public Property," which pointed out the regional limitations and absence of French-English exchange (CRTC 1974:28–9). Programs were occasionally recycled from one language into another, notably *La Famille Plouffe* (1953–59 on CBC, 1952–59 on Radio-Canada). There were a few efforts to reflect each culture to the other in the arts. *Festival* presented in English a handful of Quebec playwrights. In the 70s Tremblay permitted *Les Belles Sœurs* to be done on the CBC when Radio-Canada would not consider producing one of his scripts. But *For the Record*, the issue-oriented anthology of "journalistic dramas" (1977–83; Miller 1987:390) produced just one contemporary drama, *Don't forget: Je me souviens*, in 1980. There has been *no other* drama on this subject on the CBC in the last fourteen years.[21]

On the other hand, Radio-Canada created its own mythology through its news and current affairs department by decontextualizing and repeating months later, over and over, the "Brockville flag episode" during the Meech Lake Accord fiasco. Radio-Canada also regularly ignores the arts in the rest of Canada as well as most anglophone popular culture with a nationalist fervour that creates a deafening silence.

In fact there were a few "cross-cultural" efforts during and after the first Quebec referendum in 1980. *Riel* (1979) was shot in both languages and caused controversy in both cultures. Mini-series like the French *Duplessis*, the very successful English *Empire Inc.* and the less successful *Chasing Rainbows* (both set in Montreal, both lavish period pieces) were dubbed into the other language. However, *Lance et Compte* (1987), which was shot in both languages, turned into a litmus test of both cultures. *Lance et Compte* started on Radio-Canada with a million viewers and soon nearly tripled to 2.7 of a total viewing population of six million. There were T-shirts, mugs, a fan magazine, a book, even sweatsuits over its three-year run. Yet the same scripts, shot in English as *He Shoots, He Scores*, using the same actors, directors, producer, and crew drew only 750,000 viewers, an audience which eventually dropped to a disastrous 440,000 even though (or perhaps because?) the francophone actors' English was dubbed into more "acceptable" English (Bawden 1988). Note that despite its continuing popularity, given the high production costs, the francophone version lasted only one more season after financing from the CBC and France disappeared.

Even though there have been recent significant cross-overs of broadcasters and programs between Quebec and the rest of Canada, it is safe to say that at no time in its history did the CBC depend on a soupçon of French for a distinctive flavour. Should Quebec stay in Canada, that cross-over might continue to evolve, since a new beginning has been made. According to Tony Manera, "There must be increased exchange between our English and French networks, not simply programs that are dubbed, but actual collaborative projects" (*SCAN* May/June 1994:24). However, if Quebec leaves Canada the opportunity for shared music, drama, news reporting, sports-casts, and documentaries on a daily basis which has been wasted over the previous four decades may be one of the clearest discernible reasons for the divorce. Given that two broadcast centres were built, one in Toronto, one in Montreal, for a Crown corporation whose top executives are still housed in Ottawa, it is not surprising that two empires arose, each largely independent of and indifferent to the other (see Nash 1994).

Note that the Broadcasting Act legislated by the Conservatives in 1990 dropped the requirement that the CBC "contribute to the development of National Unity and provide for a continuing expression of Canadian Identity," substituting instead, "The programming provided by the Corporation should ... contribute to shared national consciousness and identity" (Canada 1990: sec. 3[m] vi). Symptom? Cause? Synergy?

Over all, and most reluctantly, I have come to think that in the realm of the imagination the two solitudes have become lonelier. One might say that as far as television fiction is concerned, few francophone programs translate well. To my mind it is much more problematic that no programs are made in English or French about the other culture or even the connection between the two. "Not knowing about the Other" no longer protects the peace, and there may not be much time left. However, even if Quebec leaves Canada or takes over Radio-Canada in some kind of asymmetrical arrangement, the "French fact" will continue as a significant minority in other provinces – with much to offer, if programmers choose to take advantage of it.

In the future, will the "distinctive" voice depend on the incorporation of marginalized voices? Partly. Feminist? Native? Multi-cultural? Franco-Ontarian or Acadian? Regional? Although not yet fully a part of our national symbolics, all five may become central to our perceptions of a distinctive Canadian culture. For example, we had a peaceful and successful uprising over the exclusion of women from the Charter in

1982. The documentary and the drama still wait to be made.[22] Yet although much remains to be done, in the 80s women began to take their place as TV directors, producers, and executives (Miller forthcoming). The complex issues of cultural appropriation aside, the increasing recognition of Aboriginal culture in our broadcast news, documentary, and fiction may be another distinguishing factor. The regions may be given opportunities to do genuine anthology programming without having to run every script through the Toronto blender 2000 miles away. Stories from our immigrant communities may not be confined to a ghetto-like *Inside Stories* but simply appear naturally in whatever series follow E.N.G. and *Street Legal*. Finally, our francophone minorities outside the bilingual province of New Brunswick may also demand more programming which reflects their realities.

If programs culturally specific to the First Nations, francophones, or the regions were the only distinctive flavours in Canadian television outside Quebec, I would have to conclude that the answer to, "Will distinctive Canadian television survive?" might well be, "No." However, if Canadian broadcasters fail to take advantage of these and other facts of our lives as substance for the drama from which to draw an imaginative sense of ourselves, we may well be reduced to flaunting our scenery as our only distinctive symbolic system. My guess is that this will not happen – but it might.

After twelve years spent talking to makers and decision makers at the CBC I came to the following observation: "What is absolutely necessary for making successful and worthwhile television programs of any kind for the many audiences available is a working environment where people remember their accomplishments, value their contributions, have the freedom to try new things and to fail occasionally, are consulted on policies that directly affect their work and above all share a recognizable ethos" (Miller forthcoming). That is the basic requirement for any network or program to survive in the 500 channel universe – with or without Quebec.

The other necessary condition for the survival of English television services is political will. As we have seen, the climate has thawed a bit, notwithstanding the very silly public temper tantrum CRTC Chair Keith Spicer threw in March of 1994.[23] He berated the CBC for falling ratings, ignoring viewers and for airing too many American comedies (two-and-a-half hours out of twenty-eight hours available from 7 to 11 P.M.) and predicted oblivion unless the corporation mended its ways. It is not clear to me that the chair and commissioners on the CRTC ever watch television. If the current Liberal regime decides to reform and preserve public broadcasting, high definition television, fibre optics, convergence, and information highway notwithstanding, in ten years a viewer should still be able to choose Vision, YTV, Newsworld, and more important, the more broadly based and distinctive series available to all on CTV and Global/Canwest. Radio-Canada may well disappear in its current Quebec-based incarnation. But I conclude that the network with the deepest footprint and the longest tradition of distinctive television news, current affairs, children's programming, arts, science, and drama – the CBC – will survive.

NOTES

1 Documented in Miller (1987) and Miller (forthcoming).

2 A colleague in New Mexico remarked by e-mail after I had described the content of episodes of *North of 60*, that in his opinion, as far as representation of Aboriginal people in film and on television is concerned, Canada is usually ten years ahead of the U.S. in film and television. If *Dances with Wolves, Northern Exposure*, and the "Journey's End" episode of *Star Trek: the Next Generation* (1 April 1994) are typical, he is right.

3 Nevertheless the level of anxiety felt all over the world at the dominance of American television forms is usually focused on the genres which are the most expensive; children's programs and TV drama.

4 CBC Research's 1991 internal document *How People Use Television: A Review of TV Viewing Habits* reports that Canadians in 1984–85 spent 10.8 percent of their 26.7 percent of the viewing devoted to Canadian programs on news and 4.3 percent on public affairs. In 1988–89 the percentage of viewing devoted to Canadian programming had risen to 31.6. Of that 11.8 percent was news and 5.4 percent was public affairs – or over half. Note that this statistic covers the 6 A.M. to 3 A.M. broadcast "day."

5 Personal observations verifying a local newspaper reviewer's lament. Over twelve days of viewing in 1992, confirmed in four days of viewing in 1994, there was very little material we in Canada would call news. Much of it was public relations for one kind of an event or another. There was little mention of Chicano or Native-American culture or concerns, for example, little about municipal politics or state news other than a sensational "death row" watch before an execution.

6 Barry Cooper's 1994 polemic on "shaping" the news at CBC TV posits a main and passive viewer, ignores the differences between print and a performing medium, uses the cold war rhetoric of the North American right wing, and may, I fear, preempt the balanced monograph needed on the subject.

7 For a more detailed discussion, see pp. 256–300 in Miller (1987).

8 Greenspan had already worked with CBC radio to produce a series with the same title using many of the same techniques.

9 It should be noted that the Canadian production company Alliance did well in the U.S. with the sales and ratings successes of *Ordeal in the Arctic* and *Family of Strangers*, which beat the competition in its slot in the all-important "sweeps week" – when advertising ratings for the next quarter are set. Both were also simulcast on CTV drawing over 2.4 million viewers (*Toronto Star* 24 February 1993).

10 I have examined at some length the value of regional drama programmes to the CBC over the years in a chapter called "Regional or 'what Toronto doesn't know" (Miller 1987:325–56).

11 See a conversation with Don S. Williams, executive producer of *Beachcombers*, Miller (forthcoming).

12 As far as services to Native peoples is concerned, not until the 1986 Caplan Sauvageau *Report of the Task Force on Public Broadcasting* are services in their own languages and in English explored in any depth.

13 Clarkson will not be able to show superb adult fare like the film *Le Dortoir* in her 1994–95 7 P.M. slot, traditionally a family viewing hour. When the CBC abandoned "repositioning" as a strategy, the adult slot disappeared – Canadian cinema was banished to 11:30 P.M. See also Nash (1994) in his chapter, "A Repositioned CBC," pp. 509–43.

14 See also *St Catharines Standard* (CP report), and *Globe and Mail* (4 February 1994).

15 This is why, in the costlier 80s, producers started syndicating hit sitcoms which were still in production.

16 This may be why a letter in *Starweek*, 2–8 April, lamented that the CBC was cancelling E.N.G. For that viewer it was good and therefore it was made by the CBC. Too often the reverse assumption is made.

17 CTV appealed this threat all the way to the Supreme Court. In one of the years in question they had produced one half hour of original Canadian television drama in the previous 365 days. One half hour for the year.

18 An anthology of good Canadian drama adapted from successful theatre runs on ad hoc nets of independent stations.

19 See also 463–4, 487–8, 536–8. The titles of two of Pierre Juneau's last speeches as CBC president betray the increasing desperation of the late 80s – "The CBC Just Give It the Means … And Then Watch!" (5 April 1989) and "The CBC Today – the Growing Distance Between Resources and Public Expectations" (7 June 1989). Both were delivered to chambers of commerce.

20 Later they point to dubbed versions of *The Beachcombers* and the anthology *The Newcomers*, commissioned by Imperial Oil (which was shot in both languages), as well as some music programs as evidence of their new awareness. See also the 1982 Applebaum-Hébert *Report of the Federal Cultural Policy Review Committee*, known as the "Applebert" report, Information Services, DOC, Ottawa, which recommends (six years later) "more exchange

between English and French programming" and "national viewing of materials produced by provincial television agencies" (292).

21 But then the CBC did not make a program which examined the October Crisis of 1970 in any depth until 1975.

22 However, the CBC, unlike its American counterparts, has made challenging programming for women at home since *Take Thirty* with Paul Soles and Adrienne Clarkson in the 60s.

23 See *Globe and Mail*, 24 March 1994.

BIBLIOGRAPHY

Ang, Ien, 1991. *Desperately Seeking Audience*, New York: Routledge.

Bawden, J., 1988. Toronto Star, 2 April.

Borkowski, Andrew, 1994. *SCAN* (May–June): 25.

CBC 1978. *A CBC Perspective*, vols 1–3. A Submission to the CRTC in Support of Applications for Renewal of Network Licenses. No place.

– 1989. *Budgets 1984–94: An Overview*, Publications, no place, May.

CBC Research 1991. *How People Use Television: A Review of TV Viewing Habits.* (CBC Internal Document).

Collins, Richard, 1990. Culture, *Communication, and National Identy*. Toronto: University of Toronto Press.

Cooper, Barry, 1994. *Sins of Omissions*. Toronto: University of Toronto Press.

CRTC 1974. *Radio Frequencies and Public Property*. Public announcement and decision of the Commission on applications for renewal of the CBC's television and radio license. 31 March. CRTC Decision 14–70.

Government of Canada 1986. *Report from the Task Force on Broadcasting Policy*. Ottawa: Ministry of Supplies and Services.

– 1990. *Broadcasting Act*, section 3(m)vi.

Hutchinson, David, 1993. "The European Community and Audio-Visual Culture." *Canadian Journal of Communication* 18, 4 (Autumn): 437–50.

Koch, Eric, 1986. *Inside Seven Days: The Show That Shook the Nation*. Greenwood, Ont: Prentice-Hall/Newcastle.

Lochead, Richard, ed. 1991. *Beyond the Printed Word: The Evolution of Canada's Broadcast News Heritage*. Vol. 1: *Canadian Broadcasting*. Kingston: Quarry.

Miller, Mary Jane, 1987. *Turn Up the Contrast: CBC Television Drama Since 1952*. Vancouver: University of British Columbia Press and the CBC.

– 1993. "Inflecting the Formula: The First Seasons of L.A. Law and Street Legal." In *The Beaver Bites Back? American Popular Culture in Canada*, ed. D. Flaherty and F. Manning, 325–56. Montreal: McGill-Queen's University Press.

– Forthcoming. *Rewind and Search: Makers and Decision Makers in CBC Television Drama*. Montreal: McGill-Queen's University Press.

Nash, Knowlton, 1994. *The Microphone Wars: A History of Triumph and Betrayal*. Toronto: McClelland & Stewart

Peers, Frank, 1969. *The Politics of Public Broadcasting.* Toronto: University of Toronto Press.

Rutherford, Paul, 1993. "Made in America: The Problem of Mass Culture in Canada." In *The Beaver Bites Back? American Popular Culture in Canada,* ed. D. Flaherty and F. Manning, 260–79. Montreal: McGill-Queen's University Press.

Skene, Wayne, 1993. *Fade to Black: A Requiem for the CBC.* Vancouver and Toronto: Douglas and McIntyre.

Winsor, Hugh, 1994. *Globe and Mail,* 11 February 1994.

11 The Future of English-Language Publishing

ROWLAND LORIMER

Canadian book publishing currently consists of two distinct markets, one the French-language market, the other the English-language market. Both share certain characteristics such as being part of a larger linguistic market that is dominated by more extensive, more established producers from other countries – France on the one side and the U.K. and the U.S. on the other. Since the flow of material in terms of rights sales and translations between the two Canadian linguistic markets is scant, there is no significant interdependency. Common federal policies have been developed and applied to both linguistic sectors with only minor modifications; from the point of view of the market, the likely future of neither sector depends on whether Quebec is in or out of Canada. On the other hand, should Quebec leave Canada or assume exclusive control over culture in on asymmetrical arrangement, the continuance of Canadian policy along the lines and with the attendant rationales of the past three decades is open to question.

The ability of the English-language Canadian book publishing industry to survive depends on the maintenance of gains it has made over the past thirty years. To be concise, it must continue to increase market share and maintain two revenues streams, sales and grants. Sales are a business matter that the industry seems increasingly able to manage both domestically and internationally. Grants depend upon the industry's ability to adapt to the likely political philosophy of a Canada without Quebec[1].

CANADIAN ENGLISH-LANGUAGE PUBLISHING AS A CULTURAL AND INDUSTRIAL PRESENCE

What is the current status of Canadian English-language book publishing? Generally speaking, industry and government agree (or assume) that the English-language sector controls about 25 percent of the market. However, when people think of books and reading and how much Canadian content is produced and read, they tend to think of trade books, that is, books sold in bookstores, not reference, legal, educational, or even scholarly books.

In *trade* books, *excluding mass paperbacks*, there are a number of statistics which show that Canadian participation is much higher than 25 percent. Ninety-two percent of firms publishing trade books are Canadian owned; 83 percent of new trade titles are published by Canadian-owned publishers; 86 percent of new trade titles published by Canadian-owned companies are Canadian-authored in contrast to 34 percent for foreign-owned firms; and Canadian-owned firms achieve per-title sales levels that are 73 percent of those achieved by foreign firms.[2] On the other hand, Canadian-owned publishers have a trade market share of 26 percent for their own titles. Combined with Canadian agents they have an additional share of 35 percent for agency titles and a total market share of 61 percent (Statistics Canada 1993).

Analyzing figures based on the entire range of book publishing (trade, as well as educational, scholarly, reference, and professional and technical), the average Canadian-owned firm has about 15 percent the number of employees but produced more than twice the number of titles per employee compared with foreign-owned companies[3]. And while, aggregating all titles, Canadian-owned firms sell only about one third the number of copies of each title as foreign firms, in trade books they sell just under three quarters the number of copies per title.[4]

How should these figures be interpreted? On the whole, Canadian-owned publishers dominate in numbers of firms, new title production, own-title trade sales, and publishing Canadian authors. They do so by sacrificing per-title sales, although not to any overwhelming extent. The number of firms translates into a healthy, somewhat decentralized industry operating out of many parts of the country with a range of political and cultural orientations. The high figure for title production translates into an interest and willingness to bring forward a wide range of books and authors. Given the comparative economic disadvantages of the Canadian-owned sector in attracting both authors and readers –

such as a lack of working capital to be used in part for advances, a global presence, and an aura of wealth, power, and prestige – this appears to be a creditable performance indeed. It appears even better when one considers that the Canadian-owned sector includes a very heterogeneous mix of firms across the land (73 of 310 firms are located outside Quebec and Ontario, figures are not available for the vicinities of Montreal and Toronto; Statistics Canada 1993); variability of size, genre orientation, and publishing motivation; a readiness of Canadian-owned firms to publish first-time authors; and a willingness of Canadian-owned firms to publish in low-selling genres such as poetry. It would be fair to say that Canadian-owned book publishing has become a considerable cultural force. Such a claim might be first founded on industry statistics such as those summarized above. But it might also attend to a set of secondary indicators as outlined below.

The significant secondary indicators of industry performance are the behaviour of the mass media, the orientation of educational institutions, the acquisition and collection-building practices of public libraries, the health of the professional media associated with books, and the activities of complementary media such as magazines, television, and film.

Mass Media

First to the mass media. Canadian books now command both national and regional attention in the mass media. Over two four-month periods, in eight newspapers and one weekly newsmagazine, 3,472 titles were reviewed in approximately 250,000 column lines (Canadian Centre for Studies in Publishing (CCSP) 1994). As we saw in early 1994, book publishing policy, specifically the takeover activities of Paramount, also commands attention. In short, the mass media allocate substantial resources to discussion of books both as a means to sell content to audiences and to sell audiences to advertisers. CBC radio, commercial talk-show radio, and most major daily newspapers recognize the existence of a market worth serving that is interested in knowing about books. Moreover if newspapers are any indication, about half this attention is devoted to Canadian-authored books (CCSP 1994).

Consider, for example, the book review activity in the Saturday section of the *Globe and Mail* of 19 March 1994:

TOTAL COVERAGE
a 12-page "Books and Arts" – section
a quarter-page column focusing on publishing
9 full book reviews
a children's books column

2 brief book reviews
a best seller list and book ads
Total: four full pages

NATURE OF COVERAGE:
3 Canadian authors
9 Foreign authors (U.S. = 4, U.K. = 3, Other = 2)
9 Distributed by Canadian-based firms
2 Distributed by Canadian-owned firms
1 On Canadian topics

CHILDREN'S COLUMN:
3 Canadian authors
1 foreign author
2 Canadian-owned publishers
2 Canadian-based firms

BEST-SELLERS (FROM LIST)
Fiction   5 of 10 were Canadian authors
               3 of 10 Canadian-owned publishers (all McClelland & Stewart)
Paperback   2 of 10 Canadian authors
Fiction   no Canadian-owned publishers
Non fiction   6 of 10 Canadian authors
               6 of 10 Canadian-owned publishers
Paper   3 of 10 Canadian authors
Nonfiction   no Canadian-owned publishers

ADDITIONAL:
half-page column on Ginn/Paramount

While coverage of books in the *Globe and Mail* and other major dailies has been long running, at least for the past thirty years, and specific attention to Canadian books has also been long running, the fact that it survives as a vibrant tradition in Canadian newspapers is an indication of its importance to newspaper proprietors, editors, and readers. This kind of coverage has also served as a foundation for the building of a more substantial infrastructural support for Canadian publishing that includes libraries, academe, industry periodicals, and the other media industries.

Public Libraries

The realities of building collections in Canadian libraries spending have been brought forward especially well by Francess Halpenny (1985). Halpenny provided her colleagues with an acceptable professional model for increasing Canadian holdings, thereby providing a powerful means for dissemination of Canadian ideas and images within the country. All large urban public libraries now buy Canadian books as a matter of course. Many smaller libraries have Canadian collections.

Educational Institutions

In academe a series of studies (Mathews and Steele [1969], Symons [1975], Symons and Page [1981], and Lorimer [1984]) and political and institutional responses have created a market in universities and (a slower-growing market) in Canadian schools for Canadian content and Canadian-published materials. With these studies as background, as David Cameron's report (1995) shows, learning materials and curricula reflecting Canadian literary, social, economic, cultural, geographical, geological, media, scientific and technological, artistic, historical, multicultural, First Nations, immigrant, and Northern realities are now to be found both in schools and post-secondary institutions. Certainly some of the above dimensions are underrepresented, and pockets of resistance in many guises still remain, including both institutional structure and personal prejudice. However, we are in a far different position than we were in the early 1970s when it was not unusual to find u.s. and generic realities pervasive. And Canadian authors and realities are also better represented in schools, despite the still-prevailing conception of education as a noncultural affair.

Industrial and Allied Activities

Two other secondary indicators to consider alongside mass media attention and an opening market in libraries and academe are professional industry activities and structures and complementary activities in allied industries. In publishing, bookselling, writing, and editing, Canada has a set of active and stable organizations, each with its associated provincial organizations. Each has its own newsletter, while specialty publications such as *Books in Canada*, the *Canadian Bookseller*, and *Quill and Quire* serve the industry as a whole as well as the reading public. The industry allied to books that first comes to mind is the periodical industry. There, some 120 Canadian scholarly journals, many in the humanities and social sciences, regularly take up Canadian writing and content. A variety of small magazines such the *Canadian Forum* and *This Magazine* also focus on Canadian realities. These together with the more than 500 Canadian magazine titles provide a substantial contribution to the infrastructure of Canadian book publishing (interview, Canadian Magazine Publishers Association). Television and film are also paying increasing attention to Canadian books and Canadian realities as the work of Anne Wheeler, Kevin Sullivan, and other Canadian directors and producers illustrates.

In summary, as the 1992 industry data demonstrate and as this supplementary infrastructure bears out, a sizable market for Canadian books has evolved. In sectors other than trade books, such as education, Canadian-owned publishers account for 35 percent of the school market, 13 percent of the post-secondary market, and 29 percent of the overall educational market. Since, according to Statistics Canada, 99 percent of the educational market consists of materials written by Canadian authors, there is little difference between Canadian- and foreign-owned firms.[5] Canadian collections in Canadian libraries are growing continuously, the book professions are active, and journals and magazines regularly attend to Canadian-published materials. Indeed programs specifically targeted at publishing are appearing across the country in schools, colleges where there is a technical orientation, and universities. Simon Fraser University approved a professional master's program on 14 July 1994.

CORRECTIVES TO A FINANCIAL INADEQUACY

As positive and comprehensive as the above picture is, one rather significant element is missing: the financial viability of the industry. Canadian book publishing, like other media industries, has two sources of revenue. One is direct sales to the audience. The second is derived from selling the audience. In the case of Canadian book publishing, the audience is sold not to advertisers but to those who have inherited the responsibility to encourage a literary, political, and cultural tradition, in short, Canadian governments.[6] While governments are not nearly so generous to book publishers as advertisers are to magazines, television, newspapers, and radio, the Canadian-owned book publishing industry has been reasonably successful in developing this revenue stream. For instance in 1992 direct government support (not including such programs as postal subsidies, writers' grants, prizes, etc.) amounted to just over $24 million, or 2.7 percent of book publishing revenues. For the smallest category of companies, numbering some 54 firms whose annual revenue was between $50,000 and $199,999, total grants were $2.5 million. This represented 23 percent of revenue and $46,574 per firm. At the other end of the scale are the 18 firms with revenues over $5 million who gained $4.0 million in aid. This repre-

Table 1
Types of Grants Available to Book Publishers in Canada outside Quebec

*Deficit Compensation for cultural titles	Technology assistance
– title grants	Training materials grants
– block grants	Translation grants
Book fair participation	Venture loans
Book purchase funds	Writers' grants
Canadian studies development (foreign	Writers-in-residence grants
market development)	
**Co-publishing programs	AGENCIES INVOLVED
Export market development	
**Export grants	Heritage Canada through
*Heritage grants	Cultural Industries (publishing
*Industrial development	division)
Industry promotion and distribution	Canadian Studies
*Learning materials development	Multiculturalism
programs	Bilingualism
Literary competitions	Canada Council
Loan guarantees	Social Sciences and Humanities
**Loan subsidies	Research Council
Management consulting	Foreign Affairs
Manuscript development grants	Department of Indian Affairs
*Marketing grants	Ministry of Employment and Investment
National professional association grants	Ministry of Industry
Postal subsidies	Council of Maritime Premiers
Prizes and awards	Provincial culture ministries and agencies
Professional training	(all ten provinces)
*Promotion grants	Provincial small business ministries
Readings grants	Provincial employment ministries
Regional and provincial association	Provincial heritage ministries
grants	Many large and some small municipalities
Small business development	
*Special project grants	

* These categories of assistance would appear as part of the $24 million reported by Statistics Canada.
** These categories of assistance might appear as part of the $24 million.

sented .6 percent of total revenues and $223,222 per firm. It also assisted in raising the profit level of the industry from between minus 1 percent and minus .6 percent for the two smallest categories of firms to 3 percent and 5.7 percent for the largest two categories of firms.[7]

The types of government assistance provide a sense of their integration with normal government functions and hence their likely long-term stability. Table 1 outlines the types of assistance available to book publishers in Canada outside Quebec. As table 1 indicates book publishing is supported for reasons of cultural articulation, to correct for market structure, industrial growth, and employment, cultural development, developing and maintaining our heritage, author and knowledge development, stimulating exports, providing educational materials, community development, and to promote specific political goals such as enhancing the Canadian national consciousness, bilingualism, and multiculturalism. The multiplicity of these grant forms do not get reduced to one or two in any single province or region. In Saskatchewan for instance, fourteen sources of grant revenues covering all three levels of government are used by twelve different publishers (Lorimer 1993a). Moreover, these grants do not represent merely a cosy relationship built up between government and industry. In part they are justified by polling conducted by the federal government over the years. For instance, according to some unreleased studies done by Goldfarb between 1987 and 1992, a steadily growing percentage of Canadians – 77 to 81 percent – identified Canadian ownership and control of industries producing cultural products as important or very important.

To place the industry with its two revenue sources in a general context, with the help of public funds Canadian authors and Canadian books have more than maintained a presence in Canadian life and a significant though small share of the Canadian market. In addition to entrenching themselves in the general Canadian market, at least for the time being, they have established themselves in the national and regional mass media of information and commentary, found their way into educational and library acquisitions, consolidated their status as recipients of cultural and industrial support from Canadian governments, and allied themselves for mutual benefit with the periodical, television, and film industries. They have also made inroads into exports.

Most important, if the above picture has a bias, it is a conservative one. Statistics Canada's reports are notorious underestimations of book production activity. My own research (Lorimer 1989; Lorimer 1993a) has indicated that there may be three to five times as many publishers as are reported on by Statistics Canada in every province of the nation. In British Columbia in 1989 there were at least sixty, even though Statistics Canada only reported on about twenty-four. In 1992 in Saskatchewan there were nineteen even though Statistics Canada reported only on five. A general rule of thumb in the library world is that twice the number of titles are placed on legal deposit each year as Statistics Canada reports published. Finally, a review of the catalogue of persons and institutions holding ISBN numbers, plus an examining of the new numbers each month, indicates that book publishing activity is a well-entrenched part of Canadian life.

LOOKING FORWARD FROM HERE

In contrast to dominant trends toward globalization and mass distribution of entertainment products, in book publishing in Canada an industry has developed that has specialized in the development of new products, is distinctive in being culturally oriented (to Canada), has had some growing success in establishing itself internationally, and has a significant degree of heterogeneity in terms of size, location, and genre orientation. The central question is, can the industry maintain its revenue, supportive structures, and growth in export development? An examination of sales patterns, the emergence of authors, industry activity, revenues, and market share suggests that this may indeed be the case.

There would appear to be five indicators that suggest that the industry can maintain itself and develop. First is the supply of manuscripts. Given the number of titles brought out by the Canadian sector and the relatively higher sales levels of own-titles versus agency titles, there seem to be more publishable manuscripts than publishers can publish.[8] The market performance of these publications is also nothing to ignore. Canadian-owned firms have specialized in bringing forward new titles and new authors, especially Canadian authors. The industry as a whole not only provides copious new titles each year but is also beginning, on a more regular basis, to produce market and cultural leaders. Market leaders are internationally recognized authors who win international prizes or recognition in the form of high-profile film exploitation. Cultural leaders are nationally recognized authors who are seen – by readership and book purchasing data and by media and academic attention – to be voices of nation and community. The investment in new Canadian authors, in some ways the publishing equivalent of research and development, and in other ways the spreading of risk over a wide variety of titles and authors, could serve Canadian publishers well. Certainly it serves authors, readers, and the nation well by providing constant monitoring of the concerns and celebrations of Canadians. The difficulty is that a reasonable mechanism does not exist to allow firms to hold on to authors once they have achieved some critical or market recognition. Whatever the long-term dynamics of author-publisher relations, this "talent development" should also serve as a firm foundation for export development. The international marketing role now played by Foreign Affairs is well placed for publishers to capitalize on international hits.[9]

Second, the performance of the Canadian-owned sector also provides a basis for long-term viability. Between 1988 and 1992 the market share of own-titles in Canada by the foreign-controlled sector has dropped from 42 to 40 percent. Agency sales by the foreign-controlled sector have dropped from 63 to 53 percent, while their title share has dropped from 25 to 20 percent. All these measures indicate a strengthening Canadian-owned sector.

Third, given the steady growth of grants over the past two decades and now the presence of federal, provincial, municipal, and federal/provincial grants, as well as the spreading of grants across government departments, it is difficult to imagine governments withdrawing in such a way as to cause the whole edifice to collapse.

Perhaps most significant to the survival of both revenue streams is the media, educational, and societal infrastructure. The skirmishes over Ginn that have taken place over the past five years appear to indicate that the mass media are clearly on the side of Canadian-owned publishing in any struggle against the giant transnational media and entertainment conglomerates even if the same media show no particular favouritism to Canadian firms on a day-to-day basis, that is, through selection of book to review. The antipathy to giant multinationals by journalists and the public may be apparent to the bureaucracy and politicians and, along with their polling data it may contribute to the survival and even the enhancement of necessary support programs. In addition, given the nature of the inroads made in the educational and library communities it is difficult to imagine a weakening in these markets.

At this point in history, it is difficult to imagine, despite Brian Mulroney's attempts "to sell the farm" to the u.s., that Canadians will stop being committed and interested in Canada. As the world gets smaller so, it would seem, will the value of Canadian life and society become more apparent. An historical overview suggests that our concerns for our national well-being have swung back and forth before. They show that a healthy desire to build a Canadian community that appeared for example in the 1920s (Gundy 1972) has arisen and then disappeared, only to be nurtured again. Indeed, a historical determinist would be pessimistic. However, I am neither. And there seems to exist a magical 20 percent bottom line. The history of Canadian book publishing suggests that when sales of books dealing with Canadian realities fall below about 20 percent of the market, a beginning discomfort emerges and, in the politest of ways, we Canadians appear to shuffle to our feet and raise our voices.[10]

The final indicator is that nebulous concept, the information society. Translated, this notion means that developed economies are expanding in the service and information sectors. Even the economists believe this, mostly because they have taught each other how to identify the sector and count its contribution to the economy as a whole.

Moreover, it is said that the survival of developed economies depends upon the development of information and knowledge industries. If book publishing is not an information and knowledge industry, it is hard to know what is.

The development of the book publishing industry in its current form has not been a happy accident. All the talent we see in Canadian writers together with the many emerging non-fiction and scholarly books did not happen along at the right time to be affirmed by sensitive, open, searching, knowledge and literary markets without rigidities. The development of Canadian-owned book publishing has been a result of a deliberate fostering of a writing and publishing community. Its development demanded the engendering of the confidence of writers, that if a person was struggling to learn to be a writer that she or he was doing something that mattered and might be paid attention if one could emerge with technique and a voice. The development of Canadian publishing demanded the creation of a market that saw Canadian fiction and non-fiction as important. Such deliberate fostering has taken place. The participants have been publishers, writers, booksellers, librarians, academics, the media, various departments of three levels of Canadian governments, and the Canadian public.

POLICY

And so we arrive at a reconsideration of publishing policy in the context of a Canada without Quebec. The cultural support policies of the federal government, of which publishing policy is a part, are derived from three models or philosophies of cultural development (see Lorimer and Duxbury 1994): a public service model – think of the CBC, a cultural development model – think of UNESCO and France, and a market model adjusted for cultural goals – think of merit goods, market failure, and infant industries. Book publishing has benefitted from both the cultural development and (culturally adjusted) market model. Indeed the contribution of Pierre Trudeau and Gérard Pelletier along with Marcel Masse, as unabashed champions of state intervention or willing interventionists in the case of Francis Fox, to assist cultural development through cultural industries is substantial (see Woodcock 1985:92; Trudeau 1968).

The withdrawal of Quebec from Confederation or even the assumption by Quebec of exclusive control over culture would surely change federal cultural policy significantly in the same way that the absence of these Quebecers and the Quebec bureaucrats and political operatives would substantially have affected the history of Canadian cultural policy. The evidence for predicting such a change rests in three places.

The first is in provincial policy outside Quebec. Second is in the political culture of the west, especially in B.C. and Alberta since the west would become the second force in a Canada without Quebec (see for instance, Pratt and Richards 1979). Third, some evidence can be found in an often neglected document, the Neilson Task Force Report (1985), and specifically its volume on culture and communications.

To come directly to the point, much as it may sound as if Preston Manning would banish cultural industry support, Ralph Klein has not, neither did W.A.C. Bennett, his son Bill (in spite of the Fraser Institute, which by the way cross-subsidizes its book publishing with membership fees), Bill Vanderzalm, or Grant Devine. Nor did Eric Neilson's report call for such a move. Indeed each of the above was as kind to culture and cultural industries as was Dave Barrett, and as are Roy Romanow and Mike Harcourt currently.

What is more likely is that the rationales for and perhaps the nature of support would change substantially. In short, the cultural development model would disappear in favour of a market model emphasizing small business, employment, development of the sector, and cultural goals. Calls for support of book publishers would rest on three apparently substantial foundations. The first would be market failure – the market is structured in such a way that it fails to recognize the long-term value of work written and published by Canadians. The second would derive from the fact that book publishers are small businesses who can often perform as effectively, though not as profitably, as large firms, and in doing so they create jobs. The third foundation would be the identity of book publishers as key players in an information society not only for their output but for their ability to train information workers. Supported by polls of Canadian public opinion that show support for Canadian ownership and control of industries producing cultural products, it would be reasonable to expect substantial continuity in publishing and cultural industries policy.

This may be the direction of policy in any event. Moves have already been made at the federal level to divest culture to the provinces. Federal-provincial joint programs are all industrial in nature aimed at developing publishers as small businesses. In fact the most recent program signed between Ottawa and B.C. integrates assistance for cultural industries with assistance for the development of information industries. At the same time, at a recent meeting of industry and government hosted by Simon Fraser University's Canadian Centre for Studies in Publishing, discussion focused on the development of industrial measures such as tax credits to strengthen the performance of firms in all sectors through industrial measures *within the context of cultural goals*. Such an orientation would differ from federal Department of Heritage programs which appear to set aside cultural goals in favour of (1) steering the industry into such profitable sectors as educational publishing and (2) inducing firms to increase their size and therefore encouraging concentration of ownership in pursuit of industry profitability.

CONCLUSION

André Shiffrin, former publisher of Pantheon, a subsidiary of a very rich conglomerate run by the Newhouse family which includes Random House now owns and operates a non-profit publishing company, The New Press (where have Canadians heard that name). In order to maintain a left-liberal book publishing company of the best authors both the u.s. and the world has to offer, in the world's largest and richest market, he has assembled the combined support of fourteen well-known foundations for his publishing program. Shiffrin has had to pursue this course essentially because, as the production, distribution, marketing, and consumption of books is currently organized in the u.s. Canada, the u.k., and almost every country in the world, the demands of the production of books of distinct cultural value seem incompatible with the demands for profitability. In slightly different words, the business of enlightenment and the commerce of publishing, while kissing cousins, are worlds apart. Such is Pax Americana, or maybe it is more accurately described as the heavy hand of commerce.

In this context and in the context of the ever-building information society, the cost of maintaining voices distinctive to a culture rises with a corresponding decrease in the size of the population. Such a reality is not a reason for despair but a matter for public entrepreneurship – to find mechanisms to assist Canadians to have access to Canadian voices, most obviously and justifiably through using consumption of imports to subsidize consumption of domestic products. Identifying and implementing such mechanisms is not assisted by free trade philosophy. But as the u.s. demonstrates consistently, domestic political realities should never be compromised by international trading agreements.

The existing separate French- and English-language markets within Canada suggest that whatever our future vis-à-vis Quebec, dramatic changes in the publishing industry and in government support of it are unlikely. Were Quebec to separate, the influence of France as known and reflected in Quebec would probably diminish. On the other hand, through a greater singularity of perspective, Canada might gain in resolve and effectiveness of policy. English-language producers are well-established and effective niche market producers in trade books who serve an important, coherence-building, cultural role.

They are a key element in the information sector in terms of output, job creation, and training. If anything they are a foundation for expansion which governments are beginning to recognize.

NOTES

1 The original version of this chapter contained a discussion of the influence of the changing publishing context being brought about by law, ownership, technology, and international trade. For reasons of space and specificity to Canada, but not for reasons of saliency, this section was omitted from the final version.

2 This is quite positive given that the Canadian contingent of publishers includes all kinds of publishers who are very much ideologically oriented (or producer driven) and intent on publishing what they see as important books rather than responding to market demand.

3 The average Canadian-owned firm has seventeen employees, the foreign-owned firm 111 (i.e., a Canadian-owned firm is, on average, 15 percent the size of a foreign-owned firm). Title output per employee for Canadian-owned firms is 1.51, for foreign-owned firms it is 0.64 (not including reprint and agency activity); in other words, Canadian-owned firms produce about twice the number of titles per employee compared to foreign firms. Per-title sales by foreign-owned firms are approximately three times Canadian-owned firms – what is gained in title output is more than lost in sales per title. But this is only for the aggregate of all books. In the trade sector, as noted above, Canadian-owned per-title sales are 73 percent of foreign-owned per-title sales. Taking into account both these figures, which are admittedly calculated on a different base, it may be that Canadian-owned firms are outperforming their foreign-owned competitors on the basis of both title output and sales.

4 Below are three different ways of estimating sales performance for titles published. All three are given because Statistics Canada does request in their survey sales statistics on a per-title basis and therefore there is no way to provide a single accurate estimate of per-title sales. Again these figures exclude mass paperbacks:

- per-titles sales if total trade sales are divided by new titles equal $39,370 Canadian owned and $30,640 foreign owned;
- per-title sales if total trade sales are divided by new and reprinted titles equal $23,950 Canadian owned and $22,454 foreign owned;
- per-titles sales if total trade sales are divided by titles in print equal $3,620 Canadian owned and $3,438 foreign owned.

5 It would appear that either the Statistics Canada data are incorrect or there is a mechanism allowing publishers to report a higher than expected number of Canadian-authored books in their sales. The most likely mechanism is that one of several authors is Canadian or that the vast majority of books go through a Canadian adaptation in which a Canadian author is added. It is clearly not the case that 99 percent of textbooks in Canada's educational system originated with Canadian authors for the Canadian market. One method for revealing the relative effort of Canadians would be to examine the royalties paid out to Canadians versus those paid to foreign authors.

6 I have outlined the role of a host group, organization, or society in publishing activities in Lorimer (1993b).

7 The overall industry figures do not report Canadian firms separately from all English-language firms.

8 The specialty of the Canadian-owned sector is Canadian-authored books. Canadian authors sell better than foreign authors for both Canadian-owned (3.5 times better) and foreign-owned firms (8 times better). Also, Canadian titles are a continuous feature of best seller lists.

9 The Department of Foreign Affairs runs a support program within a division called Academic Relations. It is the Canadian Studies program. Thanks to this program, Canadian authors such as Atwood, Davies, Richler, Laurence, Urquhart, Ondaatje, Shields, and many more are known in world capitals, in London, Paris, Berlin, Delhi, Seoul, Bangkok, Moscow, Warsaw, Madrid, Sydney, Rome, Vilnius, Riga, Beijing, Havana, Mexico City, Copenhagen, Stockholm, Oslo, and so forth. In some cases, such as Atwood, this has translated into substantial foreign sales. With Canadians winning international prizes and the wheels of the intellectual and information élites being well greased by Canadian diplomats, Canadian authors are beginning to gain attention, create export markets, and lead to rights and book sales abroad.

10 This phenomenon is not unique to Canada. John Curtain (1993) points out that Australian content ranges between 15 and 24 percent of the market there.

BIBLIOGRAPHY

Cameron, David. 1995. *The Cameron Report*. Ottawa: Heritage Canada.

Canada. 1985. *Task Force on Program Review (Neilson Task Force): Communications and Culture*. Ottawa: Supply and Services.

Canadian Centre for Studies in Publishing (CCSP). 1994. *Canadian Books in Review, Research Report No. 1*. Vancouver: Simon Fraser University.

Curtain, John. 1993. "Distance Makes the Market Fonder: The Development of Book Publishing in Australia." *Media Culture and Society, 15, no. 2:233–45.*

Gundy, H.P. (1972). "The Development of Trade Book Publishing in Canada." In *Royal Commission on Book Publishing* 1–37. Toronto: Queen's Printer.

Halpenny, Francess G. 1985. *Canadian Collections in Public Libraries.* Toronto: Book and Periodical Development Council.

Lorimer, R. 1989. *Book Publishing in British Columbia, 1989.* Vancouver: Canadian Centre for Studies in Publishing, Simon Fraser University.

– 1993a. *A Harvest of Books: Book Publishing in Saskatchewan – Final Report.* Vancouver: Canadian Centre for Studies in Publishing, Simon Fraser University, and the Saskatchewan Publishers Group.

– 1993b. "The socioeconomy of scholarly and cultural book publishing." *Media Culture and Society* 15, no. 2:203–16.

– with Nancy Duxbury 1994. "Cultural development in an open economy: an orientation," *Canadian Journal of Communication* 19, nos. 3 and 4.

Lorimer, Rowland. 1984. *The Nation in the Schools: Wanted, A Canadian Education.* Toronto: OISE Press.

Mathews, Robin, and James Steele. 1969. *The Struggle for Canadian Universities: A Dossier.* Toronto: New Press.

Periodical Writers Association of Canada (PWAC). (1994). "Southam Alert." 29 April. Toronto: PWAC.

Pratt, Larry, and John Richards. 1979. *Prairie Capitalism: Power and Influence in the New West.* Toronto: McClelland & Stewart.

Statistics Canada. 1993. *Book Publishing 1991–92: Culture Statistics.* Cat. no. 87–210 Annual. Ottawa: Statistics Canada.

Symons, Thomas H.B. 1975. *To Know Ourselves: The Report of the Commission on Canadian Studies,* vols. 1, 2. Association of Universities and Colleges of Canada.

– and James Page. 1981. *Reflections on the Symons Report: The State of Canadian Studies in 1980.* Ottawa: Supply and Services.

Trudeau, Pierre. 1968. *Federalism and the French-Canadians.* Toronto: Macmillan.

Woodcock, George. 1985. *Strange Bedfellows: The State and the Arts in Canada.* Vancouver: Douglas & McIntyre.

12 Native Arts in Canada: The State, Academia, and the Cultural Establishment

ALFRED YOUNG MAN

Western-created archetypes have a functional, fundamental impact on our perceptions and understanding of reality. They ultimately determine our education strategies, popular mythology, scientific opinions and definitions, and even our sense of humour. Just as important, stereotypes play an integral role in the way the West defines First Nations people, their history, and their art. This can be seen through a review of both contemporary and traditional Native art and the treatment it has received in Canada by the state, academia, and the cultural establishment, including museums.

MUSEUMS AND TRADITIONAL NATIVE ART

Displaying the skeletons of long-deceased ancestors in order to satisfy the curiosity of the public is odious at best to many First Nations people. The repatriation of skeletal remains by Indians from the world's largest "Indian grave yard," the Smithsonian Institution, has only recently become possible. Special legislation had to be enacted by Congress in order to return for reburial what had in many cases been seized through simple, senseless acts of desecration and piracy of modern and ancient Indian burial grounds on the part of exploiters and enthusiasts of early Indian culture and history.[1] It is estimated that something in the neighbourhood of over 300,000 Native bodies may have been dug up over the past 200 years.[2] The majority of the remains are stashed away in secured storage vaults in museums like the Smithsonian.

Early European explorers and adventurers who travelled west of the Mississippi River from the sixteenth to the nineteenth centuries returned home with ship- and wagonloads of randomly collected artifacts. Such people would display their collections in a glass case, known today as a "cabinet of curiosity." Modern museums such as the Canadian Museum of Civilization and the Smithsonian Institution really had their beginnings in these private cabinets.

Before the development of formal classification systems, objects were displayed as "curiosities" – without regard to their provenance other than that they came from savage, primitive peoples. "The National Institute's Cabinet which became the Smithsonian Institution exhibited Indian artifacts alongside 'the lower jaw of a sperm whale, insects from British Guiana [sic] … coral, fossils and crystal'" (Doxtator 1988:21). As time passed the original small, personal collections passed on to other personal collections, which in turn increased in size and scope through donations and various other means of acquisition. These passed on to even larger collections. The public was soon caught up in the mania of "science" and "classification" (Doxtator 1988:21).

A number of classification systems were ultimately constructed which could categorize the flood of artifacts. One such system first developed in Germany and given formal expression around 1914 in North America by Wissler in "Material Cultures of the North American Indian" was the cultural-area concept, an idea which posed its own special problems for Native people to contend with (Howard 1975:22; Wissler 1914:447-505).[3] The idea of the modern museum was being born.

Many native artists today intuitively create their aesthetic statements around this change in their world. Native academics must also struggle with erroneous conclusions about the reality behind Native art.

As an example, horse dance sticks or horse effigies were an integral part of turn-of-the-century dances where the horse itself was a primary figure. Ian M. West relates that these effigies were used by Plains Indians in such rites of passage as counting and counting coup in battle, for ceremonial clubs, and memorials (West 1978:10, 11). Among the Piegan and Blackfeet in Alberta and Montana, great religious and philosophical significance was attributed to these ceremonies. Horses were actually taken into a specially prepared arbour to dance with the people. The Smithsonian Institution's National Museum of Natural History errs in its ethnographic gallery where it reduces a horse effigy to a child's hobby horse – in a long outdated diorama. Since millions of visitors from across Canada and throughout the world have visited this particular building on the Mall in Washington, we can safely assume that over decades this particular exhibition has incorrectly influenced countless naive people.[4]

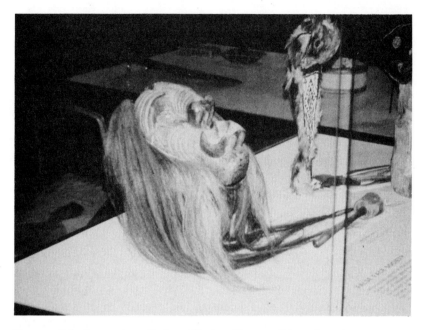

Figure 1. False face mask on display at Glenbow Museum, Calgary (1992)

The exhibition of what Native people consider sacred objects is also a contentious issue. It matters little to First Nations people whether museums and galleries consider these to be art or ethnography. The exhibition of false face masks, in particular, has given rise to a set of by-laws passed by the Haudenosaunee of Akwesasne whereby originals and replicas are strictly forbidden exhibition privileges. Nonetheless, museums continue to ignore the authority of real Indians who reserve the sole right to and sovereignty over ownership of their history and culture and therefore the autonomy and authority to state in which way their religious objects and sacraments should be used by themselves and others. One such case in which the exhibition of a false face mask raised the ire of Mohawks was the Glenbow Museum exhibition, *The Spirit Sings* (1988), in which a law suit was launched against the museum (fig. 1; not the mask in question). Mohawks from the Iroquois Confederacy who brought the suit lost the case when an uninformed Calgary judge ruled that the mask be re-instated in exhibit. Curiously, the Canadian Museum of Civilization (once again, against the wishes of the Mohawks) has made fibreglass copies of similar Iroquois masks so accurate, detailed, and aesthetically convincing that most viewers are unaware that what they are actually seeing are replicas.[5]

Plains Indians feel no differently when it comes to seeing items like medicine bundles, sacred pipes, war bonnets, rattles, and eagle bone whistles used in sun dances or other personal heirlooms irreverently displayed for public consumption and profit. When such objects are isolated behind glass, out of reach and beyond the touch and feelings of those who have made them, a vicious schism is created in those people's lives. The only way to positively bridge this violence is to have the items on display honourably repatriated to their rightful owners. This tear in the social fabric remains a problem so as long as the people who claim the objects are alive and as long as the objects remain behind glass.

The refusal of museums to legally recognize the psychological cost to Indians in this regard is unforgivable. The Assembly of First Nations/Canadian Museums Association Joint Task Force met over a period of years to discuss such concerns as repatriation of artifacts and the exhibition of sacred remains on a nationwide basis after an initial meeting in Ottawa in 1988 (Hill 1988:2).[6] Little progress has been made, however, toward meeting the pressing concerns and needs of those haunted today by such gelid museum policies. As Tom Hill wrote in *Muse*, "Museums have been manifestations of a colonial society for too long (Hill 1988:2).

THE ACADEMIC STUDY OF NATIVE PEOPLES

The invasion of waves of uninvited, uninformed, enigmatic academic guests in the early- to mid-nineteenth century doing "pure research" and other kinds of investigations must have been a curious sight to Indians of that period. These essentially nomadic academic proletarians, characteristically naïve but sincere individuals toting pencils, notebooks, cameras, paint brushes, canvases, sketch books, and more recently tape recorders, fanned out across North and South America by the thousands in earnest quest of their subject matter in whatever field they happened to specialize – art, anthropology, ethnology, psychology, religion, literature, or whatever. Some would become self-proclaimed *participant-observers*. Their ultimate aim was to leave Indian country hours, days, months, and sometimes even years later with massive documentary evidence – drawings, paintings, and photographs – of the vanishing tribal life on the "res." Some even alleged that they carried away precious notes and tape recordings about the myths, legends, songs, and languages of entire races on the verge of extinction (Deloria 1969:83).[7] For the most part these people seem to have ended their research with no greater understanding of the people they "studied" than when they began.

What were the first social scientists' plans for all that data they so laboriously gathered over the years? Did they advise their informants of their intentions? Normally, no. What was an anthropologist supposed to tell an Indian of the 1920s, 30s, 40s or 50s about anthropology's hidden agenda? Can you imagine an anthropologist telling an Indian Elder informant something like: "We are studying your people and society because you all represent a more primitive level of social, artistic, linguistic, religious, and technological development than ourselves and we plan to exhibit your primordial hide shields, rattles, drums, tipis, spears, stone tools, and whatever else we can dig up alongside our far more advanced weapons and superior technology?" The real agenda had to remain largely unknown to First Nations individuals in order to maintain "scientific objectivity" at all costs. Native informants and their children would not find out until much later how deviously and haphazardly this had all been formulated. What are theories, after all, if not incomplete dogma? It appears to be self-evident that even the principal investigators themselves, had little idea when their work was leading.[8]

Unknown to First Nations people, the knowledge they so freely gave would be used in novel and unexpected ways over the years. The Glenbow Museum in Calgary, the Museum of Civilizations in Ottawa, the Museum of Mankind in London, England, the Buffalo Bill Cody Museum in Cody, Wyoming, and the Smithsonian Institution, to name a few, exhibited virtually all of the information gathered by their specialists within the archetypal context of "primitive" versus "civilized." Had early Native informants been given the opportunity to rationalize and fully appreciate the ultimate nature and implications of their participation in such "scientific" studies, I seriously doubt that they would have taken part. Underscoring this issue is the absurd fact that in spite of all the studies done on Northwest Coast art in British Columbia (they are perhaps the most studied Indian people in North America), the province still does not have a school of Northwest Coast Indian art in any of their major art institutions or universities. Native people cannot help but wonder, "What is the point?"

CONSTRUCTING THE MYTH OF THE "REAL INDIAN"

Inevitably, artistic and political repercussions have occurred against all the theories and tabloid tales which allege to know more about Native peoples than they know about themselves. For over a century art and anthropology had the upper hand, doing pretty much whatever they pleased, whenever they pleased, in their study of these "primitive peo-

Figure 2. The ethnographic present "Indian"

ples." Had Edward S. Curtis faced the kind of Native activism found today at Kanehsatake, on the Piegan Reserve northwest of Lethbridge,
on the Queen Charlotte Islands, and on virtually every other reserve in
Canada, his famed "vanishing race" sepia photographs (which carry so
much ideological weight with the public) would have never seen the
light of day.[9] Anthropological icons like Franz Boas and Lewis Henry
Morgan would probably never have have gained any credibility with
the Kwakiutl, Haida, Blackfoot, or Haudenosaunee.

The Northwest Coast Indians protographed by Curtis epitomize the
idea of the ethnographic present Indian (fig. 2). These people were
real, of course. Their grandchildren and great grandchildren have
every reason to be proud of these photographs. I do not mean to
comment negatively upon them. However, there have been literally
millions of such cheaply produced reproductions flooding the market
for more than half a century. Books by the tens of thousands have used
such photographs to describe the "real Indian," perhaps implying in
the process that Native people today are not deserving of the same ac-
claim.

In *The Vanishing Race And Other Illusions* (1982), Christopher M.
Lyman explains in considerable detail how Edward Curtis went about
manufacturing such portraits for public consumption. The camera
did, and does, lie. Curtis' photographs consist mostly of handcrafted,
retouched images set to the theme of extinction, which of course
never happened. Nevertheless, the myth persists today and Native artists are routinely expected to look like the Indians in the Curtis photo-

graphs if they are to be taken seriously – that is, as the genuine thing. Those Indians who do happen to resemble Curtis' images sometimes exploit that resemblance, as if they also believe.

Deloria had this to say about the problems First Nations people experience in seeing themselves as a new species invented by the white man, the "Indian":

Prior to the coming of the white man, it is doubtful if any of the tribes held a conception of that racial character which today we categorize as "Indian" ... If anything the people saw themselves simply as "men," the two-leggeds, in contradistinction to the four-leggeds ... With the advent of the white man and his insistence on seeing all red men as "Indians" came the gradual recognition that the tribes had more in common than they had separating them. Yet this feeling did not transform itself into an identifiable image until modern times, when the helplessness resulting from political and economic status and the acceptance of the innate incompetence of the "Indian" was seen to represent an experience so universal among the tribes as to constitute a new species called "Indian." (Bataille and Silet 1980:49)

Needless to say, the John and Jane Q. Public who revel in Curtis' descriptions give further credence to the stereotypes through personal preference, actions, and public performance. This influences First Nations people who may also believe their ancestors were ethnographically different from what they themselves are today. "The public has been conditioned to accept anyone as an 'Indian' so long as they adhere to a few of the 'markers' of 'Indianness,'" wrote Doxtator (1988:41). These markers range from the sublime to the ridiculous. In his introduction to Lyman's book, Deloria wrote:

Everyone loves the Edward Curtis Indians. On dormitory walls on various campuses we find noble redmen staring past us into the sepia eternity along with poses of W.C. Fields and Humphrey Bogart. Anthologies about Indians, multiplying faster than the proverbial rabbit, have obligatory Curtis reproductions sandwiched between old cliches about surrender, mother earth, and days of glory. This generation of Americans, busy as previous generations in discovering, savoring, and discarding its image of the American Indian, has been enthusiastic in acquiring Curtis photographs to affirm its identity. Indeed, the many hundreds of thousands of white citizens who have discovered Cherokee in their veins since the last census seem to use Curtis pictures to verify the authenticity of their Grey Owl Trading Post buckskin costumes. (Lyman 1982:11)

It seems that little has changed since Curtis filmed *In the Land of the War Canoes* in 1914, which was also published as a book entitled *In the*

Land of the Head-hunters in 1915. Curtis wrote, "The book had its inception in an outline or scenario for a motion picture drama dealing with the hardy Indians inhabiting northern British Columbia" (Curtis 1915:vii). In both book and film Curtis claims to "give a glimpse of the primitive Americans as they lived in the Stone Age and as they were still living when the hardy explorers Perez, Heceta, Quadra, Cook, Meares and Vancouver touched the shores of the Pacific between 1774 and 1991" (Curtis 1915:vii).

Curtis further wrote: "Astonishment has been expressed that head-hunting existed among the North American Indians, notwithstanding the fact that every explorer of the North Coast region mentioned this custom" (Curtis 1915:vii).

What is most antonishing is that so many people willingly bought and still buy into that conceit. Many of the Haidas in Curtis' film were already working in the local fishing industry, taking home a weekly pay cheque so their children could attend school. By the time early European sailors reached the Haida, the Potlatch already incorporated cannibalism and head-hunting as ritualistic folk-lore and dramatic performance, entrenching the memory of such acts of barbarism into their collective history, legend, and mythology. As Curtis quite rightly and ironically writes in the book's forward, "I am guilty of its execution." Curtis was the original electronic tabloid salesman, anticipating television as a medium for sensational journalism by more than eighty years.

Indians who visit European communities where the Noble Savage still excites the imagination immediately become part of the media landscape. In Vienna an Austrian television crew came out to interview a "savage" who was travelling around Europe in 1989. World renowned museums of ethnology in Europe still categorize and exhibit contemporary Native artists according to the archaic classification systems invented in the age of Queen Victoria. It is not uncommon to find a contemporary Native artist's work being naïvely displayed alongside artifacts from the ancient civilizations of the Sumerians, Egyptians, Mayans, Persians, or Phoenicians, or with those from the modern head-hunting people of New Guinea.

The fact that the artist may have an M.F.A. from one of the finest Canadian or U.S. art schools seems to be irrelevant. While visiting the Museum für Volkerkunde in Vienna, Austria, I came across just such a scene. The Native art on display had been made relatively recently, perhaps only a few months or years before my visit. It is not difficult to imagine that in the process of creating the art the artist(s) may have watched a CBC evening newscast anchored by Knowlton Nash or Peter Mansbridge on Parliament's deficit-cutting legislation or some such

Figure 3. Contemporary Native art on display in Museum fur
Volkerkunde, Vienna, Austria (1989)

thing. In the adjoining gallery Mayan art objects and artifacts from
long "dead" civilizations were on display.[10] European anthropologists,
with their Canadian counterparts in tow, continue to perpetuate the
old stereotypes, blithely unaware of the intellectual violence of their
actions.[11] The poster to the left of the Indian-created "American flag"
(fig. 3) is one which I designed for a University of Lethbridge Native
American Studies Department conference on border-crossing issues
relative to Jay's Treaty of 1794.

In 1923 the students at Central School Auditorium in Lethbridge, Alberta, participated in a school play called *Hiawatha* which required
them to fold their arms, like the good, dumb, stoic Indians they pre-
tended to be. The irony in all of this is that they lived next to the Kainai
Indian reserve where they could very easily have seen that the locals

Figure 4. Drawing by Raymond Johnson, Navajo Nation (circa 1978)

never behaved that way. So, why did they do it? As if to prove some things never change a modern dance troop of Utah Mormons who called themselves The Young Ambassadors from Brigham Young University (they billed themselves as wholesome family entertainment) toured the Mormon Bible belt of Southern Alberta in the early 1980s publicly satirizing their conceits about Indians in "their rendition of a western hoe-down." Was this blatant exploitation of First Nations for profit, racism disguised as entertainment, Joseph Smith gone berserk, or what?

USING MYTHOLOGY IN NATIVE ART

There has been much misunderstanding about First Nations' use of metaphor to relate their mythology and legends. The two figures below illustrate two ways of saying the same thing. Both have as their fundamental function the dissemination of myth and legend, normally related orally, presented here visually. Whereas figure 4 shows how Indians see their relationship to the world of animals, birds, and insects in a way which denotes a kind of physiological transformation, figure 5 puts forth the idea that humans and animals are brothers, not in the sense that two males are brothers, but in the way all things are related, in the metaphorical sense. Jesse Cornplanter's drawing is in direct contradiction to Darwin's theory of survival of the fittest which would have

Figure 5. Jesse Cornplanter's tribute to the slain hero

Figure 6. "Deconstructivists (This is the house that Joe built)" (1990) (*Cardinal-Schubert*)

the animals in this picture eating each other; they would not meet among themselves. In Cornplanter's illustration the different species gather in harmony, all feeling the same remorse for the slain hero. These two illustrations are excellent examples of the way Native legend enters the everyday world and psychology of contemporary Native artists and the problems they face in changing from one mode of transmission of culture to another. Contrary to popular scientific theory, legends and myths do not necessarily evolve out of primitive, superstitious societies. It is quite possible that Native legends and myths more closely reflect the truth of how the universe works than do the theories of modern science.[12] Legends exist in Native societies and inform Native art. Legends and their wisdom have largely been lost to Western society.

Joane Cardinal-Schubert, a Métis from Calgary, takes this misunderstanding very seriously. Her business is to pinpoint those "messages" constructed for us by Western politics, science, and religion and recycle them, deconstructing and then reconstructing them as her art. *Deconstructivists (This is the house that Joe built)* (1990) explores these areas for the raw material which animates her tableaus (fig. 6). The results, she asserts, have been nothing short of catastrophic for Native people's culture, religions, mythologies, and land. Philosophically, Cornplanter's animals are brothers to the Indian. What are Western science and sportsmen doing to Indians through their continued violation? Who gave the animals to the white man? Controversial Western values become the text of Cardinal-Schubert's art work.

Teresa Marshall, a Mi'kmaq from Nova Scotia, uses that famous tool of capitalist history, the board game "Monopoly," in her installation of that name (fig. 7) to get her message across, a message which is similar in tone and urgency to those works of Joane Cardinal-Schubert. Another work, *Peace Order and Good Government* (1993), symbolically invokes the power of Mi'kmaq colour and design to encase a safe, a gun, work boots, and a hard hat as a trade in Indian values. Plains Cree Gerald McMaster, coordinator of contemporary Native art at the Canadian Museum of Civilization, utilizes the stuff of ambiguity and stereotype in *Savage Graces: After Images* (fig. 8). His statements often understate the humourous side of the Indian predicament. *Red Man Watching White Man Trying to Fix Hole in Sky* (fig. 9), by Emily Carr School graduate Lawrence Paul Yuxweluptun, a Coast/Salish/Okanagan artist, depicts Northwest Coast formline humans pushing in directions many people do not like, literally and metaphorically. Yuxweluptun has become controversial, to say the least. Anthropologists in particular have problems with his work, as it flies in the face of everything they believe about the survival of Northwest Coast formline design, therefore culture.

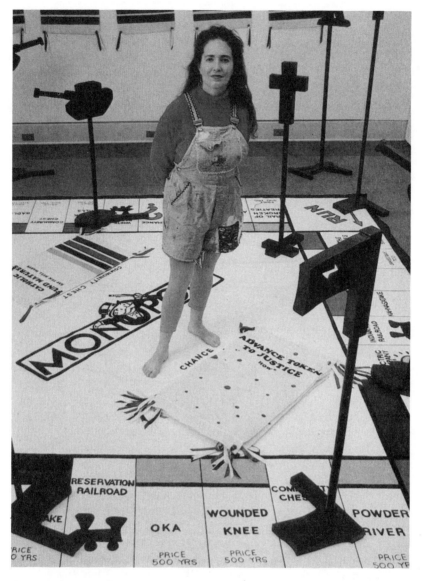

Figure 7. "Monopoly" (1991) (*Marshall*)

Rebecca Belmore from Thunder Bay was invited to Banff in the summer of 1991 to participate in *Between Views*, an exhibition of eight artists who addressed issues related to travel, place, identity, and belonging. The performance piece *Ayum-ee-aawach Oomama-mowan: Speaking to Their Mother* carried Native messages to the Earth Mother (fig. 10). The spot she had chosen was a beautiful meadow sur-

Figure 8. "Savage Graces: After Images" (1992) (*McMaster*)

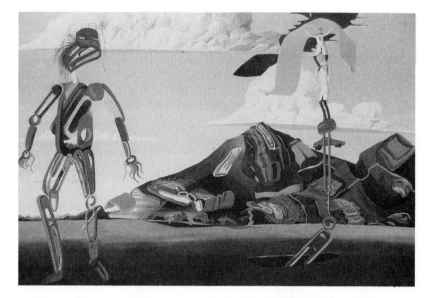

Figure 9. "Red Man Watching White Man Trying To Fix Hole In Sky"
(1990) (*McMaster*)

Figure 10. "Ayum-ee-aawach Oomama-mowan: Speaking to Their Mother"
(1991) (*Belmore*)

Figure 11. "Cowboy Time" (1986) (*Glazer-Danay*)

rounded by majestic mountains. Belmore's megaphone later appeared
on the cover of the National Gallery's 1992 catalogue of Native art
called *Land Spirit Power*. Blood artist Faye Heavyshield subtly comments
upon Christianity, sexuality, feminism, and Kainai mythology and legend in *Heart, Hoof, Horns.*

NATIVE ART AND THE CULTURAL ESTABLISHMENT

Much contemporary Native art, especially the more critical statements,
are not all that popular in public or private art galleries. Ironically, uni-
versity-educated artists find their most favourable audiences in anthropology museums. Mohawk artist Rick Glazer-Danay, for example, from
Caughnawaga (now Kanehwake), Quebec, holds an MFA from the University of California, Los Angeles. This was of no concern to the Museum
of Mankind in London, England, in the 1980s, who still chose to exhibit
his work alongside ancient Aztec artifacts. Danay is a full professor at the
University of California, Long Beach, but obviously his degree has conferred upon him neither automatic status as an artist nor membership
into the exclusive club of "civilized" artists. To look at it another way, how
many Euro-American artists with MFA's have you have seen exhibiting in
ethnographic museums lately? *Cowboy Time* (fig. 11) is a Danay's humor-
ous send up of "Indian time." Indian time is … well, Indian *time!*

Figure 12. "The End of Innocence" (1991) (*Longfish*)

In the 1970s George Longfish, a Seneca/Tuscarora from Six Nations, was among the first Native artists to challenge the dogma surrounding that decade's definition of what constituted Native art. Although he grew up in Oshweken, Ontario, Longfish chose to defy the Canadian art establishment on neutral territory (in the USA) where he also ran into stiff opposition, not only as an artist but as an art professor. So important a figure could not be left out of *Indigena*, the Canadian Museum of Civilization's 1992 exhibition of contemporary Native art. Historically he occupies a central place in the struggle of Native artists to move ahead into

Figure 13. "Legacy" (1991) (*Rivet*)

the 90s, not only in Canada but in the US.[13] *The End of Innocence* (fig. 12) is Longfish's parody of contemporary Western mythology.

Métis artist Rick Rivet, who lives on Vancouver Island, paints the conquistador as swine or wild boars who have brought the Christian syllabus to North America on the point of a spear.[14] *Legacy* (fig. 13) is not included in his newest exhibition *Directions* but can be found in McMaster and Martin's *Indigena*, where Rivet gave full expression to his political consciousness

Eric Robertson's metal wall sculpture *Bearings and Demeanours*

Figure 14. "Bearings and Demeanours" (1990) (*Robertson*)

(fig. 14) is created around the political dualism or contradictions inherent in the state versus Northwest Coast history. Works like this speak volumes about the nature of the relationship which all Native peoples have with their homelands and the state. Even though he is culturally from the other side of the country (he could be from the

Figure 15. "North American Iceberg" (1985) (*Beam*)

other side of the universe from Danay, Longfish, and other Native artists), Robertson has something in common with them through a similar political relationship with the state.

When a Native artist such as Carl Beam uses similar techniques as pop artist Robert Rauschenberg, his work is immediately labelled derivative. Strangely enough Beam's *North American Iceberg* (fig. 15) has the great distinction of being the first contemporary Native art work *ever* to be collected by the National Gallery of Canada. The gallery had for many years refused to amend its collections policy or formula concerning Native art until SCANA (The Society of Canadian Artists of Native Ancestry) came into existence. As the voice of Native artists in the early part of the 1980s (and on into the 90s), it fell to SCANA to lobby the National Gallery and other art institutions across Canada to change their collecting policies with respect to Native art.[15] SCANA clearly felt that Native art was worth collecting both as part of the Canadian state and as a way to preserve Native heritage. It can be said that until then the National Gallery did not even know there *was* a contemporary Native art heritage worth saving. The gallery simply left the unsavoury job of dealing with Indians to the anthros across the river at the Canadian Museum of Civilization in Hull.

SCANA's efforts seemed to have some effect since the National Gallery did eventually amend its collecting policy under pressure (although they would never admit it), but even today they still refuse to collect the art

Figure 16. "Coyote" (1986) (*E. Poitras*)

on the basis of it being *Native art* and a vital part not only of Canadian history but of Western art history.[16] SCANA continues to network right across the country. Many people in the art establishment still do not fully accept the concept and reality of Native art in its own right.

Coyote (fig. 16) by Métis artist Eddie Poitras is made out of coyote bones gathered from the plains. This kind of art work is valuable to Canada's Native heritage and is deserving of an honoured place in the National Gallery. Ojibway Ron Noganosh's *Canoe 92* (fig. 17) was once on exhibition at the Canadian Museum of Civilization where it was viewed by a Girl Guide troop who objected to the use of a neck scarf with their insignia. *Canoe 92* nevertheless accurately portrays the environmental degradation everyone is facing. In other works Noganosh takes note of the Oka crisis and the Lubicon protests in 1988 at the

Figure 17. "Canoe 92" (1992) (*Noganosh*)

Calgary Olympics. The *Lubicon* waterfall (fig. 18) employs liquor bottles which spell L-U-B-I-C-O-N. This controversial work was on display at the Vancouver Art Gallery in *Beyond History* in 1989 (Duffek 1989). In an unusual attack of morality the VAG refused to let Noganosh use real vodka to complete his statement. It was to be recirculated in an endless stream, through the mouth of a plastic skull placed on a tradi-

Figure 18. "Lubicon" (1988) (*Noganosh*)

tional burial platform. As the viewer closed in on the tableau one could hear a looped-tape playing and replaying the voice of a sobbing woman lost in the world of alcoholism.

Another Noganosh mixed-media work, *Shield for Modern Warriors or Concessions to Modern Society* (fig. 19), ingeniously uses a hubcap, crushed Labatt beer cans, leather, and fur. Tory Indian Affairs Minister

Figure 19. "Shield for Modern Warriors" (1989) (*Noganosh*)

Tom Siddon purportedly had this construction hanging on a wall in his office while the Mohawks fought his army.

Cree/Sioux artist Jim Logan sees himself as a social commentator on life in New Westminster, British Columbia, as he perceived and lived it as a child. Christianity, alcoholism, family ties, and personal despair all figure in his hockey series paintings which he completed especially for the *Indigena* show in 1992. *National Pastimes* (fig. 20) is Logan's contribution to Indian life in immigrant Canada.

Figure 20. "National Pastimes" (1991) (*Logan*)

APPROPRIATION OF NATIVE ART

Appropriation is of major concern to Natives today. Many Indians are protesting the use of Indian images or symbols as university mascots and so forth. The Internet news wires of the nation's computers are burning with Indians using e-mail to express their indignation about the blatant racist use of such imagery. Sports clubs are misguided in their impression that they are honouring Native peoples by making them mascots. "Just harmless fun!" says one sports announcer. Change the image to Jewish or Black people and see what happens. Is it still just harmless fun?

An issue which has major implications for education is that of appropriation of Native art by non-Natives, more specifically Canadian and American modern artists. But just what is it that was taken? Virtually everything (Rubin 1984).[17] The Surrealist Max Ernst openly declared his affinity for Northwest Coast and Pueblo Indian art forms. This attraction definitely influenced the structural qualities of his art (fig. 21). He used the Northwest and Southwest art constructs to his heart's content. He was never criticized for his attempted appropriation of another culture. *The King Playing with the Queen* (1944) seems to embody that very contention (Spalding 1979:35). Of course, that might be the surrealism he intended. Ernst avidly collected the works of African, New Guinea, and Peruvian artists in the early part of the century for clues to any artistry which might improve upon his in-

Figure 21. Max Ernst and the Northwest Coast paradigm.

sights into his own art. Modern artists routinely collected Native art by the trainload as well as that art work created by other indigenous artists, the so-called "Others" of the world, in order to enrich their lives (Rubin 1984).[18]

Native art's conventional methodology was the driving force behind much that is considered modernist invention. From the Spanish Picasso to the American Warhol to the Canadians Carr and Shadbolt we can ascertain that Native art has had a great influence. Yet textbooks on the history of the art of Canada and the Western world are just beginning to address these issues; too often the pages stand in mute testimony to this fact. Any notion that Native art might have had an impact on Euro-Canadian and American aesthetics and philosophy during this past century is still strictly qualified. Like the unrecognized historical fact that the u.s. Constitution[19] is based squarely upon the principles of government founded by the Iroquois League of Nations (Six Nations) over eight hundred years ago, Native art's rightful place in Canadian and Western art history is all but unrecognized. The debt which modernism owes Native art and the depths to which modern and post-modern art have been influenced by Native art may never be known. The West has clearly experienced a break with its past, a dangerous situation if occurring in an individual's personal life, deadly as well if found within the doctrines of the state (working on the premise of course that such an entity exists). We can only hope that the current cavalier attitude is not just "a state of mind."

CONCLUSION

To fundamentally change Native societies and culture beyond all recognition has been the quintessential quest of the Canadian state for more than a century, and it has been an unqualified failure. What about assimilation? To be sure there have been indigenous nations in Canada who have succumbed to the genocidal practices of early land- and resource-hungry pioneers and settlers who are now long dead. Saulteaux painter Robert Houle alludes to this in his paintings. Others may have met "statistical" doom but still maintain their Native roots, however improbable this may seem. Still others have simply moved beyond the borders of Canada to better places. Although there are no actual documented cases of mass assimilation, the theory has become part of our common vocabulary. We have no idea what the mechanisms may be by which whole nations of indigenous and foreign peoples become totally and unequivocally assimilated. Is it possible that the idea of assimilation is just another deception grounded and promoted in ignorance? This is appearing to be more likely every day.[20]

No doubt there is a concerted effort on the part of many Canadians to simply absorb and do away with Native Canadians. That seems to be a waste of time, especially here in multicultural Canada. But what is multiculturalism about, anyway? I once attended a national conference on multiculturalism in Ottawa. One evening a reception was held on Parliament Hill for the several hundred invited quests from the different ethnic groups. There were East Indians, Ukrainians, Polish, German, Japanese, and every other ethnic group represented. I assumed that we were all supposed to come as the people we are. I showed up in my blue jeans, cowboy boots, choker, and a ribbon shirt, with my hair tied with leather thongs in two braids in the traditional fashion of a Plains Cree man. To my astonishment, everyone else was wearing tuxedos and gowns.

NOTES

1 Canada has only recently begun to address this important issue. The legislation in question is the Native American Graves Protection and Repatriation Act 1990. Contrary to what academics routinely teach as credo not all graves were dug up for the advancement of knowledge.
2 Even here science would rather be seen as "excavating" rather than "digging up." There may be more skeletons stored away than there are live Indians.
3 Howard does a good job of bringing this fact to light.
4 The fact that West says the collector Major J. M. Bell may have observed children playing with this particular object among the Sioux captives from whom he retained it in 1893 is largely immaterial.
5 When *The Spirit Sings* went on to the Canadian Museum of Civilization in Ottawa they obligingly removed the contested mask. Catherine Bell explores this issue in more detail in "Repatriation of Cultural Property and Aboriginal Rights: A Survey of Contemporary Legal Issues" in *Native Studies*, a special issue of *Prairie Forum* (vol. 17, no. 2), 313.
6 Two other important studies which have positively contributed to the ongoing public debate over Native art are Lee-Ann Martin's "The Politics of Inclusion and Exclusion: Contemporary Native Art and Public Art Museums in Canada" (March 1991) and the Thunder Bay Art Gallery's *Mandate Study 1990–93* which is mainly concerned with the redefinition of its own policy with regards to the collection, exhibition and interpretation of contemporary Native art. Director Sharon Godwin envisions the study as hopefully having an influence on other museum and gallery policies in both Canada and the u.s. See Houle in bibliography.
7 Vine Deloria, Jr, a Lakota political scientist with Sioux relatives on both sides of the border, skewers the anthropological profession's idea and practise of "pure research" in one witty, vindictively humourous chapter entitled "Anthropologists and Other Friends." He has proved to be an even more progressively articulate, entertaining, and lucid author in other books and articles he has written since 1966. He has not exclusively afforded the Native art world the "jewels of his wisdom."
8 About now I should be getting charged with engaging in a meaningless diatribe and trivializing the old and noble professions of anthropology (known as anthropology bashing), religion, and so forth ... but press onward. No one likes to be publicly analyzed, no matter how good the intentions. This should be a lesson to those who must study "Indians."
9 He thought the people were disagreeable back then!
10 For those who may question it, I am aware that the Mayan people are not extinct, but European anthros appear not to know this.

11 This is gradually changing today, more so in Canada than in Europe although museums like the Canadian Museum of Civilization continue to misunderstand the importance of contemporary Native art and artists.

12 It is important to point out here that Indians don't have the custom of scientific theory which acts to unnecessarily cast problematical noise over otherwise pure ideas found in myths and legends which in themselves have the power to move art.

13 See Gordon, *Confluences of Tradition and Change* (1981). This important exhibition curated by Longfish would later serve as the foundation for much of the highly praised book *The Arts of the North American Indian: Traditions in Evolution* which Edwin L. Wade edited in 1986. Typically Longfish did not get the deserved credit although the editor did include one of his paintings. Some consolation!

14 See Clark, *Directions* (1992). For the most part Rivet focuses on shamanism in this latest exhibition even though the term itself is of Russian origin and has very little to do with Native spirituality.

15 The NGC today has a policy which explicitly authorizes "the acquisition of representative examples of contemporary Inuit and Indian art" ("Collections Policy and Procedures," revised 1984 and 1990, National Gallery of Canada archives, p. 57, as quoted in *Land, Spirit, Power* p. 17). SCANA has also had a great influence on virtually every other form of progress made by contemporary Native art in the past fifteen years. Its roots can be traced back at least to the 1950s (Hill 1978:34).

16 If you want to find out for yourself, do this: The next time you are in Ottawa pay a visit to the National Gallery and ask to see their Canadian Indian Art collection. In this way you can see for yourself how short sighted that institution really is.

17 The reader will see what I mean at a glance.

18 Although Rubin's invited writers do not explicitly set out to track down who appropriated what from whom, the evidence is there for all the world to see.

19 The western hemisphere's only indigenous form of government. All other forms, from Canada to Argentina, are imports.

20 As with other theories it is time to put the theory of assimilation to rest and finally admit that there are no Stone Age people in North America. Alphonso Ortiz, the Pueblo anthropologist, wonders about the archeological wisdom of pushing the dates for early occupation of North America further and further back in time. All that would finally be proved, he says, is what Indians have been saying all along, that they came from nowhere else. They simply originated here. An ancient date is essentially meaningless to the First People. For Western science it is a no-win situation. The entire exercise may one day simply be worthless, to all concerned.

BIBLIOGRAPHY

Bataille, Gretchen M., and Charles L.P. Silet, ed. 1980. *The Pretend Indians: Images of Native Americans In The Movies*. Ames: Iowa State University Press.

Bell, Catherine 1992. "Repatriation of Cultural Property and Aboriginal Rights: A Survey of Contemporary Legal Issues," Special Issue: Native Studies, *Prairie Forum* 17, no. 2:313.

Clark, Janet E. 1992. *Directions: Recent Work by Rick Rivet*, exhibition catalogue. Thunder Bay Art Gallery, 17 December 1991 – 9 February 1992.

Curtis, Edward S. 1915. (1975.) *In the Land of the Head-hunters: Indian Life and Indian Lore*. New York: Yonkers-On-Hudson, reprint: Tamarack Press.

Deloria, Jr, Vine 1969. *Custer Died for Your Sins: An Indian Manifesto*. New York: Avon.

Doxtator, Deborah 1988. *Fluffs and Feathers: An Exhibition of the Symbols of Indianness – A Resource Guide*. Brantford, Ont.: Woodland Cultural Centre.

Duffek, Karen 1989. *Beyond History*, exhibition catalogue. Vancouver Art Gallery, Vancouver, British Columbia.

Gordon, Allan M. 1981. "Confluences, An Essay," *Confluences of Tradition and Change*, exhibition catalogue. The Richard L.Nelson Gallery, University of California, Davis.

Hill, Tom 1978. "A Retrospect Of Indian Art," *The Native Perspective* 3, no. 2:34-7.

– 1988. "First Nations and Museums: Editorial," *Muse* 7, no. 3:2.

Houle, Robert, and Carol Podedworny 1994. *Mandate Study 1990-93: An Investigation of Issues Surrounding the Exhibition, Collection and Interpretation of Contemporary Art by First Nations Artists*. The Thunder Bay Art Gallery, Thunder Bay, Ontario.

Howard, James H. 1975. "The Cultural-Area Concept: Does it Refract Anthropolotical Light?" *The Indian Historian*, 8, no. 1:22–6.

Lyman, Christopher M. 1982. *The Vanishing Race And Other Illusions: Photographs of Indians by Edward S. Curtis*. New York: Pantheon Books, in association with the Smithsonian Institution Press.

Martin, Lee-Ann 1991. "The Politics of Inclusion and Exclusion: Contemporary Native Art and Public Art Museums in Canada." Report submitted to the Canada Council, March.

McMaster, Gerald, and Lee-Ann Martin. *Indigena: Contemporary Native Perspectives*, Vancouver/Toronto: Douglas and McIntyre.

Nemiroff, Diana, Robert Houle, and Charlotte Townsend-Gault 1992. *Land Spirit Power: First Nations at the National Gallery of Canada*. Ottawa: National Gallery of Canada.

Rubin, William, ed. 1984. *"Primitivism" in 20th Century Art*. New York: The Museum of Modern Art, distributed by New York Graphic Society Books, Little, Brown and Company, Boston.

Spalding, Jeffrey J. 1979. *Max Ernst*. Calgary: Glenbow-Alberta Institute.

West, Ian M. 1978. "Plains Indian Horse Sticks," *American Indian Art* 3, no. 2:58–67.

Wissler, Clark 1914. "Material Cultures of the North American Indian," *American Anthropologist*: 449–503.

PART IV

Economics: Decline of the National Economy

13 Poor Prospects: "The Rest of Canada" under Continental Integration

STEPHEN CLARKSON

If Canada has to be rebuilt without Quebec, history will not offer it much help. The four decades preceding the election of Jacques Parizeau as Quebec's second Parti Québécois – and first *pur et dur* sovereigntist – premier provide scant assurance that the rest of Canada has anything like a historical rock on which to anchor its putative nationality.

New states need economic viability, political coherence, and cultural substance as well as an international raison d'être in order to flourish, but the recent past of Canada outside Quebec shows the rest of Canada to be poorly endowed for national status in the twenty-first century. This is because much of Canada's post-war energy focused on developing a political economy that included Quebec, making it difficult retrospectively to discern an entity that can be captured by the label "Rest of the Country"(ROC). While English-Canadian politicians and officials dominated federal policy making in the first two post-war decades, French Canadians from Quebec played such a decisive role in the country's politics during the rest of the Liberal era that the economy, the polity, and even the culture of English Canada bear their imprint. Should Quebec separate, the remains of Canada would not magically rediscover themselves as a pre-existing archetype. They would have to be grafted together after radical surgery had cut out central organs from the body politic, and the prognosis for survival of the new entity would be uncertain at best.

The artificiality of ROC as an entity becomes all the clearer once we identify the dynamic interconnection of four factors:

1 the global balance of forces that prescribes the margin of manoeuvre for countries on the international stage;
2 the regime of accumulation that shapes a state's economic space and
its relationship with the world economy;
3 the mode of regulation that sets the possibilities and limits of political action;
4 the system of legitimation that defines the identity and nourishes the
consciousness of a society's citizenry.

1945-70: U.S.A. HEGEMONIC GLOBALLY, ROC HEGEMONIC FEDERALLY

The balance of forces after World War II produced a bipolar system
characterized by extreme ideological tension with a distant enemy and
unusual ideological consensus within the capitalist camp. Unquestioned
leader of the liberal industrial societies, the United States engaged in
military, economic, political, and cultural confrontation with the Soviet
Union, the leader of the centrally controlled socialist countries.

Balance of Forces: Bipolarity and Canada as Helpful Fixer

Having emerged from the devastation of war as the third- or fourth-
ranking military and economic power, Canada found itself situated not
just on the economic and cultural periphery of the United States but
as its glacis – the geographic extension of the American military system
on the direct flight path for long-range bombers between the Soviet
Union and the American heartland.

On the one hand, Ottawa *wanted* no choice: it was fully engaged
both by necessity and by will in the anti-communist cause, though it
worried about the extremes of American positions, whether that
meant General MacArthur threatening to invade communist China or
President Johnson escalating the bombing of North Vietnam. On the
other hand Ottawa *had* no choice: Great Britain's post-war economic
difficulties prevented Canada from reviving the profitable North Atlantic triangular trading relationship. It had to seek a closer relationship
with the U.S. market.

In its first quarter century U.S. economic, technological, military,
and cultural hegemony within the "free" world was overwhelming but
generous. The "special relationship" was thought to give Canadian diplomats direct access to the Washington administration and the possibility of negotiating exemptions when its policies proved unnecessarily
damaging to Canadian interests. The clash between federal mandarins
and Mackenzie King over a free trade agreement with the United States

in 1947 constituted an epiphany: Canadian officials would henceforth seek maximum possible continental economic integration consistent with their political masters' maintaining enough autonomy to sustain a self-respecting role as an autonomous state within their multilateral Atlantic alliance.

Accumulation: Continental if Possible, National if Necessary

A double-scoped regime of accumulation developed under Prime Minister Mackenzie King's chief economic minister, C.D. Howe. High Canadian tariff levels kept the Fordist production system predominantly national in its focus, but "permeable" because of high levels of foreign-controlled investment (Jenson 1989). Under the aegis of American-controlled unions, the labour movement accepted class harmony without institutional power in exchange for a steadily rising standard of living. Federal and provincial policies encouraged u.s. direct investment in Canada's resource and manufacturing sectors. Rising levels of u.s. direct investment created myriad continental subsystems at the micro-level of the corporation. The accumulation pattern was continental to the extent possible, national to the extent made necessary by a protectionist u.s. tariff structure that kept out competitive Canadian manufactured products. In adopting u.s., rather than European, technical standards for television and military equipment, Canada was recognizing and furthering its participation in a continental economic system. Infrastructure projects had nation-building objectives (Trans-Canada Highway, Trans-Canada Airlines) and were also responsive to u.s. needs (the St Lawrence Seaway, that giant zipper tying Canada to the United States, took Quebec ore to Ohio smelters; the Columbia River dam system supplied Washington state with cheap hydro generated from Canadian river power). When the national conflicted directly with the continental, the national gave way.

The Second National Policy as a Mode of Regulation

If it is true that "the role of the state in the economic life of Canada is really the modern history of Canada"(Brady in McBride and Shields 1993:5) and that the Canadian state has been the "major instrument for fostering [the Canadian nationality's] growth" (Resnick 1990:207), then the post-war mode of regulation can be understood as having been central to Canada's development. The construction of a Keynesian welfare state was a half-hearted process, Keynesian principles being observed as much in the breach as in the practice (Campbell

1987). The tax system was designed to encourage corporate growth, particularly u.s. investment. The social safety net was put in place haltingly, with modest pensions and family allowances followed by unemployment and hospital insurance. This mode of regulation developed during the King/St Laurent/Diefenbaker/Pearson era by English Canadians at the top of the vertical mosaic; the Quebec government passively objected to these federal initiatives until 1960, then aggressively pushed back as it built up its own welfare state.

A Conflicted System of Legitimation

Beyond the satisfaction with the post-war political economy that came from a standard of living which doubled over the period, Canada's legitimation system was split among four major claims on its citizenry's identity. English Canada emerged from World War II with its ruling political and cultural élites still oriented to the United Kingdom, but their diminishing British-as-mother-country identification was fast giving way to America-the-beautiful as the referent for its rising urban middle class. At the level of mass cultural, sports, and leisure activity, including much of the educational system from kindergarden to graduate school, the United States was culturally hegemonic.

Military metaphors dominated the Massey-Lévesque inquiry into the state of Canada's "arts and letters": the Canadian psyche was being invaded by American media of all sorts, particularly radio and film, with television pushing its way into the country's livingrooms. Unwilling to repulse Hollywood's monopolistic occupation of the film territory, the Canadian government's efforts were directed less toward countering that influence than to constructing a separate Canadian cultural sphere at the middle to high reaches of the information and entertainment spectrum, a kind of quiet off-Broadway eddy running beside the main current.

1971–81: TRUDEAU AND THE TIME OF TROUBLES

The global power system had been preparing to realign throughout the 1960s, but the seismic readjustment came only on 15 August 1971, when Richard Nixon announced to an astonished world that the u.s. could no longer afford to play western hegemon and was giving up its leadership in the market place.[1] Whatever the nuances, Nixonomics' uncoupling of the u.s. dollar from gold meant the end of the post-war monetary regime established by the Bretton Woods Agreement. As strategist for Republican presidents in the early 1970s, Henry Kissinger expected Sino-Soviet divisions within the socialist camp to allow the East-West standoff to moderate. Europe and Japan had rebuilt their economies and were poised to take up *le défi américain* (Servan-Schreiber 1967). The greater heft of these other large capitalist countries led to a new power sharing in the creation in 1975 of the economic summit, a club to which Washington sponsored Canada's admission in 1976 to help offset declining u.s. heft in the newly multipolar world.

Multipolarity: Canada and the Third Option

Nothing in Pierre Trudeau's intellectual armoury when he became prime minister in 1968 heralded a disengagement from Canada's quietly diplomatic continental interlock with the United States. Canada only moved toward greater autonomy because the u.s. colossus shifted from a benevolent to a more predatory stance vis-à-vis the outside world. President Nixon first aborted the special relationship by refusing Canada exemptions from Nixonomics and then by ironically declaring Canada to be independent. By dealing an equally powerful blow to the stature of the White House with his Watergate shenanigans, Nixon was forcing Canada to be free – at least for a time. In the context of a new constellation of global forces and an atmosphere of détente, the Trudeau government was offered more geopolitical space for manoeuvre than it had inherited from Lester Pearson, and it declared the Third Option strategy as an official rationale for the development and diversification of its national economy (Sharp 1972). In response to the devaluation of their assets the oil-rich countries of the Third World flexed their muscles in the OPEC cartel, and in revaluing all resource prices enhanced Canada's position in the global hierarchy, causing it in the views of some scholars to become a "principal power" (Dewitt and Kirton 1983). Premier Peter Lougheed and his blue-eyed sheiks in Alberta could dream of a diversified, petroleum-powered economy just as Premier Robert Bourassa could envisage exporting the renewable power of the James Bay watershed for an export income that could finance Quebec's economic development independently from the rest of Canada.

National and Provincial Institution Building

Freed by this greater room for manoeuvre – the intercontinental and submarine-launched ballistic missile had made Canadian air space and

Norad less important to the Pentagon – the Trudeau regime presided over what it believed was the completion of the federal state's development.

But the Third Option was premised on Ottawa's developing a nationally coherent accumulation regime. While other countries developed their industrial strategies, Canadians argued over whether to have one (Chandler 1988). As a result of this non-consensus, the new nation-building institutions – Canada Development Corporation, Petro-Canada, the Foreign Investment Review Agency – which the Trudeauites created to assert a more explicitly national orientation to federal regulatory activity, were not connected to an overarching economic strategy. Redistributive efforts by the federal government were focused less on income than on provincial equalization: large transfers were made from the rich (Ontario, the manufacturing engine of the economy) to the poor (Quebec and the Maritimes). In the same period public policy changes continued to enrich and complete the social safety net, universal medicare (1968), and an enriched unemployment insurance system (1971) being established just as the fiscal capacity of the federal state and the political will of the public to meet these growing obligations reached the limits of what was tolerable under higher levels of social distress and budgetary costs than the policy makers had anticipated. For its part the federal treasury proved unable to meet these unforeseen demands on its services. The resulting fiscal crisis took the form of the puzzling phenomenon of stagflation, simultaneously high levels of unemployment and inflation. A residual belief in Keynesian stimulation favouring deficit financing caused the national debt to explode.

Even though the demise of the Keynesian welfare state was imminent, the Trudeauites' commitment to positive liberalism prevented them from preparing an alternative. Their alleged nationalism was a compromise based on denying – and therefore doing little about – the significance of Canada's already advanced degree of continental integration but fostering a pan-Canadian consciousness through constitutional and programmatic actions designed to combat the appeal of separatism in Quebec.

Divergence within the System of Legitimation

In English Canada, with the British cultural connection reduced to little more than the Stratford Festival, space for indigenous cultural development expanded. This happened thanks to the sustenance of the existing set of institutions (Canadian Broadcasting Corporation, Canada Council, National Film Board) by a government that, while not showing particular interest in culture, did not shut off public funding. The Canadian Conference of the Arts – an umbrella organization grouping many professional creative workers into a federated lobby – symbolized the maturing of a number of identifiable cultural industries and professions.

Intensification of cultural production in the wake both of government policy and of a self-consciously nationalist generation challenged the internationalist mainstream cultural institutions (Montreal Symphony, Shaw Festival) in favour of smaller, more self-consciously indigenous forums (Tarragon Theatre, Coach House Press, *Hammersmith* magazine). This activity bore fruit with the coming of age of English-Canadian fiction (Alice Munro, Robertson Davies, Michael Ondaatje, Margaret Atwood), the high quality of indigenous theatre, and the expansion of the Canadian curriculum throughout all levels of the educational system.

Success in these sectors was limited because cultural regulatory bodies responded to new technologies with contradictory decisions. With its right hand the Canadian Radio-television and Telecommunications Commission permitted cable delivery of the three u.s. private networks plus PBS to almost every Canadian home, profoundly deepening continental cultural and informational integration (Ellis 1992) Government development of the communications network with scant concern about its contents constituted an "implicit subsidization of foreign producers while simultaneously cutting the throat of Canadian culture" (Comor 1991:243). With its left hand the CRTC supervized the Canadianization of the broadcasting industry's ownership structure and imposed quotas of Canadian content on its transmissions. Bill C-58 protected the advertising revenues of the television industry, but little was done to ensure that its broadcasting would do anything much beyond retransmitting American programming to the country's viewership.

Continental Accumulation Drains the National

By the time the Canadian government became interested in strengthening the national economy to achieve greater autonomy from the vagaries of Washington, the Canadian market was losing its national orientation. Multilateral tariff reductions from the GATT Tokyo round and bilateral sector-wide agreements for managed free trade in automobiles, defence production, and agricultural equipment had reduced the significance of tariff protection for foreign- as well as indigenously-owned enterprise.

By the mid 1970s the volume of Canadian capital moving into the u.s. economy exceeded that of American capital moving north (Rugman

1988:9). Canadian business had abandoned its earlier nationalism and statism. Transnationals in the staples and real estate sectors had freed themselves of their infant-industry need for munificence from the Canadian state. In 1975 they were mightily alarmed by the wage and price controls that Trudeau imposed. Even if wages were more controlled than prices, the prospect of increased government involvement in the marketplace was profoundly disturbing to big capital, which set up the Business Council on National Issues (BCNI) to articulate the view of continental business more coherently and effectively in the corridors of power.

By the early 1980s Canadian business had lost interest in the federal state. It spurned and scorned the national accumulation strategy offered it by Marc Lalonde's actual National Energy Program and Herb Gray's potential industrial strategy. Both were designed to promote indigenous entrepreneurs, large, medium, and small, but both were reviled by their putative beneficiaries whose priority was expanding their activities in the United States market rather than developing further in Canada. For Robert Campeau, the Reichmanns of Olympia and York, Ted Rogers, and even The Toronto Star's Harlequin Enterprises, the pot of gold lay south of the border. Entrepreneurs, who had accumulated their wealth thanks to the protective ministrations of the Canadian state, were mouthing the neo-conservative line that government had to be removed from the backs of business. Trudeau-style intervention had to be stopped. It was, and initially the job was done by the Trudeauites themselves.

CANADA AT THE END OF THE LIBERAL ERA

Although the Trudeauites came back to power in 1980 determined to introduce an interventionist economic strategy, they were driven by external forces (the fall in world commodity prices) and by internal problems (the political disaster of their 1981 tax reform budget and the huge strain put on government expenditures by an acute recession) to beat an ideological retreat. This led the federal Grits, who kept claiming to be promoting their left-Liberal agenda, to adopt increasingly business-friendly positions, which brought the policies of the Canadian government more into line with those of the colossus to the south.

Tripolarity and the North American Accord

A world of solidifying regional blocs characterized the global system of the 1980s, with North America's economic vulnerability growing as its strength declined (Deblock and Rioux 1993:24). Their morale shaken by their nation's embarrassing weakness, American politicians reacted with a new aggressiveness. The humiliation of the American withdrawal from Vietnam combined with the shamingly feeble response of the Carter administration to revolutionary Iran set the psychic stage for the radical right to bring its long campaign to take over the Republican party to a successful conclusion (Kriegler 1986:11). The u.s. may have lost its position of global economic dominance, but the neo-conservatives' genial frontman, Ronald Reagan, was determined to make the power of the u.s. felt more forcefully than ever in the western hemisphere. By expressing his startling notion of a North American accord in his presidential election campaign of 1980, Reagan reversed Nixon's repudiation of the special Canadian-American relationship. Canada became the first candidate for the Republicans' zeal in preaching the free-market gospel abroad. The northern neighbour was to be drawn into a new hemispheric sphere of influence.

Reagan's politics of nostalgia and patriotism turned out to be costly to Canada. Policies on energy and investment that had been acceptable or at least bearable to Carter's Washington became outrageous and intolerable to the Reaganauts. Washington would not accept a Cuba to the north or even a neighbour friendly to Cuba. Canada had to learn the virtues of laissez faire, at least in the areas of interest to American capitalism. The NEP, FIRA, cultural protectionism: all must give way to the level playing field, with Washington adjusting the levels.

Neo-Liberalism as an Alternative Mode of Regulation

By 1982 the welfare Liberals in the Trudeau government were in retreat, nationalist ministers being replaced in key departments by neo-liberals, who looked at the business community with less hostility than their colleagues. The interventionist industrial strategy which the Liberals had promised to win their mandate for power was scotched by the federal bureaucracy. Enhanced staple development through a series of resource mega-projects, whose linkages with the rest of the economy was to fuel an industrial renaissance, also turned out to be a non-starter once resource prices started to fall. In intellectual disarray the Trudeauites abdicated leadership to the forces that they had ostensibly battled by adopting the business community's position as articulated by the BCNI.

Strain on the System of Legitimation

Apart from excitement about their athletes' prowess at periodic Olympics and their pride in Pierre Trudeau's international efforts on behalf of his north-south and east-west causes, Canadians were mainly united by their identification with the benefits produced by the welfare state. However far the Trudeau government leaned to the right at its end, the popularity of its defence of universal medicare showed that even when the welfare state was under intense strain, the Canadian polity enjoyed strong legitimacy in the public's eye. More powerful than multiculturalism, the Charter of Rights and Freedoms had given third-force Canadians and minority groups of all kinds within English-speaking Canada a sense of their rights that was precious and attaching. The integration English Canada experienced as a result of the popularity of the Charter was not at first bought at the expense of Quebec's alienation. Trudeau's constitutional settlement enjoyed a high level of approval among francophones generally (Dion 1993:8), though Quebec's political and media élite remained dangerously unhappy.

At the end of the Trudeau era Canada outside Quebec was neither a political nor an economic entity of its own. The two solitudes persisted as separate anglophone and francophone cultures, but they were also held together by bilingual élites in government, academia, and the media. Compared with its shaky condition under Lester Pearson in the mid-1960s, the Canadian economy was more viable at the time of Pierre Trudeau's retirement, the Canadian polity more coherent, Canadian culture more substantial, and Canada more clearly differentiated as a participant in the world's major organizations. The Rest of Canada was a phrase that had not had to be invented. This situation was not to survive a radical shift in the country's political leadership.

1984–93: THE NEO-CONSERVATIVE SCOURGE

In order to assess the prospects for the Rest of Canada as an economic, political, and cultural entity, it helps to understand the powerful dynamic set in motion by Brian Mulroney's relationship with his American friends. While the Trudeau government had made straight the way for what was to follow, the abrupt reversal in Canada's historic development pattern in the late 1980s bore the stamp of a politician the likes of which had never occupied the apex of power in Canada before. Raised in the resource hinterland where continentalist values typically prevail (Cuneo 1976), learning his politics in Quebec where concerns about Americanization are anaesthetized by the protective barrier of language, and reaching the peak of his corporate career as the branch manager of a u.s. resource subsidiary, Brian Mulroney took office as Canada's most American prime minister, a comprador less attuned to the concerns of his own electorate than to the desires of his imperial master (Chodos 1988).

u.s. Multilateralism, Unilateralism, and Bilateralism

As the cold war came to its happy climax, the u.s. redoubled its strategic efforts although the cost of its military reassertion was a drastic weakening of its economic status as investor (from world creditor to world debtor) and as trader (from net exporter to net importer). While not giving up its global claims – it was to show its undisputable military supremacy in the Gulf War – the u.s. could no longer prevail economically by imposing its will on its European and Asian partners. Faced with economic crisis, the administration determined to ignore the log in its own eye but force its trade partners through unilateral retaliatory actions to remove the motes in theirs.

At the GATT's Uruguay round of trade negotiations, it adopted a rigid position demanding zero level for subsidies, the inclusion of services in the trading regime, and a drastic expansion of intellectual property rights for private enterprise. At the International Monetary Fund it demanded that the debt-ridden third world be pressured toward free-market practices by making loan relief conditional on tough structural adjustment programs.

Without the economic clout to control the multilateral agenda, the United States developed a regional fallback position to build up its position vis-à-vis its regional competitors in Europe and Asia. If the global economy was now forming as a triad of continental trading areas, Washington determined to tighten its grip on its own bloc, complementing its multilateral and unilateral strategies with a new version of the Monroe Doctrine.

Using the carrot of continued access to its market and the stick of retaliation, the u.s. set out to negotiate trade and investment agreements that would incorporate its neighbours' markets while isolating – though constraining – their political systems. The u.s. was not about to negotiate a new community of the Americas agreement on the European model. It wanted to proceed on a hub and spoke basis, using separate giant-to-pygmy negotiations with each country to obtain the maximum gains with the minimum risk of diluting its own sovereignty. The first to thrust itself into Washington's new hemispheric strategy – following prodding from corporate America – was Canada.

Trade Theory Triumphs; The Mode of Regulation is Gutted

Brian Mulroney's agenda was not immediately apparent, since he campaigned for election as prime minister more as a keep-things-as-they-are liberal for whom social programs were a "sacred trust" than as a neo-conservative dedicated to rolling back the Keynesian welfare state (Bercuson, Granatstein, and Young 1986). But within a year of his election he had adopted an agenda as politically ambitious (a transformation of the federal state) as it was historically revolutionary (achieving these goals through institutionalizing a new political subordination to the United States).

The ideas of Thatcherite and Reaganite neo-conservatism had been imported and diffused in Canada through the BCNI and other business organizations and organs. They formed the basis for an unusual business consensus that was articulated strongly to the Royal Commission on the Economic Union and Development Prospects for Canada and aimed to re-establish the special Canadian-American relationship by reuniting Canadian and American élites. This Macdonald Commission, which had been set up in 1982 to develop a new agenda for the governing Liberals, had been won over to the doctrine of free trade by its chair, the corporate lawyer and former finance minister, Donald Macdonald, and by the trade-theory guild of mainstream economists who offered a powerful rationale for free trade as a panacea for Canada's problems (Clarkson 1993).

The Canadian economy had recovered from the 1982–83 recession by the time the Macdonald Commission reported in 1985, but the report maintained nevertheless that Canada was in a double state of apprehended crisis. It declared that the Trudeau Liberals' attempts to develop an industrial strategy had failed at the national level because they were wrong in principle: intervention could never work. It also warned that growing protectionist pressures in Congress threatened to close the American market to Canada's exports, the basis of its prosperity.

A radical reversal of the direction of national policy was needed. Instead of made-in-Canada, state-led economic policies, the Macdonald report recommended a market-led solution that was continental in scope. In short, a bilateral free trade arrangement with the United States was Macdonald's tidy solution for Canada's woes. Negotiating a deal endorsed by Congress would achieve exemption from U.S. trade protectionism. It would also provide Canada with the negative industrial strategy it really needed – anti-interventionist market discipline on over-active federal and provincial governments. Canadians' political concern about getting too close to the world's greatest power was dealt with by assuming that agriculture, energy, and culture could be excluded from the negotiations. Also assumed were generous federal adjustment programs to ease the transition of workers from the losing low-productivity industries to winning high-value-added sectors of the economy.[2] Provincial legislative assent and a federal-provincial consensus on free trade were taken for granted by Macdonald as prerequisites for making his leap of faith.(Macdonald Commission 1985:383)

By October 1987 when the general outlines of the deal were revealed, it turned out that secure access had not been achieved. Far from gaining exemption from U.S. trade-remedy legislation, Canada had agreed to a dispute-settlement mechanism which legitimized the application of American (rather than GATT) rules to Canadian-American trade and perpetuated their arbitrariness by allowing Congress to change these rules at its pleasure. The one Canadian objective that would have made this situation bearable – a definition of permissible, non-countervailable government subsidy programs – was not achieved. Furthermore the conditions on which the negotiations had been premised turned out to be different from what Canadians had been led to expect. Agriculture, energy, and culture were included, not excluded: the Canadian government had made major concessions in each area, concessions for which there seemed to be few balancing benefits.

Since Canadian tariffs, low as they were by that time, were twice as high as U.S. tariffs, the reduction included in CUFTA was a greater threat to Canadian manufacturers serving their own market than a boon to exporters hoping to expand their sales in the U.S.[3]

While there seemed to be few advantages for Canada in the text even when the fine print had been published, the Canadian business community nevertheless adopted a near-unanimous position that it was a good deal. This consensus suggested that the real objective of business was something other than the agreement's trade chapters. Seen as an investment rather than as a trade agreement, CUFTA constituted a bill of rights for capital at the expense of government powers. The principle of national treatment helped level the U.S. playing field for Canadian business anxious to expand continentally. The requirement that governments wanting to nationalize a sector such as auto insurance or child care would have to compensate firms in that business not just for their present value but for foregone future earnings made it very unlikely that the politicians would be able to expand the social safety net and extend the social wage for their citizenry. Prohibitions on export or import taxes or two-price systems for commodities severely constrained future political efforts for environmental protection or resource management. Former premier Peter Lougheed happily crowed that CUFTA meant there could be no future National Energy Program, apparently unconcerned that it would *ipso facto* prevent Alberta using the comparative advantage available in its cheap energy supplies to diversify its own economy (Leeson 1988:229–30).

That the heart of CUFTA was curtailing government and liberating business was confirmed by the political response of the non-entrepreneurial segments of the Canadian polity. For some years organized labour had been trying to cope with the impact of market globalization in the form of capital mobility and corporate restructuring practices that were shedding and de-skilling labour and turning unionized jobs into part-time work without fringe benefits. It was well aware that, in the name of trade competitiveness, states everywhere were under pressure to unravel the social welfare system that had taken decades to put in place. Labour unions saw CUFTA as a disguised embodiment of these trends, a covert declaration of war against the working class. It was the manifestation of a neo-conservative mode of regulation designed to reduce the bargaining power of workers, cut wages, deregulate investment, and privatize services.

Polarization in the System of Legitimation

The unions were not alone in sensing CUFTA as a threat. Social groups of all kinds were aware that "free trade" represented a cataclysmic change for their members. In past years such social movements as feminists, pensioners, and Aboriginals had set up organizations (often with federal government funding) and devoted much of their political energy to dramatizing the inequities from which their members suffered and lobbying for more generous policies from their Liberal – and guilt-prone – governors. Faced by a financially straitened and ideologically hardened government unsympathetic to their cause, they realized the need for a new kind of social solidarity. The old everyone-for-themselves, single-interest lobbying practices were no longer effective. Yet these groups could hardly rely on the opposition political parties to defend their interests on free trade. While officially the party of the working class, the NDP was notoriously incapable of dealing with issues that raised conflicting class interests. The Liberal Party was an equally unreliable vessel when it came to dealing with issues of nationalism. Since "free trade" did both, the parties could not be counted on to come to the aid of the groups it threatened.

In response to this political dilemma, the Pro-Canada Network (PCN) formed in April 1987 as an alliance led by the Canadian Labour Congress and the Council of Canadians to bring under one umbrella labour and nationalists, the women's movement, the Assembly of First Nations, seniors' coalitions, student groups, the National Farmers' Union, international development organizations, church groups and an array of social, cultural and community organizations (Clarke 1992:3; Cohen 1992:33–4). This broad-based, cross-sectoral coalition rallied to defend the federal state of whose policies most of these groups had long been critical. The PCN heralded a new post-national politics outside Quebec where an unprecedented sense of social solidarity developed. Trade unionists lay down with pensioners, feminists with environmentalists. Although such Quebec organizations as the powerful Union des producteurs agricoles and the Confédération des syndicats nationaux belonged to the PCN, it was primarily an English-Canadian phenomenon. In a Polanyi-like movement of anticipatory reaction it was trying to prevent the neutering of the federal state's capacity to protect its population from the depredations of a globalized market.

When the 1988 federal election brought the free trade question to a head, Canada polarized both in class terms (business and the prosperous suburbs against the rest) and along regional lines with the élites in Quebec, Alberta, and British Columbia in favour, the Atlantic provinces generally opposed, and Ontario divided (with large sectors of opinion in each area bucking the official position). The Liberals and NDP were manoeuvred into angered opposition as they watched the course of Canadian history derailed by a prime minister either unable to understand or stubborn in denying the significance of what he was perpetrating.

With the opposition political parties lined up against what Mulroney had wrought, the Progressive Conservatives were in position to garner the business community's entire support for CUFTA. They needed it, since the PCN's months of consciousness-raising had swung a majority of the public across the country against the deal. Ultimately the inequities of the electoral system translated the Conservatives' minority popular support into a majority of seats in the House of Commons. CUFTA was signed by President Reagan and Prime Minister Mulroney on 1 January 1989, leaving Canada's system of legitimation severely shaken.

At the same time that the Progressive Conservatives were creating an external constitutional straitjacket on government through CUFTA and trying to downsize federal political institutions with an internal constitutional revision, they proceeded to undermine the national instititons they had inherited from the Liberals in 1984. The transcontinental passenger train was closed down. Canada Post was commercialized. Air Canada and Petro-Canada were put up for privatization.

More significant in its impact on the national legitimation system, the Canada Council and the CBC/Radio Canada became prime targets for concerted neo-conservative attack. The power of appointment was used to purge liberals from their boards of directors and executives and replace them with appointees whose credentials ranged from sheer ignorance to outright antipathy for cultural institutions (Bercuson, Granatstein and Young 1986:199–215).[4] Budget cuts meekly accepted by the new managers brought in to "downsize" and "rationalize" their operations starved the institutions of the funds necessary to sustain a noncorporate, noncommercial cultural activity at minimum efficiency. Bill C-93 to merge the Canada Council with the Social Sciences and Humanities Research Council was pushed through the House of Commons despite protests from the communities served by both councils.[5]

This effort to exert control over the cultural sector represented a destabilization of the country's shaky system of legitimation in favour of an enhanced presence for continental entertainment. The venerable Canadian Football League is expanding to the u.s. where Canadian content rules will be unenforceable and the name will probably be eliminated, and the National Basketball Association has joined the movement to increase the sale of u.s. cultural products in Canada, drain cash from the economy, and demand huge public subsidies for the stadiums, all in exchange for offering McJobs to parking attendants and fast-food stands in the local municipality.[6]

In undermining the public's few symbols of country-wide cohesion, the Mulroney government may have contributed to a sharpened sense of political vulnerability. The massive rejection of the Conservatives in the 1993 federal election and the surprising support that a nostalgic campaign for the spirit of "the good old days" yielded Jean Chrétien's Liberals suggests that values associated with the Canadian nation state had greater staying power than many had assumed.

Continental Accumulation with a Difference

For all the hype, CUFTA did not achieve the continental system of accumulation that had been promised, but this was of little concern for several types of business. For subsidiaries of American corporations, the process of continental if not global rationalization had been accelerating since the 1970s. The prospect of the complete elimination of an already low tariff simply meant that the import-substitution branch-plant had become a fossil. The Canadian market could be served from sites located anywhere on the globe (Litvak 1991).

Canadian companies seeking access to the American market could read the writing on the wall. The only way to be secure from continuing trade harassment was to move part or all of their operations across the border and have their products bear the precious logo, "Made in u.s.a." For Asian and European investors, the American customs officials' harassment of Honda car imports gave a similar, equally clear message: for full access to the American market it is more prudent to locate any new transplant in a u.s. state than in a Canadian province. For resource exporters whose supply base was fixed in Canada, CUFTA's failings remained a problem, as softwood lumbermen, fish packagers, and durum wheat or pork farmers were to find out.

Accelerated integration was the result, as intended. Rates of U.S. investment in Canada increased by 50 percent in the first four years of free trade, compared to the four previous years (Nymark 1994) though this was not necessarily of great advantage to the Canadian economy, since the purpose of takeovers in a deep recession was more likely to be to shut down competition – particularly in retailing – than to open new production facilities.

Fearful Asymmetry: A Skewed Continental Mode of Regulation

All the failings of CUFTA – as exacerbated in the North America Free Trade Agreement – might have been worth their cost had they produced a new regulatory mode for dealing with the continent's problems. But these agreements will make public policy making more difficult, not facilitate it – whether at the continental, national, or regional level.

For some time it has been possible to speak of a U.S.-driven continental mode of regulation in the sense that some institutions with North American reach have existed (e.g., the Pentagon, Hollywood) that made policy with continental effect, some élites (CEOs of transnational corporations) have had continental power, some policies (Autopact, Defence Production Sharing) have been designed to embrace the whole region, and some agenda-setting systems (Madison Avenue) have worked on the consciousness of American, Canadian, and even Mexican publics without regard for national boundaries (Clarkson 1988).

Only the new North American Trade Commission and the Commission for Environmental Cooperation and their small new secretariats have any claim to supranationality (Kirton 1993). CUFTA and NAFTA also established a number of ad hoc working groups that will operate far from the public eye. These may represent important precedents in the long term since the U.S. has long resisted any constraints on congressional sovereignty, but they point to the dearth in the present of viable continental institutions that adequately compensate Canada and Mexico for the derogation of decision-making power ordained by the agreements' constraining texts (Kirton 1993:25).[7]

Whereas the Community Charter of Fundamental Social Rights expressed the European nations' objectives as harmonious and balanced expansion, high levels of social justice, fair and equitable wages, improved living and working conditions, mutual benefit for all, and the protection of disadvantaged groups, the main goal of CUFTA and NAFTA is an economic playing field harmonized on the U.S. model of corporate freedom, possessive individualism, and minimal government regulation. Within a set of negative commandments which mainly instruct the smaller partners what they shall not do, the game implied behind the rhetoric is for each country to acquire as much benefit as it can at the expense of the other. Congress will continue to defend the interests of u.s. entrepreneurs *against* those of its partners. Rules of origin, spelled out in complicated detail, symbolize the protectionist intent of the agreements to the detriment, for instance, of the Canadian clothing industry. The external constitution that first CUFTA and now NAFTA represent for Canada is thus no giant step forward in the institutional history of humankind. Canada remains more vulnerable to arbitrary and protectionist harassment by u.s. interests than it was before making its leap of faith into the arms of a free-trading Uncle Sam.

Even if CUFTA and NAFTA have not changed Canada's position in the continent for the better, these agreements have managed to alter the delicate balance of Canadian federalism. At the same time that CUFTA and NAFTA are shifting power from government to the marketplace, the agreements are recentralizing federal power by turning the federal government into the enforcer of the market order (McBride and Shields 1993:8). Article 103 of CUFTA enjoins each signatory to "ensure that all necessary measures are taken in order to give effect to its provisions, including their observance ... by state, provincial and local governments" – the "strongest 'federal state' clause to which Canada has ever agreed in a trade agreement" (Brown 1991:97).

The predicted downward pressure that CUFTA would bring to harmonize social policies, safety and product quality standards, labour codes, and corporate taxes to u.s. levels seems to have come about (Stairs 1988:455–7). Further continental harmonization can be seen in the federal government's cutting back support for Canadian culture, relaxing foreign-ownership restrictions in Canadian broadcasting, and selling the government's shares in Telesat. A film distribution policy which would have guaranteed Canadian distributors a slightly increased share of their own market was shelved because the American distributors were able to dictate the policy they wanted directly to representatives of the Canadian government (Godfrey 1992:A1, A6). *Sports Illustrated* went behind the backs of the culture-policy officials in the Department of Communications to negotiate with Investment Canada permission to produce a Canadian edition of the magazine.(Ross 1993:C1)

Continental regulatory pressure also sabotaged the 1985 Baie Comeau policy which had been aimed at restructuring the book publishing industry by forcing the divestiture of foreign publishers' subsidiaries whenever the parent firms were bought out. The policy was made inoperative when the free-trade negotiations gave U.S. publishers a bargaining lever (Fields 1987:12, and 1988:12). By 1992 the government had beaten a full retreat. Subsidiaries of transnational publishers were no longer required to divest when their parent was bought out, and Canadian firms could be sold to foreign firms in "extraordinary circumstances of financial distress." With the GST applied to reading material and the loss of the postal subsidy for books, twenty years of efforts to develop a Canadian book industry had been reversed (Martin 1992:134).

Other cultural legislation was consistent with this retreat from concern about national cultural expression. The Telecommunications Act, Bill C–62, excluded all reference to government responsibility for the content of new telecommunications distribution services. As the Telecom Act freed up the market for new corporate players, the Broadcasting Act cleared the way for a single continental market in broadcasting. Bill C–40 made CRTC licensing decisions subject to overruling by cabinet and permitted "the importation into Canada of an unprecedented array of American broadcasting services which will compete directly with and undermine Canadian broadcasters who ... must provide a mix of Canadian and foreign programming" (Finestone 1990:A29). The Broadcasting Act also shrank the domain for public broadcasting and opened up more market share for corporate communication.

Under neo-conservatism the delegitimation of the public cultural sphere in the face of private distribution made the expression of national culture increasingly problematic – a more serious problem for English Canada than for Quebec with its greater cultural coherence.

THE PROSPECTS FOR ROC IN THE CLINTON-CHRÉTIEN ERA

With Bill Clinton's election, the Democrats' imperialism may seem more benign than did that of the Republicans, but their practice remains tough on Canada. It was no accident that President Clinton promised that the administration would use all the appropriate tools at its disposal to discourage Canadian discrimination against U.S. film, broadcasting, recording, or publishing interests.

But the global context for continental free trade has been transformed. The successful completion of GATT's Uruguay round signals yet another shift in the world balance of forces, with the United States appearing to accept rules and dispute settlement authority in the projected World Trade Organization that reduce its capacity unilaterally to impose its will on its trading partners. The new GATT text is more permissive of national government policies and less ideologically intrusive than NAFTA. Much depends on whether it will loosen the grip NAFTA has tightened round the necks of Canadian federal and provincial governments.

Even if the Mulroney era is over, its errors remain. The mounting federal debt burden severely limits Jean Chrétien's Liberal government from using the state to support the pro-active economic policy that has come back into fashion among economists.[8] The Chrétien Liberals' legitimation problems are overpowering: with a separatist party as official opposition, a regional party of western dissent speaking in the name of the ideological opposition, and a fiscal cupboard so bare that it has to continue along the road of austerity in social and cultural programs.

Even after a formal separation, Quebec would remain intimately connected with its northern neighbours, if only because it would have to negotiate with Canada as well as the U.S. and Mexico the terms of its admission to NAFTA. For the Rest of Canada the prospects are more troubling. It is not hard to envisage the shape of its federal politics (Gibbins 1993:264–73) and the mode of regulation that the former anglophone provinces would want to perpetuate. It is also easy to posit that the citizenry of the Rest of Canada would continue to identify with their state structures in the expectation that they would deliver levels of social policy superior to those provided in the United States. But in a continental context where NAFTA denies its lesser members the right to engage in nonmarket forms of state-led development, the new country's population is likely to be seriously and rapidly disenchanted. Even if its politicians were able and willing to generate a social-democratic policy thrust, it is hard to imagine how the private sector – so completely integrated in the American system and so little tied to the well-being of ROC's economy – would tolerate any new deviations from U.S.-defined continental norms.

In short, following Quebec's secession, the Rest of Canada could well have enough cultural substance and political coherence, but it would have neither the economic viability nor the international raison d'être to form a successful nation state.

NOTES

1 In the debate on U.S. hegemonic decline Susan Strange argues that, even if the United States has lost some of its *relational* power over other nations, it has maintained its global *structural* dominance in the fields of security, knowledge, production, and credit (Strange 1989:161–76). On the declinist side of the argument Robert Gilpin maintains that the imbalance

between American consumption and production as well as U.S. fiscal, exchange, and trade policies in the 1970s and 1980s indicated a secular decline similar to that of the British empire at the turn of the last century (Gilpin 364–6). Lester Thurow also challenges Strange by showing how the United States has fallen behind both Germany and Japan in per capita GNP, size of industrial corporations, and power of banks and service sector companies (Thurow 1992:29–30).

2 Harris and Cox also viewed generous adjustment programs as the sine qua non of a shift to bilateral free trade (Harris and Cox 1983).

3 Low tariffs: they averaged 3.3 percent. (Grinspun in Grinspun 1993:106).

4 The Canada Council's director, Timothy Porteous, was fired for defending the arm's length principle and replaced by a docile civil servant; its chair, the outspoken defender of an autonomous artistic community, Maureen Forrester, was replaced by the free-trade booster, Allan Gotlieb, whose cultural credentials included arguing strongly that Gulf and Western's takeover of Prentice-Hall, Canada should be permitted in violation of Canadian publishing policy and acting as lobbyist for a number of American public relations firms.

5 Not one of the submissions presented to the Standing Committee on National Finance supportred Bill C-93 (*The News*, Canadian Actors' Equity Association, 17 [July/August 1993], pp. 1–2, as cited in Burston 1994:61).

6 Professional sports cartels are a powerful Americanizing force, beginning with hockey. Once a uniquely Canadian sport, with powerful cultural reverberations throughout the country's literature, folk memory, and economy, hockey has now become a medium for U.S. values of commercialism, violence staged to attract a TV audience, and a monetarized variant of hero worship. "To what extent is a community stunted when its children play another country's national pastime," asks Bruce Kidd, "its best athletes emigrate to perform for foreign teams or it draws its symbolic representatives from other countries?" (Kidd 1991:178–84).

7 Comparing free-trading North America with the European Community (EC) provides a startling picture of what has *not* been achieved. Crucial institutions in the EC – the European Commission, the Court of Justice – are *supra*national, their civil servants and judges mandated to work in the interest of the community as a whole rather than being employed to speak for its particular members. Even in such *inter*national institutions as the Council of Ministers, weighted voting gives the smaller members disproportionately *more* power than strict representation by size would warrant (Daltrop 1982:51–69). On the assumption that social cohesion on the Continent is not compatible with severe disparities in well-being, structures and processes have been designed to ameliorate regional disparities. The European Regional Development Fund, the European Social Fund, and the European Agricultural Guidance and Guarantee Fund have mandates to

promote backward regions, promote training in areas affected by increased competition, and develop rural areas (Swann 1992:282, 130–4).

8 Giles Gherson reports Lipsey, the chief theorist of the free-trade camp in 1988, as maintaining that "the old-fashioned laissez-faire economics – free up the market and let 'em rip – is probably over ... The new-wave notion that government policy can actively foster technological innovation" is in (Gherson 1994:A22).

BIBLIOGRAPHY

Bercuson, David J., J.L. Granatstein, and W.R. Young. 1986. *Sacred Trust? Brian Mulroney and the Conservative Party in Power.* Toronto: Doubleday.

Brown, Douglas M. 1991. "The Evolving Role of the Provinces." In *Canadian Federalism: Meeting Global Economic Challenges* ed. Douglas M. Brown and Murray G. Smiths, 81–128. Kingston: Institute of Intergovernmental Relations, Queen's University.

Burston, Jonathan. 1994. "Fear and Loathing among the Kulturcrats: Brian Mulroney, the Canadian Cultural Bureaucracy, and the Neoconservative 'Revolution'."

Campbell, Robert M. 1987. *Grand Illusions: The Politics of the Keynesian Experience in Canada, 1945-1975.* Peterborough, Ont: Broadview.

Chandler, Marsha. 1986. "The State and Industrial Decline: A Survey." In *Industrial Policy*, ed. André Blais, 171–218. Toronto: University of Toronto Press.

Chodos, Robert, Rae Murphy, and Eric Hamovitch. 1988. *Selling Out: Four Years of the Mulroney Government.* Toronto: James Lorimer.

Clarke, Tony. 1992. "Welcome to the Age of Coalition Politics." *Action Canada Dossier* 37 (May-June):1.

Clarkson, Stephen. 1988. "Continentalism: the Conceptual Challenge for Canadian Social Science." *The John Porter Memorial Lectures: 1984-1987*, Canadian Sociology and Anthropology Association, 23–43.

– "Economics: The New Hemispheric Fundamentalism." In *The Political Economy of North American Free Trade* ed. Ricardo Grinspun and Maxwell A. Cameron, 61–9. Montreal: McGill-Queen's University Press.

Cohen, Marjorie. 1992. "Reflections on Organizing." In *Taking a Stand: Strategy and Tactics of Organizing the Popular Movement in Canada*, ed. Ronnie Leah, 32–4. Ottawa: Canadian Centre for Policy Alternatives.

Comor, Edward. 1991 "The Department of Communications under the Free Trade Regime." *Canadian Journal of Communication* 16:239–61.

Cuneo, C.J. 1976. "Social Basis of Political Continentalism in Canada." *Canadian Review of Sociology and Anthropology* no. 13 (February):55–70.

Daltrop, Anne. 1982. *Politics and the European Community.* London: Longman.

Deblock, Christian, and Michèle Rioux. 1993. "NAFTA: The Trump Card of the United States?" *Studies in Political Economy* 41:7–44.

Dewitt, David, and John Kirton. 1983. *Canada as a Principal Power: A Study in Foreign Policy and International Relations*. Toronto: Wiley.

Dion, Stéphane. 1993. "La sécession du Québec: Evaluation des probabilités après les élections fédérales du 25 octobre 1993," paper presented at "Les élections au Canada, 1993: Changement et continuité," Mexico City, 12 November.

Ellis, David. 1992. *Split Screen: Home Entertainment and the New Technologies*. Toronto: Friends of Canadian Broadcasting.

Fields, Howard. 1987. "Canada Free Trade Talks May End Fire Sales of U.S. Subsidiaries." *Publisher's Weekly* 23 October:11–12.

– 1988 "Free-Trade Amendment Would Ease Access to Canada's 'Cultural' Firms."*Publisher's Weekly* 17 June, 12.

Finestone, Sheila. 1990. "The gradual destruction of the CBC." *Toronto Star* 17 May, A29.

Gherson, Giles. 1994. "If Canada wants a successful economy, it needs technological innovation." *Globe and Mail*, 4 February, A22.

Gibbins, Roger. 1993. "Speculations on a Canada Without Quebec." In *The Charlottetown Accord, the Referendum, and the Future of Canada*, ed. Kenneth McRoberts and Patrick J. Monahan, 264–73. Toronto: University of Toronto Press.

Gilpin, Robert. 1987. *The Political Economy of International Relations*. Princeton, NJ: Princeton University Press.

Godfrey, Stephen. 1992. "Behind the big screen: how free trade fears made Ottawa give in on movie rights law." *Globe and Mail*, 28 March, A1, A6.

Grinspun, Ricardo. 1993. "The Economics of Free Trade in Canada." In *The Political Economy of North American Free Trade*, ed. Ricardo Grinspun and Maxwell A. Cameron, 105–24. Montreal: McGill-Queen's University Press.

Harris, Richard G., and David Cox. 1983. *Trade, Industrial Policy, and Canadian Manufacturing*. Toronto: Ontario Economic Council.

Jenson, Jane. 1989. "'Different' but not 'Exceptional': Canada's Permeable Fordism." *Canadian Review of Sociology and Anthropology* 26, no. 1:69–94.

Kidd, Bruce. 1991. "How Do We Find Our Own Voices in the 'New World Order'? A Commentary on Americanization." *Sociology of Sport Journal* 8, no. 2:178–84.

Kirton, John. 1993. "A New Global Partnership: Canada-U.S. Relations in the Clinton Era." *Canadian-American Public Policy* 15 (November):1–46.

Krieger, Joel. 1986. *Reagan, Thatcher and the Politics of Decline*. New York: Oxford University Press.

Leeson, Howard. "The Free Trade Agreement, Western Canada, and Natural Resources: A Trojan Horse?" In *Trade-Offs on Free Trade: the Canada-U.S. Free Trade Agreement*, ed. Marc Gold and David Leyton-Brown, 224–32. Scarborough, Ont: Carswell.

Litvak, Isaiah A. 1991. "Evolving Corporate Strategies: Adjusting to the FTA." In *Canada Among Nations 1990–91: After the Cold War,* ed. Fen Osler Hampson and Christopher J. Maule, 65–82. Ottawa: Carleton University Press.

McBride, Stephen, and John Shields. 1993. *Dismantling a Nation: Canada and the New World Order.* Halifax: Fernwood.

McCarthy, Shawn. 1993. "U.S. threatens trade sanctions." *Toronto Star* 6 November, C1.

Macdonald Commission. 1985. *Report: Royal Commission on the Economic Union and Development Prospects for Canada,* vol. 1. Ottawa: Minister of Supply and Services.

Martin, Carol. 1992. "Writing Off Canadian Publishing." *Canadian Forum* 70, no. 807:133–4, 136.

Nymark, Alan. 1994. lecture at the University of Toronto, March 22.

Resnick, Phillip. 1990. *The Masks of Proteus: Canadian Reflections on the State.* Montreal: McGill-Queen's University Press.

Ross, Val. 1993. "A bungee jump into culture's abyss." *Globe and Mail* 5 June, C1, C7.

Rugman, Alan. 1988. "Multinationals and the Free Trade Agreement." In *Trade-Offs on Free Trade: the Canada-U.S. Free Trade Agreement,* ed. Marc Gold and David Leyton-Brown, 4–12. Scarborough, Ont: Carswell.

Servan-Schreiber, Jean-Jacques. 1967. *Le défi américain.* Paris: Denoël.

Sharp, Mitchell. 1972. "Canada-U.S. Relations: Options for the Future." *International Perspectives.* Special Issue (Autumn):1–7.

Stairs, Denis. 1988. "The Impact on Public Policy: A Leap of Faith." In *Trade-Offs on Free Trade: the Canada-U.S. Free Trade Agreement,* ed. Marc Gold and David Leyton-Brown, 454–8. Scarborough, Ont: Carswell.

Strange, Susan. 1989. "Toward a Theory of Transnational Empire." In *Global Changes and Theoretical Challenges,* ed. Ernst-Otto Czempiel and James N. Rosenau, 161–76. Lexington, MA: Lexington Books.

Swann, Dennis. 1992. *The Economics of the Common Market,* 2nd ed. London: Penguin.

Thurow, Lester. 1992. *Head to Head: The Coming Economic Battle among Japan, Europe and America.* New York: Morrow.

14 Economic Threats to National Unity: From within and without

MELVILLE L. McMILLAN

Many people who are anxious about the continuation of Canada as a cohesive, viable and unique nation find no comfort in recent economic trends. Within the context of growing international trade, Canada-United States trade has increased and is being actively pursued, seemingly at the expense of east-west Canadian linkages. The transition, especially of policy, has been rapid. Within a decade, Canada moved from the National Energy Policy (NEP) to the Free Trade Agreement (FTA) and then to the North American Free Trade Agreement (NAFTA). There is concern that growing continental economic integration is eroding the power of the national government and undermining national unity.

I examine the issue of trade liberalization, but for reasons to be explained momentarily do not restrict myself to that subject. Although it preempts the analysis, my opinion is that freer trade offers many economic benefits and is worth pursuing. However, it is a struggle for Canada – as a small participant in a trade game with a dominant "partner" that regards itself as an opponent, largely plays by its own rules, and makes those up as it goes – to fully realize the potential gains. Still, in a rapidly globalizing world, there are gains to be achieved, and if Canadians wish to share in them there is little choice as to the direction our policy must follow. Greater economic integration, even continentally, need not seriously erode the strength of Canada as a nation if we retain distinct values and social objectives. We will be somewhat more constrained, however, in how those are to be achieved. Adjustment to international pressures has been a problem, but many of those difficulties can be attributed to inappropriate policy choices over the past twenty-five years.

The greatest threat to Canada appears to be internal rather than external. Quebec separation clearly dominates. Such an event would be so profound and the variety of potential consequences so immense that it seems most appropriate in this context simply to acknowledge the possibility. The political sorting out necessary would overwhelm and direct the economic outcomes. It is not inconceivable, however, that (to borrow from H.V. Nelles) "about the same" might characterize the subsequent state of commercial relations between Quebec and the rest of Canada.

Social policy in Canada is in disarray and in a state of flux. I will pursue this topic here because the social policy "railroad" is important in defining the Canadian identity and in binding the country, the system is in danger of imploding, it is an important determinant of the country's capacity to cope with social and economic changes, and resolution of the social policy problem certainly has intergovernmental and possibly constitutional implications. The direction in which social policy will develop is unclear, but the implications of the alternatives for social, economic, and political unity and strength differ. In contrast to the pressures of globalization and trade liberalization, Canadians have greater control over the future of their social policy.

There are two major parts to the paper. The first provides an examination of continental economic integration through the FTA and the NAFTA and the potential implications. Particular attention is given to changing domestic trade patterns. In the second part the nature, condition, and future directions of Canadian social policy are examined.[1] Because these economic pressures bear on us with or without Quebec, it is only in the conclusion that I discuss some tentative implications of them for shaping the rest of Canada should Quebec disassociate.

EVOLVING ECONOMIC LINKAGES AND THEIR IMPLICATIONS

The Move toward Liberalizing Continental Trade

During the 1970s and 1980s, numerous pressures developed to make closer economic ties with the United States attractive to Canadian business and some political interests. Those factors include expanding trade with the U.S.; diminished trade with the United Kingdom following its entry into the European Community in 1971; declining world tariffs negotiated through the General Agreement on Tariffs and

Trade (GATT), which promoted more competitive markets, larger scale production, and international integration and trade; the emergence of regional trading blocks; protectionist attitudes in the U.S.; and declining confidence in the ability of the GATT to deal with rising non-tariff trade barriers. As a result, the FTA was negotiated with the U.S., effective 1989, and subsequently Canada joined the U.S. and Mexico in the NAFTA, effective 1994.

The FTA and NAFTA – The FTA was designed to remove or reduce artificial barriers to trade between Canada and the U.S. The agreement incorporated many of the provisions of the GATT but extended beyond that with provisions for services (particularly financial services), the temporary movement of business people, foreign investment, agriculture, and trade remedy procedures. Tariffs between the two countries are to be eliminated within ten years and it started with the immediate removal of those on 15 percent of dutiable products. National treatment is to be provided to each other's businesses. Restrictions on energy trade were reduced and energy sharing extended beyond the provisions of the International Energy Agency. A bilateral trade dispute resolution mechanism was established. Although potentially superior to that under GATT and critical to enhanced Canadian access to U.S. markets, the mechanism is limited to determining whether the offending country's trade laws have been applied correctly. Cultural industries were largely exempted from the FTA.[2]

Negotiations leading to the NAFTA quickly followed the FTA. Although there was very little trade between Canada and Mexico and the existing tariffs were low, when Mexico and the U.S. initiated trade negotiations, Canada was compelled to join to protect itself from the consequences of the U.S.'s becoming the only country with trade access to all three in an expanded North American market; that is, to avoid becoming an unattractive location for businesses planning to serve the three countries. In most ways, the NAFTA paralleled the FTA but there are notable exceptions. Mexico is exempt from resource-sharing and the Mexican government essentially reserved rights to all energy investment. Protection of intellectual property rights across member countries was also included in response to U.S. concern.

The Predicted Consequences – Opinions about the free trade agreements are diverse and strong. Advocates of the FTA foresaw its yielding significant economic gains as a result of the opportunity and necessity of rationalizing the Canadian economy. Various simulation models have been developed to predict the increase in national output that would stem from freer trade. The estimates for Canada vary but more recent ones tend to cluster in the range of an increase of one to three percent of GDP. Including the impacts of the agreement with Mexico has very little effect, 0.2 percentage points, on the expected gain.[3] Most models, including those generating the above predictions, do not attempt to incorporate the improvements due to removal of non-tariff barriers. One model which does do so suggests that the gains from non-tariff barrier removal exceed those from eliminating tariffs and from the realization of greater economies of scale. Thus, while the conventional estimates are modest though not trivial, to the extent that trade liberalization reduces non-tariff barriers the gains could be improved significantly.

Those with serious reservations about the impact of freer trade argue that the projected gains are optimistic and derive support from alternative economic models. Employing what he regards as more realistic assumptions about unemployment and capital mobility (among others), Stanford (1993) predicts lower GDP (down 2.5 percent), employment, and wages. Many critics see investment and jobs moving south and blame the FTA for that and for most of the recent setbacks to the Canadian economy. They also point out that access to the U.S. market is not guaranteed. American interests are still able to harass Canadian exporters because U.S. trade law takes precedence over the FTA and those laws can be amended unilaterally.

Even ignoring possible economic deficiencies, opponents of the free trade agreements see a major erosion of national policy-making powers. In particular, the policy options of Canada (and Mexico) are diminished while those of the U.S. are affected little, if at all. A major criticism is that the agreements limit public intervention relative to its traditional role in the Canadian economy; for example, national treatment constraining the regulation of foreign capital, energy-sharing diminishing control over Canadian resources, provisions for compensation in the case of public takeovers of foreign firms being unduly generous, and Canadian social programs threatened by the harmonizing pressure of the free trade environment if not the specifics of the agreement itself. Diminishing scope for government action and independent public policy in Canada through free trade is viewed as an element of a "neo-conservative" agenda which includes deregulation, privatization, (regressive) tax reform, and less public spending. Opponents of free trade believe that Canada requires an activist state role to strengthen east-west bonds, promote national interests, and reflect Canadian values.[4]

Despite the criticism, the proponents of free trade continue to adhere to their position and have gone on to support the NAFTA. They admit that the accessibility objectives were not fully realized, but claim that the result is superior to the alternatives under GATT. They see the FTA and the NAFTA as accommodating Canada's adjustment to globalization and free trade as necessary to ensure the competitiveness and prosperity of the Canadian economy. Larger markets and expanded competition are seen as providing the opportunity and impetus for Canadian business to become more internationally competitive. Although adverse economic conditions have made adjustments more difficult, long-term gains are foreseen and, it is believed, without unduly detracting from Canadian sovereignty or identity.

Clearly, opinions and interpretations of events differ. These differences will not be resolved, but insights may be gained from reviewing recent economic developments.

Economic Trends and Performance – The dominant economic feature of the post-FTA period has been the severe and protracted recession which began in 1990. This recession hit central Canada, notably Ontario, and the manufacturing sector especially hard. Canada's unemployment rate rose from 7.5 percent in 1988 to over 11 percent by 1992. Manufacturing employment fell 16 percent and a disproportionate share of the job losses were considered permanent.

Some observers have referred to this as a "made in Canada" recession. After the 1981–82 recession, the Canadian economy grew at a solid pace until 1990. Inflationary pressures emerged by 1987 which prompted the Bank of Canada to tighten monetary policy. Interest rates rose sharply, serving to brake the economy, and the recession began early in 1990 and continued with a sharp (1.7 percent) drop in real GDP in 1991. This pattern was not unique to Canada. Parallel movements occurred in the United States and the United Kingdom which served to reinforce the Canadian cycle while the recessions in France, Germany, and Japan lagged somewhat behind ours and have probably contributed modestly to the slow Canadian recovery.

Canadian manufacturing fared well during the expansion of the 1980s despite dramatically increasing unit labour costs. Although labour productivity did not increase and fell below that of many competitors, wages rose. Augmented by a higher dollar, the unit cost of Canadian manufacturing rose from below that of the U.S. to 20 percent above by 1991. The buoyant economy of the late 1980s sheltered Canadian manufacturers and postponed productivity-improving adjustments that had been forced on U.S. firms earlier. The last recession forced Canadian manufacturers to make substantial adjustments quickly to regain competitiveness. Those adjustments are partly reflected in the employment changes. By 1989 Canadian manufacturing employment was 8.7 percent above 1978 levels. By 1992 it had dropped to 91.4 percent before beginning to recover. In the U.S., however, manufacturing employment in 1989 was at 94.5 percent of that in 1978 and it fell to 89.5 in 1992. Manufacturing employment in the U.S. northeast was 18.5 percent below its 1978 level in 1989 and 30.5 percent below in 1992. Although it has recently experienced a sharp adjustment, manufacturing employment in Canada has survived fairly well relative to that in the U.S.

Many factors influence the competitiveness of Canadian manufacturing, and the importance of each is difficult to isolate. Tremblay (1993) reports on such an effort. He attributes up to one third of the loss in manufacturing jobs between 1987 and 1991 to the appreciation of the Canadian dollar, one third to the reduced demand caused by the Canadian recession, a modest 3.5 percent to the U.S. recession, and the residual to other factors which could include implementation of the GST and the FTA, although he does not expect that the latter played a large direct role.

Trade volumes offer some insights. The constant dollar values of exports and imports have continued to grow without interruption since 1982. A study of post-FTA trade patterns indicates relative growth in trade with the U.S. in those products (notably merchandise) liberalized under the FTA in comparison to those not liberalized and growth in U.S. trade relative to that with other countries (Schwanen 1993). From 1988 to 1993 Canadian merchandise exports to the U.S. rose 41 percent, while those to other countries remained constant. For western Canada, Chambers and Janzen (1994) report a 58 percent increase in merchandise exports to the U.S., while exports elsewhere declined 14.6 percent. Strong export growth is reported in the West outside the agricultural and energy sectors. Despite trade disputes and the considerable attention given to them, trade with the U.S. seems to be growing under the FTA.

Foreign investment patterns have not changed noticeably since the FTA. Although increasing slightly in 1992, U.S. direct investment in Canada continues essentially constant in real terms as over the past 15 years. Constant dollar Canadian direct investment in the U.S. almost tripled between 1978 and 1988, but slowed after that with some resurgence in 1992. Total Canadian direct investment abroad continues steady growth with the U.S. share declining somewhat since 1988.

It is still early for the data to speak decisively on the trade impacts of the FTA. The indications appear positive, although it will be important to distinguish between changes in volumes and those in economic well-being. The implications for economic, social, and political integration will be more distant and even more obscure.

Changing Trade Patterns and the Economic Union

Canada's internal as well as external trade patterns have been changing. Comparing 1974 and 1989, Courchene (1991) noted increased foreign trade of manufactured goods and smaller interprovincial trade. Notably, Ontario's shipments abroad increased from 21 to 34 percent of total shipments, while those to other provinces fell from 28 to 18 percent. Trade liberalization is expected to promote foreign trade further. Courchene (1991:83–4) argues that:

What this suggests is that the political economy of the east-west transfer system will fall under increasing scrutiny in the context of north-south integration. In particular, Ontario's "magnanimity" in terms of existing regional transfers historically carried a healthy dose of "Ontario first." As long as trade flowed largely east-west, with Ontario being the principal north-south conduit, the second- (and future-)round spending impacts of these regional transfers generally came to rest somewhere in Ontario. Under enhanced north-south integration for Canada's provinces, the second-round spending may end up in North Carolina or California. At a political level, this will begin to erode support for regional transfers, particularly those that privilege "place" rather than people. The FTA may enhance these but they were mounting in any event.

While not denying the basic point, the problem may be less serious than initially suggested.[5] First, Courchene looks only at shipments of manufactured goods. Consider instead the movements of all traded goods and services. Canada's foreign exports increased from 14 to 19 percent of shipments while interprovincial exports fell from 19 to 18 percent (Table 1). Clearly these shifts are much more modest. Ontario's changes are still significant – from 13 to 20 percent and from 19 to 16 percent respectively – but less dramatic than those for manufactured goods.[6] In addition, even in Ontario the actual volume of interprovincial trade increased about 1.3 times, and nationally interprovincial trade grew about 1.5 times; 9 and 17 percent per capita. Second, while foreign exports became relatively more important in eight of the ten provinces, interprovincial exports also became relatively more (not less) important in six. Indeed Ontario experienced the largest decline, and given its size, accounts entirely for the lower national percentage of interprovincial exports. Still, however, Ontario has a large trade surplus with other provinces, exporting to them 55 percent more than it imports. Third, while expanding trade may cause a larger share of intergovernmental transfers to be spent on imports, outlays for imports support Canadian exports, and Ontario is now even more

Table 1
Destination of Production for Canada and by Province in 1974 and 1989 (percentage of goods and services produced).

| Province | Sold within province | | Exported to | | | |
| | | | Rest of Canada | | Abroad | |
	1974	1989	1974	1989	1974	1989
Newfoundland	61	67	7	9	32	24
Prince Edward Island	75	63	22	24	3	13
Nova Scotia	67	65	22	20	11	15
New Brunswick	61	55	21	23	18	22
Quebec	68	63	22	20	10	17
Ontario	68	64	19	16	13	20
Manitoba	66	61	23	24	11	15
Saskatchewan	52	57	19	21	29	22
Alberta	61	59	23	22	16	19
British Columbia	71	62	10	13	19	25
Canada	67	63	19	18	14	19

Note: 1974 values calculated from Whalley (1983), Tables 4 and 5; 1989 values calculated from Messinger (1993).

than before the major north-south conduit, supplying 47 (up from 39) percent of exports. Thus while expanded trade may increase the circulation through the U.S., it should not diminish Ontario's share of the return flow of intergovernmental transfers. Fourth, while goods and services may increasingly be moving north-south, people move east-west. The mobility of the vast majority of Canadians is limited to Canada. Hence they will continue to be interested in preserving the economic union and the comparative attractiveness of the provinces.

The importance of economic ties as a support for east-west transfers may be overestimated. There are significant gaps in the national web of commercial linkages. Central Canada (Ontario and Quebec) is the hub of interprovincial trade. The western and Atlantic provinces trade with the centre and among themselves, but there is very little western-Atlantic trade. On the other hand, other factors may be important in determining our trade patterns. McCallum (1993) shows that about five-sixths of interprovincial (i.e., east-west) trade is "unnatural" or "border induced." Those factors may be important also in determining support for an east-west transfer system.

While the above discussion relates to the potential international impacts of freer trade, further trade liberalization within Canada would enhance the economic and possibly the political union. Although the mobility of products, factors, and people within the country is notable, internal barriers exist, frequently irritate business, labour, and consumer groups, and are a policy concern.[7] Not all impediments to interprovincial trade are the product of provincial "province-first" strategies; many arise from federal government policies. Examples of barriers to internal trade are government procurement policies (alcoholic beverages being widely noted), transportation regulation, marketing boards, provincial investment plans, regional development and business subsidies, heritage funds, occupational licensing, and unemployment insurance. The economic costs are estimated to be 0.5 to 1.0 percent of GDP or $500 to $1000 per family; that is, in the lower end of the range of the estimated potential gains from liberalizing trade with the u.s.

Efforts to reduce barriers to interprovincial trade have been made and are ongoing. Beer marketing and procurement is a well-publicized example. Interprovincial agreements in this area have not been very successful. The FTA contains provisions (expanded somewhat under the NAFTA) to liberalize trade in alcoholic beverages. Indeed, the steps taken seem to stem largely from external trade agreements to which Canada has agreed. Movement on the beer front can certainly be traced to GATT rulings against Canadian practices. Provincial liquor board practices have also been amended in response to GATT judgments. The interprovincial agreement not to discriminate on government procurement contracts exceeding $25,000 appears to have been motivated by the FTA. Voluntary agreements among Canadian governments to relax barriers have only been realized slowly but international agreements may have hastened developments. A major draft internal trade agreement was negotiated by 28 June 1994. While significant improvements were anticipated, initial assessments found the deal unimpressive.

Expanding trade, and especially that under the FTA and NAFTA, means greater north-south movements for Canada. This has been seen as a possible threat to Canada's east-west economic and intergovernmental transfer systems. The magnitude of that threat may have been overestimated. Also, the agreements which expand international trade are an impetus to reduce internal barriers to trade and thus encourage the east-west transactions that expanding north-south trade is felt to erode.

Further Observations

Already Economically Integrated – Canada has for some time been part of the international economy. Exports now represent over 30 percent of GDP and the percentage has been growing over the past 35 years. However, much of that growth simply restored exports to their pre-1950s share of GDP. Other than during a low export period in the 1950s and 1960s, since 1926 exports have typically accounted for 22 to 30 percent of national output. Also, although the free trade agreements have drawn attention to continental economic integration, the most dramatic increase in trade with the U.S. occurred between 1945 and 1950 when the percentage of merchandise exports to the U.S. rose from 37 percent to 65 percent. The next major shift preceded the FTA when the U.S. share rose during the 1980s to the 75 to 80 percent range. International and continental economic integration are not new to Canada.

Expanded trade now means more international competition. The returns from extensive natural resources and the protection of tariffs are declining. Substitutes for natural resources are more common, capital moves easily among countries, consumers have a greater choice of quality products, inexpensive labour is available elsewhere, and trade is effectively expanding the supply of unskilled labour. More than before, the maintenance of high and growing real incomes depends on high and continuous improvements in labour productivity. The advantage of Canada and other advanced countries is the ability to invest heavily in their human resources and in turn to supply that labour with the complementary capital and technology. The world is not going to return to "normal." Better that we adjust and prepare ourselves to exploit the advantages expanded trade offers.

The Evolving Role of the State – The potential diminution of the role of the state, and especially of the federal government, as a result of trade liberalization is a subject receiving much discussion. On the one hand, provinces and international cities may be pursuing more divergent interests and seeking more autonomy and authority. On the other, transnational corporations are superseding the multinationals, and supranational institutions (GATT, FTA, NAFTA, the European Community, the International Monetary Fund) are assuming greater importance. Some political analysts see the nation state shrinking between these forces, and they are pessimistic about the consequences. But change also brings opportunities. International negotiations will demand and economic union will require a strong, single voice speaking for Canada; sometimes perhaps in collective efforts to regain regulatory and/or tax powers over international capital. Domestically, policies to enhance the quality and utilization of our human resources are of growing importance. The role of the national government is certainly evolving, but it is not necessarily diminished.

Even when international developments limit independent national action, they may constrain the means more than limit the ends. Canadian governments, not unlike those elsewhere, use the country's productive and allocative system to accomplish other goals – notably interpersonal, interindustry, and interregional redistribution. There is concern that the increased international mobility of capital and terms of the FTA (such as those limiting government procurement favouring local suppliers, protection through marketing boards, regional development subsidies, and those requiring national treatment) erode the power of the Canadian government to achieve national objectives. However, many of the policies used to accomplish those ends have strong opponents within Canada. The National Energy Policy is one of the more glaring examples as it also generated strong interregional animosities. Globalization and trade liberalization reduce the scope of national governments to implement redistributive policies through the production economy. Often, however, the objectives are worthwhile. Now governments will have to rely more heavily upon the direct tax-transfer system to accomplish those goals. Doing so is expected to force the underlying intentions to the surface and expose them to greater scrutiny, a feature many economic commentators will consider positive. The result may be that both the production economy and public sector's redistributive arm operate more effectively.

"Neo-conservative" Politics – The literature critical of trade liberalization makes frequent reference to freer trade as an instrument of a neo-conservative political movement. Ominous references to the promotion of neo-conservative agendas by powerful interests may suggest some illegitimacy or lack of popular support. I suggest otherwise. Canadians generally express dissatisfaction with their governments, and with some cause. For example, they have been buffeted by inflation and recession, witnessed unsuccessful and wasteful development efforts, experienced inefficient and unresponsive public enterprises and regulated industries, faced costly education systems which generate unimpressive results, found employment opportunities shrinking and welfare roles rising, and seen public debt reaching record levels and taxes climbing. The recent record of governments is not inspiring.[8] People are looking for alternatives. Witness the success of the Reform Party in the last federal election and of the Klein government in Alberta, which under the rationale of deficit reduction is pursuing a neo-conservative agenda. Support for neo-conservative policies is not necessarily narrowly based, and whether or not it politically dominates particular jurisdictions, neo-conservatism will influence public policy – in a way, it is hoped, that will find a suitable balance with interventionist methods.

What Binds Canada? – Canadian unity is a continuing conundrum. Unity of the rest of the country (ROC) in the absence of Quebec is an even greater question. The identity and cohesiveness of ROC, or English Canada if you wish, has been probed, and Laxer (1992) and Resnick (1994) find some evidence of emerging nationality. This is in part defined by unique values, values that are reflected in the Canadian system of social programs.

The economic link forged by the east-west railway have given way, using the Courchene analogy, to the ties of a social policy railroad. Banting (1993, 38) summarized the concept: "In Canada, social programs have been seen primarily as a means of integration across territorial lines. Social programs represent one of the few spheres of shared experience for Canadians, an important aspect of our lives which is common, irrespective of our language and region. Moreover, the interregional transfers underpinning these programs have represented an affirmation that – despite geography, economics, and demography – we are a single people, with a common set of benefits and obligations."

Unfortunately, "our social policy infrastructure appears to be in shambles" (Courchene 1992, 767). Because this problem is serious, of our own making, and so within our control, it is addressed below. Before focusing specifically on social programs, we glance at the state of the nation's finances because it contributes significantly to the deterioration of and to the prospects for the social policy network.

INTERNAL ECONOMIC PRESSURES
ON CANADIAN UNITY

The Fiscal Pits

Canadian governments are in a very difficult fiscal situation. Over the past thirty years, government expenditures have grown relative to GDP, while taxpayer contributions have been quite stable. As a result, government net debt rose from 20 to 80 percent of GDP, doubling over the past decade. Interest payments on that debt require 20 percent of government expenditures. Lender concern and taxpayer resistance make it difficult for governments to meet their financial commitments and maintain public services.

The federal government situation deserves special attention. The federal government accounts for 80 percent of government net debt, and national social programs are federally initiated even if not entirely federally funded. In 1992–93, 25 percent of federal budgetary expenditures went to pay interest on the public debt, while 75 percent went to program expenditures. Revenues amounted to 75 percent of outlays. Thus, we are paying for what we are getting from the federal government but are not yet paying for what we got. Eliminating the deficit would require increasing revenues by one third, reducing program expenditures by one third, or some mix of the two. Regardless, the effective cost of the federal government will increase. Using projections from Dungan and Wilson (1994) the dollars of program expenditure per dollar of taxes is calculated to be $0.96 in 1992 but is projected to be $0.79 in 2002, the first year in which no deficit is expected. This implies a 21.5 percent increase in the effective tax price of federal government services. Although absolutely smaller, a similar relative increase is expected at the provincial level. Taken together, these factors create a substantial increase in the cost of government to the taxpayer regardless of which deficit reduction strategy is followed.

How will Canadian taxpayers respond to the full cost of government? Events suggest that taxpayers were already unwilling to pay the full costs during the 1970s and 1980s when real and disposable incomes were rising. Taxpayer resistance has become strident as real disposable income has fallen consistently to eight percent (in 1993) below the 1989 peak. Among their impacts, these developments challenge social programs which represent about half of all government spending.

Implications for Social Programs

The extent of social programs is large. Major social expenditures by the federal government include those for old age security, unemployment insurance, transfers to the provinces to contribute to the funding of social assistance (the Canada Assistance Plan) and the finance of health care and post-secondary education (Established Programs Financing), and transfers to Native peoples, farmers, and the fishing industry. There is also the child tax credit program, which as of 1993 absorbed and superseded the family allowance. Expenditures on health, education, and social assistance dominate provincial budgets. The list could easily be extended by including smaller programs and tax expenditure measures like those for retirement savings. The size of social expenditures and the ubiquity of governments' financial problems, contributed to by federal offloading, has meant that social programs have not been overlooked by either level of government in their expenditure control/reduction efforts. The attention is not motivated only by governments' budgetary problems. As structured, the programs have not been adequately meeting changing social, economic, and political needs. Attention below focuses on the major national programs and specifically those involving major federal-provincial interrelations.

Major Social Programs and Their Problems – Federal government transfers to other governments and to persons represent more than half of federal program expenditures. The major intergovernmental transfers, divided into approximate thirds, are for Established Program Financing (EPF), the Canada Assistance Plan (CAP), and equalization. The major transfers to persons come, about equally, under unemployment insurance (UI) and old age security (OAS). Attention is directed here to EPF, CAP, and UI.

Since 1977, the EPF has supported provincial expenditures on health care and on post-secondary education through a system of tax room and residual cash transfers. The federal contribution was scaled to GDP, but because those expenditures and the tax base grew faster than GDP the federal cash contribution has steadily declined. This reduction has accelerated since 1990 with the move to restrict the change in provincial entitlements to population growth only. Although the recession has delayed the date somewhat, EPF cash transfers were expected to reach zero for Quebec before 2000 and sometime thereafter for the other provinces. Declining contributions imply declining influence. There has been little concern about the post-secondary education component since that transfer has been made unconditionally. EPF funding for health care, however, has been a lever to ensure that the provinces conform to the provisions of the Canada Health Act (universality, comprehensiveness, accessibility, portability, and public administration). In the absence of significant federal support, there is concern whether health care could maintain its national character and continue to facilitate interprovincial mobility.

From 1966 until 1990 the federal government equally shared social welfare costs with the provinces under the CAP. In 1990 the federal government introduced the "cap on CAP" which limited the growth in CAP transfers to the have provinces to five percent annually. Ontario was most severely impacted. With welfare roles ballooning due to the recession, CAP transfers to Ontario fell to only 25 percent of social assistance costs (a loss to Ontario of $1.7 billion), and this has prompted Ontario to ask for its "fair share." Courchene (1994) has argued that there has not been a federal initiative as destructive to the integrity of federal-provincial relations since the NEP.

The federal UI program has been in place since 1941. Since the 1970s it has been very much transformed from an insurance program to an interpersonal and interregional redistribution program which costs more today than EPF and CAP combined. Because UI is federal while social assistance is cost shared, there is an incentive for provinces to shift potential welfare recipients to UI if possible, and the federal government has co-operated. Reference is often made to job rotation schemes that qualify a larger number of people for UI. As a result, it is widely criticized (even by "benefiting" recipient governments) for contributing to high unemployment, undermining personal and community initiative, discouraging education, subsidizing seasonal industry, and generally impeding adjustment to economic change. UI has become a costly, misdirected program.

The UI-CAP system encourages personal and regional transfer dependency, but the structure is not suited to correct itself. UI increasingly supports those outside the work force, and CAP supports employables. Neither was intended or designed for these alternative roles. There is need to integrate the two programs, likely under a single jurisdiction, to remove the adverse incentives distorting the actions of governments, businesses, and individuals, and at the same time provide an adequate safety net. The product must be consistent with the more competitive economy. The new social policy must promote adjustment, the acquisition of skills and people's relocation to where those skills can be most effectively used. In addition, the revisions must facilitate the efficient provision of public outputs, notably education and health care. Will the recently federally initiated review of social policy lead in these directions? Various options are available.

New Directions: Mending the Social Policy System? – Important national programs could disappear, and some are not working effectively. Proposed reforms point in different directions and have quite different implications for Canadian federalism. In one direction, EPF could be left to wither and federal involvement in health care (notably) and post-secondary education eventually end. Taken to the extreme, there could be complete disentanglement. The provinces could be given full jurisdiction over health care and post-secondary (and so all) education, social welfare, and unemployment insurance and conceded extended tax room and even separate tax areas to meet the added expenditure responsibilities. Even equalization could be made an interprovincial program. In such a scenario there would be little reason to retain old age pensions and CPP at the federal level, especially when Quebec operates its Quebec Pension Plan (QPP). With all the social programs at the provincial level, the provinces (as sole and independent decision makers) would be free to integrate, rationalize, add, delete, experiment, and diversify. If this occurred, would national interests be realized, what of "national" programs, the effects on the economic union, the continuity of the Canadian social policy network, and the Canadian identity?

In the event of a reformed or expanded federal role, there would be various alternatives. The federal government could assume responsibility for *all* social assistance as well as UI and could continue transfers under EPF. Another is for a federal recommitment to EPF and CAP through expenditure-based equalization. A further option is for the federal government to carve out specific areas (e.g., child welfare and aid/vouchers/loans to post-secondary students) to support and to let the provinces design their programs around those. The lingering question with the continued, even if expanded, federal presence is how to coordinate federal-provincial objectives and decision making in those areas of joint financial involvement where that remains (health care and post-secondary education) and the interrelations among welfare, UI, and the tax system when authority is divided.[9]

Clearly, opinions diverge. The implications of the alternatives for federalism, program delivery, their national character, and the economic union are different. Unfortunately, agreement as to which option ultimately best meets our social welfare needs and facilitates national unity is unlikely.

CONCLUSION AND IMPLICATIONS FOR CANADA OUTSIDE QUEBEC

External and internal forces are challenging Canadian unity. Globalization and trade liberalization are increasingly focusing regional economic interests abroad. Yet the considerable economic forces integrating the country should not be underestimated. Internally, fiscal, economic, and political problems are threatening the continuation of a national social policy considered important for defining the Canadian identity. Maintaining a strong and competitive economy and avoiding a relative decline in the living standards that would encourage emulation of our American neighbours demands adjustment. This accommodation need not change the objectives of Canadian policy, although it may constrain somewhat the instruments available to accomplish them. The internal problems are much more of our own making and offer more scope for our own solutions. Responses to the two must be integrated. Good social and economic policies must support each other.

The issues focused upon here are Canadian problems and will be with us with or without Quebec (and with Quebec differently weighted in the federal system). Should Quebec separate, will these issues be more or less difficult for the rest of Canada to solve? Even under the very best circumstances, the transition to two separate states would be economically costly as tremendous resources would be devoted to negotiations between the parties, to defining and establishing new institutional and political arrangements within the country, and to renegotiating international agreements. All the while, important economic decisions would be deferred and output and improvements forgone because of uncertainty. Assume, however, a smooth as possible transition to a new stable situation. Although our problems might have escalated due to neglect during transition, could we be positioned differently after a separation to address them?

A post-independence Canada would be smaller and so carry less power in international affairs. This seems particularly important in the context of the NAFTA. The U.S. would likely see a smaller/divided Canada as an opportunity to further lever its own interests. Benefits might be realized because domestic interests would be somewhat more homogeneous, but these could be offset by the fact that the smaller Canada is a less important trader of products for which Quebec is an important exporter (e.g., metals, food products). While it might be possible that Quebec and Canada could cooperate in trade negotiations (perhaps even with Mexico), it is unlikely that such alliances would be sustainable. Canada is already disadvantaged in its trade relations with a much larger partner; reducing its size further will not enhance its position. Quebec, however, as the new entrant and much smaller player in the North American trade deal would be in a more tenuous situation.

Quebec-Canada trade would now be external rather than internal trade. There is no reason to believe that separation would facilitate those movements. The impacts would be greatest upon Quebec and its major Canadian trading partners, the Atlantic region and Ontario. While a portion of their trade with Quebec might be shifted to each other, the ratio of international to domestic trade would increase and could erode national ties.

It might be somewhat easier to reduce internal trade barriers in the absence of Quebec. This is not so much because Quebec's position on this front has been exceptionally difficult but rather because there would be fewer players and interests to accommodate. Any gains here, however, would be lost in the complications of trading with Quebec as a foreign country.

The impact of Quebec independence on the public debt burden and the economic and its accompanying social policy-making complications are problematic. If Quebec assumed a fair share of Canada's national debt in the event of separation, the issue would only be complicated by the significant difficulties in marketing the debt and the interest premiums stemming from the division of the country. Unfortunately, the division of the federal debt appears to be one of the more contentious issues of separation.

As Quebec is a net recipient of federal provincial and personal transfers, separation would ease the financial burden of the federal government. The expected savings are moderate; perhaps 10 percent of expenditures in those areas (Reid and Snoddon 1992). The cost of the federal-provincial equalization program could decline much more, perhaps by one third. This could assist in maintaining a strong equalization program that is important to national unity. The other transfers are primarily for social programs, and social programs are now under review.

The absence of Quebec as a province might facilitate coming to some agreement on social policy reform. In federal-provincial relations, Quebec has often had special demands (not only regarding social policy but also about taxation and regulation) and has required special arrangements. This has often undermined the sense of national programs and prompted calls for similar exceptions that may have been less well founded. Without the need for exceptional provisions for Quebec, perhaps the federal and remaining provincial governments could more readily agree on federal-provincial arrangements. For better or worse, without Quebec the provincial case for decentralization might be weakened and that for federal or federally initiated programs enhanced. On the other hand, the political institutions of a Canada without Quebec might give more authority to the regions.

With or without Quebec, core economic problems remain. Once past a potentially difficult transition, the economic cost of Quebec separation to the rest of Canada would probably be moderate, perhaps no more than the cost of living with the continual threat of separation. It is Quebec that is expected to face the relatively larger economic costs of separation (e.g., Grady 1991). If Quebec does separate, the economic consequences for a united rest of Canada are probably less significant than those of Quebec. Other long-term potential dangers emerge. What is the future of a geographically segregated Atlantic Canada? Can the rest of Canada realize a sustainable political arrangement that will avoid Ontario domination, that will successfully balance regional interests?

NOTES

Without implying any responsibility for the factual content or suggesting agreement with the opinions expressed, I thank Ken Norrie, Bruce Wilkinson, participants at the conference, and the editor for helpful comments.

1 The paper is an attempt to address a wide range of important and widely discussed topics in a short space. Those interested in more comprehensive analysis and documentation should refer to McMillan (1994) and the references cited there.

2 For further detail see, for example, Copeland (1989); Lipsey and York (1988); and Wilkinson (1991).

3 Mexico is expected to realize large output improvements. See Watson
(1993) for a survey.

4 A good survey of the free trade critics' positions is found in Grinspun and
Cameron (1993).

5 Nor is this to deny the possibility that the issue could be magnified beyond
its economic significance in political debate. See Nelles in this volume.

6 A change in auto exports does not account for the shift. Transportation
equipment represented about 54 percent of Ontario manufactured
exports in both 1974 and 1989.

7 See Brown, Lazar, and Schwanen (1992) for an overview.

8 A parallel litany of private sector failures also comes to mind but that goes
beyond the topic here.

9 For some discussion of alternatives see Courchene (1993); Hobson and
St-Hilaire (1993); Leslie, Norrie, and Ip (1993); and Watson, Richards,
and Brown (1994).

BIBLIOGRAPHY

Banting, Keith G. 1993. "Ends and Means in Social Policy." In *Income Security in
Canada: Changing Needs, Changing Means*, ed. E.B. Reynolds, 37–40. Montreal: Institute for Research on Public Policy.

Brown, David M., Fred Lazar, and Daniel Schwanen. 1992. *Free to Move*. Toronto: C.D. Howe Institute.

Chambers, Edward J., and S. Stephen Janzen. 1994. *Western Canada and the Free
Trade Agreement 1988-93*. Information Bulletin, Western Centre for Economic Research, University of Alberta, Edmonton, April.

Copeland, Brian R. 1989. "Of Mice and Elephants: The Canada-u.s. Free
Trade Agreement." *Contemporary Policy Issues* 7 (July):42–60.

Courchene, Thomas J. 1991. *In Praise of Renewed Federalism*. Toronto: C.D.
Howe Institute.

– 1992. "Presidential Address: Mon pays, c'est l'hiver: reflections of a market
populist." *Canadian Journal of Economics* 25 (November):759–91.

– 1994. "Canada's Social Policy Deficit: Implications for Fiscal Federalism."
presented at the Conference on the Future of Fiscal Federalism, School of
Policy Studies and John Deutsch Institute, Queen's University, 4–5 November. In *The Future of Fiscal Federalism*, ed. K.G. Banting, D.M. Brown, and T.J.
Courchene, 83–122. Kingston: School of Policy Studies.

Dungan, D. Peter, and Thomas A. Wilson. 1994. "Public Debt and the Economy." Discussion Paper 94-02. Kingston: Government and Competitiveness
Project, School of Policy Studies, Queen's University.

Grady, Patrick. 1991. *The Economic Consequences of Quebec Sovereignty*. Vancouver:
The Fraser Institute.

Grinspun, Ricardo, and Maxwell A. Cameron, eds. 1993. *The Political Economy
of North American Free Trade*. New York: St Martin's Press.

Hobson, Paul A.R., and France St-Hilaire. 1993. *Reforming Federal-Provincial Fiscal Arrangements: Towards Sustainable Federalism*. Montreal: Institute for Research on Public Policy.

Laxer, Gordon. 1992. "Constitutional Crises and Continentalism: Twin Threats to Canada's Continued Existence." *Canadian Journal of Sociology* 17 (June):199–222.

Leslie, P.M., K.H. Norrie, and I.K. Ip. 1993. *A Partnership in Trouble*. Toronto: C.D. Howe Institute.

Lipsey, Richard G., and Robert C. York. 1988. *Evaluating the Free Trade Deal: A Guided Tour through the Canada-U.S. Agreement*. Toronto: C.D. Howe Institute.

McCallum, John. 1993. "National Borders Matter: Regional Trade Patterns in North America." Working Paper 12/93. Montreal: Department of Economics, McGill University.

McMillan, Melville L. 1994. "Continental Economic Integration: A Perspective on the Relative Threat to Canada." Department of Economics, University of Alberta.

Messinger, Hans. 1993. "Interprovincial Trade Flows of Goods and Services." *Canadian Economic Observer* 6 (October):3.7–3.14.

Reid, Bradford, and Tracy Snoddon. 1992. "Redistribution under Alternative Constitutional Arrangements for Canada." In *Alberta and the Economics of Constitutional Change*, ed. P. Boothe, 65–105. Edmonton: Western Centre for Economic Research, University of Alberta.

Resnick, Philip. 1994. *Thinking English Canada*. Toronto: Stoddart.

Schwanen, Daniel. 1993. "A Growing Success: Canada's Performance under Free Trade." Commentary series. Toronto: C.D. Howe Institute.

Stanford, Jim. 1993. "Estimating the Effects of North American Free Trade: A Three-Country General Equilibrium Model with 'Real-World' Assumptions." Ottawa: Canadian Centre for Policy Alternatives, September.

Tremblay, Rodrique. 1993. "Macro-Based International Competitiveness with Free Trade." In *Beyond NAFTA: An Economic, Political and Sociological Perspective*, ed. A.R. Riggs and T. Volk, 143–58. Vancouver: The Fraser Institute.

Watson, W.G., J. Richards, and D.M. Brown. 1994. *The Case for Change: Reinventing the Welfare State*. Toronto: C.D. Howe Institute.

Watson, William G. 1993. "The Economic Impact of the NAFTA." Commentary series. Toronto: C.D. Howe Institute.

Whalley, John. 1983. "Induced Distortions of Interprovincial Activity: An Overview of Issues." In *Federalism and the Canadian Economic Union*, ed. M.J. Trebilcock, J.R.S. Prichard, T.J. Courchene, and J. Whalley, 161–200. Toronto: University of Toronto Press for the Ontario Economic Council.

Wilkinson, Bruce W. 1991. "The Free Trade Agreement between Canada and the United States." *Economic Bulletin for Europe* 42, no. 90:109–29.

PART V

Society: Domination and Marginality

15 Various Matters of Nationhood: Aboriginal Peoples and Canada outside Quebec

FRANCES ABELE

A nation is an association of reasonable beings united in a peaceful sharing of the things they cherish; therefore, to determine the quality of a nation, you must consider what those things are.

This sentence from St Augustine's *City of God* introduces the 1951 Massey Commission report on National Development in the Arts, Letters and Sciences.

The ability to see a "nation" of Canada in this straightforward way is characteristic of a different era, a period in which the dominant English-speaking elites were securely at the centre of what it was to be Canadian. Visions of Canada now have a much more complex and troubled character. Canada is both bicultural and multicultural, incorporating officially sanctioned ethnic diversity and the possibility of multiple, partial sovereignties.

Nationalism has a certain logic, which can be visualized as turning on two axes.[1] There is the axis of *inclusion* – once launched, the nationalist project tends to absorb all classes and all people who make the effort to "fit in." There is also an axis of *exclusion* – above all of the ethnically or "nationally" different, though ethnic difference is obviously a fluid and socially derived matter, and exclusion also of those who do not chose or who are not able to "fit in." Much of the heat and struggle of nationalist expression arises in the tension between the axes of exclusion and inclusion.

The federal polity of Canada has a straightforward focus of nationalist exclusion. The United States is nearby – large, oblivious, violent, rich, militaristic, imperialistic, and so on. As many other peoples have discovered, the u.s. is an ideal "Other" for nationalist purposes, since so many unpleasant generalizations are possible. To proclaim from whom we are different, and how, is relatively easy. The axis of inclusion has been more difficult. This is partly at least because there are two other internal "Others" with competing nationalist expressions. One of these is the collectivity of francophones living primarily in Quebec; the other Other is Aboriginal peoples, especially those First Peoples who insist upon recognition of their sovereignty. In a very strong sense, Aboriginal peoples are the ultimate internal Other, for both Québécois and the rest of Canada.

One reasonable reading of Canadian history would be to say that the main processes have been progressive inclusion of successive waves of immigrants, at the same time as there has been the progressive exclusion and dispossession of Aboriginal peoples. The Irish and the Ukrainians were nineteenth and early twentieth century "Others" who once were conceived to be different "races" and who are now not distinguishable from the general mainstream population; or rather to be Irish or Ukrainian has become to be Canadian. Aboriginal peoples have experienced double pressures from the immigrants: state and often religious policy led to assimilative (potentially inclusive) measures, while other measures, just as vigorous, worked to marginalize and exclude them. Canada did not have a frontier, but rather an "inside" and an "outside." The North, with its huge Aboriginal majority, was the last part of the country to be "brought in" (Rowley 1987).

In writing about Canada Outside Quebec, I welcome the chance to discuss unfinished business, but I do not intend to endorse separation. All parties consenting, Canada is much better *with* Quebec. Besides the intrinsic value of Quebec's traditions, culture, and language, there really is value in diversity as well as in the chance to continue to develop a new concept of a country, guided by tolerance and compromise.

JUSTICE AND HISTORICAL TRUTH

Realization of democratic Canadian nationhood will not be possible unless and until "Aboriginal issues" are thoroughly confronted and resolved. In the rest of this piece I want to explain why this is so. Much of this discussion hinges on two propositions about the reality of Aboriginal peoples and Canada outside Quebec:[2]

1 The version of Canadian history that emerges when the experience of Aboriginal peoples is remembered directly challenges many non-Aboriginal people's understanding of what happened. The truth taps at the roots of settled ideas.
2 Besides revising the historical record, the political goals of First Peoples[3] who find themselves in Canada appear to directly challenge

the main lineaments of (English) Canadian political values and traditional practices.

I want to turn these two difficult propositions to some good account as aids in thinking realistically about a better future. The discussion begins with some reflections on the nature of the polity "Canada outside Quebec" as it exists for Aboriginal peoples and the rest of us. These reflections provide a basis for considering how there might be important points of convergence in political values and goals. Throughout the discussion, the importance of establishing and recognizing historical truth to the achievement of justice and peaceful coexistence is evident. But I am not making an argument about historical guilt, the "wages of sin" or even collective responsibility. This paper is an attempt to improve communication and understanding, and thus to begin a dialogue.

It is important to mention some qualifications. This is an intervention or polemic; I am hoping to generate questions for reflection and debate rather than to arrive at clearly defensible conclusions. I do not try very hard to establish the truth of my two propositions. They share the main weakness of all grand generalizations about what people think, which is that there are important and potentially transformative exceptions. I want to start with the propositions as stated because there is enough truth in them for my limited purposes. They reflect many conversations over the years with people on matters of Aboriginal-non-Aboriginal relations. Similarly, in this essay I have occasion to offer generalizations about what might be "the Aboriginal perspective." These generalizations are based upon what I have learned over the years, and they are usually presented in a mild and tentative form, in recognition that I might easily be wrong; in any case views among Aboriginal people do differ. Finally, this paper is limited in another way, because for reasons of space I ignore some important constraints on realizing a better future, especially economic and constitutional-legal constraints. Though they are not discussed in detail here, such diverse matters as property in land ("Aboriginal title"), the need for land redistribution, the implications of the inclusion of Aboriginal and treaty rights in the Constitution, and the legal rights of Métis are all of central importance.

DIFFERING PERSPECTIVES

In *Thinking English Canada*, Philip Resnick identifies six elements "to emphasize in imagining English Canada." Resnick's list is a clear and insightful synthesis of what could be called the best common sense of contemporary scholarship, and it provides a convenient frame for some of the more important aspects of the confrontation of non-Aboriginal and Aboriginal "realities" (Resnick 1994, chap. 3 Abele 1989; Manzer 1984; Whitaker 1977). I use some ideas from Resnick's list to indicate how Aboriginal peoples' perspective of these matters might be different from the Canadian standard, if such a thing exists.[4]

Language and culture

In Canada outside Quebec, English is the common first language of all except some communities of francophones, Aboriginal peoples, and immigrants from non-English-speaking countries. A common political "culture" as carried by language has presumably come to us all with the words, concepts, parliamentary institutions, practices, and certain political values embodied in the language and the history we have all been taught and that originate in England. This is far from the end of the story, though: the "culture" of Canada outside Quebec is also heterogeneous. The varied backgrounds of immigrants and the regionally specific expanse of the country have engendered diversity and helped it to grow. Actual Canadian political culture is a redolent and hearty stew, reflecting the political kitchens of most of the world. To offer just one illustration: the particular character of what was once the strong prairie wing of the Cooperative Commonwealth Federation is probably a blend of the communalism of immigrant peasant cultures wedded through principle and self-interest to the ascetic but determined tradition of Methodist charity and mutual aid. The mix is what has helped to create a distinctively Canadian socialism.

For Aboriginal peoples there are at least two issues that must be addressed in a discussion of language and culture. The first concerns maintenance of their own languages. The normal universalizing pressures of life in the twentieth century bear on the First Peoples as on us all: intergenerational transmission of minority languages is a difficult practical matter, especially when the overall number of speakers is small.[5] Beyond and going much deeper than these problems, though, is the history of deliberate efforts by the state and religious authorities to suppress Aboriginal languages and to prevent their intergenerational preservation. Speaking English with "the rest of us" is thus not a neutral experience but a politically and emotionally charged one for most Aboriginal people who are now adults.[6]

The second issue concerns Aboriginal peoples' experience of the institutions of liberal democracy. Immigrants to Canada from the United Kingdom and from some Commonwealth countries (such as Australia and New Zealand) take the main features of the Westminster model for granted, and find in the constitutional tradition the source of their own rights and liberties. Immigrants from non-parliamentary countries learn about these rights and make a (more or less) conscious choice to live with what is here, to build on it, or at least to find a viable way to live here in light of the official ideals.

Aboriginal peoples have had a quite different experience of Canadian democracy than many of the rest of us. First, they have seen their own governing traditions challenged, eroded, and outlawed; those whose ancestors lived in democratic societies saw democracy replaced by domination.[7] If they are the descendants of treaty signatories, they have seen the federal and provincial governments walk away from agreements; they have seen their negotiated rights ignored, misrepresented, and dismissed; they remember the days when "registered" Indians were not allowed to vote or even to leave reserves without written passes from the Indian agents. Aboriginal peoples whose ancestors did not negotiate treaties with the newcomers (and this large group includes all Inuit, almost all Métis, and all other Aboriginal people in British Columbia and significant parts of the other provinces and the northern territories) were "administered" by state officials, and ignored when they were out of the way, to a degree not common in the experience of most Canadians.

Obviously, for Canada to include Aboriginal peoples in a non-tyrannical way, the absolute minimum starting point is the recognition of Aboriginal peoples' original sovereignty, revision of the "general idea" most people carry about Canadian history to reflect what really happened, and the wide discussion of the strikingly partial realization of liberal democratic ideals today. These points are easy to make analytically – and very difficult to realize, for many reasons. This is illustrated as Resnick moves between a discussion of language and culture (just reviewed) toward a discussion of Canada's relative tolerance of difference (later in his book) by way of some very mildly nationalist myth-building with respect to geography (Resnick 1994: chap. 3).[8]

Territory or space

Resnick rings many familiar bells in this ironical evocation of our odd lack of historical foundation myths and parallel attraction to geography:

What sets Canada apart from others on the globe is the particular territory it occupies in the northern part of North America, the three oceans – Atlantic, Pacific, and Arctic – that is touches, the mythos of harsh climate, endless winter, tundra and shield with which Canadian like to regale themselves.

For a long time, geography served as a substitute for history. Not only was history on the English-Canadian side (outside the Maritimes) relatively new, dating from after 1759, but it seemed rather undramatic when compared to the national histories of the United States, France or Great Britain ... Canadian geography, by comparison, was unique and challenging. (Resnick 1994:27)

While these remarks are salient for many English-speaking Canadians, since they may capture our educational experience and adult perceptions, in important ways they obscure the truth. The history of Canada (in or outside Quebec) did not begin, of course, in 1759 or with European settlement. Human history in North America began many thousands of years before 1759. And while the landscape may have evoked very interesting and important reactions in the immigrants who started to come here from Europe in the sixteenth century,[9] geography has quite a different meaning for the nations of peoples who were already living here.

Many Inuit, for example, did not find the climate of their homeland particularly harsh. While the tundra and shield were "endless" they were far from featureless: each people had a home territory, in which each feature was named, and for which the names evoked genealogical knowledge, history, and religious experience. Inuit gatherers' and hunters' knowledge is highly specific to place and type of species, reflecting encyclopedic and extremely detailed scientific understanding – all related to climate and place. This is an entirely different experience of the natural world from the "mythos" identified by Resnick, though it is certainly comprehensible to non-Aboriginal Canadians and even familiar to some. The general point here is that the old, prevailing or "common sense" dominant myths will go, as Aboriginal peoples' history and their perspective on the contact period, is brought forward – or brought *in*.

RE-EXAMINING THE HISTORICAL RECORD

The elaboration of a new national myth about place and politics, suitable to Canada outside Quebec, is, I believe inevitable. That is not to say, though, that it will be comfortable. The historical reality of First Peoples' experience of the migrants and settlers makes a disturbing basis for nation building and disrupts any prospect of the migrant society's establishment of a founding myth, in light of the other features of prevailing political culture. Seen from most points of view, though, the founding myths are not strong anyway, and many of the dominant ones lack salience outside of southern Ontario and Ottawa. We must begin with an understanding of the historical record – but not with guilt – and proceed to work on the immanent political problems.

How should this be done? One way to think the matter through is to consider the need for changes in a number of related areas, which can be tackled in series or at once. (The order in which I have listed them indicates neither priority nor desirable sequence.)

The Constitution

Part of the strange comfort of thinking about "Canada outside Quebec" instead of thinking about Canada and Quebec is the freedom from fussing about the contradictions and dangers of fragmented nationalism within a federation such as ours. And for many of us, the last three or four decades of constitutional negotiations have been sufficient. While it does seem that at least some aspects of a political resolution in Aboriginal-Canada relations entail constitutional change, it is really not clear whether anyone has the heart or the good will for another constitutional round, especially in light of the general deterioration of the Canadian economy, the public service, the educational establishment, and many other important institutions.

Constitutional change might be essential to the complete resolution of First Peoples-Canada relations, though there is considerable disagreement about this. Many Mohawks, for example, hold that their relationship with Canada was settled long ago, with the treaty recorded in the Two Row Wampum, which described peacefully co-existing, equal but separate polities. Other peoples are quite interested in constitutional entrenchment (and thus protection) of their self-government agreements with Canada. Anyway, further constitutionalization of First Peoples' political agenda is almost inevitable in light of the continued lack of resolution in Quebec-Canada relations. It would seem to be uncontroversial that constitutional change is insufficient. Within either the current constitutional framework or a new one, there is a need for citizens of the rest of Canada to address many other political matters. (Here I am speaking almost entirely of the work that remains for non-Aboriginal people in the rest of Canada; Aboriginal peoples all over have established their own agendas for change.)

History

One large outstanding item of business concerns adjusting the popular understanding of Canada's beginnings to bring it closer to what really happened. What is required at first is something less than the necessary detailed and constant revision that is the common labour of historians (structured by debates concerning interpretations of specific events and periods). This essential scholarly work will generate the building blocks of a new vision of the country. In the case of the popular versions of Canadian history and the "mythos," though, a major first step would be much more gross. It would involve simply the wide recognition of Aboriginal peoples' long history before they encountered migrants to North America (and the dissemination of knowledge about what life in North America was like then) and an understanding of the continuities between the "pre-contact" and "post-contact" periods. Their discovery of the newcomers is a major watershed for each Aboriginal nation, but usually there are other world-shaking events in their history, and the legacy of the pre-contact past illuminates the present. To understand what came before, the rest of us must lift our eyes from the period of colonialization and settlement but it matters very much how this is done.

One of the most pointed demonstrations of the difference history makes was the recent experience in the British Columbia Supreme Court of the Gitskan and Wet'suwet'en, who argued for their land rights on the basis of their own well-preserved and relatively accessible historical record. The oral historical record was heard in the courtroom but rejected in the judgment.[10] As Doug Elias (1991:126) explained:

The Chief Justice felt bound by judicial concepts of aboriginality. Courts have typically stripped aboriginality of any sense of change or history; any aboriginal matter must literally be pre-historic. Thus, rights and expressions of right are frozen at some ancient time, and anything since that time is more or less of a deviation from aboriginality. The Gitskan and Wet'suwet'en claims to sovereignty were struck down because what the Indians described as the contemporary form of self-government could not be shown to have a form identical to whatever existed in prehistoric times.

All other political institutions, and any claims to sovereignty of any collectivity on this continent, would fail this test.

Changing the "mythos" for the rest of Canada based upon an adjustment of the "general understanding" of the past is not simply a matter of educating those people who do not have post-secondary educations. It will involve changes in the perspectives and assumptions of lawyers, judges, teachers, artists, journalists, and others. And of course it will necessarily be a long and disorderly process: I am not recommending requiring everyone to learn the Truth and pass it on, but rather urging them to begin their reflections about what it means to be Canadian in the recognition of Aboriginal peoples' perspectives on their own histories – and their experience of "contact." There are signs everywhere that this is important business for the rest of us: "socially aware" television programs and popular movies probe the painful episodes of the past; the urban landscape bears many "appropriated" Aboriginal names – attached to sports teams, city streets, and (in Ontario at least) even post-secondary educational institutions; children often develop a fascination with Aboriginal culture. These signs are like the shadows on the wall of Plato's cave, except that we can all turn around to see the reality, without penality. The rest of Canada outside Quebec needs to understand the past.

The Past Recovered

Developing a more accurate general understanding of Canadian history will have direct material consequences. The appropriation of indigenous peoples' lands, and the establishment of a land tenure system suitable to the settlers, has been a major part of the global expansion of European nations during the last several centuries. In Canada this has been a protracted and uneven process.

Aboriginal–non-Aboriginal "contact" and then (mainly) European settlement across the continent occupied nearly three centuries. In the course of this long meeting, a variety of solemn agreements were reached. Normally, these agreements are called treaties. There is still considerable distance between the interpretation by British-Canadian jurisprudence and by Aboriginal parties to the treaties of their significance, meaning, and original intent. In recent years, however, a vital and difficult debate has begun to occur concerning these differences; it is too early to celebrate, but it is hard to believe that there will not be some convergence in understanding over time.[11]

Practical resolution of some other outstanding matters related to land ownership is already leading to a change in the architecture of federalism. There are large areas of Canada where no treaty was ever signed. The federal government's 1973 decision to commence negotiation of the so-called "modern treaties" – comprehensive claims agreements – recognized Aboriginal peoples' enduring rights in these "unceded" lands. Federal insistence that the comprehensive claims agreements "extinguish" all Aboriginal interest in the land, however, has led to the protraction and in some areas the total failure of the claims negotiation process. Where the process has not totally collapsed, First Peoples have forced into claims agreements a series of political arrangements. Despite federal resistance in principle and after the fact in practice, these agreements will ultimately change the face of federalism. To take just the most obvious example, consider that the federal legislation to create a territory in the Inuit homeland – to create Nunavut by the turn of the millennium – is reflected in a provision of the negotiated land claim settlement of the Inuit of the Northwest Territories. When that particular negotiation began twenty years ago, the federal Cabinet insisted that there would be no negotiation of political arrangements but strictly a cash and land settlement in which Inuit "claims" to a large territory would be exchanged for some money and fee simple ownership of very small bits of territory. Inuit negotiated the cash and land settlement, but they also managed to gain the consent of the rest of us to create a political jurisdiction in which they will be the very large majority for the foreseeable future, and in which they will have the all-important control over wildlife, water, and land management in order to protect their productive base.

The matter of land and the need for more just and peaceful co-existence on it arises in equally pointed fashion for those areas of Canada where earlier treaties have been negotiated. For example, the numbered treaties of western Canada were understood by the Aboriginal signatories to outline a basis for regularized joint occupancy of territories that were formerly exclusively Aboriginal. Besides the relatively small bits of "reserve" land (which were reserved for exclusive Indian residency), there were much larger territories traditionally used by Aboriginal people and now to be shared with the newcomers: a common explicit provision guaranteed continued traditional use of the territory, involving hunting and fishing. The reserves were created (though not always protected in full from encroachment); the larger territories of traditional use were shared in a most unequal fashion. They remained accessible to continued Aboriginal use only until a competing use was identified: cities, mines, dams, and farms all now occupy this "shared" land.

Clearly the matter of shared land use among Aboriginal peoples and the citizens of the rest of Canada must be addressed in just and practical ways. Experiments are under way across the country. "Co-management" of shared resources is being tried everywhere from the Arctic to the Shushwap territories in what is now British Columbia. Co-management usually involves first a closely negotiated agreement, which is inevitably itself heavily circumscribed by current law on Aboriginal rights and policies of the governments involved, both based in part at least in the unrevised version of Canadian history. These agreements do generally provide the basis for governments representing Aboriginal and non-Aboriginal "resource users" to establish management regimes that regulate competition and stock depletion. Flawed as they are (especially in being based upon "unequal" versions of how the resources came to be shared), the various types of co-management experiments across the land do suggest that peaceful coexistence can be institutionalized.[12]

Institutionalization of peaceful coexistence is essential. The recent experiments with co-management regimes are only a hopeful sign. There are many cases of outright conflict over land use every year in the rest of Canada. Where blocades or other forms of nonviolent direct action are taken by First Peoples, the problem is often land use. The painful and expensive confrontation at Oka revolves around a relatively small but precious area of land called "the Pines," which is where the municipality chose to build a golf course and which the Mohawks have a special responsibility to protect. In the evil cycle of escalating confrontation that preceeded the seige of 1991 and which continues to spin disorder and conflict today, there is an example of how important the serious discussion of land rights and history that awaits us really is.

THE NEED FOR ECONOMIC SOLUTIONS

It is impossible to generalize about the economic circumstances of Aboriginal communities. Some communities and some reserves are relatively healthy and prosperous; not all are the stuff of alarming stories on the national news. Most Aboriginal communities (including those in cities) do struggle with a shortage of jobs for a rapidly growing population of young people. The land bases are almost all inadequate; community economies are limited by the laws that apply to reserve lands.[13] Many reserves and predominantly Aboriginal communities are remote from markets and out of range of many of the services, such as banking, required by small businesses.

Resolution of outstanding land issues will go some distance toward improving the economic viability of Aboriginal communities. Even given stable and more just arrangements concerning land, however, there will be major economic difficulties for many Aboriginal communities.

These are being confronted now with a variety of locally specific strategies. Nations located near major population centres are able to take advantage of the economic opportunities such centres present. For example the Wyandot territory, Wendake (formerly known as Huron Village), is contiguous with Quebec City; it has become a sucessful small manufacturing centre, even providing a small number of jobs to nonresidents of the reserve. Housing developments serving nonresidents, recreational opportunities, services, sales, and tourism have all been exploited by the nations who live near virtually every site in western Canada. In the northern regions where over one third of Aboriginal people live, eco-tourism, quarrying of fine stones, various forms of art (such as soapstone carving and print-making), handicraft production, luxury food marketing and many other "small impact" measures are being tried. No one activity on its own can provide sufficient economic opportunities, but all generate a certain amount of cash to households who still produce a great deal of their own food by hunting, fishing, and gathering.

Most of the work of economic recovery and development will be undertaken by the people who live in each Aboriginal territory. In common with most Canadians everywhere, they will benefit from economic and social policies that build upon the traditions of redistribution and positive state involvement, to the extent that any government is ever able to provide these again.

SURVIVING TOGETHER

Recent events on virtually every continent illustrate the ugly side of ethnic identification and the human misery that is produced by irridentist claims to original occupancy and ownership of territory. Reflecting on these ill effects, a well-intentioned person well might ask, is it wise (or necessary) to make any adjustments at all to ensure the survival of Aboriginal peoples as collectivities? Ought we all not to live as Canadians, citizens equal before the law and non-committal (or at least private and non-political) about our differences?

These are important questions, but they are quite beside one important point. The question is not *whether* adjustments "should be made" for Aboriginal peoples to exist as collectivities. The fact is that Aboriginal peoples (as peoples, nations, collectivities) exist now, as they have for thousands of years. That we know of indigenous history, that we hear Aboriginal languages spoken, that more and more indigenous peoples' knowledge of the natural world is being recovered and applied, are all evidence of their *collective* existence.

The future of Aboriginal collectivities depends now as it always has upon what Aboriginal peoples themselves do; it is not fundamentally a matter for public policy or constitutional engineering. But it is important that discussions of these matters be informed by respect for the importance of culture and society.

A shared linguistic and conceptual context, a shared experience of meaning and memory sustains all human beings as individuals and keeps us whole. Virtually all contemporary Aboriginal people share the conceptual context, and the culture, of other Canadians – that is, they speak the same language as their non-Aboriginal neighbours and understand the key features of public life in similar ways. But most Aboriginal people also participate in another conceptual sphere, expressed in an Aboriginal language and grown in the history of their original people of nation. The future will grow from the well-being of this indigenous conceptual sphere, as much as Aboriginal peoples' just inclusion depends does upon the growth of the other.

FINAL THOUGHTS

I believe that there is only one direction for building a nation in Canada, whether or not that nation ultimately includes Quebec. It will have to be launched in light of and with thorough reference to the long-standing political purposes of Aboriginal peoples, for prudential not moral reasons: the nature of nationalism itself requires this. If Canada outside Quebec fails to *include* those who were here before and displaced, as well as those who keep coming, then it will exclude them. With exclusion will come mutual elaboration and entrenchment of "Otherness," with all the risks of vilification, mistrust, and civil conflict.

Although the Aboriginal side of the relationship of Otherness has not been my focus here, it is obvious that a parallel initiative is necessary within Aboriginal nations and communities. Aboriginal peoples are coming to terms with Canada. As individuals and communities, citizens and neighbours, we often live together. The challenge is to create a polity that reflects and supports the best of the relationships already prevailing in civil society.

How may we proceed? Not with the goal of assimilation, for that is only one aspect of the force that has driven Aboriginal peoples to the margin. I think, paradoxically, that the discussion must begin with the recognition of original sovereignty and of the reality that now Aboriginal peoples and everyone else share the territory, the institutions, and the urgent need to begin to understand what Augustine's vision might mean if everyone's self-determination were to be respected. There must be a process of respectful negotiation and – where the ground is properly prepared – of development. This work is going to have to proceed without certainty of outcome, in an open-ended and unfinished fashion that is familiar to Canadians as their natural approach to national development. It is full of unavoidable risks for non-Aboriginal as well as Aboriginal people. Aboriginal and non-Aboriginal peoples alike may begin to glimpse a new kind of nationhood, based on equality, tolerance, fairness, peace, order, good government, and mutual inclusion.

NOTES

Although I recently worked for the Royal Commission on Aboriginal Peoples, the ideas here are my own. They are not necessarily shared by the commission. I want to thank Joyce Ford, Katherine Graham, and Phoebe Nahanni for sharing their insights on these matters. For insight and for many probing conversations, I am grateful also to my husband, George Kinloch, who continues to be *sine qua non.*

1 This discussion and, less directly, several others in this paper are developments of ideas found in Anderson, 1983.

2 These two propositions are true equally in Quebec and the rest of Canada, though the political values and assumptions that are challenged do differ, and certainly the history that needs revision is different for Quebec than for the rest of Canada.

3 I use First Peoples and Aboriginal peoples interchangeably to refer collectively to all nations descended from the original inhabitants of northern North America. For convenience, I use 'non-Aboriginal' to refer to everyone else, wherever her or his ancestors came from. None of these terms is really very informative. They do draw a sort of a line (between the original inhabitants and the descendants of the newcomers), but they conceal as much as they reveal of the complex history of this continent. Wherever possible, I do refer to nations by their proper names – Dene, Cree, Innu, Inuit, Inuvialuit, Métis, Wyandot, and so on. Achieving informative clarity about the nature of the newcomers is even more complex and difficult, due to our extreme heterogeneity.

4 I do not deal with his whole list; there is not proper attention to all the subtle points Resnick makes, and sometimes my characterization on a particular point goes beyond what he has said.

5 The prospects for a language like Inuktittut (the language of Inuit) are fairly healthy; it is likely that the transmission of this language to successive generations will continue. Many more Aboriginal languages are in rapid decline because they are not spoken widely by young people.

6 The statements of the current generation of Aboriginal political leaders (who in their thirties, forties, and fifties now) may not reflect the experience or the interests of the next generation of Aboriginal people, now in their teens and twenties. This group is enormous (in 1991, 58 percent of Aboriginal people in Canada were under the age of 24, compared to about 30 percent for the general population), and there is some early evidence that their political views and social needs are quite different from those of their elders.

7 There is much more to say about the process of political conquest of the Americas than can even be alluded to here. A convenient and beautifully

clear overview appears in Ronald Wright, *Stolen Continents*. This book are also contains many useful references.

8 I use Resnick because his attempt to "think English Canada" is consistently aware that Aboriginal peoples are important to consider as well; in the entire book, he never fails to mention the Aboriginal exception where this is appropriate. My comments proceed from the ground he lays, by showing just how difficult is the task toward which he has gestured. There are many easier targets, who ignore the Aboriginal and frequently the immigrant reality entirely. Cf. the aging but still relatively relevant Abele and Stasiulis (1989).

9 Something important is captured in the Stan Rogers song, *Northwest Passage*. Many people have remarked that this heroic and beautiful celebration of the hardiness of the mariners who sought a passage through the Arctic archipelago from the Atlantic to the Pacific should become Canada's national anthem. A different sort of European reaction in dissected in Griffiths (1987).

10 A powerful discussion of these matters appears in Culhane (1994 and 1992). The quotation from Elias obviously does not address all the reasons for the judicial decision in this case. See Delgamuukw v. The Queen, [1991] unreported decision of the Supreme Court of British Columbia.

11 There is much too much to be said about treaties to make it useful to generalize here. The Aboriginal parties to treaties largely heard rather than read what they were signing, and it seems clear that problems of translation and cross-cultural understanding compounded what were also very clear differences of interest and mandate in all the parties.

12 A widely studied and relatively effective co-management initiative is the Porcupine Cariboo Management Board (which involves the Aboriginal cariboo harvesters) in the United States (Alaska) and Canada.

13 For example, many small businesses are financed by mortgages on the owners' homes and other property; because land on reserve is held in common, individuals are unable to mortgage such property. After many attempts at revisions and reform, the Indian Act still assigns considerable control over economic affairs on reserves to the Department of Indian Affairs. Change in this area is likely to be gradual.

BIBLIOGRAPHY

Abele, Frances. 1989. "Canadian Contradictions: Forty Years of Northern Political Development." *Arctic* 40, no. 4 (Winter).

– and Daiva Stasiulis. 1989. "Canada as a White Settler Colony: What About Natives and Immigrants?" In *The New Canadian Political Economy*, ed. W. Clement and G. Williams, 240–77. Kingston and Montreal: McGill-Queen's University Press.

Anderson, Benedict. 1991. *Imagined Communities*. London and New York: Verso.

Culhane, Dara. 1992. "Adding Insult to Injury: Her Majesty's Loyal Anthropologist." *B.C. Studies*, no. 92 (Autumn): 66–92.

– 1994. "Delgamuukw and the People Without Culture: Anthropology and the Crown." PH.D. diss. Department of Sociology and Anthropology, Simon Fraser University.

Elias, Peter Douglas. 1991. *Development of Aboriginal people's Communities*. North York: Captus Press.

Griffiths, Franklyn, 1987. "Where Vision and Illusion Meet." In *Politics of the Northwest Passage*, ed. Franklyn Griffiths. Kingston and Montreal: McGill-Queen's University Press.

Manzer, Ronald. 1984. "Public Policy-Making as Practical Reasoning." *Canadian Journal of Political Science* 17, no. 3:577–94.

Resnick, Philip. 1994. *Thinking English Canada*. Toronto: Stoddart.

Rowley, Graham. 1987. "Bringing the Outside Inside: Towards Development of the Passage." In *Politics of the Northwest Passage*, ed. Franklyn Griffiths. Kingston and Montreal: McGill-Queen's University Press.

Royal Commission on National Development in the Arts, Letters and Sciences. 1951. *Report*. Ottawa: Queen's Printer.

Whitaker, Reg. 1977. "Images of the State in Canada." In *The Canadian State: Political Economy and Political Power*, ed. Leo Panitch, 28–68. Toronto: University of Toronto Press.

Wright, Ronald. 1993. *Stolen Continents: The New World through Indian Eyes since 1942*. Markham: Viking.

16 Multiculturalism and Identity in "Canada outside Quebec"

C. MICHAEL LANPHIER AND
ANTHONY H. RICHMOND[1]

This chapter examines ethnic pluralism and multiculturalism in Canada outside Quebec (COQ). It distinguishes among language, nation, and state as ways of defining collective identity, and emphasizes the regional variations within the countr. It asks, "How English is English Canada?" and concludes that COQ is in the process of becoming a postmodern state in serious danger of fragmentation.

LANGUAGE, CULTURE, NATION, AND STATE

There are complementary images of the state as *Staatsnation,* focusing on the legal forms and *Kulturnation* which emphasises common values, heritage, and symbols (Meinecke 1970). Language is often regarded as the critical link, but this overlooks other dimensions of ethnicity, such as "race,"[1] religion, and ancestry, which persist even when a single language is in use. There are important connections of language, culture, and nation but they are not synonymous terms (Fishman 1989).

Canada is a post-industrial society with a positive immigration policy which officially promotes bilingualism within a multicultural framework. When Trudeau enunciated this policy in 1971, he emphasized the importance of recognizing that French Canadians lived from the Atlantic coast to British Columbia and were not limited to Quebec. He was criticized by Claude Ryan (1971), who argued that the two official languages of Canada were "the expression of two cultures, two peoples, two societies which give Canada its distinctive shape." Such a view ignores the reality of multiculturalism in COQ and the impact of globalization.

POSTMODERNISM AND GLOBAL CULTURE

The ethnic diversity of almost all post-industrial societies today raises the question whether equality of opportunity and the coaptation of immigrants, with each other and with indigenous populations, can be reconciled with the maintenance of separate identities and cultural pluralism. The viability of "multiculturalism" as a policy designed to accommodate the needs and interests of minorities is being questioned (Bibby 1990; McLellan and Richmond 1994). Two hundred years of industrialism and state formation in both democratic and authoritarian regimes have failed to suppress the diverse languages, religions, and aspirations for self-determination of ethnic minorities throughout the world. The expressive dimensions of ethnicity are not exclusively primordial, but they are profoundly related to identity, and as such they are powerful motivators. When socio-economic status and ethnicity come together in relations of economic and political domination, the resulting *ethclass* conflicts explode in violent confrontations on a global scale (Richmond 1994). As Robertson (1990:57) points out, "National societies are increasingly exposed, internally, to problems of heterogeneity and diversity and, at the same time, are experiencing both external and internal pressures to reconstruct their collective identities along pluralistic lines."

There are competing reference points for individuals in terms of ethnicity, culture, and religion and, as Robertson explains, the system of international relations is becoming more and more fluid and "multipolar." The United States, like many other countries, is ethnically stratified and culturally pluralistic, and as a consequence there is no single "American way of life" into which immigrants must eventually be assimilated. Australia, Britain, and various European countries, as well as Canada, have adopted educational and social policies specifically defined as "multi-cultural." There is much debate and uncertainty, however, concerning what such policies and programs mean in practice (Burnet 1987; Bullivant 1981; Foster and Stockley 1988; Zubrzycki 1986).

The possible secession of Quebec from the Canadian federation and the varying ideas of provincial rights evident in the western provinces lend some support to the view that the COQ is not sufficiently cohesive and integrated to resist the combined centrifugal and centripetal forces of globalization and ethnic pluralism. It is tempting to conclude that "English Canada," as a homogeneous community, a unitary nation and a single state, exists only in the imagination of Quebec separatists!

REGIONAL DIVERSITY AND MULTICULTURALISM IN CANADA OUTSIDE QUEBEC

Sociologists have noted for over a half century the decentralizing effect of regions (Dawson 1936; Driedger 1989; Matthews 1980). Regional distinctiveness nevertheless stands as a hallmark of Canadian social organization, especially with respect to the relation of ethnicity to culture. Driedger (1989) identifies six such regions: Atlantic, Quebec, the North, the Bilingual Belt, Upper Canada, and the West, which have a degree of homogeneity of ethnicity and language. However, there are significant variations within and among these regions. These include questions of resources and socio-economic organization (discussed in other chapters) as well as ethnic diversity.

Atlantic Provinces

The population of the Atlantic Provinces has remained distinctive in the high proportion of persons of British, Irish, and Scottish descent in Nova Scotia, Prince Edward Island, and Newfoundland – nearly four-fifths overall. English is the mother tongue of the large majority in these provinces. Only in New Brunswick does more than a third of the population claim French heritage. Overall, the proportion claiming an ethnic origin other than English or French hovers around 10 percent, most of whom live in Nova Scotia.

Gilad (1990) records a poignant chapter in Newfoundland life: the arrival of refugee claimants through the international Gander airport during the mid- and late-1980s. The official apparatus for processing claims is available there, no less than at any other port of entry. Likewise, basic services of governmental and nongovernmental agencies (NGOs) were either in place or rapidly developed to serve newcomers, mainly in St John's, the only urban centre with sufficient infrastructure to provide settlement services. The newcomers represented diverse origins. Eastern Europeans (citizens of the former USSR and other Eastern Bloc states), Cubans, and Vietnamese constituted the major groups of arrivals. These newcomers were well received by Newfoundlanders, despite their unfamiliarity with families from such diverse backgrounds. Overcoming formidable difficulties, housing was located, English language classes were arranged, and orientation to Canada initiated. However, there was little success in placing these newcomers in the labour force. Few jobs were available in the period of the declining fishing industry. The resident population was experiencing the negative effects of structural adjustment. Nor was the other principal form of social organization (kinship) available as an integrational mechanism. The only available alternative was out-migration. This was not a result of a xenophobic reaction by the local population: surprisingly little was evident. There simply was no room in a society in which a "sense of place" was clearly rooted in attachment to land and sea among kin groups who supported each other.

Despite the competition between them for increasingly scarce resources, the fishing communities of the Atlantic provinces have more in common with their maritime counterparts in France, Spain, and the Portuguese Azores than they do with other Canadian regions. The Atlantic region faces an imminent collapse of their traditional community style as economic "safety nets" regressively yield as little as those fishing nets so long the mainstay.

The North

Although living on reserves has the advantage of preserving Native language and many traditions, compared with the rest of Canada, social conditions in the North show high rates of disease, infant mortality, alcoholism, drug abuse, crime, violence, and suicide, reflecting varying degrees of anomie and alienation. The suicide rate for Native peoples under the age of twenty-five, living on reserves is six to twelve times higher than the national average in Canada (*Gazette* 27 July 1992). High unemployment, poverty, and loss of nonrenewable resources due to the rapid growth of industrialization, poor housing, inadequate health care, family breakdown, and feelings of isolation are typical. The case for greater autonomy leading to some form of self-government is overwhelming (Mercredi and Turpel 1993).

Although the North has a diverse population, about 53 percent of the people there are of Inuit origin. Living mostly in secluded settlements or in villages with populations of 200 to 1,000 inhabitants, they speak languages indigenous to the region, such as Eskimo-Aleut, Athapascan, and Algonquian (Frideres 1983). Population density ranges from zero to sixty persons per hundred square kilometres (Driedger 1989:115). The Inuit live a traditional style, hunt in semi-nomadic bands and use sleds for local transportation. Despite recent changes in the boundaries and forms of government, the Inuit have not gained complete autonomy, but they remain largely isolated, geographically and socially, from the rest of Canada. Some have moved to the southern industrial developments for better employment opportunities. There they perforce adapt a bureaucratic and urban lifestyle, often indistinguishable from that of their neighbours in other regions of Canada.

Thus, while multiple cultures inhabit the North, and to that extent multiculturalism is practised in day-to-day life, Native peoples and the Inuit lead separate existences, although increasingly linked by commercial and telecommunication networks that enable them to communicate with their counterparts in other northern countries, such as Norway and Russia. The North displays a "multiculturalism of separation."

Ontario

Ontario is able to support social and multicultural services as an outgrowth of its diversified and relatively prosperous economic performance, even in recent years of structural adjustment and high rates of unemployment.

In addition to federal multicultural programs, the Province of Ontario has its own policies, with emphasis upon employment equity and mandated nondiscriminatory practices in service deliveries by all agencies that receive provincial funds. The overall objective of the policy is "mainstreaming," that is, helping newcomers to make a transition from services specifically directed to their particular ethnic, language, or nationality group, to services generally available to all residents of Ontario (Fleras and Elliott 1992:80–5). Many municipalities, for example, make translation services available both in print and voice in several major languages of newcomers. Special funding is available for cultural events. The Municipality of Metro Toronto sponsors a "Refugee Awareness Week," which enlists participation from non-governmental organizations and the multicultural public. Well-publicized and supported by civic groups, this week contributes to greater multicultural sensitivity on the part of front-line public services, especially the police force.

These extensive programs in Ontario and its municipalities are contingent upon the availability and continuation of funding which in turn depends on the economic prosperity of the province. More than 40 percent of all immigrants to Canada annually settle in Ontario. The high volume of intake requires service deliveries of a varied nature with accommodation of language and cultural practices common to the newcomers. Moreover, the province has contributed to funding NGOs committed to advocacy for newcomers.

Multicultural programming has created a mini-industry which has become self-perpetuating. While loosely coordinated with federal initiatives, the provincial programs operate quite autonomously, with their own system of funding. Provincial sources characteristically subsidize the same agencies which receive federal funding, for example, and demand separate accounting for expenditures. The potential for conflict and confusion (as well as a taxpayer backlash) is obvious.

After a series of clashes between Black youths and the police, together with other violent outbursts, the Premier of Ontario commissioned the noted parliamentarian Stephen Lewis to formulate recommendations for immediate remedial action. Despite haste in preparation, Lewis addressed a breakdown of institutional control in the metropolitan area with the highest concentration of persons of colour in Canada. Not only did Lewis receive reports of systemic anti-Black discrimination throughout southern Ontario, members of minorities of colour themselves expressed distressed puzzlement at delays in implementing policies relating to race relations based on legislation already in place. Nor did Black members of the community feel that the world outside their individual households could be navigated with any sense of public safety (Lewis 1992:2–3).

Despite strengthening institutional and formal governmental mechanisms already available as legal or administrative instruments, Lewis felt still more were needed: committees of review (e.g., a community-based monitoring and audit board for reviewing police activity) and action-initiating committees (e.g., curriculum review) to reflect multicultural changes in Ontario. Such reform has to cross-cut levels of political administration (local through provincial) and traverse the total sphere of social institutions: the criminal justice system, education, employment, community organization. All such institutional-control changes proceed notoriously slowly.

Lewis' report evidences a lack of effective multicultural sensitivity throughout the whole of (Ontario) society. It serves as a stinging indictment of public administration as well as of public concern in reflecting the multicultural policy enunciated federally some twenty years earlier.

Ontario is dominated by its metropolitan south. As an emerging "global city," Toronto more closely allies with Montreal and New York than its own urban-rural hinterland. Its cosmopolitan population experiences tensions no different from its multiracial, polyethnic counterparts throughout the world. Toronto quintessentially represents the arena of "politics of recognition." Multiculturalism too often becomes a battleground of competition for power and resources.

Prairie Provinces

The Prairie provinces comprise a diversified cultural mix, principally of European origins, particularly German, Ukrainian, and to a lesser extent French. The Prairie provinces trace their roots through several languages and cultures from Métis, through European settlers now including German, Ukrainian, Mennonite, Hutterite, Doukhobor, and Mormon communities. In addition, American links remain strong, partly from the immigration influx after the turn of the twentieth century.

Ethnic enclaves are scattered throughout urban and rural areas, although English is used far more frequently than other languages, even at home (Driedger 1989:126–31). Despite their historical roots the French, as well as others of non-English ancestry, are considered merely one of several minorities in the region, not deserving special language accommodation, although the courts have upheld some claims to official language rights by francophones (Vallee and deVries 1978). Native peoples, however marginalized, form part of urban as well as rural culture, so that there are many ethnocultural specificities to be taken into account.

However equivocal the past record, all Prairie provinces have formally endorsed multicultural policies in recent years. In Saskatchewan the institutional sectors of education and employment have been identified as targets for multicultural policy implementation. Manitoba has introduced a multiculturalism secretariat with a diversified implementation policy. Alberta has developed a three-tiered policy to foster economic integration through equal opportunity (Fleras and Elliott 1992:80). Throughout the Prairies, multicultural services are principally available only in major metropolitan areas and through a restricted number of agencies. While there appears willingness to provide initial multicultural services for newcomers, it is tempered by availability of resources and personnel, both in scarce supply, and often dependent on sources other than government.

British Columbia

British Columbia entered its modern historical period with the strongest claim to "English" heritage, albeit qualified by the rich Native heritage and those of other minorities, including German and Doukhobor settlements. Since the end of the Second World War, British Columbia has received significant numbers of newcomers of languages other than English or French. In recent years the Asian influx has been notable (Driedger 1989:179). Significantly more persons in British Columbia than elsewhere in Canada endorse a "melting pot" over a "mosaic" model of social pluralism (Driedger 1989:334). Newcomers and Canadians of Asian background experienced a series of attacks in the 1980s. The Klu Klux Klan distributed their propaganda and harassed visible minorities. The B.C. Organization to Fight Racism was established. It was composed of members from the South Asian community, supported by various ethnic communities, Native peoples, labour groups, and left-leaning political groups, including some organizations with communist affiliations. This group established a common front, with demonstrations and representations to civic groups and councils. It attempted to disengage from its anti-capitalist ideological roots to create a wider base of grassroots support from a wide variety of minorities who experienced discrimination, and realized temporary success with some 1,500 dues-paying members (Sharma 1991). Because of the lack of a permanent institutionalized base, however, this alliance all but disappeared with the tapering of these confrontations. No formal assistance came from official sources. As a result the movement has remained in virtual eclipse since 1983.

In March 1994 the district of North Vancouver struck down a series of recommendations from its own task force commissioned over a two-year period to bring forth a municipal policy on multicultural and other equity issues. Local area politicians complained that such recommendations reflected special-interest groups and were not a proper use of public resources (Matas 1994). Multicultural policy has thus received a distinctly more passive endorsement in British Columbia. A policy removing barriers to employment opportunity represents a positive thrust, but this strategy appears weak in face of a complex economy.

Given the province's orientation to Asia and the Pacific, combined with a vigorous north-south commerce with Washington, Oregon, and California, there are many economic factors which set B.C. apart from COQ. The greatest socio-economic impact derives from the accelerating Pacific orientation, apace with globalization. Vancouver has become a proverbial "commuter suburb" for Hong Kong, Tokyo, and even Taipei. It also retains strong links through its long-established South Asian (particularly Sikh) community. The Rocky Mountains serve as no less a psychological than physical barrier, all the more to ensure that Vancouver and its environs strengthen ties with the emerging global economic giants of the Pacific.

In sum, the official policy of multiculturalism has been variously interpreted in different regions of Canada outside Quebec. These interpretations have responded to different challenges of mutual adaptation of newcomers and various ethnic minorities in each region. Whether these different forms of multiculturalism can be integrated sufficiently into a more or less consistent policy throughout all regions is a challenge which may bring forward elements of collective identity. Prominent among these elements of the supposed common denominator that Canada outside Quebec shares its "English" cultural background. It is to this challenge that we now turn.

FIGURE 1
Ethnic Origin Responses in Canada, 1991

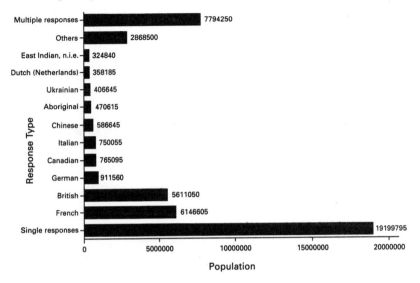

Source: Statistics Canada, *The Daily*, February 23, 1993

HOW "ENGLISH" IS ENGLISH CANADA?

The term "English" has several connotations depending upon context. Quebec francophones tend to view the COQ as quite homogeneous in terms of language and ethnicity. As we have seen, this is far from the case. Less than a quarter of the population of Canada outside Quebec reported a single response, "English," in the 1986 and 1991 censuses. The incorrect perception of English dominance has been reinforced by the propensity of census takers to combine the English, Welsh, Scots, and Irish (and their descendants) into a single classification: "British." Even so, only 26 percent of the population of COQ was of exclusively "British" ethnic origin in 1991. When Quebec is included, the proportion is reduced to 21 percent (Statistics Canada, 1993b, see figure 1). Regional differences in ethnic composition are significant, reflecting the varied experience of early colonial settlement and later waves of immigration. The reality in Ontario, and the in West, is an increasing ethnic diversity, a consequence of the waves of immigration since the end of the nineteenth century. The situation is further complicated by the extent of intermarriage and the emergence of multiple ethnic origins as a norm. Figure 2 shows the distribution of multiple and single responses and the most frequent single responses in each region. Multiple origins were least often found in Quebec and most often in the Prairie provinces and British Columbia.

FIGURE 2A
Ethnic Origin Responses, Atlantic Region, 1991

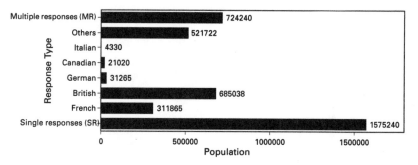

Ethnic Origin Responses, Quebec, 1991

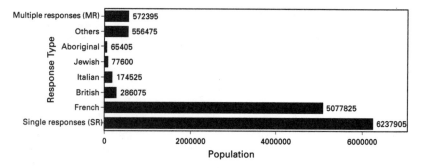

Ethnic Origin Responses, Ontario, 1991

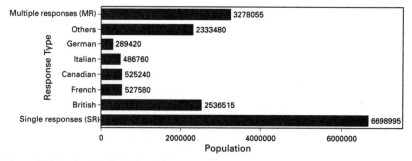

Source: Statistics Canada, *The Daily*, 23 February 1993

Using the ability to speak one of the two official languages as a basis of classification gives a deceptive appearance of English dominance. It overlooks the pluralistic basis of ethnic identity. Gender, age, colour, language, "race," nationality, and religion are among the ascriptive bases on which people define their identities. The plural noun, "identities,"

FIGURE 2B
Ethnic Origin Responses, Prairies Region, 1991

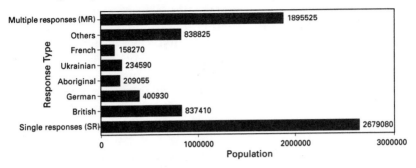

Ethnic Origin Responses, British Colombia, 1991

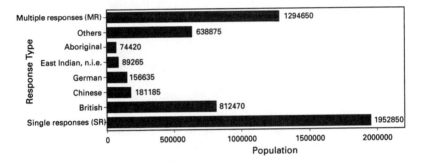

Ethnic Origin Responses, Territories, 1991

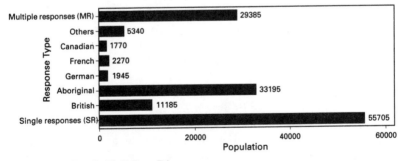

Source: Statistics Canada, *The Daily,* 23 February 1993

appears more appropriate because individual identities are multiple, influenced by context, and situationally determined. They are reflexively organized and redefined subjectively over time. Self-definitions do not always correspond with the identities attributed by others, which may be based upon different criteria and perceptions (Richmond 1994).

Exogamy and Multiple Ethnic Origins

Until the 1986 and 1991 censuses in Canada, respondents were forced to use a "paternal ancestry"criterion for defining ethnic origin, and only single-origin responses were tabulated. Dual or multiple origins were edited out, and a response of "American" or "Canadian" was disallowed. Even when, in the last two censuses, reporting more than one ethnic origin was permitted, computing limitations have obliged Statistics Canada to publish only "Single" and "Dual" responses. In censuses it is clear that multiple ethnic origins are characteristic of contemporary societies, such as the u.s. and Canada, that have experienced substantial waves of immigration over long periods. There has been extensive intermarriage between ethno-religious groups, with consequent diversification of the population even though complete "assimilation" to the characteristics of the majority of dominant group has not occurred (Richard 1991).

In 1991, 29 percent of the population reported more than one ethnic origin, and over a million people insisted on describing themselves as "Canadian," although this was not an option on the census form. Earlier studies suggested that the preference for describing oneself as Canadian, rather than defining specific ethnic ancestry, was particularly characteristic of third and subsequent generation Canadian-born respondents who were not of British or French ethnic origin (Richmond and Goldlust 1977).

Using the 1986 census, Krotki and Odynak (1990) demonstrated a substantial increase in the reporting of multiple ethnicities. Overall, since 1981 there was a 21 percent decline in the number of people reporting "single origins" (these groups reported multiple ethnic affiliations in greater frequency). The largest drop was among those of East European origins, followed by those of West European and British (including English, Welsh, Irish, and Scots) origins. The propensity to marry out of one's ethnic community is, in part, a function of the absolute size of the group in question: the smaller the numbers, the greater the statistical probability of finding a partner of a different ethnicity. Therefore, the English *might* be expected to have a lower rate of multiple ethnicity reporting than others. Yet in the 1986 and 1991 censuses, almost half those reporting "English" were multiples, that is, they also reported one or more other origins. Of the Irish, 81 percent reported multiple origins, as did 79 percent of the Scots. The propensity to report more than one origin was common among North, West, and Eastern European groups, all of them exceeding 50 percent (Statistics Canada, 1993b; see figure 3).

FIGURE 3
Multiple Responses for Selected Ethnic Origins

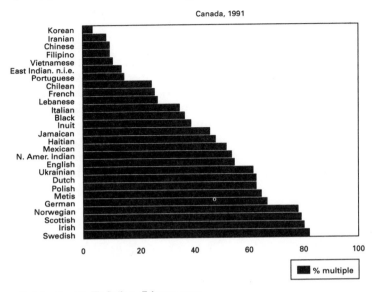

Canada, 1991

Source: Statistics Canada, *The Daily*, 23 February 1993

English language use

Recognition of the multiple nature of ethnic identity does not detract from the importance of language as a medium through which ethnic identity is communicated. Language, religion, and nationality combine in different ways to form ethno-cultural groupings and ethno-national political movements. Language plays a critical role, not only as an ethnic signifier in its own right but also as the medium through which ethnic consciousness and ethnic groups are formed (Fishman 1989; Richmond 1994). Therefore, it is necessary to examine the distribution of English language use as well as English ethnic origins.

Those reporting English as mother tongue in 1991 were a majority in all provinces except Quebec, but the proportion varied from 56 percent in the North-West Territories to 99 percent in Newfoundland. Both Ontario and British Columbia experienced a decrease in the relative size of the anglophone population between 1986 and 1991. When home language is considered, the number speaking a non-official language (in Canada as a whole) was 2.3 million in 1991, half of whom were living in Ontario (Statistics Canada 1992). Linguistic and ethnic diversity was greatest in the metropolitan areas. More than a fifth of the population of the Toronto metropolitan area spoke a language other than English at home; in Vancouver the corresponding proportion was 17 percent (Statistics Canada 1993a).

CANADA WITHOUT QUEBEC

There is no obvious way to provide a power base for ethnocultural groups, whose multiplicity provides a more complex scenario than that of "two founding peoples." The Canadian Multiculturalism Act (1988) cites the Canadian Human Rights Act, the International Convention on the Elimination of All forms of Racial Discrimination, the Charter of Rights as it applies to visible minorities and aboriginal peoples, as well as the Official Languages Act. It is important that entitlements and access to governmental institutions and services cannot be reserved to peoples of any single origin. By implication, groups having been declared equal need no further claim to entitlement, although affirmative action may be required to redress past inequities. The myth of two founding peoples can no longer be sustained. An emphasis on rights of the individual, which cuts across all ethnocultural groups provides, in principle, access to government services, the courts, and employment in the public and private sectors for all citizens.

Waves of immigration from all over the world and the official acknowledgment of this diversity in official legislation indicate that multiculturalism is now accepted in theory, if not always in practice. Not only the sheer proliferation of languages, religions, customs, and folkways, but the recognition of their legitimacy raises questions concerning the management of such diversity in the interests of political unity and social peace. Departments of immigration and secretary of state and multiculturalism (and their various more recent incarnations) established various advisory councils on ethnocultural relations in an attempt to contain the potential conflict. Initial concerns about forging political unity out of cultural diversity have given rise to further questions concerning the transformation of second-class status. Concerns over distributive justice have persisted. Expression of these principles is usually found in the concrete complaints of individual minority members that discriminatory practices have deprived them of essential rights. However, the question of *collective* rights is also raised by Native communities and by some religious groups (Turpel 1990:3–45; Morris and Lanphier 1977).

Many of the problems outlined would exist whether or not Quebec separated from the rest of Canada (Morris and Lanphier 1977). But political and territorial separation would add social, political, and organizational consequences. If separation occurs, another form of organization will have to emerge to allow for the multiplicity and cross-cutting nature of ethnocultural relations. Such a social structure cannot be territorialized; it is more likely to take the form of extensive networking (*Verbindungsnetzschaft*) using postmodern communications technology (Richmond 1969; 1988).[2] The links thus established do not replace territorially based communities or formal organizations typical of Canadian bureaucratic organization; such networks superimpose themselves on these communities and organizations. They focus upon relationships as an interconnected network and ongoing process, rather than as an overarching set of functional and normative principles as exemplified in institutional integration and codified law. *Verbindungsnetzschaft* depends upon communication more than transportation networks for integration. This decentralized form depends upon the impetus of the individual or group to initiate and to continue an exchange. What emerges out of the exchange is indeterminate. Rather than reflecting ethnocultural identity, feedback would occur in a form recognizable by anyone in the network, so that ethnocultural particularities would be less likely to be transmitted. Coalitions would form for particular, more or less functional purposes in which the accretion of numbers appears more important than the identity of the groups constituting that coalition (Boissevain 1974). Thus the "mixing" of ethnicities, as demonstrated in recent Canadian data on ethnic origin indicated above, serves as a harbinger of future ethnicities in Canadian "culture" in what may be Canada Outside Quebec. Although each exchange is purposive and itself part of a network of communications occurring in proliferation, the totality of such communications, or at one level remove, networks, would reflect less overarching Canadian concerns than other social pressures of immediate interest to the participants in the network. These may be local, or they may reflect global concerns, of which COQ acts as a bit player. The centripetal forces of Canadian unity appear to be overtaken by those centrifugally oriented, either from the micro-organization of units within or, more likely, from those which masquerade as global. While an emergent social organization is possible, it may not coincide with the territory that is now Canada Outside Quebec.

CONCLUSION

This paper has examined the question of social and cultural cohesion in Canada if Quebec decides to separate, assuming that the transition to separatism and independence for Quebec would be a peaceful one. This should not be taken for granted. Already there are signs that the Mohawk and the Cree in Quebec would prefer their own sovereignty, or a closer association with COQ, to remaining subordinate in a French-(Quebec-)dominated state. Few signs of unity are evident. COQ is splitting; the fissures run north and south as well as east and west. The process of globalization has impacted all parts of the nation state, albeit in different ways.

Culturally, whatever "English" social character which may once have existed has by the late twentieth century been supplanted by ethnic mixing through successive waves of immigration from various world regions and consequent intermarriage. Many Canadians, especially from Ontario westward, consider themselves affiliated with more than one ethnic origin. No single ethnicity has numerical dominance.

The structural outlines and social dynamics of multiculturalism have remained tentative and ambiguous. A single unified conception has eluded social planners and ideologues alike. Nevertheless, multiculturalism has continued as official Canadian policy, both at federal and provincial levels, with the significant exception of Quebec, where a parallel policy of *interculturalisme* has informed official policy and planning.

Demographic and social changes have not always occurred peacefully. There has been inter-racial conflict in cities. Aboriginal populations have confronted the police and the army from B.C. to Labrador. Already, transnational networks link Native peoples with other "fourth world" communities in the Americas, and in the case of Inuit, to their counterparts in the circumpolar regions. Similar linkages are maintained by other ethnic minorities (such as Buddhists) with their counterparts elsewhere in the world, using the latest communication technologies.

Canada has viewed this wider and expanding cultural mix with passive tolerance, political indifference, and occasional popular hostility. Multicultural policies have suffered from fiscal restraints, but money alone will not overcome the difficulties. Overall, multicultural policy has failed to address the problems created by the continuing waves of newcomers from varied origins and the claims of established minorities for greater recognition and autonomy.

New ties, which depend upon interpersonal networks supported by electronic and conventional forms of communication as well as advanced modes of transportation, know no political boundaries. They are now global in their reach. In Canada Outside Quebec, as in any other postmodern state, this *Verbindungsnetzschaft* provides a form of relating that is particularly appropriate for cultural survival and change. It can grow with demographic expansion throughout the world and can represent culture instantaneously in visual and auditory as well as in written form. It is as accessible to kinship networks and communal groups as it is to governmental and multinational corporate structures.

Thus while a social organizational form appears to overarch COQ, it respects no political boundaries. This particular challenge, therefore, lies in the possible dispersion of organizational (and cultural) focus along network, rather than geopolitical lines. Ironically, cultural distinctiveness will continue to expand spatially as information networks expand. Multiculturalism will assume more varied forms and disperse into separate cross-cutting networks in the course of such development.

As Jameson (1991:17) contends, a proliferation of social codes relating to ethnicity, gender, colour, religion, and class have led to a rejection of dominant bourgeois ideologies. As a result, "advanced capitalist countries of today are now a field of stylistic and discursive heterogeneity without a norm." Canada, no less than any other nation state, clearly typifies such heterogeneity.

A 1993 Canadian studies conference in Cambridge, UK, raised the question, *"Canada: The First Postmodern State?"* The answers mirrored the uncertainty and confusing reality of Canada itself. Yet in a keynote address, Anthony Giddens countered the postmodern thesis of disintegration and fragmentation, leading to anarchy and alienation. Adopting a more optimistic viewpoint, he recognized modernity as inherently globalizing and replete with serious risks. Human beings, nevertheless, are capable of reflexive action and thereby can effect institutional transformation, guided by a "realistic utopian vision" of a postmodern, global society. Such a vision comprehends ideals of equality, self-actualization, and a positive response to the needs of the local as well as the world system (*cf.* Giddens 1990:92–100).

The argument thus comes full circle. To Giddens, no less than to Meinecke, a nation state contains within its own organizational form the capacity to guarantee human rights, equality of opportunity, and social justice, while fully recognizing cultural sensitivities. If that conception has merit, Canada Outside Quebec may respond to the challenge and set an example to the world of how to achieve "unity in diversity." If the pessimistic alternative proves to be more realistic, future historians may consider that, just as the railway in the nineteenth century bound eastern, western, and central Canada together, so the "Information Highway" of the twenty-first century may tear them apart!

NOTES

We acknowledge, with thanks, the bibliographical research assistance of Mehran Banaei, and the editorial help of Freda Richmond.

1 "Race" is not a formal term in current sociology. It is popularly used to connect ethnic origin, nationality, or colour. These more precise terms will be used in this article.

2 The term *Verbindungsnetzschaft* (literally "network connected social system") complements Tönnies' (1957) concepts of *Gemeinschaft* (territorial-based community) and *Gesellschaft* (formal organization).

BIBLIOGRAPHY

Adelman, H. 1992. "Ethnicity and refugees." *World refugee survey – 1992*. Washington, D.C.: U.S. Committee for Refugees, 6–11.

Bibby, R.W. 1990. *Mosaic Madness: The Poverty and Potential of Life in Canada*. Toronto: Stoddart.

Boissevain, J. 1974. *Friends of Friends*. New York: St Martin's Press.

Breton, R. 1994. Keynote address, Conference: "Intercultural, Interethnic and Interracial Relations: Canadian and German Perspectives," Toronto, 9 March.

Bullivant, B. 1981. *The Pluralist Dilemma in Education: Six Case Studies*. Sydney: George Allen & Unwin.

Burnet, J. 1987. "Multiculturalism in Canada." In *Ethnic Canada: Identities and Inequalities*, ed. L. Driedger. Toronto, Copp Clark Pitman.

Canada. House of Commons. 1988. Bill C–93: *Canadian Multiculturalism Act*.

Dawson, C. 1936. *Group Settlement: Ethnic Communities in Western Canada*. Toronto: Macmillan of Canada.

Driedger, L. 1989. *The Ethnic Factor: Identity in Diversity*. Toronto: McGraw-Hill Ryerson.

Durkheim, E. 1893. *De la division du travail social*. Paris: F. Alcan.

Fishman, J. 1989. *Language and ethnicity in minority linguistic perspective*. Philadelphia: Multilingual Matters.

Fleras, A., and J.L. Elliott. 1992. *Multiculturalism in Canada: The Challenge of Diversity*. Scarborough, Ont: Nelson.

Foster, L., and D. Stockley. 1988. "The Rise and Decline of Australian Multiculturalism." *Politics* 23, no. 2:1–10.

Frideres, J. 1983. *Native People in Canada*. Scarborough, Ont: Prentice-Hall.

Gazette. Montreal. 1992. 27 July.

Giddens, A. 1990. *The Consequences of Modernity*. Cambridge, UK: Polity Press.

Gilad, L. 1990. *The Northern route*. St John's: Institute for Social and Economic Research, Memorial University of Newfoundland.

Jameson, F. 1991. *Postmodernism: or the cultural logic of late capitalism*. Durham, NC: Duke University Press.

Krotki, K., and D. Odynak. 1990. "The Emergence of Multiethnicities in the Eighties." In *Ethnic Demography: Canadian immigrant and Ethnic Variations*, ed. S.S. Hall, et al. Ottawa: Carleton University Press.

Lewis, S. 1992. *Report on Race Relations in Ontario*. Queen's Park: Province of Ontario.

Matas, R. 1994. "Race Relations, Ideology Collide." *Globe and Mail* 5 April.

Matthews, R. 1980. "The significance and explanation of regional divisions in Canada: Towards a Canadian Sociology." *Journal of Canadian Studies* 15:43–61.

McLellan, J., and A.H. Richmond. 1994. "Multiculturalism in Crisis: A Postmodern Perspective on Canada." *Ethnic and Racial Studies* 17, no. 4:662-83.

McRoberts, K. 1991. *English Canada and Québec.* Downsview, Ont: Robarts Centre, York University.

Meinecke, F. 1970. *Cosmopolitanism and the National State.* Princeton: Princeton University Press.

Mercredi, O., and M.E. Turpel. *In the Rapids: Navigating the Future of the First Nations.* Toronto: Viking Penguin.

Morris, R., and Lanphier, C.M. 1977. *Three Scales of Inequality.* Don Mills, Ont: Longmans.

Richard, M. 1991. *Ethnic groups and Marital Choices, Ethnic History and Marital Assimilation in Canada 1871–1971.* Vancouver: UBC Press.

Richmond, A.H. 1969. "Sociology of Migration in Industrial and Post-industrial Societies." In *Sociological Studies, 2: Migration*, ed. J. Jackson, Cambridge: Cambridge University Press.

– 1988. *Immigration and Ethnic Conflict.* London: Macmillan.

– 1994. *Global Apartheid: Refugees, Racism and the New World Order.* Toronto: Oxford University Press.

Richmond, A.H., and J. Goldlust. 1977. "Factors Associated with Commitment to and Identification with Canada." In *Identities: the Impact of Ethnicity on Canadian Society*, ed. W. Isajiw, 132–53. Toronto: Peter Martin.

Robertson, R. 1990. "Mapping the Global Condition: Globalization as the Central Concept." In *Global Culture: Nationalism, Globalization and Modernity*, ed. M. Featherstone, London: Sage.

Ryan, C., 1971. "L'aide aux groupes ethniques: exige-t-elle l'abandon du biculturalisme?" *Le Devoir*, 9 octobre; trans. and quoted in K. McRoberts, *English Canada and Québec*, 30.

Sharma, H. 1991. "Beyond ethnicity and Class: Uniting *people* in the Fight Against Racism." In *Immigrants and refugees in Canada*, ed. S. Sharma, *et al.* Saskatoon: University of Saskatchewan. 111–33.

Statistics Canada. 1992. "More Canadians have a non-official language as mother tongue." *The Daily* Tues. 15 September.

– 1992/93. *Canadian Economic Observer.*

– 1993a. "Increased numbers speak a language other than English and French at home." *The Daily* Tues. 12 January.

– 1993b. "Nearly one in three respondents reported am ethnic background other than British of French." *The Daily* Tues. 23 February.

Tönnies, F. (1957). *Community and Society.* ed. and trans., L.P. Loomis. East Lansing: Michigan State University Press.

Trudeau, P. 1968. Speech to Quebec Liberal Convention, 28 January. Quoted in K. McRoberts, K., *English Canada and Québec*, 15.

Turpel, M.E. 1990. "Aboriginal peoples and the Canadian Charter: Interpretive Monopolies, Cultural Differences." *Canadian Human Rights Year Book.* Ottawa: University of Ottawa, Human Rights Research and Education Centre.

Vallee, F., and J. deVries. 1985. Issues and trends in bilingualism in Canada." In *Advances in the study of Multilingualism,* ed. J. Fishman, The Hague: Mouton.

Zubrzycki, J. 1986. "Multiculturalism and Beyond: The Australian Experience in Retrospect and Prospect." *New Community* 13, no. 2:167–76.

17 The Women's Movement outside Quebec: Shifting Relations with the Canadian State

JANINE BRODIE

During the past twenty-five years English-Canadian politics has witnessed the unprecedented growth of what is commonly termed the "second-wave" of the Canadian women's movement. From its meagre presence in the early 1970s as a small and influential cabal of urban, WASP, middle-class women, it has emerged as a powerful social movement which has assumed the role as one of few remaining progressive voices of politics in Canada outside Quebec. Much like the "first-wave" of English-Canadian feminism, which flourished in the first decades of this century, this social movement took root outside the party system and has pursued a political trajectory quite distinct from its counterpart in Quebec. Indeed, the English-Canadian and Quebec women's movements have disagreed on many of the key political debates which have rocked Canadian politics in recent years, among them the Canada-U.S. Free Trade Agreement (CUFTA) and the Meech Lake and Charlottetown accords. The two movements have pronounced quite distinct visions of the future of Canada and the ideal configuration of Canadian federalism. I will argue in this chapter that these different visions can be traced, in large part, to the manner in which the second wave of English-Canadian feminism was constituted in the post-war years by the federal Keynesian welfare state. Moreover, during the 1980s the English-Canadian women's movement, unlike its Quebec counterpart, found a new and strengthened identity as "Charter Canadians" in the Charter of Rights and Freedoms.

After the defeat of the Meech Lake Accord front-line organizations such as the National Action Committee on the Status of Women (NAC) attempted to bridge the gulf between the English and Quebec women's movements by becoming strong advocates of the right of the people of Quebec to self determination and of asymmetrical federalism. The latter would see a significant devolution of powers to the Quebec provincial government and, at the same time, retain a strong national government in the rest of Canada. With this creative response to the constitutional crisis, the English-Canadian women's movement may be poised to take a leadership role in deciding the future shape of Canadian federalism when the issue of Quebec's status in Confederation erupts again, as it surely will. Nevertheless, I suggest in this chapter that the future of the English-Canadian women's movement is far from secure in the politics of the late 1990s and beyond. Its major challenge is less the potential dissolution or the radical reshaping of Confederation but instead the current shifts in political discourse and state form which are occurring in all western liberal democracies. This restructuring is eroding the very political identities and public spaces that empowered the second wave of English-Canadian feminism and distinguished it from its turn-of-the-century counterpart. The current era, in other words, invites, indeed demands, that the English-Canadian women's movement engage in new strategic thinking about the very meaning of the public and the discursive foundations of its potential "third wave" – with or without Quebec.

THE ENGLISH CANADIAN WOMEN'S MOVEMENT AND THE FEDERAL STATE

The Laissez-Faire State

This chapter emphasizes the changing relationships among state form, gender relations, and the historical preoccupations of the English-Canadian women's movement (ECWM). By drawing these linkages, I want to show that women and the women's movement are both producers and products of their political culture and of historically specific state forms. The laissez-faire state, for example, made women the objects of policy long before they were officially recognized in law as legitimate political actors (Phillips 1991:87). It inscribed the private sphere with a particular construction of gender and gender relations which, in time, provided the basis for women's entry into the formal political sphere. Women were contained in the private sphere by denying them legal personhood and citizenship rights. Their economic dependence on men was secured through a series of gender-based restrictions on education, employment, and property ownership. For most of its reign, then, the laissez-faire state constructed women as "pre-political" subjects – a public excluded from "the public" (Chapman 1993). The legislatively enforced and rigid boundary between the public and private served to constrain and limit the terrain of politics, enclaving, and shielding most gender issues and relations from political contestation and negotiation (Fraser 1989).

Canadian women's enfranchisement (1917–21) and the winning of the Person's Case (1929) are sometimes recounted as historic mileposts in the ECWM's long march toward gender equality. This perspective, however, largely misrepresents its dominant characteristics in early twentieth century Canada and how women initially engaged with the public sphere as recognized political actors. English-Canadian women were not called into the public on the same basis as men, that is, as members of a gender-neutral community of citizens. A small proportion of the early feminists did struggle for the equal treatment of the sexes in all spheres of life. These women, however, were marginalized within both the Canadian women's movement and the turn-of-the-century Victorian social reform movement.

Maternal feminism was the dominant current in the early ECMW and its advocates embraced rather than challenged the prevailing patriarchal family form and cultural representations of women (Ursel 1992:80–2). These early feminists, as well as their opponents, shared the same assumptions about women's supposed "nature" and the "natural" gender order. Women belonged in the home and it was from there that all "good" women – daughters, wives, and especially mothers – exercised their inherent moral superiority and reproduced the race. As such they became powerful allies of the social reform movement which was also deeply imbued with the values of temperance, Protestant moralism, and British imperialism, if not outright anti-Catholicism and racism (Valverde 1992). This coalition, nonetheless, was a powerful force in English Canada, motivating a series of protective reforms for women and children – reforms which laid some of the foundations for the post-World War II welfare state (Ursel 1992). The political force of this coalition also was instrumental in the enfranchisement of women nationally and in the provinces almost three decades before the same rights were granted to women in the Quebec provincial electorate (Brodie 1985: chap. 1). The social reformers and British imperialists were willing to grant women the vote in order to draw protestant morals and white middle-class values into the public sphere.

The "first-wave" of the women's movement was a key player in early twentieth-century Canadian politics, but its claims to citizenship rights were largely a product of its reformism rather than the reverse. With the vote, maternal feminists soon came to focus on law reform, especially provincial welfare, family, and labour protection legislation, as a way to empower women and recognize in law their "special needs and distinct qualities" (Chunn 1995:180). In contrast, Quebec women remained only a potential political force during this period, having neither a similar progressive movement with which to align nor fledging secular women's organizations such as the National Council of Women to lobby government for social reform. In Quebec, social welfare remained in the hands of the church and the community.

The Welfare State

During the immediate post-war years, Quebec and Newfoundland women gained formal citizenship rights at the provincial level (the national and provincial franchise continued to be withheld from Aboriginal women and men). A distinctly Canadian variant of the Keynesian Welfare State (KWS) also came to occupy and politicize many of the spaces that laissez-faire liberalism previously had declared to be unalterably, naturally, and universally private. The emergence of the welfare state was another instance of restructuring during which the boundaries between the economy and state and the public and the domestic were fundamentally realigned (Brodie 1994). It realized a radical expansion of the public through regulation and direct intervention in the economy, and by subjecting the family and other aspects of private life to new forms of state scrutiny and assistance (Andrew 1984:667; Abbott and Wallace 1992:17). This new state form was in part the realization of the visions of the Victorian social reform movement as well as those of oppositional movements which gained force in Canadian politics during the Great Depression of the 1930s and the war years. Despite this legacy the welfare state was grounded on quite different assumptions about the proper role of the state and the rights of citizens.

Jane Ursel calls this new understanding "welfare ideology" and argues that it was "an achievement of public consensus equal in significance, but substantially different to the Victorian Social Reform Movement" (Ursel 1992:205). It also altered the constitution of the gender order and women's place within it. The new order rested on a very particular model of the workplace and the home. It presumed a stable working/middle class, a nuclear family supported by a male breadwinner, a dependent wife and children, and the unpaid domestic labour of women. Each of these cultural forms was in turn supported and reinforced by the Keynesian Welfare State (KWS) (McDowell 1991:400-2).

If the KWS reinforced a particular family form and gender order, it also hailed women into politics, at least initially, in a complementary way. Instead of casting women as the moral force of politics and the mothers of the race, the KWS largely spoke to women as mothers framed within the context of a nuclear family headed by a male wage-earner. After the war, women were actively encouraged, if not forced, to leave the work-force and return to the home and all the unpaid domestic labour it entailed. Feminist state theorists are quite correct in identifying the discourses around welfare and its provisions as central to the construction of the gender order and women's subordination during the post-war years (Pringle and Watson 1990:235). The new welfare ideology shifted the emphasis of state discourse and practice from regulation to provision, from the protection of women and children to the administration of income and social services for the family.

The Family Allowance Act (1944; i.e., mother's allowance), for example, was Canada's first universal social welfare program and unique among social security measures considering that its major beneficiaries never campaigned for it (Ursel 1992:205, 190). Designed to shore up the family wage, this welfare provision recognized women primarily as mothers and homemakers. The KWS readily transferred money from working women who did not fit the dominant cultural model to the women who did – mothers (Pringle and Watson 1990:236). In a very real sense, then, welfare policy was less directed at women as a social category than *through* mothers in order to reinforce a particular family form and the post-war organization of the labour force and the economy.

The family was differently constituted under the welfare state, opening up for policy consideration and political negotiation many aspects of the everyday which had previously been considered private and therefore incompatible with political intervention. In the process, new public spaces for women were opened, but these spaces often rested on the assumption that "women's interests" and "family interests" were one and the same. There was little recognition that the family could be a site of political conflict and a source of women's subordination. However circumscribed, these new political spaces did enable Canadian women, both inside and outside Quebec, to organize, to make political claims, to lobby the state for better services for the family, and eventually to demand state action to improve the condition of women in all aspects of social life. These projects gave rise to a myriad of women's organizations, often state financed, that shaped a collective identity and increasingly drew the overtly political arm of the women's movement into new state-centred "progressive" coalitions. Importantly, these developments forged a strong and self-interested bond between the ECWM and the federal government. In contrast, the lines of coalition in Quebec were more commonly established among the women's movement, Quebec nationalists, and the provincial state, particularly after the Quiet Revolution transformed and secularized the provincial state and the delivery of social services (Lamoureux 1987). As Fraser puts it, the welfare state brought new forms of social control *as well as* new forms of conflict, new social movements, and new conflict zones (Fraser 1989:132). Within the specific context of Canadian politics, however, this new state focus also meant that the emergent second wave of the women's movement in Quebec and the rest of Canada would follow quite different paths and look to different places within the federal system to advance their shared goal of gender equality. The women's movements in Quebec and English Canada were created and subsequently matured within the context of the "two solitudes" (Bégin 1992:23).

The Royal Commission of the Status of Women

In its early years, the second wave of the ECWM took a variety of different forms ranging from intimate consciousness-raising groups and radical and socialist feminist collectives to rape crisis centres and equality-seeking groups (Adamson, Briskin, and McPhail 1988). Most commentators, however, trace the development of its most public face to the establishment of the Royal Commission of the Status of Women (RCSW) in 1967. The idea of establishing such a commission had been contemplated by many English-Canadian women's groups for a number of years, especially after a similar task force had been appointed in the United States during the Kennedy administration. In 1966 English Canada's Committee on Equality (CEW), a temporary regrouping of over thirty women's groups, joined forces with the newly formed Federation des femmes du Québec to demand that the federal government establish a royal commission to investigate the status of women in Canadian society and to recommend policy responses (Bégin 1992:23–5). The Pearson government responded positively six months later by appointing the Royal Commission on the Status of Women under the direction of journalist Florence Bird. The government expected the commission to "recommend what steps might be taken by the Federal Government to ensure for women equal opportunities with men in all aspects of Canadian society" (Canada 1970:vii; Findlay 1987:34–5).

In all it took the RCSW three years to complete its report and another two years before the federal government gave it lukewarm approval "in principle." The commission made 167 recommendations, some 122 of which were defined exclusively as federal responsibilities, (Findlay 1988:5–6). These recommendations, however, did not reflect an overtly feminist subtext. Instead, the commission applied an equal opportunity framework which depicted women's subordination as a problem of inadequate access, unwarranted discrimination, and lack of education (Findlay 1987:33). This absence of an explicitly feminist analysis reflected both the theoretical underdevelopment of the fledgling movement and the distance of the commission from that movement. As Monique Begin, who served as the commission's research coordinator explains: "The commission did not benefit from discussions generated within the women's movement because we did not know what was going on, except through rare public demonstrations ... These were often quite radical and difficult to understand from outside the movement and without the help of written manifestos" (Bégin 1992:28).

The RCSW which reported in late 1970, however, is widely recognized as having set the political agenda for the ECWM for the 1970s and beyond (Burt 1986). It identified "the problems" and offered tangible solutions for federal government intervention in most sectors of Canadian society. More than this, it provided a checklist around which the women's movement could mobilize for immediate action and measure the federal government's progress toward and commitment to women's equality. But it also directly impacted on the politics and strategies of the ECWM. During these early years, the movement was often divided by debates concerning whether it was better to work inside the system for change – the so-called "liberal feminist" position – or struggle outside the mainstream in order to avoid co-optation and to bring about a complete transformation of the system itself. This latter strategy was more often advocated by radical and socialist feminists. The timing of the royal commission, coming as it did in the early years of the second wave, served to strengthen the liberal feminist position. One of the less visible outcomes of the RCSW, then, was that "a majority of women came to believe that the government would respond to their concerns if faced with appropriate pressure." As a result, English-Canadian feminists began to develop their expertise in many policy fields, particularly social welfare, and to adopt formal lobbying skills. In the process, "liberal feminism became the 'public face' of the women's movement" (Findlay 1988:6–7).

The royal commission also provided the impetus for the very formation of key representational institutions for women both inside and outside the federal bureaucracy. The early 1970s witnessed the proliferation within the federal government of offices and agencies assigned to improve some aspect of women's lives. Among these were the Women's Bureau in Department of Labour, the Office of Equal Opportunity in Public Service Commission, the Office of the Co-ordinator of the Status of Women in the Privy Council Office, the Canadian Advisory Council on the Status of Women (CACSW), and most important, the Women's Program in the Secretary of State. Some provincial governments also established a women's bureau. At the same time, the RCSW encouraged the consolidation of women's organizations outside the federal government. The 1972 Strategy for Change Conference saw the formation of the ECWM's key frontline organization, the National Action Committee on the Status of Women (NAC). This conference, as well as the founding of NAC, reflected the organizers' resolve that an organization outside the federal government was needed in order to pressure it to implement the recommendations of the royal commission (Findlay 1987:37–9).

The Second Wave of the English Canadian Women's Movement

During the 1970s NAC and other women's organizations repeatedly lobbied for the expansion of the social welfare system and make it more responsive to their conception of women's needs. And the federal government appeared to respond, especially in the years immediately following International Women's Year in 1975. In these years, which Findlay identifies as the "consultative period," the agencies of the federal state invited the organized women's movement to consult on a broad range of issues from pay equity to rape to divorce reform (Findlay 1988:7). This federal consultation strategy, while producing only limited reforms, won many allies within the ECWM, strengthening their gaze on the federal state. As Findlay explains, "Such affirmations of political commitment to improve the status of women in Canada were sufficient to win new allies to the liberal feminists' view that the women's movement must tailor its strategies to work with the state in a collaborative and consultative manner" (Findlay 1988:7).

Throughout the 1970s, then, the dominant target of the ECWM and NAC, its most important umbrella organization, was the state, specifically the national government. Most Canadian feminists saw "the state more as a provider of services, including the service of regulation, than as a reinforcer of patriarchal norms, and most seem[ed] to believe that services, whether child care or medicare, [would] help" (Vickers 1992:45). And the federal government increasingly recognized the organized women's movement as a legitimate lobby group which was entitled to consultation in the policy-making process, gender-designated funding and programs, and special points of access within the federal bureaucracy. In other words, the ECWM became an recognized participant in federal politics as a representative of a social category with a corporate interest in the federal state and, in particular, its post-war presence as the director and underwriter of the Canadian *welfare* state.

Indeed by the early 1980s women's organizations found themselves increasingly entangled in the federal government's political agenda, "working hand in hand," as Findlay puts it, "to implement its commitment to the status of women" (Findlay 1988:7).

The constitutional crisis of the early 1980s only served to strengthen this relationship, although this outcome was far from certain during the protracted constitutional negotiations. At first, the federal government appeared to be a strong supporter of constitutional guarantees for sexual equality when it was trying to build popular support for its unilateral constitutional initiatives. Ultimately, however, the women's movement was both shocked and betrayed to discover that, after months of pressure, the Trudeau government was prepared to make the constitutional guarantee of sexual equality subject to the override clause. As Gotell suggests, there is evidence that some provinces demanded the weakening of sexual equality clause as the price for their support of the constitutional package (Gotell 1993:198). A massive lobbying effort ensued, and the sexual equality clause was ultimately placed beyond the reach of the notwithstanding clause in the Charter of Rights and Freedoms. This episode, nonetheless, was an expansive moment in the history of the ECWM, both mobilizing many women who had never before been part of the women's movement and providing a sense of empowerment to women's organizations. It also helped new organizations such as the Legal and Education Action Fund (LEAF) to use the sexual equality provisions in the Charter in the courts to improve the substantive condition of Canadian women (Gotell 1993). This enthusiasm, however, was not shared by the Quebec women's movement, which alongside other groups in the province, viewed the charter as a betrayal of Quebec and a threatening federal imposition on the provincial government. The 1980–82 constitutional episode, in other words, provided yet another illustration that the women's movements inside and outside Quebec were products of and interacted within quite distinct political cultures and political/institutional matrices.

By the mid-1980s, the English-Canadian women's movement approached the apex of its influence within the federal government. During the 1984 election campaign, for example, NAC was obviously perceived to hold enough influence among women electors that the three major parties readily agreed to participate in a NAC-sponsored federal leadership debate on women's issues (Brodie 1984). In retrospect, however, it is important to emphasize that the legitimacy of the women's movement during these years was almost entirely attached to their ability to speak to "women's issues," which in turn, within the context of the welfare state, effectively meant social policy matters. As arjorie Cohen, a feminist economist long active in NAC, recounts, by the 1980s government and employers had accepted women's intervention in issues like equal pay, maternity leave, and the movement of women out of traditional occupations. They also accepted our right to speak on day care, reproductive choice, pornography – anything that could be seen as a women's issue"(Cohen 1992:217). Later in the decade, when the women's movement began to discuss issues lying outside a narrow definition of social policy such as macro-economic policy their interventions were interpreted as "takeaways." Cohen observes that women's contributions to these broader debates were always treated "as a discussion of welfare policy, not economic policy" (Cohen 1992:218). By the late 1980s, she continues, when "we began to talk about economic issues like the budget, trade policy, privatization, deregulation, and the general structure of the Canadian economy, we were going too far. These were not women's issues: women were not 'experts' and therefore our criticism had little credibility" (Cohen 1992:218–19).

So long as the welfare state remained unchallenged, the organized English-Canadian women's movement could and did expand its sphere of influence, particularly inside the federal state itself. Nevertheless, as the chapters by Clarkson, Cohen, and others in this volume describe, the mid-1980s saw a breakdown in the post-war consensus about the role of the Keynesian state, the federal government, and its welfare ideology. After a decade of "restructuring" with its attendant shifts in discourse and state form, it has become increasingly apparent that the very political spaces within which the contemporary women's movement found much of its cohesion and empowerment are disappearing. Social welfarism is rapidly being displaced by an as yet unfinished discursive struggle about the very meaning of the public and private.

THE WOMEN'S MOVEMENT AND POLITICS OF RESTRUCTURING

The New Governing Orthodoxy

During the past decade, Canada and all western democracies have undergone a profound shift in state form and governing practices. Keynesianism, which provided for a strong federal government and informed the politics of the post-war years, has incrementally, but surely, given way to a new governing orthodoxy. This new orthodoxy rests on the fundamental proposition that the changing international political economy puts roughly the same demands on all governments:

- maximize exports;
- reduce social spending;
- curtail state economic regulation and participation in the economy;
- empower capital to reorganize national economies as parts of transnational trading blocs. (Friedman 1991:35)

Whispers of these new tenets of governance could be heard in the dying days of the Trudeau administration in the early 1980s. The landslide electoral victory of the Mulroney Conservatives in 1984 and the release in 1985 of the report of the Royal Commission on the Economic Union and Development Prospects for Canada (the Macdonald Commission), however, marked a watershed in emerging new order. The Macdonald Commission successfully advanced the position that free trade with the United States was the *only* economic development strategy left to Canada. Canadians were told to close their eyes and take "a leap of faith" because the globalization train had already left the station. Canada had no choice but become competitive in the international political economy. In addition the commission advised all governments, federal and provincial, to pursue a market-driven industrial policy, to create new opportunities for private sector growth and to redesign the social welfare system to facilitate adjustment (Brodie 1990:218–23).

This neo-conservative worldview came to dominate the Mulroney government's front benches, especially after its re-election in 1988 and the implementation of the Canada-u.s. Free Trade Agreement in 1989 (cufta). Throughout the late 1980s the federal government used the alleged imperatives of "competitiveness" and "deficit reduction" as uncontestable rationales for cutting back on the welfare state and transfer payments to the provinces. These new tenets of governance have guided shifts in public policy priorities and regulatory regimes and have increasingly informed new institutional forms (Brodie 1995b). Canadian governments, for example, have abandoned as futile the post-war policy goals of full employment and an inclusive social safety net in order to achieve the illusive and abstract states of flexibility, efficiency, and international competitiveness (Cox 1991:337). In the process, the post-war pattern of politics has been pushed aside, revealing in stark relief the uncertain and contested political space we now occupy. Familiar political understandings, institutions, and political actors are being sidelined by the politics of restructuring. They are being replaced with strangers to the post-war political terrain with decidedly different visions of politics, the public sphere – indeed of the future of the country itself (Brodie and Jenson 1995).

As the chapters in this volume eloquently testify, these developments have had a profound and unsettling impact on Canadian politics. Relatively little attention has been paid, however, to the question of how this fundamental transformation in governing practices has affected and will affect social movements and the shape of oppositional politics (Brodie 1995a; Cohen 1993). The following section examines the fortunes of the ECWM within the politics of restructuring.

The English-Canadian Women's Movement in the 1980s and Beyond

The ECWM has not stared passively in the face of the emerging new order. Women's organizations in English Canada have been in the forefront of the broad-based political coalition – the so-called "popular sector" – opposed to neoconservative ideology and governing practices (Cameron 1989). They have also been among the few political actors to emphasize that restructuring has been enacted precisely on the field of gender (Bakker 1994). Feminist academics and women's organizations have linked restructuring to the intensification and feminization of poverty, especially among single mothers and elderly women. They also point out that women have been disproportionately affected by ever-growing cuts to social welfare spending and the reduction of the public sector. Lastly, the women's movement has been among the first to demonstrate that the gendered impacts of restructuring are highly uneven among women themselves, exacting the heaviest toll among young women, women of colour, and working class women (Leger and Rebick 1993). As Judy Rebick, former president of NAC, explains, "All the 'vanguard destructive forces' of the right are hitting women first – teleworking, part-time work – all of that hits women first" (Rebick 1994:62).

As important, key front-line organizations such as NAC clearly recognized that the neoconservatives' vision of a minimalist state and unfettered global capitalism threatened the very foundations of the ECWM's equity agenda. As we have seen, the dominant current of the ECWM in the post-war years consistently linked the achievement of gender equality with federal state activism, whether through the elaboration of the social safety net or through the regulation and law reform. Key feminist policy demands such as universal and affordable childcare, income security for single mothers and elderly women, the protection of women from male violence, affirmative action, and pay equity call for more not less government and public funding (Gotel and Brodie 1991:62). It is hardly surprising then that, after the election of the federal Progressive Conservative Party in 1984, NAC and other prominent women's organizations expended ever-increasing quantities of their political currency defending the federal state and, more specifically, its post-war role in the creation and funding of the welfare state. Key elements of the ECWM challenged the so-called "Tory agenda" and were in the forefront of the popular coalitions which protested Free Trade, the Meech Lake Accord, the Conservative government's constitutional proposals for the Economic Union prior to the Charlottetown Accord, the Charlottetown Accord, and the North American Free Trade Agreement (NAFTA). In each case, the protest has centred around the protection of the rights women achieved in the Charter of Rights and, increasingly, a defence of the welfare state and federal power itself.

Women's concerns about free trade, for example, initially revolved around concerns that the deal would have a disastrous impact on women workers, many of them immigrant women, in vulnerable sectors such as textiles (Ontario 1987). Soon, however, Women Against Free Trade (WAFT) which included, among others, representatives of NAC, the Ontario Federation of Labour (OFL) Women's Committee, the New Democratic Party (NDP), and the daycare coalition, issued a manifesto arguing that free trade would lower the standard of public services in Canada and threaten the decision-making capacity of Canadian governments (Burstyn and Rebick 1988). The Meech Lake Accord obviously held the potential to cause a massive rupture between the English and Quebec women's movements; thus, official pronouncements against the deal were few and cautious. Nonetheless, ad hoc women's committees did make presentations outlining their concerns to various provincial inquiries. The dominant themes in their arguments were that the process had been unrepresentative and undemocratic. More important, they argued that the specific provisions of the accord put women's Charter rights in risk, potentially elevating cultural rights over equality rights (Ad Hoc Committee of Women on the Constitution 1988:143–4).

The ECWM's most explicit defence of the federal state and the post-war model of welfarism came with its unprecedented opposition to the Charlottetown Accord. To the shock of many Canadian women both inside and outside NAC, its traditional allies such as the Canadian Labour Congress (CLC), the NDP, and the reigning political elite, the NAC executive announced in the fall of 1992 that it would be urging Canadians to vote "No" in the forthcoming referendum on the accord. With this move, NAC appeared among unlikely allies – the Reform Party and the Quebec sovereigntists. Nevertheless, NAC made it clear from the outset that its reasons for not supporting the accord were fundamentally different from the others standing in the "No" camp.

Similar to the Meech debacle, NAC registered its disapproval of the male elite-dominated process which crafted the accord and to the proposed Canada Clause which potentially could be used to override women's Charter guarantees (Day 1993). However, the hub of NAC's "No" campaign revolved around the accord's failure to protect universal social programs and to ensure that the federal government maintained its power to establish new ones (Fudge 1993:8). Speaking for NAC, then president Judy Rebick argued that "the Charlottetown Accord [would] lead to a dismantling of national social programs and more division and more disunity over the years" (Rebick 1993:106). In so doing, NAC emerged from the debate and the ultimate defeat of the Charlottetown Accord as one of the few organizational lonely supporters of Canada's post-war welfare regime and the federal power, although many individual Canadians still support the post-war regime. In a sense it was less a representative of women, although an explicit construction of "women's interests" informed their rejection of the accord, than the last-ditch defender of the post-war consensus. Again, Judy Rebick elaborates on this point: "The force from the Referendum [on the Charlottetown Accord] that NAC represented was not women really. It was progressive people who wanted to see democratic reform; progressive people concerned with the devolution of power; progressive people concerned with the domination of collective rights over individual and group rights" (Rebick 1994:69).

Backlash Politics

During the past twenty-five years the ECWM has grown from an influential group of middle-class women concerned with equity issues to a recognized lobby group with special access to the federal state, including constitutional protections as a "Charter" group to part of a broad-based coalition opposed to the new economy and the emerging post-Keynesian state form. Increasingly, however, the politics of restructuring and the demise of the post-war welfare state have put the women's movement in an untenable position which both marginalizes it within mainstream political discourse and threatens its identity as we have come to know it – indeed, as it has come to know itself. The politics of the past decade, while inescapable, left the ECWM in the paradoxical position of having to defend the same welfare state that it had previously criticized for being inadequate, sexist, classist, and racist (Abbott and Wallace 1992:22). It was the same welfare state that the neoconservatives had successfully blamed for the prolonged economic crisis and for growing public sector debt; it was the same welfare state that the Mulroney government had progressively dismantled through the budgetary process and the negotiation of CUFTA and NAFTA. In the process, the terrain and language of Canadian politics has shifted in such a way as to write women out of the script and to brush the women's movement off of the political stage. As Rebick puts it, "The framework of the deficit ... completely marginalizes women's issues, because, of course, most concerns of women either require government expenditure or intervention and both things are really out of fashion right now" (Rebick 1994:58).

The challenges facing the ECWM involve much more than passing fashions, however. The ascendency of neo-conservatism in all liberal democracies, including Canada, has been accompanied by a sustained attack on feminism, women's claims to equality, and public perception of the legitimacy of the women's movement. This hostility was particularly evident during and after the national referendum on the Charlottetown Accord. NAC was accused of being part of a self-interested coalition of special interests groups which "threatened Canadian consensus," indeed, were "enemies of Canada" (Fudge 1993, 9). This hostility was only part of a broader concerted attack on – some would say a backlash against – feminism and the Canadian women's movement, especially during the Mulroney government's second mandate. During these years, journalists commonly joked that feminism had become the new "F-word" on Parliament Hill. More tangibly, the Mulroney administration broke a longstanding tradition of meeting with NAC officials annually to discuss their policy concerns and the government's progress toward achieving gender equality. It also used deficit reduction as a pretext to cut its support for NAC and to dismantle some of the women's movement's important strategic resources, including women's centres, women's journals, and the Court Challenges Program which provided the financial underpinnings for LEAF.

It would be a strategic mistake, however, to interpret these cuts merely as a financial "slap on the wrist" wielded by a vindictive neo-conservative government or for that matter part of its failed efforts at deficit reduction. Since the election of the new Liberal government, there has been no obvious attempt to come to a new understanding with women's groups. Although the Chrétien government met with NAC officials after their 1994 annual meeting, it has also demoted the minister responsible for women to the junior ranks of the cabinet and continued to cut funding for women's groups. All these changes are symptoms of redefinition and displacement of the women's movement as we have come to know it in the post-war years.

The Politics of Marginalization

Comparative experiences suggest that the politics of restructuring attempts to marginalize and deconstruct emancipatory movements, such as the women's movement, in at least two critical ways. One form of marginalization is to deny the movement's universal significance, making it appear instead as a sectoral and self-interested lobby group. The other form is to constitute particular members of the women's movement as lying on the outer limits of the norm or the "ordinary." They are recast as disadvantaged groups for whom special provision is to be made (Yeatman 1990:130).

These marginalizing moves obviously echo the Canadian experience in the 1990s. It has become increasingly common to argue that feminist organizations such as NAC do not represent the mainstream of Canadian women. This sentiment was first expressed by REAL Women (Realistic, Equal, and Active for Life) in the mid-1980s in order to gain federal funding made available for groups that "promote the advancement of women." The federal Conservatives judged that REAL Women met this standard even though the organization actively opposes, among other things, equal pay for work of equal value, reproductive choice, and greater constitutional protection for women's rights. Later, PC leadership candidate, Kim Campbell, vowed that when she became prime minister she would stop giving money to "advocacy groups" such as NAC, arguing that they should be funded by their private constituencies (*Globe and Mail 1993*:A6). This sentiment was revisited in the Liberal government's first budget of 22 February 1994 which reduced group funding by 5 percent and promised to review the question of whether the federal government should get out of the business of funding "lobby groups" altogether. Finally, the Reform Party raised the spectre of the special interest group as its reason for refusing to meet with NAC officials in the summer of 1994.

Although the women's movement is broad based, inclusive, and emancipatory, the new politics attempts to label it and other new social movements as "special" – and by implication unrepresentative and self-interested. More than this, the new politics attempts to cast social movements which seek to empower marginalized people as threats to democracy itself. It is argued that they threaten to hijack the political agenda and disrupt the political process (Phillips 1993:6). Barbara McDougall, a former minister in the Mulroney cabinet, for example, concluded that the problem of governing in the 1990s is that "so many single or limited interest groups have established their presence on the national political scene that it is virtually impossible for any government to undertake a comprehensive policy platform" (quoted in Phillips 1993:12).

The new political order goes further than denying the legitimacy of organized voices in democratic politics. It attempts to minimize the relevance of gender itself. Increasingly, the social category "women," which found some unity, however misleading, in the welfare state and post-war feminist discourse, is being deconstructed. Women, it is argued, do not have similar interests. At the same time, some women are being redefined as members of specially disadvantaged groups which require "targeted" social programs to address their "unique" needs (Yeatman 1990:134).

The idea of targeting is entirely consistent with the hollowing out of the welfare state. The overt rationale is that, in an era of fiscal restraint, scarce resources are best targeted at those who need them the most. Thus universal entitlements such as family allowance which constructed mothers as gendered citizens are transformed into a child tax credit available only to those the government defines as truly in need. Similarly, initiatives designed to combat violence against women are structured to target what are deemed to be high risk groups such as, for example, Aboriginal women, women of colour, lesbian women, and women with disabilities. Women's different experiences of oppression and the effects of heterosexism, race, and class cannot be denied or ignored. Targeting, however, may have the effect of pathologizing difference instead of exposing the structural links among race, gender, poverty, and violence. It disassembles and diffuses the collective claims of the women's movement, recasting it as a "ghetto of disadvantaged groups" (Yeatman 1990:134).

The women's movement, a historical-moral-political concept with an evolving vision of political inclusion, democracy, and equality is deconstructed into a series of disconnected statistical and administrative categories which require some sort of therapeutic intervention to produce self-sufficient individuals. Many of the new welfare pilot projects, for example, target single mothers for re-entry into the workforce by providing them with training and work incentives instead of a comprehensive childcare program. This sends the clear message that a single mother is poor because she lacks motivation or job skills even through there is a shortage of good jobs and few and often costly alternative child care systems (McFarland 1993).

The new politics seeks to disempower and dislocate women and the women's movement by contrasting them with the favourite son of the emerging order – "the ordinary Canadian." This is not his first incarnation in federal politics. The NDP raised his presence in the late 1970s in order to contrast its support for ordinary "working people" instead of corporations (Brodie and Jenson 1988: 309). The current juxtaposition between the "ordinary Canadian" and "special interests" evokes a very different and disturbing politics. To designate the women's movement as a "special interest group," for example, somehow implies that its demands are not in the general interest. "Special interest groups" don't speak for the ordinary Canadian, but instead, demand privileges which are unearned and violate the new norms of citizenship (Brodie 1994). Special interests are the opposite, indeed, the enemies of equality. Similarly, defining "special" need groups and targeting them for intensive state intervention casts them outside the community of ordinary citizens who presumably are able to attend to their own needs.

The "ordinary Canadian" in his current manifestation has appeared only recently on the federal political stage. He was hailed by the Spicer Commission as the source of Canadian values and the holder of the key to national unity; he was invited along with experts to attend the Mulroney government's constitutional forums prior to the referendum on the Charlottetown Accord; and he became a regular on the CBC's 1993 "townhall meetings" election coverage. The ordinary Canadian also figures prominently in the rhetoric of the Reform Party, and it is here that we perhaps see most clearly his role in the politics of restructuring. The Reform Party won fifty-two seats in the 1993 election and placed second in some fifty-seven Ontario ridings, in part because its leader, Preston Manning, skilfully and repeatedly evoked the opposition between the ordinary Canadian and special interests. According to Manning, for example, bilingualism and multiculturalism have created conditions of special status which are incompatible with citizen equality. Moreover, he accused the Mulroney government as being dictated by a "tyranny of minorities" (Patten 1994:18, 33–4). The role of the individual citizen in federal politics in the 1990s, however, does not end here. The ordinary Canadian was cast as the star, in fact the only one invited to the Liberals' pre-budget consultation meetings that were held in five cities in early 1994. In contrast, officials rejected the participation of NAC President Sunera Thobani at the Toronto budget consultation on the grounds that she was too high profile – too visible.

Although the ordinary Canadian is increasingly evoked in political rhetoric, his identity is elusive, defined primarily by the things he is not. The ordinary Canadian is disinterested, seeking neither special status nor special treatment from the state. He is neither raced, sexed, nor classed: he transcends difference. But how do we interpret the ordinary Canadian's rapid ascendency to the centre of the political stage – a stage which the political elite suggests is congested with organized special interest groups which threaten to hijack the political agenda and pervert the common good (Leger and Rebick 1993:95)?

The "ordinary Canadian" clearly is a metaphor for something. None of us is ordinary or, put differently, all of us are special in some way or another. So what does it mean for us to defer to the voice of the mythic ordinary Canadian? For one thing, this dichotomy between the "ordinary" and the "special" sends the clear message that regular people don't require state assistance and protection. Moreover, it asks us to be silent about our differences even if these differences are the product of structural and therefore politically contestable biases. As Iris Marion Young suggests contemporary politics increasingly grants political legitimacy to persons "on the condition that they do not claim special rights or needs, or call attention to their particular history or culture" (Young 1990:109). This discursive move effectively reinforces privilege by silencing those deemed to be different. As Young (1989:257) explains, "In a society where some groups are privileged while others are oppressed, insisting that as citizens persons should leave behind their particular affiliations and experiences to adopt a general point of view serves only to reinforce that privilege."

In other words, the current discourse in English Canada on the ordinary and the special serves to delegitimize and silence all those who declare themselves to be different, marginalized, and structurally or historically disadvantaged. This new politics, therefore, is obviously a threat to the ECWM as well as all other groups which suffer from systemic discrimination in Canadian society.

CONCLUSION

I am not suggesting that the politics of the English Canadian Women's Movement in recent years have been misguided or that it is doomed to political extinction. Instead, I want to emphasize that social movements, including the women's movement, are part of the complex matrix of cultural and political forms that are transformed during an era of fundamental restructuring. The passing of the welfare state has displaced many of the sites and objects of political struggle for the women's movement outside Quebec. This does not mean, however, that gender is no longer important, even if neoconservatives protest to the contrary. Neither does it mean that the women's movement vision of social equality or its potential political force has disappeared. Instead, the current transformation in state and cultural forms challenge the women's movement to adjust its political sites by recognizing both the constraints and the liabilities of the emerging new order.

Haraway has argued that the present post-Keynesian moment is premised on an "oxymoronic structure of women-headed households" and an "explosion of feminisms" and "the paradoxical intensification and erosion of gender" (Haraway 1991:167). Haraway is underlining the changing gender and political order which confronts the ECWM and those of other liberal democracies. Many of the assumptions and practices which have guided the women's movement and structured its relationship with the post-war welfare state have much less force today. Women, for example, are no longer primarily housewives supported by a male wage-earner and a politically negotiated family wage. The so-called "private sphere" is now populated by an infinite variety of family forms ranging from the stereotypic but rapidly disappearing male wage-earner model to sole parent families to same sex couples and families. Moreover, the vast majority of Canadian women, whether mothers of young children or not, combine the increasingly onerous responsibilities of paid work and unpaid domestic and childcaring labour. In other words, the post-war gender order, the "Ossies and Harriets," are quickly becoming cultural artifacts.

Similarly, neither the women's movement nor the state can any longer rest comfortably with concepts such as women, women's interests, or women's experience. The past decade, as Haraway puts it, has witnessed "an explosion of feminisms" which rightfully belie the notion of a singular women's experience and a singular feminist truth. Again, this explosion marks a shifting political terrain for the ECWM, one which is both difficult and absolutely necessary to successfully navigate. Restructuring has brought about numerous gendered effects, but the most serious are often experienced by women who, until recent years, have not been highly visible within the women's movement. It is primarily women of colour, working class women, and immigrant women who have had to "adjust" to deindustrialization, homework, and cutbacks in government services.

One of the most empowering slogans in the early days of the second-wave of the women's movement was "The Personal is Political." This message was meant to forge a solidarity among women by conveying the idea that their personal lives were imbued with political relations, specifically patriarchy and an oppressive gender order. The personal continues to be political, but the personal takes different forms and these invite different feminist struggles. In fact, many of our so-called "personal" life choices – such as, for example, hiring an immigrant nanny, buying designer clothes made in sweatshops, shopping at non-unionized department stores, obtaining an abortion or in vitro fertilization at a private clinic, buying private health coverage, sending our children to private school, etc. – are highly political. Moreover, many of these "choices" are no longer choices in the sense that there are alternatives. Nevertheless by exercizing these "choices," we simultaneously deny them to other women who remain trapped in a complex maze of racism, sexism, and classism. These latter terms are clearly recognized as political and in a sense invite us to reverse the slogan. More than ever, "The Political is the Personal."[1] The task of the women's movement in the 1990s and beyond is precisely to embrace both this perspective and its mirror opposite.

This brings us to Haraway's final, and I think most insightful, observation: that the new order is premised on the simultaneous erosion and intensification of gender. Herein lies the greatest challenge. In many ways, the present era has been marked by an erosion of gender as we have come to understand it in the post-war years. Women, for example, are no longer trapped in the home. They have constitutional guarantees of their equality with men as well as laws which enforce pay equity. In the meantime, work itself is said to be increasingly feminized. Stable full-time high-paying jobs are rapidly being displaced by part-time and precarious employment – the kind of work that marked the gendered division of labour in the post-war years (Haraway 1991:166–8). Although the pay gap between men and women remains, the current period has seen both increasing income imbalances among women and a trend toward harmonization among men and women. This has led some to suggest that gender is no longer a viable base for political organizing (Wilson 1988). Others suggest that declining labour standards, employment, and wages mean "we are all becoming women workers regardless of biological sex" (McDowell 1991:418). Finally, as I have argued here, on the political front the new politics attempts to erode gender by denying its relevance, by marginalizing the women's movement as a "special interest group," and pathologizing women with needs as lying outside the realm of the ordinary.

If we chose to view the world through the myopic and phallocentric lens of neo-conservatism, our inquiry could end here. To do so, however, would require us to ignore or deny the intensification of gender and the reconstitution of the gender order. This reconstitution is guided by what Fraser calls reprivatization discourse – a discourse which seeks to push issues of social well-being back into the private sphere and to create the illusion that social welfare is an individual rather than a community or collective concern (Fraser 1989:172). Privatization puts renewed emphasis on the so-called "feminine" sphere of the home and the "feminine" qualities of sacrifice, nurturing, and caregiving. The new order stresses self-reliance, the responsibilities of families to look after their own, and the necessity that state policies be directed to that end (Abbott and Wallace 1992:2). In the meantime, cutbacks in social welfare effectively download these responsibilities to the private sphere where it is simply assumed that women will take up the slack. This often means that middle-class women have to buy childcare and caring labour, and in so doing only further entrench the

growing racialization of the division of labour. Others simply have to re-
tire from the workforce, often into the depths of poverty or violence, in
order to fill the gaps left by an eroding public sector.

The current era provides the ECWM with a fundamental challenge –
to interrogate restructuring discourse and to reveal the new cultural
and political forms that it advances. In a sense, it must make clear to
Canadian women that the increased stress, longer working hours, inse-
cure employment, declining benefits and wages, the increasing commodification and racialization of domestic and caring work are
everyday examples of how the personal is political and, conversely, how
the political is indeed very personal. It is perhaps the opportune moment for the women's movement to capture the political space that has
been closed in recent years. It is perhaps time to begin to build a new
consensus about social responsibility, equality, and public morality.

NOTES

1 I thank my friend and colleague, Hamani Bannerji, for this critical insight.

BIBLIOGRAPHY

Abbott, Pamela, and Claire Wallace. 1992. *The Family and the New Right.* Boul-
der: Pluto.

Adamson, Nancy, Linda Briskin, and Margaret McPhail. 1988. *Feminist Organizing For Change: The Contemporary Women's Movement in Canada.* Toronto: Oxford University Press.

Ad Hoc Committee of Women on the Constitution. 1988. "We Can Afford a
Better Accord: The Meech Lake Accord." *Resources for Feminist Research* 17,
no. 3:143–6.

Andrew, Caroline. 1984. "Women and the Welfare State." *Canadian Journal of
Political Science* 27, no. 4:667–84.

Backhouse, Constance, and David Flaherty, eds. 1992. *Changing Times: The
Women's Movement in Canada and the United States.* Montreal: McGill-Queen's
University Press.

Bakker, Isabella, ed. 1994. *The Strategic Silence: Gender and Economic Policy.* London: Zed Books.

Bégin, Monique. 1992. "The Royal Commission on the Status of Women in
Canada: Twenty Years Later." In *Changing Times: The Women's Movement in
Canada and the United States,* ed. Constance Backhouse and David Flaherty,
21–38. Montreal: McGill-Queen's University Press.

Brodie, Janine. 1990. *The Political Economy of Canadian Regionalism.* Toronto:
Harcourt, Brace, Jovanovich.

- 1994. "Shifting Public Spaces: A Reconsideration of Women and the State in the Era of Global Restructuring." In *The Strategic Silence*, ed. Isabella Bakker, 46–60. London: Zed Books.
- 1995a. "Politics in a Globalized World: New State Forms, New Political Spaces." In *The Future of Nations and the Power of Markets*, ed. Robert Boyer and Daniel Drache. Montreal: McGill-Queens.
- ed. 1995b *Women and Canadian Public Policy*. Toronto: Harcourt, Brace and Company.
- and Jane Jenson. 1988. *Crisis, Challenge and Change: Party and Class in Canada Revisited*. Ottawa: Carleton University Press.
- 1995. "Piercing the Smokescreen: Stability and Change in Brokerage Politics." In *Canadian Parties in Transition: Discourse, Organization and Representation*, ed. Alain Gagnon and Brian Tanguay, 24–44. Toronto: Nelson.
Burstyn, Varda, and Judy Rebick. 1988. "How 'Women Against Free Trade' Came to Write its Manifesto." *Resources for Feminist Research* 17, no. 3:139–42.
Burt, Sandra. 1986. "Women's Issues and the Women's Movement in Canada Since 1970." In *The Politics of Gender, Ethnicity and Language in Canada*, ed. Alan Cairns and Cynthia Williams, 111–70. Toronto: University of Toronto Press.
- 1994. "The Women's Movement: Working to Transform Public Life." In *Canadian Politics*, 2nd ed., ed. James Bickerton and Alain Gagnon, 207–23. Peterborough, Ont: Broadview.
Cameron, Duncan. 1989. "Political Discourse in the Eighties." In *Canadian Parties in Transition*, ed. Alain Gagnon and Brian Tanguay, 64–82. Toronto: Nelson.
Canada. 1970. *The Report of the Royal Commission on the Status of Women*. Ottawa: Information Canada.
Chapman, Jenny. 1993. *Politics, Feminism and the Reformation of Gender*. New York: Routledge.
Chunn, Dorothy. 1995. "Feminism, Law and Public Policy: Politicizing the Personal." In *Canadian Families: Diversity, Conflict and Change*, ed. Nancy Mandell and Ann Duffy, 177–210. Toronto: Harcourt, Brace and Company.
Cohen, Majorie Griffin. 1991. *Women and Economic Structure*. Ottawa: Centre for Policy Alternatives.
- 1992. "The Canadian Women's Movement and its Efforts to Influence the Canadian Economy." In *Changing Times: The Women's Movement in Canada and the United States*, ed. Constance Backhouse and David Flaherty, 215–24. Montreal: McGill-Queen's University Press.
- 1993. "Economic Restructuring Through Trade: Implications for People." Paper presented at the Shastri Indo-Canadian Seminar on Economic Change and Economic Development, New Delhi, December.

Cox, Robert. 1991. "The Global Political Economy and Social Choice." In *The Era of Global Competition: State Policy and Market Power,* ed. Daniel Drache and Meric Gertler, 335–49. Montreal: McGill-Queen's University Press.

Day, Shelagh. 1993. "Speaking for Ourselves." In *The Charlottetown Accord, the Referendum, and the Future of Canada,* ed. Kenneth McRoberts and Patrick Monahan, 58–72. Toronto: University of Toronto Press.

Drache, Daniel, and Meric Gertler, eds. 1991. "Introduction." In *The New Era of Global Competition: State Policy and Market Power,* ed. Daniel Drache and Meric Gertler. Montreal: McGill-Queen's Press.

Findlay, Sue. 1987. "Facing the State: The Politics of the Women's Movement Reconsidered." In *Feminism and Political Economy: Women's Work, Women's Struggles,* 31–50. Toronto: Methuen.

– (1988) "Feminist Struggles with the Canadian State, 1966–1988." *Resources for Feminist Research* 17, no. 3:5–9.

Fraser, Nancy. 1989. *Unruly Practices: Power, Discourse and Gender in Contemporary Social Theory.* Minneapolis: University of Minnesota Press.

Friedman, Harriet. 1991. "New Wines, New Bottles: The Regulation of Capital on a World Scale." *Studies in Political Economy* 36 (Autumn): 9–42.

Fudge, Judy. 1993. "NAC for Change: Women's No Transformed Debate." *This Magazine* (January/February): 7–9.

Gotell Lise. 1993. *The Women's Movement, Equality Rights, and the Charter.* PH.D. diss., York University.

– and Janine Brodie. 1991. "Women and Parties: More than an Issue of Numbers." In *Party Politics in Canada,* 6th ed., ed. Hugh Thorburn, 53–67. Toronto: Prentice-Hall.

Haraway, Donna. 1991. *Simians, Cyborgs and Women: The Reinvention of Nature.* New York: Routledge.

Lamoureux, Diane. 1987. "Nationalism and Feminism in Quebec: An Impossible Attraction." In *Feminism and Political Economy: Women's Work, Women's Struggles,* 76–99. Toronto: Methuen.

Leger, Huguette, and Judy Rebick. 1993. *The NAC Voters' Guide.* Hull: National Action Committee on the Status of Women.

Maroney, Heather, and Meg Luxton, eds. 1987. *Feminism and Political Economy: Women's Work, Women's Struggles.* Toronto: Methuen.

McDowell, Linda. 1991. "Life Without Father and Ford: The New Gender Orderof Post-Fordism." *Trans. Institute of British Geography* 16:400–19.

McFarland, Joan. 1993. "Combining Economic and Social Policy Through Work and Welfare: The Impact on Women." Paper presented to the Economic Equity Workshop, Status of Women, Ottawa, April.

Ontario. 1987. *The Free Trade Agreement and Women.* Toronto: Ontario Women's Directorate.

Patten, Steve. 1994. "A Political Economy of Reform: Understanding Middle-Class Support for Manning's Right-Libertarian Populism." Paper presented at the Annual Meeting of the Canadian Political Science Association, Calgary, June.

Phillips, Anne. 1991. *Engendering Democracy*. Pittsburgh: Pennsylvania State University Press.

Phillips, Susan, ed. 1993. *How Ottawa Spends, 1993–93: A More Democratic Canada?* Ottawa: Carleton University Press.

Pringle, Rosemary, and Sophie Watson. 1990. "Fathers, Brothers, and Mates: The Fraternal State in Australia." In *Playing the State: Australian Feminist Interventions*, ed. Sophie Watson, 229–43. London: Verso.

Rebick, Judy. 1993. "The Charlottetown Accord: A Faulty Framework and a Wrong Headed Compromise." In *The Charlottetown Accord, the Referendum, and the Future of Canada*, ed. Kenneth McRoberts and Patrick Monahan, 102–6. Toronto: University of Toronto Press.

– 1994. "An Interview With Judy Rebick." *Studies in Political Economy* 44 (Summer):39–72.

Ursel, Jane. 1992. *Private Lives, Public Policy: 100 Years of State Intervention in the Family*. Toronto: Women's Press.

Valverde, Mariana. 1992. "When the Mother of the Race is Free: Race, Reproduction and Sexuality in First-Wave Feminism." In *Gender Conflicts: New Essays in Women's History*, ed. Franca Iacovetta and Mariana Valverde, 4–33. Toronto: University of Toronto Press.

Vickers, Jill. 1992. "The Intellectual Origins of the Women's Movements in Canada." In *Changing Times: The Women's Movement in Canada and the United States*, ed. Constance Backhouse and David Flaherty, 36–60. Montreal: McGill-Queen's University Press.

Wilson, Elizabeth. 1988. *Hallucinations: Life in the Postmodern City*. London: Radius.

Yeatman, Anna. 1990. *Bureaucrats, Technocrats, Femocrats: Essays on the Contemporary Australian State*. Sydney: Allen and Unwin.

Young, Irish Marion. 1989. "Polity and Group Difference: A Critique of Universal Citizenship. *Ethics* 99:248–65.

– 1990. *Throwing Like A Girl and Other Essays in Feminist Philosophy and Social Theory*. Bloomington: Indiana University Press.

18 Francophone Minorities: The Fragmentation of the French-Canadian Identity

PHYLLIS E. LEBLANC

In the course of the conference that gave rise to this book, repeated reference was made to the role of symbolism in Canadian nationhood. Professor Nelles asked whether, beyond economic or material conditions, Canadians may be perceived as having a state of mind that would serve to define Canadian nationhood. Others noted the absence of a symbolic identity as a basic element of Canadian nationhood. In general, our discussions acknowledged (and regretted) the absence of a common definition – beyond the political state – of what constitutes Canada as a nation. This sad state of affairs is attributed a priori to the political instability our country is experiencing, and which would seem to have begun with Quebec's fundamental questioning regarding its future.

Quebec is still debating the possibility of transforming itself from a *nation* in the original sense of the word, that is, a *"people,"* to a nation in the political (and sovereign) sense, that is, a nation state. Meanwhile the rest of the country must address the questions associated with re-building the political nation, and beyond the political realm, rebuilding a Canadian national awareness.

An essential element in building a national awareness is collective identity. This concept refers to a collective feeling of belonging. In the case of Canada, it seems obvious that culture is (or at least is proposed to be) the basic tool for producing this feeling of belonging and hence the collective identity. Gaétan Gervais describes the concept in these words: "Culture rests on a past, a history, a continuity; it brings together a community that has a shared experience, a collective existence, an overall vision of the future. What are these feelings of belonging to be based on, if not a collective awareness of what the community has been and what it wants to become?" (Gervais 1994:165).

Thus I propose here to interpret how francophone identities have evolved in Canada. Let us begin by admitting that the francophone experience in Canada tends to support the hypothesis of a definitive fragmentation of the Canadian collective identity. To support this hypothesis, I propose to develop this study in three stages. I shall first provide a very brief summary of the evolution of the *historical* construction of Canadian and French-Canadian collective identities. I shall then discuss the current situation of French-speaking minorities in Canada. Finally I shall deal with several of the issues which continue to confront French-speaking minorities in Canada Outside Quebec and which are preventing the development of a Canada-wide francophone identity.

EVOLUTION OF CANADIAN AND FRENCH-CANADIAN COLLECTIVE IDENTITIES

Collective identity is one of the most important elements to be taken into account in reconstructing Canada's past, and it is certainly the issue most wrestled with by historians. Collective identity is logically associated with nationalism and the need to define a distinct Canadian identity. It has consumed so much energy in constructing the historiography concerning Canada (including Quebec) that one of Canada's best-known historians, Ramsay Cook, has likened this preoccupation of historians to "Portnoy's Complaint" (Cook 1972).

For generations, historians have tried to define Canadian identity, seeing this as a concrete way to project a common vision of Canada. That there were at least two main schools of historical interpretation was obviously a major obstacle in achieving this objective. Until recently, Canadian historians propounded two separate visions of Canada's national evolution – labelled the "two solitudes" – depending on whether they rooted themselves in the French- or the English-speaking community of historians.

Thus in French Canada (more precisely in Quebec), historians initially and for quite a long time defined language and the Catholic religion as symbols of the French culture and as foundations of an identity described as *French Canadian*. Francophone-minorities outside Quebec participated in this broad definition of the French-Canadian nation because they embraced the basic elements of the collective identity – the Catholic faith and the French language – historical factors that explain the feeling of shared belonging with Quebec, the vital core of

French-Canadian culture and survival. In "English" Canadian (more precisely in Ontario) historians have long seen the evolution of Canada (both as a geographic entity and as a country in the hearts of its citizens) as originating in the St Lawrence Valley. In both cases the evolving identity was defined on the basis of a national image that was generally mythical but also positive. This image was essentially *positive*, because the different visions of the construction of the Canadian nation were not yet on a collision course; in French Canada (in Quebec as elsewhere), there was recognition of the stages of marginalization of francophone society and culture, but this was seen favourably, as proof (and sometimes even as a guarantee) of the survival of the minority culture. This image was also *mythical*, because the national image thus created could not reconcile the fundamental differences in historical experience between anglophones and francophones in order to construct a national identity acceptable to contemporary Canadian society.

If we accept the principle that the primary role of a historian is to construct an identifiable image of the past that society can incorporate into its collective memory (Mathieu 1991:264), then Canadian historiography has failed to achieve this purpose. In 1969 J.M.S. Careless argued that the sustained efforts of the two cultures' "national" historians to construct a national identity had had the opposite effect.[1] Given the obvious contradictions in interpretations of Canada's past, he recommended that historians instead turn their attention to analyzing more modest units (within Canada) in order to arrive at acceptable generalizations on collective identity.

With the explosion of both historical fields and methods in the 1970s, Careless' comments began to bear fruit. The development of the field of social history had the effect of shifting analysis away from political history; the individual was replaced by society as an object of analysis, with a major emphasis on social relations. More complex historical methods would in turn replace the descriptive approach with serial and quantitative analysis. But despite the splintering of historical fields into subfields and the application of new methods to the analysis of the past, social historians were, as before, concerned with defining national identity and with models of cultural interaction; the difference was that these were now analyzed from the perspective of social practices.

Regional studies was among those areas of research that benefitted from the explosion of historical fields in Canada. Regional history rejected a priori the traditional definition of national identity based on the St Lawrence nexus and the alliance of two races and two cultures. The task this field assigned itself was nothing less than reconstructing

Canadian history on new foundations of identity.[2] However, the identity paradigm continued to be at the centre of the exploration of the past; moreover, the impact of work in the regional sphere on Canadian historiography would not be uniform. On the whole, regional studies research helped to redefine Canadian history or, at the very least, to offer new interpretations that added to the construction of the national history.

Social history, when applied to regional history, has undoubtedly had a decisive impact on the way historians look at francophone minorities (and other subgroups such as ethnic groups). According to historian Bruno Ramirez, ethnicity was "discovered" as a phenomenon that permeates social relations and produces distinct models of social change (Ramirez 1991:3). As in regional history, the output and the impact of historiography dealing with francophone minorities were not uniform. These new studies followed the historical evolution of francophone societies in their respective communities. Researchers increasingly defined culture as a social construct arising from objective factors and specific social practices. This led them to the inescapable conclusion that francophone regional identities outside Quebec were fragmented and differentiated from one another.[3] Thus belonging to the same French linguistic community was no longer enough to establish a shared sense of belonging. As historian Gaétan Gervais noted: "To reduce the whole of French Canada to a 'francophone collection' is to offer it an alienating self-image anchored neither in time nor in space; it is in short to deny, in its very specificity, the existence of the historical French community that has been living in Canada for four centuries" (Gervais 1994:165).[4]

This short historiographical overview serves two functions here. First, it confirms the priority assigned to the national or "identity" objective in Canadian historiographic output. More important, it supports the hypothesis that for a Canadian society seeking to redefine its national identity, the experience of French-speaking minority linguistic groups is increasingly one of fragmentation. French-speaking communities are fragmented among themselves, but each French-speaking community is also fragmented in relation to its natural (defined territorially) and social (defined by economic, political, cultural and other structures) environment. The first form of fragmentation gives rise to the marginalization of the minority group in relation to the majority group within the territory identified; the second form encourages the formulation of a myth of homogeneity of the group under study.

The predominance given to "identity" in Canadian historiography precludes in-depth treatment of the paradigms that go beyond the specific object of the analysis. This observation applies as much to Quebec, Acadia, and French-speaking Ontario as elsewhere. According to some researchers, this is attributed to the "minority" status of the group. In a study on the changing patterns of Quebec historiography, historian Gérard Bouchard observed that "the feeling of the fragile minority nation induces a militancy with respect to identity: the nation is represented on the one hand as something pure, perfectly homogeneous, and on the other hand as intrinsically different from the societies that surround it" (Bouchard 1990:255–6). In other words, the identity of the group is defined by its particular experiences, and these same experiences explain its alienation from others.

The second form of fragmentation that arises from the importance of the identity function assigned to history is the presumption of homogeneity as a basic tenet of the science of history. The history of minorities too often falls into this error of underestimating the complexity of social structures and conflict relationships within a society or community. Historian Fernand Ouellet associates this weakness with the nationalistic aims of Canadian historiography: "Fundamentally, all of Canadian historiography, whether francophone or anglophone, has for over a century found its inspiration and organizing concepts in nationalism. The need for homogeneity and sense of community that imbues this literature encourages readers to minimize the importance of exploitative mechanisms in society and to exaggerate the influence of forces that tend to reduce social conditions and individual destinies to a common denominator" (Ouellet 1991:6).

FRENCH-SPEAKING MINORITIES: THE CURRENT SITUATION

The first section of this paper identified the fragmentation of a Canada-wide national identity and the proliferation of regional, ethnic, and linguistic identities. This second section examines their contemporary significance.

The most recent Canadian census (1991) noted that only 23.8 percent of the 27,296,860 Canadians enumerated had French as their mother tongue. Of those, 84.5 percent (or 5,746,630) live in Quebec, which means that French is the mother tongue of only a little over 15 percent of Canadians outside Quebec. These people are unevenly distributed throughout the country. New Brunswick has proportionally the largest francophone population, that is, 34.5 percent of a population of 723,900. Ontario has more francophones, but this population is proportionally less significant: 547,300 persons reported French as their mother tongue in 1991, but they constituted only 5.4 percent of the population of that province. Elsewhere the figures and the relative proportions are demographically less significant: in Nova Scotia, Prince Edward Island, and Newfoundland, francophones represent respectively 4.2, 4.8 and 0.6 percent of the total population. In the west, in Manitoba, Saskatchewan, Alberta, and British Columbia, Francophones account for respectively 5, 2.5, 2.5, and 1.8 percent of the total provincial population (Statistics Canada 1991). Studies of demolinguistic trends in Canada confirm the trend toward a greater concentration of francophones in Quebec and a greater concentration of anglophones everywhere else (Statistics Canada 1991; Lachapelle 1989).

Despite major variations in the relative weight of minority francophone communities across the country, at the federal political level these minorities have since 1969 enjoyed official linguistic recognition. In spite of both the resistance of some provinces and regional hostility (Boudreau and Nielson 1994:7), this formal recognition was recently reinforced by section 41 of the Official Languages Act, which states that the federal government "is committed to (a) enhancing the vitality of the English and French linguistic minority communities in Canada and supporting and assisting their development, and (b) fostering the full recognition and use of both English and French in Canadian society" (Canada, Commissioner of Official Languages 1993:112). Indeed the federal government recognizes "the linguistic equality of its national language minorities" (Boudreau and Nielson 1994:7).

Despite the legal recognition and even the constitutional recognition accorded to the two national linguistic communities, the most recent report of the Commissioner of Official Languages noted that no federal institution had yet developed an effective strategy for fulfilling the federal government's commitment regarding section 41 of the Official Languages Act (Canada, Commissioner of Official Languages 1993:112). It is disquieting that there is thus no "strategic plan" that would ensure fulfilment of the Canadian government's formal and constitutional commitment toward its linguistic minorities.

The lack of an overall policy is especially troublesome considering that the federal government now plays (and is expected to continue to play) the greatest role in building national identity within which language is judged to be an essential component. The government can at least theoretically go beyond benevolence in applying national language policies in promoting its own national aims. This brings us back to the concept of a national identity or awareness, and in contemporary society this identity function is assigned to the state. As sociologist W.D. Denis observes: "The state creates and re-creates national unity and its own legitimacy within the nation/society through its discourse and through government projects created to maintain the balance of social forces within society" (Denis 1994:133-5).

However, very practical constraints, such as budget cutbacks, can have a decisive (and negative) impact on the achievement of national objectives, and they show the vulnerability of government strategies. For example, the Commissioner of Official Languages recently pointed out that federal grants to organizations representing official languages minority communities were cut by 10 percent in 1993 and another 10 percent in 1994 (Canada, Commissioner of Official Languages 1993:112). This reduction in funding has serious consequences, considering that it is mainly through two intermediaries – the language communities' official organizations and formal agreements with the provincial governments – that the federal government plans to apply policies to ensure respect for the French-speaking communities and to guarantee their survival (Denis 1994:133–5).

Yet the federal government is not alone in supporting French-speaking communities. Various provinces have since 1969 discussed and at least tried to develop policies that affirm the duality of the two national languages. New Brunswick is the most often-cited example in this regard. Canada's only bilingual province, New Brunswick recognized the equality of the two linguistic communities in 1981 and since then has had the rights of these communities enshrined in Canada's constitution.

The example of the Acadians of New Brunswick supports the hypothesis of a "provincialization of identities" among francophones in recent decades as a reflection of a desire to assert identity (Bernard 1990). It is of course quite predictable that the provincial governments would wish to participate in the development of strategies designed for the linguistic minorities within their territory, and for the relative weight of the francophone group to serve as a measurement factor in shaping provincial strategies. On the whole, however, researchers have thus far found that the provinces "lack policies to assist their minority or encourage it to develop" (Gervais 1994:163). Thus, beyond stating interest and willingness, most provinces have yet to establish concrete ways to back up these statements of intent.

Furthermore, several francophone organizations have pointed out the dangers of allowing provincial governments full responsibility for enhancing the vitality of their francophone minorities. Among the numerous examples is the 1979 manifesto by the Fédération des francophones hors Québec (FFHQ), *Pour ne plus être ... sans pays*, which posed the political problem of francophone communities (FFHQ 1979). The FFHQ called for "the power of community initiative" as the only solution to the problem of determining where responsibility lay for the development of Canada's French-speaking communities. This strategy supports the concept of "parallelism" maintained by the Acadians of

New Brunswick to give that French-speaking minority a greater share of responsibility in the administrative structures of the province.[5] A number of provincial francophone associations have since adopted this vision of community responsibility. In a more recent study, the Fédération des jeunes Canadiens français indicated its support of the very same strategy (FFHQ 1992).

ISSUES FACING FRENCH-SPEAKING MINORITIES OUTSIDE QUEBEC

It is futile to claim that the future of French-speaking minorities can be dissociated from the future of Quebec. There is no denying that the political and social changes which have occured within Quebec during the past generation have fully justified its abandonment of the traditional definition of its identity as French Canadian in favour of a new definition based on the concept of distinct society. Quebec no longer identifies itself, at least in its political discourse, as the cradle of a French-Canadian identity. It instead projects a distinct Quebec identity, which in its pure form includes any society, language, or culture within Quebec – an identity which, in order to flourish, must achieve the status of *nation* in the sense of sovereignty.

The development of a Quebec national awareness has undeniably caused tensions between Quebec and Canada's other French-speaking communities. The latter have been profoundly shaken by the changes in Quebec society, changes that moreover have continued to this day, without, however, leading to definitive actions that go beyond often-contradictory political strategies and discourse. While the fragmentation of minority French-speaking communities is one of the consequences of the historical evolution of French-speaking communities, and while the marginalization of their linguistic minority status is a result of the fragmentation of minority French-speaking communities, the fact remains that these communities will maintain these characteristics so long as they do not find the means to go beyond the narrow parameters of their own communities to finally tackle common problems, regardless of the choices Quebec makes regarding its national destiny.[6]

In 1989 the Institut québécois de recherche sur la culture (IQRC) organized a symposium to assess the state of deliberations on Quebec and Quebecers thirty years after the Quiet Revolution. The researchers asked themselves this fundamental question: "What is our current position for interpreting the upheavals of the past and the current situation?"[7] In my view, Francophones elsewhere in the country should undertake a similar intellectual exercise. The Fédération des jeunes

Canadiens français has as its overall strategy to "restore a Canada-wide sense of belonging, of relatedness ... We must resist the tendency to withdraw into identities that are everywhere undermining solidarity and increasing the sense of alienation" (Gervais 1994:167). This constitutes a major challenge, one Quebec francophones may not wish to undertake and other francophone minorities may be unable to meet.

Concretely, only the Acadians of New Brunswick have succeeded – admittedly to a modest extent – in guaranteeing the equality of the province's two linguistic communities, a logical but important consequence of New Brunswick's recognition of its – and Canada's – official bilingualism. This is much more than has been accomplished by Canada's other French-speaking communities, but it is certainly not sufficient to guarantee a secure future for New Brunswick Acadians in a Canada that no longer includes Quebec. Even a constitutional guarantee will not survive the process of redefining the Canadian nation (Denis 1994:134) which will surely take place if Quebec withdraws from the federation.

If this study has achieved any goal, it is perhaps that of offering evidence that history does indeed repeat itself. Only temporarily did we set aside the paradigm of a national identity which was originally defined as Canadian but to which, from the beginning of the interpretation of our national history, two undeniably different visions of this concept have been grafted. Sociologist J.-Yvon Thériault (1994) argues that the minority linguistic communities are still at the stage of fragmentation and indecision as to their identity, and he concludes that Canada's French-speaking minorities do not constitute a coherent whole, a comprehensive social reality. It may perhaps be concluded that the Quebec nation may, more than "The Rest of Canada," need to identify what characterizes it and what makes it different. For it is Quebec that is determining its destiny, and the rest of the country that remains in a holding pattern, awaiting further developments.

NOTES

This text was originally written in French. It and the quotations it contains have been translated by MacKenzie Birrell. The author would like to thank the School of Graduate Studies and Research of the Université de Moncton for their financial assistance in the production of this paper.

1 In his own words, Careless spoke of "expectations and discouragements out of keeping with realities" (Carless 1969:5–6).
2 This is the thrust of William Westfall's interpretation (Westfall 1980).

3 For an example of this proliferation of francophone identities, see Bernard (1988).

4 Also see Jacques-Paul Couturier's excellent analysis of Acadian historiography (Couturier 1987).

5 Of primary interest on this subject are the comments of Léon Thériault in FFHQ 1984:48.

6 This, moreover, is one of the conclusions that emerged from the meeting of the Etats généraux de la recherche sur les minorités francophones au Canada, held in Ottawa from March 24 to 26 1994 under the auspices of the Regroupement des universités de la francophonie hors-Québec.

7 This symposium resulted in the publication, under the direction of sociologist Fernand Dumont, of a very interesting study (Dumont 1990).

BIBLIOGRAPHY

Bernard, R. 1990. *Le déclin d'une culture*, vol. 1 of a study on the future of the French language and culture in Canada. Ottawa: FFHQ. Ottawa.

Bernard, Roger. 1988. *De Québécois à Ontarois: la communauté franco-ontarienne.* Hearst: Les Editions Le Nordir.

Bouchard, Gérard. 1990. "Sur les mutations de l'historiographie québécoise." *La société québécoise après trente ans de changements*, under the direction of F. Dumont, 255–6. Québec: Institut québécois de recherche sur la culture.

Boudreau, F., and G.M. Nielson. 1994. "Francophonies minoritaires. Identités, stratégies et altérité." *Sociologie et sociétés* 26, no. 1:3–14.

Canada, Commissioner of Official Languages. 1993. *Annual Report.* Ottawa: Supply and Services Canada.

Careless, J.M.S. 1969. "Limited Identities In Canada." *Canadian Historical Review* 50, no. 1:5–6.

Cook, Ramsay. 1972. "Nationalism in Canada or Portnoy's Complaint Revisited." *The Maple Leaf Forever.* Toronto: University of Toronto Press.

Couturier, Jacques-Paul. 1987. "Tendances actuelles de l'historiographie acadienne (1970–1985)." *Historical Papers*, Canadian Historical Association, 230–50.

Denis, W.B. 1994. "L'Etat et les minorités: de la domination à l'autonomie." *Sociologie et sociétés* 26, no. 1, 133–53.

Dumont, Fernand, ed. 1990. *La société québécoise après trente ans de changements.* Québec: Institut québécois de recherche sur la culture.

FFHQ 1979. *Pour ne plus être ... sans pays.* Ottawa: FFHQ.

– 1984. *Etat de la recherche sur les communautés francophones hors Québec. Actes du premier colloque national des chercheurs.* Ottawa: FFHQ.

– 1992. *Vision d'avenir* project, 4 vols. Ottawa: FFHQ.

Gervais, Gaétan. 1994. "Le Canada-Français: un phare allumé sur mille citadelles." *Francophonies d'Amérique*, no. 4.

Lachapelle, Réjean. 1989. "Evolution of Language Groups and the Official Languages Situation in Canada." *Demolinguistic Trends and the Evolution of Canadian Institutions*. Special Issue, Canadian Issues series of the Association for Canadian Studies, 7–33.

Mathieu, J. 1991. "Le sens de l'événement. Un événement fondateur: la découverte du Canada. Le personnage de Jacques Cartier et son évolution." *Événement, identité et histoire*, ed. C. Dolan, 264. Sillery, Qué: Septentrion.

Ouellet, Fernand. 1991. "The Formation of a New Society in the St Lawrence Valley: From Classless Society to Class Conflict. *Economy, Class & Nation in Quebec, Interpretive Essays*. Toronto: Copp Clark.

Ramirez, Bruno. 1991. "Émigration et Franco-Américanie. Bilan des recherches historiques." *Le Québec et les francophones de la Nouvelle-Angleterre*, under the direction of Dean Louder. Québec: CEFAN, Presses de l'Université Laval.

Statistics Canada (1991).

Thériault, J.-Yvon. 1994. "Entre la nation et l'ethnie. Sociologie, société et communautés minoritaires francophones." *Sociologie et sociétés* 26, no. 1:15–32.

Westfall, William. 1980. "On the Concept of Region in Canadian History and Literature." *Journal of Canadian Studies* 15, no. 2:3–15.

PART VI

The Future of Canada outside Quebec

19 A Difficult Transition: English-Canadian Populism vs Quebec Nationalism

ABRAHAM ROTSTEIN

I would like to begin with a favourite story which I hope not too many people have heard. It's from my old mentor Marshall McLuhan and it seems to be particularly appropriate for this big moment in Canada's history. The scene is the middle of the ocean, where a research vessel is stationed. It is measuring fish and waves, depths and so on, and it sends down a deep sea diver to probe the bottom of the ocean. Suddenly this diver gets an urgent communication from the ship: "Surface immediately. The ship is sinking!"

Somehow, I have a sense that we've been summoned here at the moment when the ship is sinking and Ken McRoberts is telling us to surface immediately and confront the crisis.

I think this volume has some excellent contributions. I particularly enjoy Philip Resnick's chapter about a nation unable to say its name and to be itself. I enjoy Roger Gibbins' chapter very much and find that the news is marginally brighter on the West than it was in the past. I take from his chapter a sense that over the years the belligerence and the adversarial rebuff against central Canada have modulated. The other great surprise is how much we've advanced culturally. I somehow think that going back as I do to the late 60s, I bring a sort of a Rip Van Winkle effect to these discussions. Thus it is encouraging to read Mary Jane Miller's, Ted Magder's, and Rowland Lorimer's chapters.

I would like to focus on the last election for my own contribution to this book. To repeat the obvious, this was an earthquake in English-Canadian, in Canadian political experience: the virtual disappearance of the Progressive Conservative Party and the downgrading of the NDP, plus the eruption of two forces which weren't altogether new, but which became very prominent: populism, represented by the Reform Party, and Quebec nationalism, which made the Bloc Québécois Her Majesty's Loyal Opposition.

After the election the consternation was complete. How, we asked, could we have our official ("loyal") opposition committed to the dismantling of the country? And did the "Goths and Visigoths" (as the Reform Party seemed to some) want to override all the accepted modes of political discourse with which the old-line parties had soothed us for so many years? And finally, why was all this so sudden – why did all the pollsters and the political cognoscenti fail to warn us against this unprecedented opening of the San Andreas fault so to speak, of Canadian politics? Would we survive this "revenge of the regions?"

In this piece I attempt a speculative analysis of these forces of political change. We are still trying to assimilate these events and achieve a clearer focus on what happened and why. What follows is a preliminary and necessarily personal analysis.

The consistent undercurrents flowing beneath the surface of Canadian politics have always intrigued me more than the overt duelling of the established parties in the system. The two major undercurrents are nationalism in Quebec and populism in the rest of the country. These have been the perennials of Canadian politics; the underlying forces that have periodically burst through and provided the momentum that resulted in the shifts in electoral fortunes of the mainline parties.

Some of these same forces have recently echoed across the globe. In many countries the populace is alienated and disaffected with the established parties and existing political institutions. One has only to recall the recent upheaval in Italy and the success of the right-wing populism of Berlusconi, the roughly similar echoes in Russia with Zhirinovsky as well as in the Ukraine and earlier in Peru, to sense a common wave moving through many countries. Perhaps these are all the stepchildren of that most prominent of right-wing populists, Ross Perot.

The ripple effect of these Perot-like themes need not be overstated. It falls far short of the wave of global revolution the u.s. initiated in 1776 and again in the Berkeley Free Speech Movement in 1964. Still, we may ask, why is the populace everywhere so disparaging and dismissive of its politicians and its political institutions within the last decade? The experience of every country varies and in the end is rooted in its own indigenous situation. But in aggregate I believe the populace senses again and again that its politicians are helpless against the tide of global economic forces. These have drastically curtailed the autonomy of most nation states and with it the power of their politicians.

The "politics" the public observe looks like a series of empty gestures and endless posturing while basic problems such as unemployment and the public debt crisis linger on and show no prospects of being resolved. Speaking generally, then, the global disaffection with existing democratic procedures has its roots in a pervasive scepticism present throughout many countries: they share the tacit conviction that their politicians are impotent.

This is a populism that may be heavily mixed with nationalism, such as we see in the Ukraine, or it may give way entirely to extreme nationalism as in Bosnia. Perhaps this nationalist component – if one can generalize at all – is rooted in a groping attempt to close ranks and set up a buffer against an array of external disruptive forces. The aim is to safeguard something of a "core" community against a series of random shocks. In that broad sense nationalism and populism have something in common in so far as they are both militant reactions to external disruptive forces.

In Canada, it seems, we have – as usual – done the decent and orderly thing. We have had a division of labour rooting our manifest nationalism in Quebec and our populism in the rest of the country (but mainly in the West). This geographic and linguistic division is a great help to political theorists who might otherwise have to unscramble complex strands that have been hopelessly intertwined. In short, while recognizing the global parallels that are echoed in Canada, it is to the specific and indigenous political forces particular to Canada that we must turn to better understand the origins of the recent electoral upheaval.

Populism and Quebec nationalism have been the deepest undercurrents of the Canadian political culture virtually from the time of birth of the two constituent nations. For example, the rebellions of 1837, one in each community virtually mirror these separate (and related) political manifestations.

Recourse to more strident forms of political discourse is usually the result of stress on the body politic. We have recently had the disruptive effects of the two free trade agreements, the ongoing unemployment, the intractable deficit, the constitutional crisis (around the Charlottetown agreement and the Meech Lake Accord), the growing divisiveness around immigration policy, and so on. The disillusion and disaffection that these have created has given a new momentum to the two latent strands of the political culture that I have mentioned, populism in English Canada (to use a short-hand label) and a more militant nationalism in Quebec. This is not to negate the mediating role of the main political party, the Liberals, who provide so to speak the role of the "brake" on the political engine while the other two movements act as the "accelerator."

Our subject here is two fold: a short profile of both Quebec nationalism and Western populism as well as the likely result of their interaction. These forces are regarded here as a proxy for the more dynamic political forces now operating on the Canadian scene.

The Reform Party and the Bloc Québécois are the political conduits for both prior and new political cross-currents. The Bloc's position takes the form of a rounded and developed nationalist expression that has been gestating in its modern phase since the mid-1950s. (I refer to the influence of Father Lévesque on a founding generation of Quebec intellectuals and politicians.) Its focus is on the organic and coherent nature of Quebec society and on the linguistic and cultural legacy that it sees as continually in jeopardy. Its classic watchword has been "la survivance" – national survival. Civil liberties and the classical liberal individualism of Anglo-Saxon cultures have a low priority with the Bloc in the face of a self-image that is communitarian and integral in its expression.

This nationalism has had some difficulty positioning itself clearly and precisely in relation to the rest of Canada. It has on various occasions adopted such ambiguous watchwords as sovereignty-association or "separatism" rather than outright "independence." The latter would involve a surgical severance with all Canadian institutions, including the Canadian dollar. That would be the outside point on the range of options, and much of the debate on tactics and choice of specific policies is in flux in both parts of the country.

Turning to the content of the Reform Party's platform, we discover some fundamentally different propositions from those of the Bloc Québécois. The historical sentiments are those of right-wing Canadian populism, namely an abiding sense of grievance against the central authority in Ottawa and against the financial and cultural institutions in Toronto. This sense of historical injustice is rooted mainly in the unfair burden borne by the West from the time of the National Policy of 1879. This has resulted in belligerent mistrust of the electoral process because the West is left with an inadequate voice on the national scene. Populists thus view Canadian society not as a collectivity, but as a collection of hard-done-by individuals. The ingredients of present-day populism comprise one part nineteenth century liberalism, one part tax revolt, and one part rejection of multiculturalism. Tossed together you have the scent of this new brew that has been wafting through the country.

The most recent expression of populist sentiment during the election includes something of a nationalist tinge embodied in its slogan "The West Wants In." This approximates a 90 degree turn from traditional Western populism which lacked any national focus and seldom went beyond reciting its "rosary" of grievances and complaints against the federal government. The Reform Party now wishes to reconceive Canada as a home for "unhyphenated Canadians" (the English-Canadian version of the québécois "pur laine" or unadulterated québécois from the founding group). It espouses as well fiscal probity including balanced budgets and lower taxes, a commitment to reduce expenditures on welfare programs and regional assistance, more direct democracy, and no collective privileges of any kind either to Quebec or any ethnic minority. (The recent watchword to accommodate Quebec, "asymmetrical federalism," is anathema to the Reformers.)

Thus we see that in Reform's attempt to extend its appeal from a strictly regional to a national party, there is a muted and unfocused sense of nationalism that is new. It is largely based on the self-image of Canada as an integral territory – embodied in the old motto "Dominion from sea unto sea." But it is an impoverished or poor man's version of Canadian nationalism. There is, for example, no particular concern with policies vis-à-vis the United States – its economic and cultural dominance of Canada – little support for domestic cultural policies, little sympathy for the Canadian Broadcasting Corporation, and so on.

The foregoing has been a thumb-nail sketch of the positions of the two new and dynamic parties that are rapidly overtaking the Canadian political scene. What does the growing confrontation of these two parties or political forces portend for the future?

Real politics in Canada seems to have overtaken us recently while the established parties were making other plans. That makes it all the more hazardous to attempt to extrapolate the future from the recent past. One would have to anticipate the role of more factors than can be handled in this paper, including the strategy and credibility of the ruling Liberal Party, the response of ethnic communities in Canada to both Quebec and the Reform Party, the emerging political prominence of the Aboriginal peoples, and the economic situation including the lifting of the recession with lingering unemployment.

But setting these important and tangible issues aside for now, what are the likely dynamics that may emerge in a Quebec represented by the Bloc and the Parti Québécois on the one side and the rest of the country falling behind the type of approach advocated by the Reform Party?

On a personal note let me say that I formed part of a small group on the progressive left in Canada that for many years expressed a good deal of sympathy for the evolving aspirations of a Quebec moving toward self-determination. It was Quebec's democratic right, we felt, to determine its own fate. The rest of the country should give it a free hand to do so – that is, to stay in Confederation or to leave as it saw fit.

(See for example the 1977 statement of the Committee for a New Constitution, issued after the 1976 election victory of the Parti Québécois.)

The basis of this position was the concept of "parallel nationalisms" in English Canada and Quebec that would have some empathy for each other's goals as well as pursuing some common aspirations. The hope (however naïve or innocent it may seem today) was for the two societies or "nations" to evolve in tandem but to stay under some common rubric called Canada.

That goodwill toward Quebec of the 1970s and 1980s has largely eroded, and little support remains on the progressive left. This is emblematic of a hardening of position across the political spectrum toward the aspirations of the Quebec independence movement. There is little positive sympathy for this movement anywhere in the rest of Canada. There is in fact a growing determination that Quebec should pay a price for its exit – either financial (its share of the national debt) or territorial (not to include in the new Quebec the area where aboriginal peoples live, for example). The mood in English Canada is increasingly belligerent and abrasive toward the prospect of an independent Quebec. This mood seems to continue the momentum of the populist politics that resulted in the defeat of the Meech Lake Accord and the Charlottetown agreement.

Add to that an impression (difficult to document) that those who speak on behalf of the provincial Liberals within Quebec lack any positive conviction in their support of the federal alternative. This seems to be true among both the key civil servants and the politicians.

Meantime, informal reports indicate that many large corporations whose headquarters are in Montreal are preparing alternative offices in Toronto, often leaving only a legal shell behind in Quebec and quietly transferring their assets out of the province.

Putting these factors together in this admittedly impressionist analysis, the prospects for a united Canada do not bode well for the future. One can envision that should the Parti Québécois win the forthcoming referendum it would not face a sympathetic counterpart in the rest of Canada with whom to negotiate its independence. Certainly if the mood represented by the Reform Party becomes more widespread – with its individualistic, egalitarian values entirely at cross-purposes with those of the communitarian Parti Québécois – there will be little common basis for the parties to come to some agreement. In effect, Quebec and English Canada are out of synch. They're not talking "the same language," nor are they talking about recognition of each other's survival as a nation. With such discussions running at cross purposes, their interaction will likely result in the escalation of political tensions.

It may be too early to write such a scenario of successive stages of escalation and belligerence on both sides, but such a possibility cannot be dismissed given that the circumstances surrounding such negotiations will be less than ideal. One has only to mention, for example, that the Ontario election will likely follow closely on the Quebec election in order to see what may be in store. Quebec separation is bound to become an election issue in Canada's most populous province. There will be a great temptation for a provincial government that is reeling at the polls to take a hard line with Quebec as much out of response to the popular mood and its changing internal convictions as for reasons of sheer electoral expediency.

As it stands on the threshold of this new chapter in its political life, English Canada rediscovers its weak sense of itself – its own identity and aspirations. These unresolved questions are, as most people are aware, long standing. Attempts at further self-definition are certainly enhanced by the new cultural achievements, particularly those of a brilliant generation of writers that has now attained international eminence. But the main component of English Canada's self-image, I venture, is still the territorial dimension of its existence rather than its cultural self-awareness and social cohesion.

These unresolved issues are now being submerged by the bandwagon movement toward "globalization," the new international ideology that invites us to abandon this search for national self-definition in the name of a universalism that is still over the horizon.

I conclude I am afraid, on a sombre note. The separation of Quebec and the dismantling of Canada as we know it is not inevitable. But I believe – with much personal pain and consternation – that for the foregoing reasons, the dismantling of Canada is more than likely.

20 The Meristonic Society: Restructuring and the Future of Canada outside Quebec

MARJORIE GRIFFIN COHEN

Just north of Ottawa in the Gatineau Hills there exists a lake which is an ecological oddity. It consists of distinct layers which do not interact in any way: the very ancient forms of life at the bottom have never been exposed to sun or air or even to the forms of life at the upper levels of the lake. The life forms nearer the top do receive a lot more oxygen and light, but these advantages are not transmitted to the lake's bottom layers. Because the various layers of this lake have no interaction, this lake has not evolved over time and has remained virtually unchanged for eons. It is called a meristonic lake.

In this paper I am using the term "meristonic society" to characterize the type of society toward which Canada is moving as it responds to the imperatives of economic restructuring. The irony of restructuring is that while economic, political, and social systems are becoming more homogeneous throughout the industrialized world, the inequalities in social systems are solidifying. We are in the process of creating a type of social organization, the *meristonic society*, which is highly stratified with little possibility of movement between those on the bottom and those on the top. My interest is in understanding the distinct form that restructuring will take in Canada and what it will mean for disadvantaged groups – for disadvantaged women and for disadvantaged minorities.

THE INSTABILITY OF CANADA OUTSIDE QUEBEC

The main task of the contributors of this book has been to examine the impact of recent trends in Canada outside Quebec. We were asked specifically to look at the extent to which economic fragmentation has been offset by political, social, and cultural forces of mobilization and integration. I want to respond to this by focusing on the ways in which the tools for mobilization and integration are being destroyed: the normal political tools of democracy are less directly applicable to the sweeping changes under way than we are accustomed to acknowledging. As a result, there appears to be an inevitability to the political fragmentation of our social order, as typified through the welfare state, despite the homogenization of economic policy.

Throughout this process the public has not been passive, but has actively participated in the debates about the future directions of this country. People identified with the left have espoused support for a strong central government which would maintain inclusive social programs and shape the economic directions of the country in the future. Those identified with the right have argued for less government altogether, but with specific emphasis on more autonomy for local and provincial governments. They favour more reliance on market forces not only for easily identifiable economic activity, but also for supplying and delivering activities associated with social welfare. The most successful efforts at mobilization (in practical terms, that which leads to changes in public policy) have been those that advocate policies which tend to accentuate the fragmenting tendencies of the social order. For example, the privatization and "free market" theme of the Reform Party accentuates fragmentation of the social order because its proposed solutions to social program failures necessitate the dismantling or downsizing of programs and their removal, in most cases, from federal control.

All groups recognize a need to respond in some way to the enormous changes which are under way. That these changes are dramatic is indicated by the very terms used to describe them: globalization, restructuring, the new international economic order, post-Fordist regime, new international division of labour, information based society, post-welfare state, age of global capital, new world economy, and so on. These are all terms which convey several things: the vastness of what is occurring as well as the inclusiveness of this change (involving everybody in the world) and also its inevitability. The political message associated with change – the arguments we are repeatedly given by politicians and business leaders – is that the timid (who we might call the "economically challenged" if we were to use this kind of language) shy away from the dislocations that retructuring brings. But those with courage understand that whatever pain is caused is part of a necessary process. While Joseph Schumpeter's words aren't used, the notion of "creative destruction" is the justification for moving in very unpalatable directions (Schumpeter 1950). The old order might be falling apart, but this destruction has a silver lining because along with this tearing down of the old institutions is a simultaneous building up of new and better forms of organization. Destruction becomes a part of the growth process and the old familiar pain, but gain reasserts the belief in the positive and progressive features of change.

My basic point is that Canada is headed on a specific course, and whether or not Quebec is part of the country will not markedly change this reality for the rest of Canada. I certainly do not mean that whether or not Quebec is part of Canada is irrelevant or unimportant to us. Stephen Clarkson says this very clearly in the beginning of his contribution: the economy, polity, and even culture of the rest of Canada bears the imprint of Quebec and there is no denying that. Rather, I see the forces pushing Quebec in a specific direction, toward greater homogenization of its economic and social institutions to conform to international imperatives, as essentially the same as those which are shaping the future of the rest of Canada. The political reality is that through the Canada-u.s. Free Trade Agreement (FTA) and the North American Free Trade Agreement (NAFTA), Canada's sovereignty has been circumscribed to an unwarranted degree. As the opponents of these trade agreements have argued, the u.s. government can now determine the legitimacy of government polities in Canada (Drache and Gertler 1991; Cameron 1993). The question then is, What remnants of control can Canada maintain and how can this country continue to determine how best to meet the needs of its own people? We may be compelled to accept what appears to be obvious, which means that policy makers will have to accept globalization and all its ramifications, simply because "Canada cannot opt out of this process" (Globerman and Walker 1993). But this does not mean that it is impossible to confront threats to the nation posed by globalization.

We will undoubtedly argue about the best ways to deal with globalization, but it seems clear to me that having a strong, unified, articulate sense of nationhood is a prerequisite for any action to protect the interest of people in this country. This absence of a strong sense of nationhood in Canada (without Quebec) has contributed to the destabilizing effect of the new trade-centred regimes.

In saying this I realize that I am going against the general tenor of most of the contributions to this volume. Throughout our deliberations of the topic of Canada outside Quebec, there has been a tremendous sense of optimism: even with Free Trade and with Quebec gone, things will probably stay the same – or almost the same or not too different. There have been some exceptions to this, but my general perception is that most of the contributors want to believe that the future will be a bright one and that all the doomsday scenarios of the anti-free traders or the federalists are neglecting the inherent resiliance of the rest of Canada. I think this is a dangerous line of thinking. Things can get a lot worse and they can stay a lot worse. There is nothing inherently positive about the globalization process, and for many nations which have got caught up in its web, the results have been anything but positive.

Canada without Quebec is not an inherently stable entity. The logic which is leading to economic integration within North America is the logic which also leads to political disintegration and fragmentation. The supremacy of market forces over political ones makes strong central governments obsolete, and Quebec's efforts to gain independence from the centralizing aspect of federalism have established a precedent for the rest of Canada – not exactly to separate, but certainly to disengage. As each province attempts to achieve some kind of distance from federal control, the sense of a need to stand together as a nation evaporates. There are not too many reasons for various sections of this country to hang together if our collective politics is replaced by the market. The reduction of federal political institutions to a couple of Thatcherite and Reaganite functions – mainly the administration of justice and the protection of property – can occur without the overarching control of a nation state.

As the market becomes the sole arbiter of economic and social policy, certain sections of the country are likely to exhibit even more impatience with what is perceived as the liability of Atlantic Canada. Whatever sentiment exists toward a unified continent will disappear when Atlantic Canada is physically separated from the rest of Canada. (Nor is the international precedent for happy outcomes for countries which are physically divided encouraging.) In the west, particularly in British Columbia, there is much more discussion of north-south links than there has been in the past. B.C. Premier Harcourt talks about the "evergreen corridor," and the notion of a whole new region encompassing the U.S. and Canadian pacific northwest, "Cascadia," has captured some attention as a plausible new direction for political and economic viability in the region. While this notion is not yet part of any party's political platform, granting distinct status to B.C. has considerable public appeal. Harcourt went out of his way, during the debate over the Charlottetown Accord, to maintain that the federal system is too centralized in certain aspects. And his insistence, during recent discussions about Quebec and sovereignty, that nothing be accorded to Quebec that is not given also to other provinces, was well received within B.C. and elsewhere in the West. My point in raising this is not because I believe that the current B.C. government has separatist tendencies, but rather to demonstrate that in the West the prospect of disengaging from central Canada is popular. In some parts of western Canada the hostility to Ontario is as strong as and sometimes even greater than the hostility to Quebec. It is hard to imagine how this western hostility would accommodate Ontario if Quebec is no longer part of the nation.

THE REST OF CANADA AS A NATION STATE?

It is always difficult to describe what it means to be Canadian, mainly because we usually define the term by reference to what we are not. But it seems to me that we are more than an economic entity characterized by a market mechanism, more than a geographic space, and certainly more than Viv Nelles' characterization of the nation as a "state of mind." What stands out and makes this nation a cohesive unit relates to all these things, but it also has something to do with the culture which has built up around the market-correcting institutions that have been established to protect the people in this country. The very existence of these institutions enables Canada to be a nation state, rather than simply a nation. I make this distinction because a nation can be a "state of mind," in the way that Scotland is a nation, where the idea of cultural distinctness is retained, but political and social autonomy is absent. In contrast, a nation state is a place where people can actually determine the way they live and how they interact with each other. It is a political entity which is autonomous, which exercises self-determination without undue pressure from outside forces. In Canada self-determination and autonomy have resulted in establishing a whole set of policies and institutions which have produced results the economic system could not have achieved on its own. The very existence of these policies rests on the necessity to correct and supplement the way the economic system works and is guided by a morality which does not coincide with the objectives of a market system. Canada is a nation state which binds diverse people together because a social policy exists which, in varying degrees, meets people's needs.

The destabilizing political tendencies in the rest of Canada are directly related to the forces threatening this social policy. Three of these are most significant.

The first are the forces associated with Quebec's struggle for greater autonomy. The main problem here is not so much Quebec's action, but the ways in which the rest of Canada reacts to Quebec. We have seen how the will to retain a federal concept, and specifically a national social policy, has evaporated as each premier and each province outside Quebec pursues separate and distinct jurisdiction over the same areas as Quebec.

The second is the desire of the central government to disengage from its obligations to the rest of Canada. This shift in political will is related to Canada's international competitive position initiated by trade liberalization. The severe debt crisis has made decentralization and privatization more attractive, and this has been bolstered by a shift in ideology whereby the market is perceived as the most efficient way of ordering almost all social institutions. Since politicians see raising taxes as political suicide, and all governments seem to have to prove to the public their seriousness by instituting deficit-reduction measures, shifting costly programs like health and education to the provinces or privatizing and deregulating transportation and communication systems makes sense.

The third threat to social programs and a strong national social policy is the international trade agreements. Through the FTA and NAFTA a single market has been created but without a corresponding political institution to exert discipline on this market. These agreements have been established to the great advantage of international corporations, primarily because while they used to have to deal with national governments within the confines of any market in which they operated, this form of control is rapidly losing its force. The trade agreements have established one market, but the only supranational institutions being created related to this market are those which facilitate the formation of the market itself and which lead to greater capital mobility. These new institutions are not being created to exert discipline on the market, in the way in which nation states were able to do over the course of the development of the welfare state, and their objective is not to function as instruments of market correction. All the market-correcting functions are left to nations, and since the major purpose of the trade agreements has been to limit the power of these national entities, their ability to prevent some of the greatest dislocations and unhappy consequences of the "free market" is considerably reduced.

TOWARD THE MERISTONIC SOCIETY

I want to focus on the impact this ideological shift will have on democracy and the ways in which embracing a "free market," through the international trade agreements, affects the redistributive goals of the disadvantaged in Canada.

Most of the political activity of marginalized and disadvantaged groups has centred on correcting the unequal results which are brought about when the market operates without restraint. For many groups the expansion of political institutions to greater reflect the diverse nature of people's experiences in the society has been an important political exercise. In some respects, this has succeeded, particularly as greater numbers of people representing women, Native people, and different races and ethnic backgrounds have achieved political recognition. However, now it seems that just as these groups have begun to understand how to be effective within the existing political institutions, the significance of these institutions themselves is waning. So, for example, while there may be more women and people from racial minorities in parliament than ever before, the nasty reality is that because of the constraints of the international trading agreements, parliament is less and less able to pursue policies which can benefit these disadvantaged groups.

Since the power of nations over the market is not being replicated in the international arena, the target for political activity for popular sector organizations has become very nebulous. There is no international mechanism which must respond to democrative demands of citizens. At best international institutions are comprised of bureaucrats who are appointed by national governments. But these bureaucrats, as is the case of those appointed to adjudicate disputes arising through NAFTA, have no contact with the public and are not accountable to public desires, pressure, or disapproval.

As Janine Brodie says in her chapter, within nations popular sector organizations have become caught up in issues that are really superceded by international events and the traditional forms of protest become less and less relevant. The feminist involvement in the debate over the Charlottetown Accord is a case which reflects this. The feminist movement's position on the constitutional issue was incredibly important for giving people who were progressive in their political outlook a rallying point against the Charlottetown Accord. Because all political parties and the trade unions supported the accord, and because the main voices against it were either identified with separatists from Quebec or right-wing Reform Party types, the position of the women's movement was significant for those who worried about the consequences for a strong federal government. In particular, women's groups (as articulated through the National Action Committee on the Status of Women) focused on the dangers of decentralizing important social institutions and the ways in which this would occur, should the referendum on the Charlottetown Accord be won. My point in raising this is not to say that the position of women's organizations was a misguided one, but rather that the very consequences which were feared would occur through the Charlottetown Accord, are coming about because of the free trade agreements. The lesson to be learned from this is that even though groups may have considerable success within the national political arena, this may ultimately have little effect on what happens within the country. This success may make absolutely no difference to the ability of disadvantaged groups to bring about a more democratic society and to have their wishes translated into political action.

The functions of the state are being reduced considerably and are likely to centre on controlling its own population's behaviour to conform to international rules. With a reliance on the market as the main international regulator of social interactions, states are less and less likely to act as advocates on behalf of the interests of popular sector groups. This function for states coincides very well with the Thatcherite and Reaganite notions of the minimalist state and what the state should and should not be doing. Most notably the redistributive functions of state actions will have fewer and fewer ways of being effective. The results will be the confirmation of rigid economic and social distinctions between groups of people with little chance of movement between groups.

OTHER POSSIBILITIES

People in Canada have been aware of the dangers of globalization for sovereignty and democracy. This has been evident through the vigorous ways in which the Canada-u.s. Free Trade Agreement and the North American Free Trade Agreement were opposed by popular sector groups. However, since these agreements where entered into without popular support, progressive groups have found it increasingly difficult to argue on behalf of national sovereignty: it becomes almost contradictory to push for the sovereignty of a state in an international arena when the state itself is not responding to popular sovereignty. The major issue then becomes finding ways to ensure that the domestic government responds to the will of the people. Without the entity of the state as the advocate for national sovereignty in the international arena, the possibility is remote for Canadians having any influence in bringing about international rules which would either exert sufficient control over capital or would allow for diverse economic policies within countries.

The mose dramatic opposition to the dictates of the international trading regimes is coming from the actions of the very poorest people in the world, not from protests by people in wealthy countries like Canada. The threats to the very poor on this earth are life threatening, in that they affect the very ability to grow food. In this respect, it is not surprising that it is the people in Chiapas, Mexico, and farmers in India who recognize the dangers of ways in which international trade agreements like the GATT and NAFTA restrict their ability to feed themselves. These groups are protesting both the morality of the agreements and the substance of their restrictive requirements for national economic policies. So far these groups have not had much success in changing the direction of international policy, but the important first step of dramatizing the problem has been made.

In Canada and the u.s. some hope is given to the possibility of enacting some kind of governance over international capital through the establishment of supplemental codes of conduct, such as the Social Charter in Europe. While virtually everyone who is concerned about the effects of free trade on labour and the environment recognizes the ineffectiveness of NAFTA's supplemental agreements on the environment and labour, the hope is often expressed that at least this is a first step from which we might build. I do not think this will ever be an effective route. These supplemental agreements do not set up any international institutions to compel any nation to behave according to a set of international regulations. Rather, they merely require that each country enforce its own laws! Even the Social Charter in Europe, which goes considerably further than anything proposed for North America, is not binding and is less effective than an old document like the ILO Labour Convention, which has considerably more power than the Social Charter.

So far there are no international institutions to govern capital and there is no avenue through which these institutions can be developed right now. I would argue that trying to create international institutions to govern capital is not the best route to take. At best the process will be too slow to eliminate the very worst features of exploitation internationally. At worst the regulatory institutions will never really materialize. The most important direction for action now is to influence international trade laws in such a way as to permit diversity among nations' economic policies. It is the insistence on uniformity in economic policy that is at the heart of the free trade agreements. As a result of this, there is no way in which poor countries can compete internationally if they must abide by employment and environmental standards of wealthy countries. Yet they have no way to organize their society other than through the neo-liberal institutions which are insisted upon by the trade agreements.

The real task of the future is to find ways to democratize our own countries so that they, on behalf of people, can insist on tolerance for variation in social and economic policy internationally. Obviously this is not a short-term project, particularly considering the strength of international capital to force nation after nation of capitulate to its logic. But there is something which politicians, business interests, and even academics cannot predict: how people are able to change their own circumstances. The point of the trade agreements is to limit the effect people in the future can have on government policy: as Michael Walker, of the Fraser Institute approvingly noted, "A trade deal simply limits the extent to which the u.s. or other signatory government may respond to pressure from their citizens." Setting up institutions which govern people's lives and which cannot be controlled by national governments, changes in ideology (as a result of elections), or pressure from citizens contravenes most people's notion of what governments should do. It will not be long before people see the effects of this, and particularly feel the effects of the rigidities of inequalities in society. Perhaps then governments will be forced to take seriously the demands for a different social order and for change.

BIBLIOGRAPHY

Drache, Daniel, and Merc S. Gertler, eds. 1991. *The New Era of Global Competition: State Policy and Market Power.* Montreal and Kingston: McGill-Queen's University Press.

Globerman, Steven, and Michael Walker, eds. *Assessing NAFTA: A Trinational Analysis.* Vancouver: The Fraser Institute.

Grinspun, Ricardo, and Maxwell A. Cameron, eds. 1993. *The Political Economy of North American Free Trade.* Montreal and Kingston: McGill-Queen's University Press.

Schumpeter, Joseph. 1950. *Capitalism, Socialism and Democracy,* 3d ed. New York: Harper & Row.

21 *Staatsnation* vs *Kulturnation:* The Future of ROC

THOMAS J. COURCHENE

I am interpreting my contribution to this volume as that of a combination forecaster and rapporteur, that is, assessing the future of the Rest of Canada (ROC) both in its own terms and in terms of some of the ideas and issues contained in these chapters. I have accordingly structured my comments as follows: the first section will focus on a range of impacts on ROC if Quebec opts for sovereignty. In section 2 I shall argue that, regardless of what Quebec chooses to do, ROC is in for significant political and socio-economic changes emanating from the new global economic order. The third section then addresses the *Staatsnation* vs *Kulturnation* distinction raised in the chapter by Lanphier and Richmond, but applies this distinction to the broader set of issues arising from the various papers. The final two sections contain a few peripheral but probably provocative observations relating to the contributions by Morton on the Charter of Rights and Gibbins on the West and the Reform Party. A brief conclusion completes the comments.

One final introductory note. The volume constitutes an extremely valuable snapshot of the status quo of ROC across a wide range of fronts – economic, regional, literary, publishing, cultural, the arts and media, etc. To my knowledge, this exercise is unique and it is certainly welcome and timely. I shall argue at least in part that an equally important issue is how these various characteristics of ROC will be altered if Quebec opts for sovereignty. I recognize that this is somewhat unfair since the authors were asked to prepare a report card on the status quo and not to focus on what the future holds. But my assigned role is to focus on the future.

THE IMPACT OF THE HOLE ON THE PARTS

I do not profess to know the precise socio-cultural or political-economy characteristics or values underpinning ROC's identity as it currently exists. Therefore, it is all the more difficult to forecast what it might be like were Quebec to achieve sovereignty. There is, however, a way around this. Regardless of the inherent features of ROC, one can probably assess the nature of the *directional* changes were Quebec no longer to be part of the Canadian family. Indeed, economists are quite familiar with these sorts of analyses, since the issue essentially becomes: What is the impact on ROC, at the margin, if Quebec decides to leave? Or as the heading suggests: What is the likely impact of the "hole" on the parts?

While it will be relatively easy to isolate selected *qualitative* characteristics, it is much more difficult to assess their *quantitative* impacts. I shall make some guesstimates, but by and large what follows is a qualitative exercise. Among the influences of Quebec on the federation and, therefore, among the ways in which Canada without Quebec will be influenced are the following:

1 Quebec brings legal and institutional pluralism to Canada. The former relates primarily to the civil law tradition, while one aspect of the latter relates to Quebec's "opting out" of various policy areas. Thus, at the margin, ROC becomes much less legally and institutionally pluralistic or, in the way that we are used to expressing this, much less asymmetric. This may not be good news for the First Nations: How much of our apparent willingness to accomodate alternative institutional/constitutional arrangements for the First Nations is a reflection of the *existing* degree of pluralism? With Quebec gone, will ROC remain as accommodating?

2 The taste for regional redistribution is likely to erode. The argument here is that the magnitude of interpersonal and interregional transfers has been influenced in no small way because one of the "founding nations" was also a "have-not" province.

3 ROC will probably be more centralized. Quebec is the clear leader in terms of decentralization, whether in terms of revenue (with its own separate personal income tax system) or expenditure (with its continuing requests for greater powers). It is true that there are other decentralist forces in the system. Alberta is a "closet" decentralist, with the closet door open in direct proportion to the price of energy. British Columbia will eventually exercise its decentralist impulse as it integrates with the Pacific Rim. But in the interim, a Quebec exit will increase the centralist nature of ROC in comparison to the status quo.

4 With Quebec in the family, the tensions in the federation revolved around federal-provincial or territorial axes. With Quebec gone, these may be eclipsed to some degree by pan-ROC and nonterritorial cleavages – that is, the tensions will relate more to Charter interests vs vested interests or what Morton refers to as the confrontation between the Court Party and the Reform Party. While this is related to the centralist issue in point 3 above, I believe that it is conceptually distinct.

5 More speculatively, I have always viewed our approach to "official" multiculturalism as a response, in part at least, to official bilingualism. The support for both will surely erode in ROC. Viv Nelles may be correct in suggesting that Ontario and Quebec will work out some accommodation in this and other areas, but these will be in the nature of bilateral, not pan-ROC, arrangements.

6 Quebec is the bastion of "collective rights." With Quebec out, the focus will shift more toward individual rights. I recognize that the collective rights in the Charter may appear to offset this, but later I will argue that the impact of the Charter will also move in the individual rights direction.

7 Relatedly, one might distinguish a "communitarian" capitalism (Japan, Continental Europe) from Anglo-Saxon and especially U.S. "individualist" capitalism. Apart from the West's experimentation with "cooperative" capitalism (the coops and wheat pools) and Canada's earlier enchantment with Crown corporations, Quebec is the leading exponent of communitarian capitalism – the caisses populaires, the Caisse de dépôt, the European universal banking model, the concern about domestic ownership, etc. Perhaps this should not be surprising because it is probably linked to the collective rights and civil law aspects of Quebec. Elsewhere I have labelled this approach "market nationalism." In any event, ROC will shift in the direction of individualist capitalism.

This list could easily be extended, but it is sufficient for present purposes. What is striking is that *each and every one of these implications represents a move in the direction of the American creed.* That is, a move toward embracing "life, liberty, and the pursuit of happiness" rather than "peace, order, and good government." This is significant because the rather positive assessments of the state of ROC culture, literature, publishing, etc., articulated in this volume are, as alredy noted, really snapshots of the status quo and not necessarily the reality that would obtain in a truncated Canada. Moreover, apart perhaps from the focus on the alternatives to U.S.-style capitalism, none of the above analysis relates to the typical "Americanization" fears of many participants, namely the neo-conservative thrust, NAFTA and the FTA, and the general drift toward continentalism.

Now that I have broached these larger forces, which are quite independent of whether Quebec becomes independent, I want to devote some attention to them.

THE GLOBALIZATION CHALLENGE

The world is undergoing one of its epic transformations. I have referred to this as "globalization and the information/knowledge revolution." Harris (1993) calls it a fundamental shift in the "wealth-creation process," while Lipsey (1994) claims that we are witnessing the emergence of a "new technoeconomic paradigm."

However one chooses to label these developments, the essential point is that ROC with or without Quebec is in for some major changes that will have significant impacts across a broad range of societal fronts. Rather than attempt to detail these, I am attaching two tableaus that are intended to capture the implications for social policy of globalization (tableau 1) and the knowledge/information revolution (tableau 2). Although these tableaus are intended to be self-contained, two points are worth highlighting. The first is that the pressures, at least as I interpret them, are in the direction of greater decentralization, north-south integration, and east-west flexibility, including wage flexibility. The second is to bolster the argument for decentralization by providing (figure 1) some further evidence for the non-synchronization of our regional business cycles. As is clear from figure 1, the commodities recession in the early 1980s devastated Alberta and British Columbia while the 1990s recession took its toll on the heartland, among other areas, with Alberta and B.C. skating through relatively unscathed. One could mount a case to the effect that the combination of the trend toward greater north-south trade relative to east-west trade and the non-synchronization of regional business cycles means that Canada is no longer an optimal currency area. But I do not need to go this far (although I have in other articles). Rather, I will limit myself to the statement that it is highly likely that Quebec sovereignty would mean the end of the Canadian currency. A debt-ridden Quebec using the Canadian dollar would render the Canadian currency unsustainable. And if Quebec opts for its own currency or, more likely, for the U.S. dollar, then ROC will be probably be also forced to use the U.S. dollar, either directly or indirectly via some rigid sort of exchange relationship. The impacts of this would go beyond the economic realm.

Table 1
Globalization and Social Policy: A Subjective "Tour d'horizon"

General Implications

- At its most basic level, globalization is the internationalization of production. Even at this level, it represents a severe challenge to social policy because welfare states in all countries were geared to their respective national production machines. What is the optimal nature of the social policy envelope when production is international?
- It is the international private sector that is globalizing, not the international public sector. Thus, economic space is transcending political space. In countervail fashion, some functions of the economic nation-state are being passed upward (free trade, the European Union, the Bank for International Settlements).
- Power is also flowing downward both to citizens and to international cities since it is largely via the latter that "institutions" are globalizing. The European regional science literature now focuses on the "regional/international" interface and not only the national/international interface — that is, economic regions are cutting across traditional political boundaries.
- Globalization as represented by free trade pacts has other social policy implications. With freer markets, delivering social policy via cross-subsidization is more difficult. Distributional (that is, tax transfer) instruments, not allocative instruments, must now deliver social policy. This is a welcome development.
- Relatedly, with the spread of free trade deals, whether in Europe or America, social policy issues are coming under the rubric of competition policy — hence, the increasing use of the term "social dumping."

Relevance for Canada

- As trade increasingly flows north-south, Canada will cease to be a single economy and become a series of north-south, cross-border economies. What will then bind us east-west is more of a social policy railway than an economic policy railway. The emerging challenge is how to mount an east-west transfer system over an increasing north-south trading system.
- In particular, the political economy of transfers will alter. When the second-round spending effects of equalization and interregional transfers tend to go south, rather than back to the "golden horseshoe", how will this alter Canadians' (or Ontarians') taste for transfers?
- In an increasing number of areas, a central vision emanating from the center will no longer be acceptable — the regions will be too economically diverse in that the requirements for a Great Lakes economy like Ontario will differ from those for a Pacific Rim economy like British Columbia. Part of the solution will likely be one or all of greater decentralization, greater asymmetry and greater east-west flexibility (including wage flexibility).

In terms of the subject matter of this volume, I draw three implications from the changed, and still changing, global order. The first is that the combination of powers flowing both upward and downward from nation states is fully consistent with an integrating global economy and a splintering global polity. This is so because "distinct societies" have become much more viable since they can now bypass their national governments and latch on to the emerging international infrastructure (e.g., Quebec and NAFTA or Scotland and Europe 1992

Table 2
The Information Revolution and Social Policy: A Subjective "Tour d'Horizon"

- The information revolution is inherently decentralizing in that individuals can now access, transform, transmit and manipulate data and information in ways that governments are powerless to prevent. This will make old-style governance more difficult for governments of all stripes.
- With knowledge at the cutting edge of competitiveness, aspects of social policy become indistinguishable from economic policy. Regardless of what the Constitution may say, it is inconceivable that the federal government will be relegated to the sidelines of social policy if national competitiveness is at stake.
- Drucker's predictions (1986) are holding up well — the manufacturing sector is becoming uncoupled from the resource sector (that is, GNP is becoming less raw-materials intensive) and, within manufacturing, production is becoming uncoupled from employment. The latest version of the latter is the prediction for a low-employment-growth recovery.
- Despite its generous resource endowments, Canada cannot avoid making the transition from a resource-based economy and society to a knowledge-based economy and society. Further success in the resource areas will progressively require the application of knowledge and high-value-added techniques.
- The middle class in this new era will include versions of technologists and information analysts. But Canada remains a professional society. — hence, the disappearing middle class. Social policy has a critical role to play in this inevitable shift from boards and mortar to mortar boards.
- In tandem with globalization, the information revolution is altering much of the old order:
  - Interregional transfers will have to tilt from "place prosperity" to "people prosperity." To the extent that place prosperity remains important, it ought to be a provincial, not a federal, matter.
  - There is emerging the notion of a global "maximum wage" for certain activities. Wages beyond this maximum wage will shift the activity offshore. As Drucker (1993) notes, this is a powerful argument for "contracting out" — that is, to enhance the productivity of these activities.
- This is turning the original British North America Act on its head. Some of the line functions, such as forestry, fishing, mining, and, energy, can and probably should be devolved to the provinces (in any event, they will continue to be driven by global imperatives) and some of the traditional provincial areas, such as education and training, will have to take on national, if not federal, dimensions. Since not all provinces will be able or willing to take down these areas, asymmetry will likely increase.
- We will witness an exciting and perhaps bewildering set of provincial experiments across the full range of the social envelope. Ottawa's role is to provide the framework within which this experimentation can take place and to ensure that there is information with respect to the successes and failures. In the same way that Saskatchewan's experimentation led to medicare a quarter of a century ago, the ongoing process is, Schumpeterian-like, creating or re-creating key elements of our new social order.

FIGURE 1
Employment Recovery after Two Recessions

A. *1980s Recession:*
Employment Recovered Four Years Later?

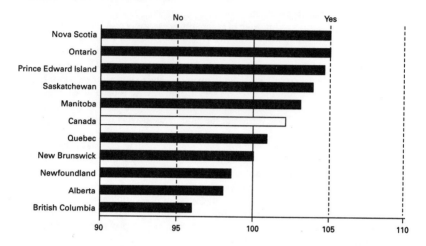

B. *1990s Recession:*
Employment Recovered Four Years Later?

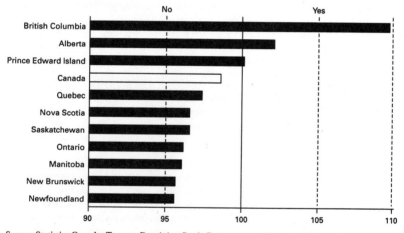

Sources: Statistics Canada; Toronto-Dominion Bank, Department of Economic Research.

and soon Maastricht). It is in this sense that these global forces are facilitating Quebec's aspirations toward sovereignty and a few years down the road they will also facilitate a Western Canadian "distinct society" linked to the Pacific Rim.

great deal who does the negotiating for ROC – Ottawa or th[e]
inces? Were Ottawa to be the key negotiator, the result wou[ld]
ably be a more centralized ROC in the immediate afte[r]
Quebec exit. But what happens in the event that there is a l[e]
tinuity, however temporary, in the transition? My guess is [that]
capital, including Canadian capital, would step into any [s]
vacuum. And this is beyond the current influence of the in[ternational]
capital markets, given that we are about to hit the proverbi[al]
The key point is that the transition would likely be critica[l]
that ROC comes out the other end as one country necessita[ting]
address the challenges of the transition. It is of course fair t[hat]
characteristics of transition that would mesh well with one'[s]
long-run equilibrium, but the transition cannot be ignored.

THE CHARTER OF RIGHTS AND FRE[EDOMS]

I now turn to a few general points relating to the insightful [of]
Morton and Gibbins. In terms of the former, the Charter of [Rights and]
Freedoms can be viewed as Trudeau's *beau risque* with our [for]
starters, the Charter effectively spelled the end of the *deux n[ations]*
ception of Canada because the most significant constitutio[nal amend]
ment since Confederation (and one that actually reduce[d Quebec's]
powers) carried without the consent of one of the two "fo[unding na]
tions." At the same time the Charter has given a new an[d powerful]
sense of identity to English Canada or in Morton's words, "h[as become]
the leading institutional symbol of the new pan-Canadia[n national]
ism." In the process this is making life even more unpalatab[le for Que]
bec, especially in the context of the Charter-influenced co[nception of]
Canada that espouses equality of citizens and of provinces. A[symmetry,]
which in reality has been an admirable solution and indeed [one of the]
contributions of Canada to the art of federalism, has now c[ome to be]
viewed as a problem and even a defect in our approach to g[overnance,]
with important reverberations back on Quebec.

In a much more speculative vein, let me assert that ROC [could also]
become profoundly disillusioned with the Charter. Thus fa[r we have]
accommodated the cleavages it has generated by spending [a great deal]
of money on them, in much the same way that we have a[pplied more]
money as a solvent to the regional cleavages. But there i[s no more]
money. Under a constrained fiscal position, enhancing equa[lity for in]
dividuals or groups will progressively mean the "levelling do[wn" of oth]
ers rather than levelling up or giving more money to the e[xisting or new]
equity-seeking groups. More important, and rephrasing pa[rt of Mor]
ton, individual rights and equality of opportunity are more [likely to]

The second observation is that, in this larger framework, the FTA and NAFTA are hardly the monumental events that many observers, including those writing here, would claim. Rather they are natural (and probably inevitable) extensions of the set of forces that are already at play. Indeed, the "national treatment" provisions of these arrangements will eventually be seen as an incredibly creative institutional innovation for accommodating national sovereignty within free-trade arrangements. Certainly, they are to be preferred to the "homogenization" of national policies that will arise under the "single passport" approach in the EU. This will especially be the case if we embrace some version of a currency union.

The third point is more in the nature of a personal observation (as is, no doubt, this entire set of comments). Based on my interpretation of the nature of the underlying global forces, my proposals for Canada's future political economy *are the same* whether Quebec is in or out: greater decentalization with a stronger federal role in preserving and promoting the internal socio-economic union. This puts me well away from many of the writers here who, I think, espouse a dual decision matrix – a willingness to tolerate some greater decentralization or asymmetry provided Quebec commits to staying in the federation, but a preference for a much more centralized ROC with Quebec out. With respect, I believe that this misreads the message coming from the new global order.

But not all the powerful forces constraining our future are external to Canada. By borrowing from the future to the extent that we did, the crushing weight of the interest charges are beginning to dictate domestic policy. Whether we like it or not, Alberta-type spending cuts will have to spread through the country – the alternative will be for economic activity to move south. While this fiscal burden is daunting enough under the status quo, the exit of Quebec would clearly exacerbate the impact.

Thus, the challenge on the cultural front for ROC is not simply to overcome any effects of Quebec sovereignty, but as well to come to grips with the rather dramatic implications that will be unleashed from the global economy and our own fiscal profligacy. By and large, both were ignored in the papers (except those focusing on economic issues).

STAATSNATION VS KULTURNATION

With this backdrop, I now turn to what is probably the core of my comments, a focus on the interplay between *Staatsnation* and *Kulturnation*. In their chapter, Lanphier and Richmond define *Staatsnation* as "that aspect of a nation state which articulates a legal system which unites a people in some form of equality" and *Kulturnation* as "that aspect

which provides definition in terms of values, common herita[g]
symbol systems." With some degree of misrepresentation, I shall
ate state with *Staatsnation* and nation with *Kulturnation*.

One of difficulties ROC has in coming to grips with the Quebe[c]
is that, for most of Quebecers, their nation is Quebec and thei[r]
try is Canada, and contrary to some of my earlier points and as
to the underlying premise of the conference which led to this
they will not likely give up either. The same is true for most of th[e]
Nations: their nation is the relevant First Nation and their cou[ntry]
Canada. Most residents in ROC do not make this distinction – C[anada]
is both their nation and their country.

Actually, the first part of Resnick's recent book, *Thinking [About]
Canada* (1994), contains an excellent discussion of this distincti[on]
tween state and nation or, in effect, between *Staatsnation* and *Ku[ltura-]
tion*. However, Resnick's contribution to this volume argues with
enthusiasm that not only is there a socio-cultural identity inher[ent in]
English Canada (a *Kulturnation*) but that this should be the ba[sis for]
designing an optimal state structure that would embody these
In other words *Kulturnation* should drive *Staatsnation*.

I doubt whether this is possible, let alone desirable. For one t[hing I]
do not think that there is anywhere near the needed degree of c[onsen-]
sus in terms of ROC's value system – this is Morton's Court Party
form Party again. Moreover the values that now exist are inform[ed in]
an important way by the presence of Quebec in the Canadian f[amily.]
The relevant question is, What are the alternative long-run cu[ltural]
and value equilibria once Quebec is out of the equation, and h[ow will]
these steady state alternatives be influenced by the range of p[ossible]
scenarios for the critical transition period? The analyses of th[e eco-]
nomics of Quebec separation have tackled these issues. The anal[ysts of]
Kulturnation must also begin to address them as well.

Therefore, while I do not believe that there is a shared vision i[n ROC]
in *Kulturnation* terms, I think that there is close to universal accep[tance]
of Canada in terms of *Staatsnation*. Moreover, as Abe Rotstein [points]
out, it is far from certain that ROC would survive as a single co[untry.]
Thus the primary concern if Quebec opts for sovereignty must [be to]
preserve the country, replete with a set of agreed-upon processes[, consti-]
tutional arrangements, incentives, etc., through which we can in[divid-]
ually and collectively filter our conceptions of who we are and w[hat we]
want to be. In other words, *Staatsnation* must take precedence ove[r *Kul-*]
turnation or we risk losing both.

Returning to the question of transition, it is almost surely the [case]
that the nature of the transition would have a powerful influen[ce on]
ROC, at least over some medium term. For example, would it ma[tter to]

with globalization and the knowledge/information revolution than
are group rights and equality of result. Under the onslaught of powerful external forces, of fiscal constraint, and of well-financed private-sector challenges, I believe that the Charter will eventually be interpreted
as an individual rights document. This is easier to comprehend if, as a
result of Quebec's exit, the negotiations between the Court Party and
the Reform Party on the future of ROC lead to the inclusion of "property rights" in the Charter. But the pressures will exist even without this
amendment. This is admittedly sheer assertion on my part, perhaps
motivated by a desire to be consistent, since elsewhere I have argued
that over the long-term the Charter rather than the FTA will be the
more republicanizing and Americanizing intitiative.

THE REFORM PARTY

This reference to a republican influence is a convenient entry for an
elaboration on Gibbins' insightful chapter on the West and the Reform Party. My perspective on Reform is that Albertans have for some
time now espoused some version of "representative" rather than "responsible" government in order to protect their interests. Their first attempt at this was to abandon the Liberals in the wake of the NEP.
When the Tories showed themselves to be no more respectful of their
views (Senate stacking and the GST), Albertans' interest shifted to a
Triple E Senate. When this also foundered, they did the next best
thing, namely to destroy the national parties. A fragmentation of national parties, particularly if there is the possibility of recall, clearly introduces more checks and balances into the parliamentary system.
With the Charter impinging on parliamentary supremacy from the
outside, and with national party fragmentation working from within,
the net result will be a much altered system of governance. This is relevant to the issues raised in this volume because a good deal of what
passes for our identity, however defined, has been the result of the operations of national parties (including a degree of party discipline
much more strict than that which characterizes Westminster). We may
not be facing parliamentary gridlock, but it probably is the case that
the grand "compromises" of old will be much harder to come by. This
will pose a challenge to reconstituting a truncated ROC if and when
Quebec achieves sovereignty. And it provides an alternative rationale
for a more decentralized future.

CONCLUSION

If Quebec leaves, ROC will be faced with three challenges – assessing
the status quo across a broad range of fronts, outlining alternative

longer-term futures for ROC, and focusing on how to get there, that is, addressing the transition. This volume has admirably addressed the first of these challenges. What I have done is to outline the nature of some of the forces, internal and external, that would have to be addressed in coming to grips with the other two challenges. Phrased differently, this is the research agenda facing ROC.

My final comment is that the premise of this volume is wrong. Quebec will probably not go its own way. It is too economically weak to ensure its continued viability. And a weak economy is likely to be a prelude to an unwinding of aspects of its identity. But one cannot be absolutely sure of this, so that the research this collection of essays begins is essential. The larger point is that even with Quebec remaining in the Canadian family, both the economic and socio-cultural challenges for the future of Canada remain daunting.

BIBLIOGRAPHY

Courchene, Thomas J. 1994. *Social Canada in the Millennium.* Toronto: C.D. Howe Institute.

Harris, Richard G. 1993. "Trade, Money and Wealth in the Canadian Economy." Benefactors' Lecture, C.D. Howe Institute, Toronto.

Lipsey, Richard G. 1994. "Markets, Technological Change and Economic Growth." Paper presented to the Tenth Annual General Meetings of the Pakistan Society of Development Economics, mimeo, Department of Economics, Simon Fraser University.

Resnick, Philip. 1994. *Thinking English Canada.* Toronto: Stoddart.

PART SEVEN

Postscript

22 After the Referendum: Canada with or without Quebec

KENNETH McROBERTS

Within months, perhaps even weeks, of the publication of this book, Quebec voters are supposed to have decided whether Quebec should become "a sovereign country." In fact, the Parti Québécois (PQ) government of Jacques Parizeau has already defined the broad outlines of its sovereignty project and begun an elaborate process of popular consultation leading to the referendum. A proposed version of the referendum question has even been made available. In addition, over the last few months some important new studies have been published about the processes through which Quebec might become sovereign, and their consequences for Canada Outside Quebec (Gibson 1994; Monahan 1995; Young 1995).

In this postscript I will attempt to apply the many findings of this book to the specific prospect of Quebec sovereignty presently before us. In the process I will also seek to provide the readers with some thoughts about how the transition to Quebec sovereignty might affect Canada outside Quebec, in effect partially taking up the challenge raised by Thomas Courchene in the preceding chapter. Finally, I will outline how the findings of the book bear upon the future of Canada Outside Quebec if, as seems likely, sovereignty is rejected in the upcoming referendum.

Before doing so, however, I must stress that this analysis is very much my own and does not represent the collective judgment of the contributors to this book. At the conference from which the book emerged the focus was very much upon "taking stock" of the contemporary state of Canada outside Quebec. As Thomas Courchene has already noted, the participants did not discuss at any length the details of Quebec sovereignty or the specific processes through which Quebec might be sovereign. They certainly did not come to any collective conclusions about how Canada should react to a referendum vote for sovereignty. Undoubtedly, many of them would strongly disagree with the arguments that I am about to present.

QUEBEC'S REFERENDUM PLANS

According to plans presented early in December 1994, the referendum will call upon voters to approve a bill both declaring Quebec's sovereignty and spelling out its basic features. A draft version of that bill has been circulated to households throughout Quebec and will be the focus of public consultation through a series of commissions to be held in sixteen regions of Quebec as well among two specific categories of the Quebec population: youth and senior citizens. (Aboriginal peoples are planning to stage a separate consultation process.) The results of these consultations are to be presented to a special committee of the Assemblée nationale, which will decide on the final version to be submitted to the Assemblée. Upon receiving approval there, the bill would then be submitted for popular approval in the referendum. Only if the referendum should be successful would the bill be enacted.

Between the time of writing, February 1995, and the referendum much could happen. The draft bill may well be modified through the consultation process. There are proposals that the referendum question not be restricted to approval of sovereignty, less radical options might also be included. There is even continuing speculation that the referendum might be postponed beyond 1995 or indefinitely. Nonetheless, for present purposes we will assume that the referendum will indeed be held in 1995 and that it will focus upon approval of a bill that is quite similar to the draft bill presently in circulation.

On this basis, Quebec voters would be asked to approve a bill that begins with the declaration that "Québec is a sovereign country" (Québec 1994:sec. 1). The rest of the bill would be devoted to spelling out some of the conditions of Quebec's sovereignty: Quebec would use the Canadian dollar as its currency; Quebec citizens would be entitled to retain Canadian citizenship should the Canadian government allow; a constitution would, among other things, guarantee anglophone and Aboriginal rights; and so on. In addition, the Quebec government would seek to negotiate an agreement with the Canadian government "to maintain an economic association" (Québec 1994:sec. 2). Finally, Quebec would accede to sovereignty within one year of the referendum, if not sooner.

At this point it is difficult to predict whether a referendum on these terms will succeed. The terms of the election of the Parti Québécois on 12 September 1994 were not auspicious, falling well short of PQ expectations. The PQ won an overwhelming majority of seventy-seven seats in the 125-seat Assemblée nationale, but its popular vote of only 44.7 percent barely exceeded the Liberals' 44.3 percent. Part of the explanation lay in the surprising strength of Mario Dumont's Parti action démocratique (PAD) which won one seat (Dumont's) but secured 6.5 percent of the popular vote. Support for the PAD, which envisages a "sovereignty" for Quebec in a continuing political relationship with the rest of Canada, would suggest that some Quebec nationalists were distinctly uncomfortable with the PQ's plans.

Moreover, opinion surveys continue to predict a majority "No" vote in a referendum based upon the PQ's proposals. The most recent estimates call for a "No" vote of 54–55 percent (Mackie 1995a; O'Neill 1995). In particular, they demonstrate continuing apprehension over the economic consequences of Quebec secession (Mackie 1995b).

Nonetheless, the Quebec government has several potential advantages in the upcoming referendum. Not only is the government popular, but it may benefit from an expected economic upturn, and its plans for decentralization of power may win local notables to the "Yes" side. The federal government, led by a prime minister who is personally unpopular in Quebec, is both politically and financially constrained from any spending campaign to secure Quebeckers to the federalist cause. Most important, after the twin debacles of Meech and Charlottetown, federalists cannot credibly use the tactic that was so useful in defeating the 1980 referendum on sovereignty-association: to promise that should Quebec vote "No", the Canadian constitution would be revised to meet Quebec's aspirations.

Responding to a "Yes" Vote

A majority "Yes" vote in the upcoming referendum may not be the more likely outcome, but it remains a distinct possibility. Thus there is more than enough reason to pose the question: What would happen to Canada outside Quebec should the referendum succeed? More to the point, what would be the interests of Canada outside Quebec and what strategies would best maximize them? The following constitutes my personal response to these questions.

A first issue to be addressed is whether Canadians outside Quebec should recognize such a referendum result. Over the years, a general understanding has developed among Canada's political leaders that if the majority of Quebec voters express their approval of sovereignty then the rest of Canada should accept the result and enter into good faith negotiations with the Quebec government over the terms of sovereignty. This understanding was explicitly or tacitly acknowledged by all three parties in the last Parliament and was recently endorsed by Reform leader, Preston Manning, in the present Parliament (Whitaker 1995). While over recent weeks Prime Minister Chrétien has avoided publicly acknowledging this understanding, he did affirm it in his 1985 best-seller autobiography (Chrétien 1985: 137). And his justice minister, Alan Rock, has recently stated that while the Quebec government's draft bill is unconstitutional, "what matters is more the will of Quebecers" (Wells and Authier 1994).

In most formulations this understanding has required that the approval be registered in a referendum that (1) is democratically conducted and (2) presents sovereignty in clear and unambiguous terms. The plans outlined by the Parizeau government clearly would meet these conditions. With respect to the first condition, the referendum would be conducted under Quebec's general referendum law, allowing a vote for all Canadian citizens residing in Quebec. Moreover, it would have been preceded by a large-scale public consultation over the text to be presented in the referendum. Some critics have objected that these consultations will neither give equal time to federalist options nor afford equal representation to advocates of federalism. Yet they fall squarely within established Canadian political practice. For instance, when it created the Spicer Commission on national unity the Mulroney government neither named separatists among the commissioners nor included a discussion of Quebec sovereignty in its mandate. As to the second condition, a clear definition of sovereignty, we have already seen that the bill refers to Quebec being "a sovereign country." For that matter, at two places in the explanatory notes to the draft bill sovereignty is clearly defined as the exclusive right to pass laws, collect taxes, and sign treaties (Québec 1994).

To be sure, not all Canadians subscribe to this general understanding to accept the democratically expressed approval by Quebeckers of sovereignty. Some commentators have insisted on the fact that there is no provision for secession under the Canadian constitution and that Quebec can dispose of no unambiguous right to claim sovereignty under international law (Coyne 1995; Finkelstein and Vegh 1992; Williams 1992; Monahan 1995). Yet, these points need not *preclude* Quebec sovereignty. For instance, the Canadian constitution might be amended to exclude Quebec. More importantly, there appears to be little public support for what would seem to be the clear implication of this position: if Quebec sovereignty is illegal, then the federal government is both entitled and obliged to use force to prevent it from happening (Young 1995: 186).

I will try to demonstrate below that in the face of a clear majority approval of the Quebec government's sovereignty project it would be in the best *interest* of Canada Outside Quebec to enter into good faith negotiations over the terms of Quebec's accession to sovereignty. Without a settlement of these questions, Quebec might still seek to become sovereign unilaterally.

A CANADA WITHOUT QUEBEC

On this basis, the prospect of a Canada Without Quebec is a real one. Thus, to return to the question we posed at the beginning of this book: how cohesive would Canada be if Quebec were no longer part of it? In other words, can there be a Canada without Quebec, or would the process of disintegration continue?

The Will to Maintain a Canada

As I noted in the introductory chapter, most of the foregoing chapters clearly suggest that most Canadians would continue to subscribe to the idea of Canada and would support efforts to keep the country together. Public opinion surveys confirm this judgement (Banting 1992:173; Young 1995:192). Although this commitment might be strained by some of the challenges outlined below, it would at least form the initial reaction to Quebec's departure.

Most of the contributors to this book agree that Canadians outside Quebec would remain united by a strong national sentiment. In his analysis of Ontario, H.V. Nelles insisted that the idea of a Canada is so deeply rooted in the psyche of most Ontarians that they would not contemplate abandoning it even for other arrangements that might be more to their economic advantage, such as Ontario sovereignty or a loose political arrangement with the United States. By the same token, they would be prepared to assume both economic and political concessions necessary to secure the unity of the new country. Similarly, Roger Gibbins demonstrated that not only have Western Canadians long shared a strong Canadian nationalism but the departure of Quebec would bring Canada more in line with the Western Canadian vision of the nation as a culturally homogenous community. And Robert Finbow argued that Atlantic Canada's long-standing loyalty to Canada would continue to be reinforced by the region's economic precariousness and consequent dependence upon the central government.

More generally, without Quebec Canada would approximate more closely the idea of an English-Canadian nation which Philip Resnick argues is the basis for a strong sense of identity. "The nation that dares not speak its name" would become, simply, "Canada." Finally, F.L. Morton's piece showed how, unlike Quebec francophones, English Canadians have come to see the Charter of Rights and Freedoms as a central element of Canadian nationhood. Without Quebec, this sentiment would be given freer reign. Morton did argue that English Canadians are in fact divided over the terms of application of the Charter but suggests that this cleavage might well straddle the new Canada rather than pit region against region.

Beyond this continuing bond of national sentiment many Canadians might also remain united by their membership in specific communities that are pan-Canadian in scope and historically have looked to the federal government to advance their interests. For instance, as Joyce Zemans' chapter suggested, the Canadian cultural community could be expected to defend the integrity of its national cultural institutions. Indeed, without Quebec's presence it would be more fully united in doing so. Similarly, Janine Brodie's analysis of the women's movement showed how it has had a long history of drawing together women outside Quebec and of defending a strong role for the federal government as well as such national institutions as the Charter of Rights and Freedoms.

Nonetheless, this initial will to maintain a Canada without Quebec would soon face severe challenges that, if not properly handled, could weaken the cohesion of the new Canada – perhaps fatally. One set of concerns involves defining the new relationship with a sovereign Quebec; the other involves finding a balance among the parts of the new Canada.

Defining the New Relationship with Quebec

The Quebec government has very clear ideas as to how the relationship between Canada and a sovereign Quebec should develop. It presumes that within a fairly short period of time, no more than a year, Quebec and Canada could resolve all the issues involved in Quebec assuming sovereignty, including its responsibility for part of the federal debt. Beyond that Quebec proposes that once it becomes sovereign the two states not only would conduct amicable relations but would allow free movement of goods across their borders and provide dual citizenship and passports for those who qualify. In addition, Quebec intends to use the Canadian dollar as its own currency (Québec 1994).

As Rotstein argued in his chapter, this agenda would have little appeal for most Canadians outside Quebec. Many of them would greet Quebec's departure with a sense of loss or bitterness or both. After close to 130 years of cohabiting the same country and an almost interminable effort over the last three decades to find a new *modus vivendi*, English Canadians and Quebec francophones would have "failed." Moreover, in leaving Canada Quebec would be propelling the rest of Canada into a new condition filled with uncertainties that most of its residents neither desired nor anticipated. They hardly would be in the mood for building a new amicable relationship with a sovereign Quebec (Banting 1992:167). Openly confronting Quebec and even seeking vengeance for its "betrayal" of Canada might help to solidify Canadians in their shaken sense of national community.

Beyond that, many of the issues that would have to be addressed in negotiating the terms of Quebec's accession to sovereignty are highly complex and difficult to resolve. What is Quebec's "fair" share of the debt? What should be the boundaries of a sovereign Quebec? Moreover, the very process of organizing the negotiations could be difficult. How, for instance, could the federal government represent the rest of Canada?

Nonetheless, I would argue that the new Canada's interests would in the last analysis lie in a speedy resolution of the terms of Quebec's accession to sovereignty. By the same token, galling as it might be to many Canadians, they would have an interest in amicable relations with a sovereign Quebec, extending to free trade and perhaps even joint citizenship.

If negotiations over the terms of Quebec's accession to sovereignty were to fail, then Quebec could secure its sovereignty only by declaring it unilaterally. Canada would have no interest in allowing such a situation to develop. Clearly, a unilateral declaration of sovereignty by Quebec without recognition by the federal government would cause enormous concern in business circles, both Canadian and foreign. They would be bound to re-examine their holdings not just in Quebec but in any part of Canada and to postpone any future investment until the situation is clarified. One observer has claimed that "the economic dislocation in parts of the country would be far greater than that experienced ... in the Great Depression" (Monahan 1995:29). This may be an overstatement, but the economic crisis would clearly be of major proportions.

It could be argued that a unilateral declaration of independence would impose a greater economic price on Quebec than it would on the rest of the country. While Canadian leaders might be tempted to call Quebec's bluff by refusing to agree on the terms of sovereignty, they would be running a risk that Canada could ill afford.

Even if Canada were to decide its interest lay in a negotiated settlement, securing this objective would not be easy. Patrick Monahan has recently insisted that the hurdles are so great that a negotiated settlement is virtually impossible (Monahan 1995). I would argue that this overstates the case. Most of the hurdles he cites can either be circumvented or may not be so great as he claims. Indeed, there is a contradiction between, on the one hand, contending that a unilateral declaration of independence by Quebec would have catastrophic consequences for Canada and, on the other hand, insisting that efforts to avoid such an eventuality are virtually doomed to fail. Both Quebec and Canada would have powerful incentives to reach an agreement.

A first issue is the number of provincial legislatures that would have to approve a constitutional amendment to make Quebec's secession legal, removing Quebec as a province. Some scholars insist that the agreement of all provinces would be necessary and that consequently securing the necessary amendment would be virtually impossible (Finkelstein and Vegh 1992:8; Monahan 1995:5–8). However, a province might have great difficulty in exercising such a veto in defiance of Ottawa and all the other provinces given the interest they would have in securing a negotiated settlement with Quebec (Young 1995:249). In any event, some constitutional scholars either insist that the agreement of only seven provinces, with 50 percent of the population, would be necessary (Woerhling 1991:56–7; Brun and Tremblay 1990:236) or state that this would probably be so (Hogg 1992:126). On this basis, beyond Quebec only six other provinces would have to agree.

A second question is whether, as Monahan insists, Aboriginal peoples would need to give their formal consent to any such change. Clearly, the federal government has a fiduciary responsibility for Aboriginal peoples anywhere in Canada, but other scholars, such as Vegh and Finkelstein, conclude that this responsibility requires consultation but not necessarily consent (Vegh and Finkelstein 1992:25). And Vegh and Finkelstein only characterize as "arguable" the claim that consent is required by constitutional convention (Vegh and Finkelstein 1992:31). For his part, Young both declares unequivocally that the necessary amendments can be made without Aboriginal consent and also predicts that with sovereignty Quebec would commit itself to constitutional guarantees of Aboriginal rights that go far beyond those contained in the Canadian constitution (Young 1995:253).

A third set of issues has to do with the structures through which Canada outside Quebec would negotiate the terms of Quebec's accession to sovereignty. The Quebec government would expect to negotiate directly and exclusively with the federal government, as representative of the rest of Canada. Yet a series of concerns have been raised. First, some commentators contend that the federal government could not assume such a role since it would have no explicit mandate to do so. Moreover, the process of securing such a mandate would be exceedingly difficult: a federal election would have to be held in all parts of Canada, Quebec included; a referendum might be restricted to Canada Outside Quebec but would be extremely divisive (Monahan 1995:17). Yet under our parliamentary tradition governments are fully entitled to respond to situations that emerge without securing a specific mandate, and regularly do so. Second, it is claimed that the rest of the country would not grant the present federal government the right to negotiate on their behalf given the role that Quebeckers occupy within it, including the key functions of prime minister, minister of intergovernmental affairs, and finance minister. Yet there is nothing to prevent the Liberal government from reconstituting itself with a prime minister and other key ministers from outside Quebec, should this be politically necessary, just as it might draw Reform MP's into a "national unity" government.

A final contention is that other political actors, especially provincial governments and Aboriginal leaders, would claim for themselves the right to participate in, if not conduct, the negotiations. Gordon Gibson has recently taken this argument the furthest, claiming that with a referendum victory for sovereignty, the federal government would lose all moral authority – "If our federal gladiators lose, you don't reward failure" (Gibson 1995:8) – and would lose much of its financial authority: "Most foreign lenders" would boycott Canadian governments bonds "because the very continuity of Canada and its government would be in question" (Gibson 1995:11). As a result, "the provinces will likely become the repository of political legitimacy in ROC" (Gibson 1995:13). Clearly, this overstates the case. If a referendum victory might discredit federal leaders in the eyes of English Canadians it need not undermine attachment to the federal government as an institution. Moreover, as we have seen, the leaders could be replaced through normal parliamentary procedures. As for federal borrowing, the government clearly would have to pay a premium on its bonds. But it should still be able to find takers, as long as it is acting to ensure that the issues surrounding Quebec sovereignty will be quickly resolved and political stability will return.

The federal government could ill afford to ignore the demands of provincial and Aboriginal leaders to have some say in the negotiations, if only because of their potential role in any constitutional amendment process. This claim could be accommodated through a negotiating authority with provincial and Aboriginal representatives, as a task force established by the Ontario government has already proposed (Monahan and Covello 1992:99).

Another hurdle to a negotiated settlement has to do with the arrangements by which the Quebec government assumes responsibility for a share of the federal debt. A first issue is determining Quebec's "fair" share. The two sides are bound to start from very different positions, but with a firm commitment they should be able to settle on a compromise. A second issue has to do with the precise arrangements through which Quebec assumes its share. The Quebec government proposes to pay the federal government predetermined amounts that would cover Quebec's share of Ottawa's interest payments. The debt would remain Ottawa's legal responsibility. As Monahan points out, confronted with this new arrangement the holders of the Canadian debt might insist that Ottawa pay a risk premium (Monahan 1995:23–4). Ottawa might claim that Quebec cover the amount of the premium; Quebec might refuse. Yet, sharing the cost and settling the question would surely be preferable to facing the financial chaos of a unilateral declaration of sovereignty (Young 1995:217).

A final hurdle, perhaps the most difficult, is agreeing on the boundaries of a sovereign Quebec. In recent years considerable sentiment has developed, mainly among Canadians outside Quebec, that Quebec's boundaries need not be those it holds as a province. It is argued typically that they should define a considerably smaller area (Bercuson and Cooper 1991:139–57). Beyond a variety of historically based arguments has been the contention that communities within Quebec, especially those dominated by Aboriginal peoples, should be able to decide whether the territory they inhabit should remain part of Canada rather than becoming part of a sovereign Quebec (McNeil 1992; Turpel 1992). On the other hand, the Quebec government has been adamant that the boundaries be unaltered. Thus, to cite the draft bill: "Quebec shall retain the boundaries it has within the Canadian Confederation at the time section 1 [the declaration of sovereignty] comes into force" (Québec 1992: section 4). The leader of federalist forces in Quebec, Daniel Johnson, affirmed the same position last spring while he was still premier of the province.[1]

Clearly, if negotiations become focused upon the issue of boundaries, they will fail (Covell 1992:30; Gibson 1994:128; Young 1995: 213). Canadians are bound to be concerned about the welfare of Aboriginal peoples and linguistic minorities in Quebec; indeed, as already noted, the federal government has a fiduciary responsibility for Aboriginal peoples in Canada as presently constituted. But this concern could be met in other ways than seeking to impose an adjustment in boundaries. In particular, Quebec and Canada might enter into reciprocal accords whereby they are both bound to respect the rights of Aboriginal peoples and linguistic minorities within their respective territories (Armstrong 1992; McRoberts 1992:186).

In sum, despite the contentions of some, negotiations over the terms of Quebec's assumption of sovereignty *could* succeed, provided there is a will on both sides that they do so[2]. There is no *guarantee* that they would succeed or indeed that confronted with a referendum victory for sovereignty the federal government would enter into good faith negotiations and would have the support of the rest of the country. The shock of a referendum victory could trigger a deep emotional response among English Canadians, including anger against Quebec for "betraying" Canada and fear for the survival of Canada without Quebec. Under these conditions, some Canadians might want to deny Quebec the possibility of becoming sovereign or to ensure that it would do so under conditions that would be as detrimental to Quebec as possible. Much will depend upon the direction given by Canada's political leaders.

Beyond that, as Alan Cairns has recently argued, public opinion in Canada outside Quebec would not have been prepared to deal with a Quebec vote for sovereignty, and the implications that follow from it. Indeed no political leaders outside Quebec would have had an interest in doing so. Yet, the public would have to grant the federal government the authority to negotiate, in collaboration with provincial governments and other interests, the terms of Quebec's accession to sovereignty. And, given the Charlottetown Accord precedent, the public would have to approve these terms in a referendum. (Cairns 1995)

What can be stated with certainty is that with a clear expression of support for sovereignty in Quebec the *interest* of Canada outside Quebec would lie in entering negotiations with the clear aim of securing a smooth and reasonably expeditious transition to Quebec sovereignty.[3] (I stress that this is my personal conclusion and is not necessarily shared by the contributors to this volume.) If the negotiations were to fail, or if Canada were to refuse even to enter into them, the resulting uncertainty, if not chaos, would impose heavy economic and political costs on both Quebec and the rest of Canada. We must hope that, confronted with a victory in the upcoming referendum, government officials would provide the necessary leadership.

Yet if Canada would have an interest in the rapid resolution of the issues surrounding Quebec's accession to sovereignty, would it have an interest in entering into the joint arrangements proposed by the Quebec government, such as economic association and dual citizenship? With respect to "economic association" the Quebec government's draft bill would authorize the government to conclude with the federal government "an agreement the purpose of which is to maintain an economic association between Québec and Canada" (Québec 1994: sec. 2). So far, however, the Quebec government has proposed no more than a free-trade arrangement that would fall under the terms of the NAFTA agreement.

Such an arrangement clearly would be in the interest of the new Canada, albeit more of some parts of the country than others. Atlantic Canada would favour any measure that secured its trade links to the rest of Canada. Nelles notes that while Ontario's trade with Quebec has slipped to 5.89 percent removing Quebec's trade would still be "a big shock."[4] On the other hand, Western Canada would see little interest in protecting trade links with Quebec and would likely expect some compensation from the rest of Canada. In any event, even if Canada were to be divided over the question, the United States could be expected to tip the balance in favour Quebec's membership in NAFTA if only to stabilize the situation on its northern borders (Young 1995:112, 206). However, Lemco (1994:160) insists that the United States would defer to Canadian opposition.

Of course, an economic association could extend well beyond trade relations. So far, however, the Quebec government has made no specific proposals to that effect. In the 1979 proposal made by the Quebec government of René Lévesque, Quebec and Canada would have shared a common currency (Québec 1979:63). Partly as a result of English Canada's fierce rejection of that arrangement, this time the Quebec government is proposing no common arrangement: Quebec would simply use Canadian currency. Opinions differ, but it appears that Canada would have the capacity to prevent Quebec from doing this only through measures that would be prohibitively costly (Laidler and Robson 1991:27–9; Young 1995:46).[5] At the same time, commentators suggest that if Quebec were to continue to use Canadian currency, it would be in the interest of Canada as well as Quebec that Quebec should participate in its management (Donner and Lazar 1992; Laidler and Robson 1991, chap. 3; Young 1995:238).

On the other hand, Canada would have to decide whether to accept Quebec's proposal in another area: that Quebec citizens should be allowed to hold Canadian citizenship as well, should they wish. In the bitterness that would accompany Quebec's departure many Canadians may see this an intolerable concession. Yet, they might respond to the appeals of Quebeckers who are opposed to sovereignty and do not wish to lose their Canadian citizenship.

In the last analysis, I would argue, Canada's interest would lie in a rapid agreement on the terms of Quebec accession to sovereignty and in the pursuit of amicable relations which would allow the free movement of goods and people across the borders. The obstacles to attaining these objectives are very substantial. But with determination on both sides, and a bit of luck, they could be reached. The new Canada would still be faced with a second challenge: securing its internal cohesion.

Linking the Parts Together

First and most obviously, with Quebec no longer a province, Canada would be divided into two sections. In part, the challenge would be psychic. As Abraham Rotstein noted a good number of years ago, Canadians tend to comprehend their country first and foremost in geographical terms: an enormous (and typically pink) mass on the map (Rostein 1978; Whitaker 1992:75). Thus while they may have been prepared to accept American invasions of Canada's economic and cultural independence, Canadians have been vigilant when it comes to threats to Canada's territorial integrity. On the basis of this "mappism," a gaping "hole" in the Canadian territory could significantly diminish Canada's sense of nationhood.

Beyond that, the separation of Atlantic Canada from the rest of the country could constitute a major practical problem, impeding the movement of goods and people between Canada's two parts. This problem could be eased in two ways, with radically different implications for relations between Canada and its new neighbour. One approach would be to eliminate the problem through some type of "land bridge" through Quebec. Indeed, Ian Ross Robertson has proposed that the Atlantic Canada be linked to the rest of Canada by a corridor "in the range of thirty to fifty kilometres," perhaps along the Quebec-U.S. border (Robertson 1991:170).

Yet, as Finbow noted in his essay above: "It is unlikely that his [Robertson's] proposal ... could be realized without a high degree of conflict, possibly violent, which the majority of Canadians would likely dismiss as not worthwhile."

The other approach would be to secure free movement of people and goods across the Canada-Quebec borders (Covell 1992:31). This, of course, could be accomplished through the Quebec government's proposal that Quebec and Canada be linked within the NAFTA free trade agreement, combined with a separate agreement allowing free mobility for non-work purposes. At the same time, a joint immigration policy would probably also be required.

A second danger to the internal cohesion of the new Canada lies in the exacerbation of regional rivalries and suspicions. The mere fact of Quebec's departure might lead some Western Canadians to take a fresh look at their region's options. Quebec's example might seem quite compelling to Western Canadians, especially in Alberta and British Columbia, who are convinced that remaining part of Canada would carry a heavy price thanks to Central Canadian political and economic dominance (Leslie 1991). To be sure, Quebec's departure would lower the burden of fiscal transfers through equalization and other programs. But in any reasonably hard-nosed calculation of flows of fiscal federalism, B.C. and Alberta would still be losers.

Moreover, resentment of this dominance would be exacerbated by the fact that with Quebec's departure Ontario would alone constitute half Canada's population. Yet with such heightened demographic weight, Ontarians may see even less logic in schemes, such as a "Triple E Senate," to equalize regional representation in central political institutions.

Nonetheless, even the residents of B.C. and Alberta would not be initially disposed to follow Quebec's example and actually secede from Canada (Covell 1992:14, 26). Any serious consideration of secession would be inhibited not only by a continuing attachment to Canada but by the inevitable economic costs of the transition to full sovereignty. While these potential costs might by contained by opting not for full sovereignty but incorporation in the United States, under normal conditions the American system would have much less to offer such provinces than does Canada. Their political weight within American political institutions would be infinitesimal: for instance, each would enjoy only two senators within a Senate of over 100 members. Moreover, as a state Alberta would no longer control revenue from energy reserves (Whitaker, 1992:74). This presumes, of course, that American statehood would in fact be available – which, in the case of Atlantic Canada and its chronic economic dependence, would in all likelihood not be the case.

Thus, even provinces such as B.C. and Alberta would need compelling reasons to formally secede from the new Canada. However, such a reason could be provided by the economic and political instability that would arise if, for whatever reason, Quebec and the federal government fail to arrive at a settlement on Quebec's accession to sovereignty. Under such conditions the advantages of remaining part of Canada would quickly erode.

The motivation to secede might even be provided by a refusal of Ontario to consider a reorganization of federal institutions to afford better regional representation. Since any such measure would be explicitly designed to attenuate the power that Ontario would be able to wield on the basis of representation by population, the abiding commitment to Canada that Nelles ascribes to Ontarians would be sorely tested. Perhaps the solution would lie in preserving representation by population in the House of Commons but reforming the Senate to equalize territorial representation and introducing congressional modes of functioning to both the House and the Senate (Gibbins 1993:267). Even if Western Canadian secession should not be a real possibility, Canada Without Quebec could ill afford to allow its national cohesion to be undermined by regional grievances, given the challenges it would face on other fronts.

Without the presence of Quebec as a province, this Canada outside Quebec would be quite different from the one that presently exists. In particular, the absence of Quebec would have a profound effect on its internal political complexion.

First, the structure of Canada's national party system could be markedly affected by Quebec's departure. The Liberals would lose what historically has been their strongest regional base. And without the need to win seats in Quebec, the Reform Party would be in a much stronger position. Indeed it could not only claim to be a "national" party but could challenge the capacity of the old-line parties to understand the "new" Canada, especially if the break-up of Canada had been a highly acrimonious one. With Reform occupying the government, or credibly threatening to do so, the discourse of Canadian politics would undergo even more of a rightward shift than it is at present. Of course, without the need to have a Quebec base, the NDP would also be better placed to claim national leadership. But it would first need to overcome its current unpopularity in Canada outside Quebec to be able to capitalize on this.

Second, the structure of Canada's political institutions would also be affected. We have just noted how Parliament would have to be modified to afford better regional representation. In his piece, Thomas Courchene argued that without Quebec's presence Canada would show less tolerance of legal and institutional pluralism, multiculturalism, and official bilingualism, and would become more oriented to individual rights and an individualist conception of capitalism.

Third, a variety of commentators both in this volume and elsewhere predict that Quebec's departure would lead to a centralization of Canadian federalism, presuming mechanisms are adopted for better regional representation in federal institutions (Gibbins 1993:270; McRoberts 1992:54; Young 1995:chap. 7). Without Quebec, Canada would be more culturally homogeneous. Many Canadians might be more comfortable with national institutions once they have lost the trappings of linguistic dualism. Without Quebec vigilantly protecting provincial jurisdictions on the basis of principle, Ottawa would be able to respond to public support outside Quebec for such measures as national standards in education or environmental regulation. The sense of crisis surrounding Quebec secession and the emergence of a new Canada could actually strengthen the hand of federal leaders.

As we have already seen, Gordon Gibson does not share this analysis. Starting from the premise that a referendum victory for sovereignty would deprive Ottawa of all moral and financial authority, he argues that already strong decentralizing pressures in such "have" provinces as British Columbia and Alberta would hold sway and force a radical decentralization of the new Canada (Gibson 1994 1995). Yet this underestimates the likelihood that the shock of Quebec sovereignty would induce a rallying around Ottawa and that terms of regional accommodation might be found in national institutions.

Finally, as Nelles notes, without Quebec even the location of the national capital might change. The westward shift of the geographical centre of Canada would produce pressure to move the capital in the same direction.

Still, as I have argued, the prospects of survival for Canada without Quebec, even in this modified form, would be heavily dependent upon meeting two fundamental challenges. The first is to resolve in a fairly rapid manner the issues surrounding Quebec's transition to sovereignty while at the same time establishing the framework for amicable relations between Canada and sovereign Quebec. This is a tall order: the issues to be negotiated are complex and difficult, the very process of negotiations poses substantial institutional difficulties, and as Rotstein reminds us the emotional climate in which all this must be done would be problematic, to say the least. The second challenge is to find the bases for an internal cohesion of the new Canada both by countering the new physical separation of Atlantic Canada from the rest of Canada and by accommodating apprehension both in the West and the East over Ontario's new demographic weight. Moreover, as we shall see below, the national government of the new Canada would not have the fiscal capacity to maintain the social programs and other measures that have been so important to cementing national cohesion.

These two challenges are closely interrelated. If a new relationship with Quebec, based on sovereignty, cannot be secured both rapidly and in a way that is generally acceptable to Canadians, then the authority of the federal government and the appeal of Canada itself might decline. Regions such as Alberta and b.c. might start considering other options. Conversely, failure to secure Canada's internal cohesion could have ramifications for Canada's relations with a sovereign Quebec. For instance, without confidence that their concerns will be satisfactorily represented in central institutions, Western Canadians might be very hostile to any broadening of the terms of Canada's economic collaboration with Quebec. They would be quick to see measures to do this as merely attempts on Ontario's part to resurrect the old Central Canada.

CANADA WITH OR WITHOUT QUEBEC

The future of Canada Outside Quebec will be determined not just by whether Quebec secedes, and, if it does, whether the above two challenges can be met. This book has another equally important lesson to offer: the future of Canada outside Quebec will be even more fundamentally shaped by forces that will operate whether or not Quebec remains part of Canada.

As Melville McMillan observes, once the transition to Quebec sovereignty has taken place, "the economic cost of Quebec separation to the rest of Canada would probably be moderate." However, he warns: "With or without Quebec, core economic problems remain."

The same conclusion applies to each of the other areas we have examined. In each instance, Canada outside Quebec faces challenges which are largely the same with or without Quebec. Moreover, in most cases these challenges will present themselves differently in Quebec and in Canada outside Quebec. Thus, even if Quebec stays, they will require responses that come from within Canada outside Quebec. Even if Quebec remains a province, Canadians may need to think increasingly in terms of a Canada "beyond Quebec".

Sustaining A Vigorous Cultural Life

We have seen how over recent decades there has been a dramatic growth in all forms of cultural activity in Canada outside Quebec. Within this activity, the specific contribution of Native arts has yet to be properly recognized – as Alfred Young Man demonstrated. The cultural production of Canada's francophone minorities also must be taken into account. Nonetheless, the fact remains that most cultural achievement in Canada outside Quebec has occurred in the English language (or, in the case of the visual arts, has been produced by anglophones). What is the future of this activity? The answer will be largely the same whether Quebec remains a province or not.

First, and most obviously, anglophone cultural production is largely based in Canada outside Quebec despite Anglophone Montreal's rich cultural milieu. The relative balance of English speakers guarantees that: 96 percent of Canada's anglophones live outside Quebec.[6] By the same token, English-language television broadcasting is centred in Toronto where both "national" networks, CBC and CTV, have their primary facilities. Feature film production is centred in Toronto and Vancouver. With some important exceptions (including the publisher of this book!) English-language book publishing is also based outside Quebec, and is centralized in Toronto.

Second, the contributors have noted how these structures function largely without reference to Quebec. This in part reflects market pressures. Ted Magder showed how independent English-language television production is primarily geared not to the Canadian market but to the United States. Even if English were its predominant language, Quebec would hardly be significant in those calculations. But attitudes must also be involved. Mary Jane Miller showed how even the CBC, which is primarily geared to Canadians and indeed has a mandate to strengthen unity among them, has largely functioned without reference to francophone Quebec and its Radio-Canada counterpart. The CBC has produced few programs on its own that deal with Quebec and has made few Radio-Canada productions available to Canadians elsewhere. In the case of the publishing industry, cultural production does seem to transfer more readily. Several leading publishers have produced French translations of Quebec works. (Of course, some Quebec anglophones have published with Toronto publishers.) But this remains very secondary in their operations.

Finally, whereas anglophone cultural activity is heavily dependent upon state support, the Quebec provincial government does not figure significantly. Provincial governments in general are secondary actors. The primary support comes from the federal government; this has served to wed the anglophone cultural community to strong defense of the role of the federal government.

To this extent, the presence or absence of Quebec as a province is not central to the future of cultural activity in Canada outside Quebec. Quebec's departure could have some indirect effects. For instance, if the reconfiguration of Canada's political landscape meant new prominence for the Reform Party, the federal government's commitment to support cultural production might be weakened.

However, the basic challenges remain the same and will find their answers within Canada outside Quebec. As Magder noted, the most compelling rationales for state support of film production lie in artistic rather than political considerations. Canadian film could no better assure the unity of a Canada without Quebec than it has the unity of one with Quebec. And the commercial viability of English-language Canadian television production will be largely determined in the American market; Quebec's status has no bearing on that. Mary Jane Miller argued that the future of English-language broadcasting is dependent upon both political will and the fostering of a supportive environment – with or without Quebec. Lorimer claimed that book publishing has a promising future provided that public entrepreneurship finds the appropriate mechanisms of support. The departure of Quebec would not materially affect the likelihood of this occurring. Indeed, "through a greater singularity of perspective, Canada might gain in resolve and effectiveness of policy."

Beyond such considerations as public commitment and commercial viability, the future of cultural production in Canada Outside Quebec will also be closely shaped by the intense pressure upon the federal government to reduce spending in all areas, culture included. Driven by both neo-liberal attacks on state intervention and concern with the level of Ottawa's debt, these pressures promise to remain intense even if Quebec stays.

As for the future of native arts in Canada, Alfred Young Man has amply demonstrated how the primary determinant lies with the attitudes of Canada's cultural establishment. Within that establishment he drew no differentiation between anglophones and francophones or Quebec and the rest of the country. According to his analysis, the obstacle to recognition of native art lies with the attitudes of white society, or, more precisely, its cultural elites. Thus the obstacle will remain whether Quebec is a part of Canada or not.

Developing a Coherent Social Identity

We have seen how there are continuing controversies regarding the nature and relative status of the different elements that compose the society represented by Canada outside Quebec. In each case these debates have taken a particular form in Canada outside Quebec that will persist even if Quebec should remain a province.

In her essay Janine Brodie traced the historical processes through which the definition of women's identity has undergone fundamental changes and continues to do so. She showed how these changes were rooted in the relationship between the women's movement and the state. At the turn of the century, the state still relegated women to the private sphere; the first women's movement, rooted in maternal feminism, defined itself in these terms. In the post-World War II period women were able, through the construction of the Keynesian welfare state, to secure a wide range of measures based upon the definition of women as mothers. Now, as the state is being rolled back, under the twin pressures of globalization and neo-conservatism, women are losing any specific claim to state action and their movement is being marginalized.

At the same time, Brodie showed how throughout this historical process of shifting relations with the state and redefinition of women's identities, anglophone women have acted quite separately from their Quebec francophone counterparts. Whereas the former focused upon the *federal* state, the latter have geared their struggles to the Quebec provincial state. Indeed, during the Meech Lake debate anglophone women were led by their historical relationship with the federal state, and solicitude for its powers, to oppose measures that threatened to shift power or status to the Quebec state. In the process, anglophone and francophone women became opponents. As anglophone women continue to resist the neo-liberal redefinition of their relationship to the state and their place in society, their struggle will remain separate from that of Quebec women: focused upon the federal arena and based in Canada outside Quebec.

The leaders of Aboriginal peoples have tended to draw a distinction between Quebec and the rest of Canada, singling out Quebec for particular concern. This sentiment has been shared by much of non-Aboriginal public opinion outside Quebec. Yet Frances Abele demonstrated that within the sense of community that dominates Canada outside Quebec, namely that shared by most English Canadians, there is as yet little role for Aboriginal peoples. The notions of language and culture, the sense of territory and space, and the understanding of history shared by English Canadians all exclude the perspectives held by Aboriginal peoples. In effect, for Canadians outside Quebec Aboriginal peoples constitute "the ultimate internal Other." With or without Quebec, the challenge remains the same.

Lanphier and Richmond demonstrated how at both the federal level and among the provinces outside Quebec multiculturalism has become the basic framework within which the state seeks to address the many dimensions of ethnicity among its residents: language, culture, race, and ancestry. They pointed out that these policies have been only partially effective in resolving the tensions linked to ethnic diversity, and even this effectiveness has varied greatly from jurisdiction to jurisdiction. Moreover, the challenge of ethnic diversity to Canadian unity is now being reinforced by globalization, which is serving to create new ethnic networks that transcend territory. Thus, Lanphier and Richmond wondered whether Canada outside Quebec will be overcome by fragmentation.

The authors also noted how, from its initial promulgation by the Trudeau government in 1971, the framework of multiculturalism has been rejected by political and intellectual leaders in Quebec. Not only have Quebec governments resisted the presumption that Quebec's place in Canada can be comprehended within the terms of multiculturalism, but in articulating policies to deal with ethnic diversity within Quebec itself they have sought, with varying success, to develop an alternative to multiculturalism. Thus whether Quebec stays or leaves the debate over multiculturalism will be a debate among Canadians outside Quebec and will find its resolution there.

Phyllis LeBlanc's examination of the francophone minorities under-lined the extent to which the condition of francophones and their lan-guage is fundamentally different outside and inside Quebec. In Quebec, francophones constitute the overwhelming majority at 82 percent. Outside Quebec their presence ranges from 34.5 percent in New Brunswick to 1.8 percent in B.C., and 0.6 percent in Newfound-land, to use Leblanc's figures based on mother tongue. (In provinces other than New Brunswick, the percentages actually using French as their primary language at home are substantially lower.)

To a much greater extent than the francophones of Quebec, the francophone minorities of the rest of Canada must face economic, so-cial, and even political pressures to assimilate that can be overwhelm-ing. Yet recent decades have seen a profound fragmentation of Canada's francophone population. With the rise of Quebec national-ism, francophones outside Quebec have lost the overarching institu-tions and support of a French-Canadian identity. Despite their new provincially based identities, whether Franco-Ontarian, Acadian, or Franco-saskois, as minorities they cannot rely upon their provincial governments to protect and promote their cultural and social well-be-ing in the way Quebec's francophones do. Instead they must rely heavily upon the federal government. In short, in Canada outside Que-bec both the condition of francophones and the strategies to improve it are fundamentally different than in Quebec. Quebec's departure would vastly heighten the challenge the francophone minorities must face but its continued presence in Canada cannot eliminate that basic fact.

Continental Integration and a Diminished National State

As for the Canadian political economy, Canadians face severely dimin-ished prospects whether Quebec leaves or stays. Not only has the Cana-dian economy ceased to function as a "national" economy but the capacities of the Canadian state have been drastically reduced. The structual basis of Canadian cohesion has been severely weakend.

As Stephen Clarkson demonstrated, the FTA and NAFTA have served to integrate Canada within a continental economy while at the same time greatly constraining the ability of Ottawa and the provinces to intervene in the market or to maintain a system of social programs. In-deed that was the primary objective of the Canadian corporate promoters of continental integration. As a result, if Quebec were to separate Canada would have difficulty functioning not just because of the consequences of Quebec's departure, but more fundamentally be-cause of what has already happened. Even if Quebec stays, the Canadian state will be unable to maintain the distinctive social policy and state-led economic development to which Canadians have been accustomed.

By the same token, as Marjorie Griffin Cohen argued, this decline in the capacity of the Canadian state is part of the general processes of globalization which have shifted power from states to international capital. As a result, the state has become increasingly irrelevant as a site for social and economic struggle.

Melville McMillan may have offered a more sanguine view about the effects of continentalization and globalization on Canada, and thus its prospects without Quebec, but he too sees a decline in the capacity of federal state. He assigned responsibility primarily to domestic factors, namely the heavy indebtedness of the federal government. This constitutes a fundamental threat to Canada's cohesion since it has undermined the capacity of the federal state to maintain the range of social programs that it developed in the post-war years.

In short, whether Quebec leaves or stays, Canadians will have to learn to live with a seriously diminished state and to function within a continental economy. Beyond that, Canadians outside Quebec tend to view these issues in terms that are not shared by most Quebeckers. These developments may equally affect Quebec and the rest of Canada, but they clearly carry different meanings to the populations of these two parts of the country.

First, many Canadians outside Quebec see the decline in the capacity of the federal state in terms of a diminished ability to maintain national standards. On this basis, it is less able to function as their "national" state. Yet in Quebec a decline in Ottawa's capacity to impose national standards tends to be welcomed, precisely because for most of Quebec's population the federal state is not their "national" state. To be sure, some Canadians outside Quebec would also welcome a decline in Ottawa's capacity to impose national standards. But this springs from a desire for decentralization or general rollback of the state, rather than any sense that Ottawa is not their national government.

Second, continental integration is seen in quite different terms in Quebec and in the rest of Canada. This was clearly revealed by the 1988 federal election, in which the Canada-u.s. free trade agreement was the central issue. The difference in the relative success of the parties in the two parts of the country reflected quite closely the substantial opposition to the FTA among Canadians outside Quebec and general support for the FTA in Quebec. Also striking was the degree to which social forces in Quebec that were nominally opposed to the FTA were relatively passive, whereas the rest of Canada saw the emergence of the Pro-Canada Network, a broad-based coalition which Clarkson characterizes as "primarily an English-Canadian phenomenon" which heralded "a new post-national politics outside Quebec."

Adapting Canadian Political Institutions

Finally, whether or not Quebec remains a province, Canadians in the rest of the country will continue to be divided over the shape of the country's political institutions. Moreover, this debate will continue to be structured in terms that are distinctive to Canada outside Quebec, even if Quebec should remain a province.

First, Canadians outside Quebec are divided over whether the federal system should be decentralized, unlike Quebec francophones who broadly support enhanced power for the Quebec government as their "national" government (Winsor 1994). Clearly, as Marjorie Griffin Cohen noted, significant forces outside Quebec are calling for radical devolution to the provinces. In provinces such as British Columbia or Alberta provincial leaders have openly embraced this goal. This is the basic message of Gordon Gibson's *Plan B*, published by the Vancouver-based Fraser Institute (Gibson 1994). Beyond regions that have historically resented Ottawa's power, the cause of decentralization has an appeal to neo-liberals who, critical of state intervention in general, see decentralization as a way of stripping down Ottawa's "excesses." The hand of advocates of decentralization is, of course, greatly strengthened by the present fiscal crisis of the federal government.

We have already seen that in the rest of Canada there remain strong defenders of the federal role. Ontario can be expected to support an important federal role, as Nelles suggests, just as will economically vulnerable provinces, especially in Atlantic Canada. Beyond that we have identified a variety of groups that have a strong interest in defending the federal role: the women's movement, the cultural communities, francophone minorities, etc. Indeed within Canada outside Quebec there could well be support for an enhancement of the federal role to establish national standards in areas such as education. Similar forces are difficult to find in Quebec.

Second, Canadians outside Quebec will continue to be confronted with a need to reform central institutions in Ottawa so as to better represent regional interests. As Gibbins argued, many of the jurisdictions that are crucial to Western Canadians, such as tariff policy, must necessarily remain in federal hands. Thus any revision of Canadian federalism must include reform of central institutions, whether or not Quebec remains a province. Unlike the Ontario government, which in the name of national unity reluctantly accepted the notion of a "Triple E" Senate during the Charlottetown negotiations (McRoberts 1993:251), the Quebec government can be expected to fiercely resist such a measure whatever party is in power.

Third, as Morton's piece demonstrated, Canadians outside Quebec will continue to be divided over how the Charter of Rights and Freedoms should be interpreted and applied, with some arguing that the general directions followed to date should be radically changed. Here too the debate is particular to Canada outside Quebec. Critics of the Charter in francophone Quebec come from quite a different angle: rather then calling for a particular approach to interpreting the Charter, they claim that Quebec's specificity requires a relaxation of the very application of the Charter.

If Quebec should remain a province within Canada, its presence could affect the relative balance of power between these competing positions. For instance, the need to accommodate Quebec is a highly effective argument for decentralization of powers (Gibson 1994).

However, Quebec's presence does not guarantee that the forces for decentralization will prevail. If support for a major federal role should persist among Canadians outside Quebec, and continue to have little echo in Quebec, then Canadian federalism may yet need to be transformed to a structure that explicitly recognizes this difference in conceptions of Ottawa's role. Two possibilities have been widely discussed: asymmetrical federalism and confederalism. Each has its advantages and disadvantages (McRoberts 1991; Resnick 1994; Webber 1994; Whitaker 1993). Given their potential importance in maintaining the cohesion of Canada outside Quebec, we need to examine these options briefly.

Asymmetry and Confederalism

Under asymmetrical federalism some of the federal government's functions would, in the case of Quebec, be exercised by the Quebec government. The federal government would continue to discharge them in the rest of the country. Thus asymmetrical federalism does not involve the creation of new institutions. The respective needs of Quebec and Canada outside Quebec would be met simply by respecifying the role of the federal government. Quebec's government would be able to exercise the additional powers its residents desire, while Canadians outside Quebec could continue to look to the federal government to discharge its established functions. Indeed, under this formula Ottawa might be assigned additional functions, such as responsibility for post-secondary education, which it would exercise in all parts of Canada but Quebec. The best-known instance of such asymmetry is the Canada Pension Plan. Using provisions in the act which created the plan, Quebec established its own Quebec Pension Plan.

Yet the institutional simplicity of asymmetry is also the root of its most persistent criticism: what is to be the status of MP's from Quebec when Parliament debates measures that establish or modify programs that do not apply to Quebec? Are they to be allowed to vote on such bills? By the same token, could MP's from Quebec assume cabinet portfolios which entail responsibility for programs that do not apply to Quebec? In point of fact, Quebec MP's have voted on such bills, as with the legislation to establish the Canada Pension Plan. Moreover, two Quebec MP's, Monique Bégin and Marc Lalonde, have even assumed responsibility, as minister of health and welfare, for administration of the Canada Pension Plan even though it does not apply in Quebec. Some scholars contend that under certain conditions it is perfectly appropriate for Quebec's representatives to vote on such measures (Webber 1994:281–3). The majority view seems to be that they should not. This prospect does raise an interesting possibility, however. If MP's from Quebec are precluded from voting on a measure then Central Canadian dominance would be broken; Atlantic and Western Canada would secure the enhanced representation that they have been seeking (Laxer 1992).

Another common criticism of such asymmetry is that it might appear to be offering a "special status" to Quebec but nothing to the rest of the country. In point of fact, if Quebec MP's are precluded from voting, such asymmetry would give Canada outside Quebec total control over Parliament for certain purposes. In any event, the terms of asymmetry might be defined in a way that makes it available to all provinces but with conditions that would prevent provincial politicians from using it frivolously: a two-third's majority in a provincial legislature or approval in a popular referendum.

Under confederalism Quebec and Canada outside Quebec each would have governments with identical sets of powers. In addition, a new government would exercise a limited number of powers over Quebec and Canada outside Quebec. In effect, most of the powers that the federal government presently holds would pass to the separate governments of Quebec and Canada outside Quebec; the remaining ones would go the new common government.

Such a scheme would avoid the institutional problem associated with asymmetry: all members of the common parliament would vote on the limited range of matters before it. Indeed, if asymmetry were applied extensively the difficulties surrounding the status of Quebec MP's might be such that confederalism would be the only viable option (Resnick 1994: 84). On the other hand, confederalism would bear an institutional problem of its own: it would require the creation of an additional level of government. Thus, Canadians outside Quebec would need to contend with governments (beyond their municipal government: a provincial government, a federal government of Canada Outside Quebec,. and a confederal government.

Yet, serious as the difficulties of each of these schemes may be, they may well be preferable to Canada Outside Quebec than the radical decentralization that might be needed to meet Quebec's demands should it remain within Canada. They may also be highly preferable to the many difficulties that would be raised by Quebec sovereignty. They would be high on the agenda of the Estates General proposed by Philip Resnick, whether it be based on English Canada or Canada Outside Quebec.

CONCLUSION

Whatever happens in the upcoming referendum, Canadians outside Quebec will need to think increasingly in terms of their part of the country. If Quebec opts for sovereignty, Canadians will be forced to deal with the simultaneous challenges of pursuing their common interests in building a new relationship with Quebec and securing cohesion within the new abbreviated Canada.

The challenges that will face Canada outside Quebec even if Quebec stays will also determine the cohesion of the new Canada. In particular, they will be looking to a federal state whose capacities have been greatly weakened through the twin processes of continental integration and indebtedness.

In the last analysis, however frustrated Canadians outside Quebec may be with "the Quebec question," few of them would welcome Quebec's departure. Nor, for that matter, do the contributions to this book reflect enthusiasm for the prospect of a Canada without Quebec. Many contributors raise profound concerns about the notion. Yet it is also clear that confronted with Quebec's loss, most Canadians would want to maintain what remains of their country. Their resolve would be severely tested.

Alternatively, if Quebec should opt to remain within Canada, Canadians outside Quebec will still be confronted with a series of challenges that are specific to them or at least which they interpret in different terms than do Quebeckers: conserving Ottawa's role as the "national" government, maintaining anglophone cultural activity, reworking the terms of multiculturalism, assuring the future of francophone minorities, making the federal government more responsive to the concerns of Western and Atlantic Canada, debating the terms on which the Charter of Rights and Freedoms should be applied, and so on. Thus, even then, this book's "stock taking" of Canada outside Quebec should provide needed direction for a good many years to come.

NOTES

1 Johnson declared that "the position of all those elected to the Quebec legislature, the premier, the government and obviously the opposition is to defend everywhere and forever the territorial integrity of Quebec" (Montreal *Gazette* 19 May 1994, as quoted in Young 1995:214).

2 All these issues are discussed in much greater detail in Young 1995).

3 A similar position is taken by Monahan and Covello in their 1992 proposals to the Ontario government, based on the York University Constitutional Reform Project:

In the event that a majority of Québécois clearly and freely indicates that they no longer wish to remain a part of Canada, it would be folly on the part of the rest of the country to attempt to suppress or deny that desire … We recommend that, in the event that a majority of Québecers clearly and democratically express a desire to leave Canada, the rest of the country undertake negotiations with Québec in good faith … designed to arrive at an agreement which permits Québec to leave on terms that are just and reasonable. (Monahan and Covello 1992:98–9)

4 To quote Monahan and Covello:

The creation of a free-trade zone between Canada and Québec would be particularly important from the perspective of Ontario. Québec is by far the largest recipient of Ontario's exports to other parts of Canada, Ontario has the most at stake in ensuring the existing trade patterns are disrupted to the smallest extent possible. In fact, we believe that the arrangement of a free-trade zone between Québec and the rest of Canada is absolutely essential. (Monahan and Covello 1992:112)

5 Grady presents a more positive view of Canada's capacity to prevent Quebec's unilateral use of its currency (Grady 1991:147–48).

6 Calculated from *Census, 1991* data presented in Canada, Commissioner of Official Languages 1993:17. Based on home language.

BIBLIOGRAPHY

Armstrong, Pat, et al. 1992. "Three Nations in a Delicate Balance" *Toronto Star* 4 February, A17.

Banting, Keith. 1992. "If Quebec Separates: Restructuring North America." In *The Collapse of Canada?*, ed. R. Kent Weaver, 159–78. Washington, DC: Brookings Institution.

Bercuson, David J., and Barry Cooper. 1991. *Deconfederation: Canada Without Quebec.* Toronto: Key Porter.

Brun, H., and G. Tremblay. 1990. *Droit constitutionnel*, 2ᵉ éd. Cowansville: Editions Yvon Blais.

Cairns, Alan C. 1995. "Suppose the "Yes" Side Wins: Are We Ready?" unpublished paper.

Canada, Commissioner of Official Languages. 1993. *Annual Report, 1992*. Ottawa: Supplies and Services.

Chrétien, Jean. 1985. *Straight From the Heart*. Toronto: McClelland & Stewart-Bantam.

Covell, Maureen. 1992. *Thinking About the Rest of Canada: Options for Canada Without Quebec*. Study No. 6. North York, Ont: York University Centre for Public Law and Public Policy.

Coyne, Andrew. 1995. "It's no 'narrow' legalism to ask if Quebeckers want a law-based state." *Globe and Mail*, 23 January, A15.

Donner, Arthur, and Fred Lazar. 1992. "The Case for a Single Currency and a Reformed Central Bank." In *Negotiating With a Sovereign Quebec*, ed. Daniel Drache and Roberto Perin, 127–50. Toronto: Lorimer.

Finkelstein, Neil, and George Vegh. 1992. *The Separation of Québec and the Constitution of Canada*. Study No. 2. North York, Ont: York University Centre for Public Law and Public Policy.

Gibbins, Roger. 1993. "Speculations on a Canada Without Quebec." In *The Charlottetown Accord, the Referendum, and the Future of Canada*, ed. Kenneth McRoberts and Patrick J. Monahan, 264–73. Toronto: University of Toronto Press.

Gibson, Gordon. 1994. *Plan B: The Future of the Rest of Canada* Vancouver: Fraser Institute.

– 1995. "In Cold or Hot Blood? A Response to the C.D. Howe Forecast of the Post-referendum World." *Fraser Forum* [Fraser Institute] (February): 5–20.

Grady, Patrick. 1991. *The Economic Consequences of Quebec Sovereignty.* Vancouver: Fraser Institute.

Hogg, Peter. 1992. *Constitutional Law of Canada*, 3rd ed. Scarborough, Ont: Carswell.

Laxer, Gordon. 1992. "Distinct Status for Quebec: A Benefit to English Canada." *Constitutional Forum constitutionnel*, vol. 3 no. 3 (Winter 1992), 57–61.

Lemco, Jonathan. 1994. *The Quebec Sovereignty Movement and its Implications for Canada and the United States*. Toronto: University of Toronto Press.

Leslie, Peter. 1991. "Options for the Future of Canada: The Good, the Bad and the Fantastic." In *Options for a New Canada*, ed. Ronald L. Watts and Douglas M. Brown, 123–40. Toronto: University of Toronto Press.

Mackie, Richard. 1995a. "Quebeckers Cling to Views, Poll Finds." *Globe and Mail,* 27 January, A4.

– 1995b. "Tax Hike Feared in Separate Quebec" *Globe and Mail,* 28 January, A4.

McNeil, Kent. 1992. "Aboriginal Nations and Quebec's Boundaries: Canada Couldn't Give What It Didn't Have." In *Negotiating with a Sovereign Quebec*, ed. Daniel Drache and Roberto Perin, 107–23. Toronto: Lorimer.

McRoberts, Kenneth 1991. *English Canada and Quebec: Avoiding the Issue*. Sixth Annual Robarts Lecture. North York, Ont: Robarts Centre for Canadian Studies, York University.

– 1992. "Protecting the Rights of Linguistic Minorities." In *Negotiating with a Sovereign Quebec*, ed. Daniel Drache and Roberto Perin, 107–23. Toronto: Lorimer.

– 1993. "Disagreeing on Fundamentals: English Canada and Quebec." In *The Charlottetown Accord, the Referendum, and the Future of Canada*, ed. Kenneth McRoberts and Patrick J. Monahan, 249–63. Toronto: University of Toronto Press.

Monahan, Patrick, and Lynda Covello. 1992. *An Agenda for Constitutional Reform.* North York, Ont: York University Centre for Public Law and Public Policy.

Monahan, Patrick. 1995. *Cooler Heads Shall Prevail: Assessing the Costs and Consequences of Quebec Separation*, No. 65. Toronto: C.D. Howe Institute.

O'Neill, Pierre. 1995. "Près de la moitié (44%) des Québécois la trouvent confuse." *Le Devoir*, 26 January A1.

Québec, National Assembly. 1994. *Draft Bill: An Act Respecting the Sovereignty of Québec.* Québec: Québec Official Publisher.

Québec. 1979. *La nouvelle entente Québec-Canada.* Québec: Editeur officiel du Québec.

Resnick, Philip. 1994. "Toward a Multinational Federalism: Asymmetrical and Confederal Alternatives." In *Seeking a New Canadian Partnership*, ed. Leslie Seidle, 71–90. Montreal: Institute for Research on Public Policy.

Robertson, Ian Ross. 1991. "The Atlantic Provinces and the Territorial Question." In *"English Canada" Speaks Out*, ed. J.L. Granatstein and Kenneth McNaught, 162–71. Toronto: Doubleday.

Rotstein, Abraham. 1978. "Is There an English-Canadian Nationalism?" *Journal of Canadian Studies* no.13:109–18.

Turpel, Mary Ellen. 1992. "Does the Road to Québec Sovereignty Run through Aboriginal Territory?" In *Negotiating with a Sovereign Quebec*, ed. Daniel Drache and Roberto Perin, 93–106. Toronto: Lorimer.

Webber, Jeremy. 1994. *Reimagining Canada: Language, Culture and Community and the Canadian Constitution.* Montreal and Kingston: McGill-Queen's University Press.

Wells, Paul, and Philip Authier. 1994. "Sovereignty illegal Rock says. But Justice minister calls decision of voters more important." Montreal *Gazette*, 16 December A1.

Williams, Sharon. 1992. *International Legal Effects of Secession by Quebec.* Study No. 3. North York, Ont: York University Centre for Public Law and Public Policy.

Whitaker, Reg. 1992. "Life after Separation." In *Negotiating with a Sovereign Quebec*, ed. Daniel Drache and Roberto Perin, 71–81. Toronto: Lorimer.

– 1995. "Quebec's Right to National Self-Determination, the Aboriginal Right to Self-Government: Conflict and Reconciliation?" In *Is Quebec Nationalism Justified?* ed. Joseph Carens. Montreal and Kingston: McGill-Queen's University Press.

Winsor, Hugh. 1994. "Provincial Role More Important to Quebeckers." *Globe and Mail*, 20 May, A2.

Woehrling, José. 1991. "Les aspects juridiques de la redéfinition du statut politique et constitutionnel du Québec." In *Elements d'analyse institutionnelle, juridique et démolinguistique pertinents à la révision du statut politique et constitutionnel du Québec*, 1–110. Document de travail no. 2. Québec: Commission sur l'avenir politique et constitutionnel du Québec.

Young, Robert A. 1995. *The Secession of Quebec and the Future of Canada*. Montreal and Kingston: McGill-Queen's University Press.

Contributors

ABELE, FRANCES. Associate professor of public administration, Carleton University. Publications include *Gathering Strength, The Politics of Competiveness: How Ottawa Spends, 1991-92* (ed.), and *The Politics of Fragmentation, 1990-91* (ed.).

BRODIE, JANINE. Professor of political science and past holder of Robarts Chair in Canadian Studies, York University. Publications include *The Political Economy of Regionalism, The Politics of Abortion* (co-author), *Politics on the Margins: Restructuring and the Canadian Women's Movement,* and *Women and Politics in Canada.*

CLARKSON, STEPHEN. Professor of political economy, University of Toronto. Publications include *Canada and the Reagan Challenge: Crisis and Response* and *Trudeau and Our Times,* vol. 1: *The Magnificant Obsession* and *Trudeau and Our Times,* vol. 2: *The Heroic Delusion.*

COHEN, MARJORIE GRIFFIN. Professor of political science and women's studies, Simon Fraser University. Publications include *Women's Work, Markets and Economic Development in Nineteenth Century Ontario, Canadian Women's Issues,* vol. 1, 2 (co-author), and *Free Trade and the Future of Women's Work.*

COURCHENE, THOMAS J. Jariskowsky-Deutsch Professor of Economic and Financial Policy and director, John Deutsch Institute for the Study of Economics, Queen's University. Publications include *In Praise of Renewed Federalism, Rearrangements,* and *Canada in the Millenium.*

DAVEY, FRANK. Carl F. Klinck Professor of Canadian Literature, University of Western Ontario. Publications include *Canadian Literary Power, Post-National Arguments: The Politics of Anglophone-Canadian Fiction Since 1967, Reading "KIM" Right,* and *Karla's Web: A Cultural Investigation of the Mahaffy-French Murders.*

FINBOW, ROBERT. Associate professor of political science, Dalhousie University. Publications include articles in *Canadian Journal of Political Science* (1993; 1994).

GIBBINS, ROGER. Professor and chair of political science, University of Calgary. Publications include *Government and Politics of Alberta* (co-editor), *Conflict and Unity: An Introduction to Canadian Political Life* (3rd ed.), and *Parameters of Power* (co-authored with Keith Archer, Rainer Knopff, and Leslie Pal.

LANPHIER, C. MICHAEL. Professor of sociology, York University. Publications include chapters in *The International Refugee Crisis: British and Canadian Response* and *Immigration and Refugee Policy: The Australian and Canadian Experiences.*

LEBLANC, PHYLLIS E. Director, Acadian Studies Centre and chair, Department of History and Geography, Université de Moncton. Publications include chapters in *Moncton, 1781-1929: changements socio-économiques dans une ville ferroviaire, Papal Diplomacy in the Modernage,* and *Egalité* (1992; 1994).

LORIMER, ROWLAND. Director, Canadian Centre for Studies in Publishing and professor of communication, Simon Fraser University. Authored books include *Mass Communication in Canada* (with Jean McNulty), *Mass Communications: A Comparative Introduction,* and *The Nation in the Schools.*

MCMILLAN, MELVILLE L. Professor and chair of economics, University of Alberta. Publications include papers in *Review of Economics and Statistics, Journal of Urban Economics, American Journal of Economics,* and *Constitutional Forum.*

MCROBERTS, KENNETH. Professor of political science, York University. Publications include *Quebec: Social Change and Political Crisis,* third edition with postscript, *English Canada and Quebec: Avoiding the Issue,* and *The Charlottetown Accord, the Referendum, and the Future of Canada* (co-editor).

MAGDER, TED. Associate professor, division of Social Science and director, Mass Communications Programme, York University. Publications include *Canada's Hollywood: the Canadian State and Feature Films* (1993), chapter in *Building on the New Canadian Political Economy* and an article in *Canadian Journal of Communications* (1993).

MILLER, MARY JANE. Professor of film studies, dramatic and visual arts, Brock University. Publications include *Turn Up the Contrast, Rewind and Search: Conversations with Makers of Canadian Television Drama*, and chapters in *The Beaver Bites Back* and *Documents that Move and Speak*.

MORTON, F.L. Professor of political science, University of Calgary and 1995 Bora Laskin Fellow in Human Rights. Publications include *Morgentaler vs. Borowski: Abortion, the Charter and the Courts, Charter Politics* (co-author), and *Law, Politics and the Judicial Process in Canada*.

NELLES, H.V. Professor of history, York University. Publications include *Southern Exposure* (co-author), *Monopoly's Moment* (co-author), and *Politics of Development*.

RESNICK, PHILIP. Professor of political science, University of British Columbia. Publications include *Thinking English Canada, Towards a Canada-Quebec Union, and The Mask of Proteus*.

RICHMOND, ANTHONY H. Professor Emeritus of sociology, York University. Publications include *Global Apartheid: Refugees, Racism and the New World Order* and *Immigration and Ethnic Conflict*.

ROTSTEIN, ABRAHAM. Professor of economics and political science, University of Toronto. Publications include *Rebuilding from Within: Remedies for Canada's Ailing Economy*, and a chapter in *The New Era of Global Competition*.

YOUNG MAN, ALFRED. Associate professor, Native American studies, University of Lethbridge. Publications include articles in *Fuse* magazine and *Parallelogramme*, chapter in *Indigena* and *Allen Sapp, A Retrospective* (exhibition catalogue).

ZEMANS, JOYCE. Professor of fine arts and co-director of the M.B.A. Programme in Arts and Media Administration in the Faculty of Administrative Studies at York University. Publications include article in *Journal of Canadian Art History* (1995) and chapters in *Free Expression, Public Support and Censorship: Examining Government's Role in the Arts in Canada and the United States* and *The Idea of the University, 1789-1989*.